To Ben
from
Dan
March 2021

Wholesome Nutrition

Wholesome Nutrition

For
Mind, Body and Microflora

The Goal of
Lacto-Vegetarianism

(Recipes of Udipi Cuisine Included)

YAMUNA LINGAPPA, PH. D.
B. T. LINGAPPA, PH. D.

ECOBIOLOGY FOUNDATION INTERNATIONAL
WORCESTER, MASSACHUSETTS
1992

THE PURPOSE OF ECOBIOLOGY FOUNDATION INTERNATIONAL IS TO PROMOTE A VARIETY OF RESEARCH PROJECTS (Library, Laboratory and Field) AND EDUCATION IN LACTO-VEGETARIANISM AS AN INTEGRAL PART OF ENVIRONMENTAL PROTECTION. LACTO-VEGETARIANISM IS A WAY OF LIFE THAT IS DEDICATED TO LIVING IN HARMONY WITH THE ENVIRONMENT, BOTH NONLIVING (the mountains, rivers and the earth) AND LIVING (the people, animals and the plants). THE FOUNDATION WILL PURSUE THIS OBJECTIVE BY SOLICITING DONATIONS OF FUNDS AND TALENTS IN ORDER TO ENGAGE IN WRITING, PUBLISHING (books, newsletters, journals), LECTURING (offering courses), FUND RAISING, RECRUITING DONORS AND VOLUNTEERS, SETTING-UP DEMONSTRATIONS (by purchasing, planting, raising, and otherwise maintaining and promoting biodiversity on farms, gardens, forests), EXAMPLES OF LIFESTYLES, PRODUCTION AND DISTRIBUTION OF LITERARY, ARTISTIC (visual, audio-visual), AND THEATRICAL PRESENTATIONS, AND BY ANY OTHER NOBLE MEANS, TO PROMOTE LACTO-VEGETARIAN LIFESTYLE WORLDWIDE.

Library of Congress Cataloging in Publication Data

ISBN 0-9634999-0-4

CIP 92-74581

Printed in the United States of America.
Printed by BookCrafters.
Printed on Recycled Paper.

Published by
ECOBIOLOGY FOUNDATION INTERNATIONAL
4 McGill Street, Worcester, Massachusetts 01607

Address all enquiries relating to the book and current and future plans of the movement to the FOUNDATION.

This book is dedicated to our mothers and grandmothers who toiled to raise us with a wholesome traditional diet. That diet was based on bulk and variety of plant products and was always supplemented with milk and yogurt. We owe our relatively resilient bodies and minds to that type of diet. We hope this kind of nourishment will gain popularity in the world so that more people will live to enjoy healthy, active, creative, and youthful old age.

". . . By instinct and upbringing I personally favor a purely vegetarian diet, and have for years been experimenting in finding a suitable vegetarian combination. But there is no danger of my decrying milk until I have obtained overwhelming evidence in support of a milkless diet. It is one of the many inconsistencies of my life that whilst I am in my own person avoiding milk, I am conducting a model dairy which is already producing cow's milk that can successfully compete with any such milk produced in India in purity . . .

". . . I submit scientists have not yet explored the hidden possibilities of the innumerable seeds, leaves and fruits for giving the fullest possible nutrition to mankind. For one thing the tremendous vested interests that have grown round the belief in animal food prevent the medical profession from approaching the question with complete detachment. . . ."

– Mahatma Gandhi, *Diet & Diet Reform,* 1949.

Contents

PREFACE

This book is the culmination of 40 years of personal inquiry into a basis for the optimal human diet. At the outset, this quest was that of an immigrant couple from India trying to make sense of the contradiction between Western medical advice in the 1950s versus the traditions and culture of our Indian heritage. When our first child was born in 1954, we had to make critical dietary decisions. Raised in traditional Indian vegetarian families, we knew that it was possible to maintain good health on a diet of plant products and milk. Yet our American physician, following the accepted teachings of that time, recommended a diet high in meat, eggs and seafoods to provide "good nutrition" during pregnancy and after child birth. The dilemma of choosing between time-tested cultural practices and questionable modern "scientific" advice led us to investigate the basic nutritional issues. We came to the conclusion that many dietary practices in America are based not on solid physiological principles, but are, in the words of Mark Hegsted, an Emeritus Professor of Nutrition at Harvard School of Public Health, "... a happenstance related to our affluence" (Eating in America. Dietary Goals for the U.S.; 1977 P. 3).

Starting nearly thirty five years ago, we carried out modifications in our family's diet giving attention to the principles of homeostasis and holistic or wholesome nutrition. This has been done by questioning and searching, moderately and cautiously, without embracing fads or rituals, but paying careful attention to nutritional science. YL remained a strict traditional lacto-vegetarian throughout the stressful years of graduate school, developing a professional career, through three pregnancies and raising three children. YL thus went through puberty, child-bearing, and menopause without eating any meat, fish or poultry. It is notable that she was not only healthy throughout, but furthermore had almost no need of many common prescribed or over-the-counter medicine. BTL, on the other hand, took to a more typical American lifestyle, developed certain typical health problems (e.g. mild hypertension). Changes in both diet and lifestyle have resulted in significant improvement in his health. Our children, who have grown up in the American culture, did not avoid meat, poultry or sea foods entirely. However, their intake of these foods was occasional. In general, our family diet has been low in protein and fat and high in complex carbohydrates, according to the concepts discussed in the chapter on "protective foods". We always supplemented our diet with milk and yogurt. While our personal experience is anecdotal and thus does not lend itself to statistical or reductionist analysis, it is nevertheless impressive. The family medical and dental bills have remained minuscule. We have had no need for laxatives, antacids and tranquilizers. None of us has suffered from a major illness in over three decades. Our children have grown into adulthood in excellent health.

For the last 20 years the major focus of our quest for insight into the optimal human diet has been the practical and theoretical formulation of an alternative perspective to that of commercial nutrition so widespread in our society. The theoretical basis has derived from our study of culture and science through distant and recent human history. It has led us to appreciate why the lacto-vegetarian diet on which we were raised half a century ago is superior to the diet based on animal products and refined foods being popularized today the world over. The practical venue for developing our view of optimal human nutrition has been our vegetarian restaurant, Annapurna, located in Worcester, Massachusetts.

A number of our relatives, six families of men and women 20-65 years old, came from India after 1975. Many of them subsequently worked in Annapurna. Faced with the potential for dietary excess upon immigrating to this country, they chose to maintain a lacto-vegetarian diet similar to that espoused in this book (plant staples, low in protein and high in complex carbohydrates supplemented with milk and water soluble vitamins B-complex and C). At the time of their arrival, almost all of them showed signs of varying degrees of malnutrition, and had a variety of minor complaints ranging from recurrent headaches to stomach cramps, skin and hair problems, foot odor and lethargy. In the course of a year the children showed tremendous increases in overall growth and alertness as well as resistance to diseases and colds, while the adults resolved many of their minor health complaints with minimal use of medications. Two women who became pregnant gave birth to three healthy children, two girls went through puberty and one woman went through menopause. Two individuals who were heavy smokers developed medical problems. One of them was also overweight and developed mild diabetes mellitus at age 60. Modification of his diet has brought his diabetes under control with mild medications. Furthermore, none of the Annapurna employees, including the individual with diabetes, have had need for a single day of sick leave during the course of more than 16 years of daily operation of the restaurant.

While we cannot prove that this maintenance of health was due to nutrition modification, our experience suggests, at the very least, that a practical alternative to the prevailing American diet does exist. At best, it indicates a way of escaping the nutritional debacle in which sedentary American society finds itself. By making unprocessed plant products and milk rather than meat and highly processed foods the staples of our diet, we may prevent many chronic health problems, both minor and serious, that are common in American society today. Moreover, we may also be able to uplift the dietary standard of people in developing countries. By emphasizing bulk and variety rather than "the food groups", a single scientific dietary standard would provide more choices to all people than the two unhealthy standards existing today: one of overindulgence and degenerative disease the other of malnutrition. Affluent people who wish to curtail their intake of calories ought to eat more plant products, as should persons who cannot afford to buy rich foods, especially meat, for economic reasons.

By viewing meat, poultry, fish and cheese, as condiments and seasonings to provide flavor and palatability rather than as staples, the world can set a scientific standard in nutrition that is adaptable to people of a wide range of cultures, tastes and economic strata. Nutrition education should enable an individual to eat according to his or her physiological needs. Adopting this perspective may help to fill the gap that exists between cultural and scientific diets as well as between "the haves and the have-nots."

We are not the first proponents of a "wholesome nutrition" nor to argue for health maintenance through nutrition management. The nutritional holists of an earlier era applied these principles and succeeded as well. Their approach fell into disfavor during the last half century not because it lacked scientific merit, but rather, because of a variety of historically specific reasons. These reasons included i) the fascination among both scientists and the public with reductionistic rather than holistic approaches to human problems, ii) the trend towards pharmacologic intervention rather than assisting the body to maintain itself (homeostasis), and iii) the influence of propaganda from certain food industries and their influential supporters. In the words of the late Dr.René Dubos of The Rockefeller University, "The dietary factors most effective in the production of meat, milk, and eggs also bring about a rapid growth of children; but growth rates are not the most significant values of human life. Life span, resistance to disease, intellectual performance, emotional responsiveness and perceptiveness, etc. are characteristics that cannot be measured on a weight scale and are of little relevance to the production of market pigs or chickens, yet should be of paramount importance in judging the value of a diet for man".

The Annapurna experience gave us a confidence (that can come only from such an enterprise), in the lacto-vegetarian diet as both economically feasible and subjectively palatable to a broad section of the American public. Over the centuries many different cultures have developed wholesome lacto-vegetarian diets that are both varied and tasty. Yet, many Americans have been misled into believing that unless a diet is based on meat staples it is inadequate and monotonous. The conventional notion of a vegetarian as someone who must live on carrot sticks and cottage cheese is absurd! We have demonstrated for nearly two decades at Annapurna Restaurant that it is possible to eat each and every day a wholesome, filling and tasty diet suitable to meet the needs of one's "physiological economy" without wasting our food resources or stressing our body functions.

This book has been written to share our conclusions with others who may be concerned about the nutritional roots of the health problems here in the U.S. and around the world. We hope that this work will help others not only understand the modern nutrition debacle, but also recognize what can be done to correct it. Accomplishing these goals was complicated by the fact that we wished to provide a text that was both intellectually rigorous and yet accessible to interested individuals who may be lacking a background in scientific subjects such as biochemistry, physiology or microbiology.

We have organized this book into five sections that are quite different from those of most books on nutrition. Each section consists of several chapters related to a particular nutritional theme. Each chapter begins with an abstract that summarizes its key conclusions.

Section A,"Wisdom of the Body", defines the components of our bodies and the processes by which life is possible. Then the nutritional needs of the brain, other body organs and intestinal microflora are interrelated as part of a physiological economy in which complex carbohydrates play a central role. Finally this view is contrasted to the modern state of American nutrition.

In section B, "Dietary constituents: Subsaturation is Optimal", we downplay the importance of protein in determining the value of a diet. Similarly, we de-emphasize the current obsession with calorie counting. Instead, the importance of consuming variety and bulk in the form of plant staples is emphasized. Such a diet provides needed nutrients such as protein, complex carbohydrates, and others as well as fiber that are essential to maintain health and well-being. Yet, such a diet is automatically lower in calories than usual high protein diets. We present the arguments first articulated three generations ago by Professor Russell Chittenden of Yale University that "a diet which conforms to the true nutritive requirement of the body must necessarily lead toward vegetable foods" (Chittenden, p.291, 1907). Other dietary components including fats, vitamins, minerals and fiber are also considered. The true dietary villain is seen not to be fat or protein per se, but rather concentrated excess of any nutrient. Only a complex carbohydrate-rich diet is seen to provide needed nutrients with bulk, variety and moderation.

The section C of this book, "Our Internal Environment" focuses on the importance of events that take place in the gastrointestinal tract, especially in the colon, in maintaining or disrupting health. While our normal intestinal microorganisms synthesize nutrients beneficial for themselves and for our bodies, microbial population altered by improper diets can synthesize increased amounts of toxins and carcinogens that may debilitate and destroy parts, or the whole body.

Having presented our perspective on the bodily systems and functions affected by nutrition, and the problems with current concepts of nutrition, in section D, "A Diet Tailored By Evolution", we present our views on the optimal human diet. Human milk is used as a model to illustrate the principle that all nutrients including proteins should be present in variety and moderation rather than in high nutrient density.

Section E, "Philosophy, Culture and Nutrition" tries to narrow the recently created gap between vegetarian and non-vegetarian diets. Culturally, these categorizations were not treated as watertight compartments. Meat, poultry and seafoods used to be minor components of traditional plant staple-based diets, even for many non-vegetarians.

Section E is followed a summary of key concepts and by two appendixes which are drawn from our experience in establishing and operating our practical showcase, Annapurna Restaurant. The appendixes provide model recipes of Udipi Cuisine and answers to some common questions. The choice of recipes reflect our family background and experience. However, equally wholesome diets can be derived from plant-based recipes of cultures around the world.

This book is based on the belief that nutrition modification is an important adjunct to preventive medicine. By changing our eating habits we can safeguard our health while making our personal contribution to alleviating world hunger. Our efforts, however small, are a working model. We have utilized a legacy of 4,000 years of cultural practice, investigated its credibility in the nutritional literature, practiced it in the American environment in our own family for a full generation, and demonstrated its viability with the general American public at Annapurna Restaurant.

Philosophically we have a commitment to the broad issue of lacto-vegetarian lifestyle. We consider it an ultimate commitment to protection of the environment; a declaration of living in harmony as an integral part of nature. We have been fooling ourselves, for a long time, in trying to become masters of nature. We believe that by being lacto-vegetarians we will be living the life of interdependence with nature. Such a lifestyle, we believe, will turn us away from all kinds of self-destructive personal and interpersonal activities and pave a way towards non-violence and harmony.

Our indebtedness goes to many, only a few of whom we will mention by name. Some are still involved in Annapurna, others have moved in other directions physically or philosophically, and some have passed away. Some are in the U.S. and some are in India. They all have played parts either in inspiring us to undertake this project or in contributing to its development. They include our teachers, grandparents, parents and friends whose teachings contributed to a philosophy that sustained us through cultural turmoil in our adopted country. Likewise we are indebted to our professional and academic American colleagues who gave us strength through intellectual development. We regard this book a working paper, an interim report. It needs considerable refinement, editorial and pedagogical. We could have done a better job of providing forceful arguments, comprehensive discussions, tables, illustrations and bibliography. The time had run out.

We are grateful to the dedicated librarians at the College of the Holy Cross, Mr. Anthony Stankus and Ms. Carolyn Mills, and also to the librarians of the University of Massachusetts Medical School Library, Mr. Paul Julian and others, for years of assistance and access to their wonderful collections. We thank the administration of the College of the Holy Cross for generous access to facilities of the college. Finally we wish to thank the many people who made running Annapurna possible including those who came from India.

Thanks go to Richard C. Turek for the gifts of the cover painting of this book and the insignia of the Foundation. We are thankful to Mr. Nicholas Kanaracus for providing book design and production knowledge and for completing the final pages using Ventura Publisher on the PC.

Special thanks goes to our chef and his wife, Ramachandra and Vishala Rao, and to others who struggled with us in serving the cause of Annapurna for the past seventeen years. To our three children, Vishwanath, Jaisri and Jairam, and our daughter-in-law Krista Farey, we owe more than thanks. It was they who coaxed us to dream of, and ultimately, to complete, this project. Finally, it is gratifying to note that our very healthy 18 month-old granddaughter, Usha, consumes a lacto-vegetarian diet consistent with the nutritional principles espoused here, with gusto.

Y.L. and B.T.L.
November, 1992
Worcester, Massachusetts

PART A
Wisdom of the Body

1

Understanding the Human Body and Its Three Entities

Abstract: From a nutritional perspective, a human being consists of three interacting and interdependent entities: i) the brain, ii) the rest of the organs of the body and iii) the normal intestinal microflora. The brain as coordinator of all bodily activities, gets first priority in allocation of nutrients. The body is comprised of nine systems (musculoskeletal, respiratory, cardiovascular, digestive, lymphatic, excretory, reproductive, endocrine and nervous systems). These systems are responsible for carrying out the activities necessary for survival. The normal intestinal microflora refers to the microorganisms that populate the healthy colon. They play a special role in nutrition (as will be discussed in detail in Chapter 13). Together, the brain, body and intestinal microflora help to create, and are in turn influenced by, the internal environment within our bodies. Nutrition is a crucial determinant of the quality of this internal environment, affecting all three entities. In part this reflects the intricate hierarchies of structure and function in the human body; in part this reflects the interplay of genetic and environmental influences on the growth, development and maintenance of cells, tissues and organs, over the course of evolution. Because of these relationships between the three entities of our bodies, manipulation of nutrition is a means of maintaining health, fighting disease, and promoting longevity.

The human body, a truly amazing machine, is an integrated system made up of trillions of living cells and their products. Each cell of the human body has the potential to exist independently. Yet, in a healthy body these cells are interdependent, functioning in harmony and contributing to the welfare of the organism.

The integrated functions of the human body have been compared to those of machines, cities, and computers among other things. However, as all scholars agree, nothing human-made can be compared to a thinking, feeling, healthy and working human being. The American scientist, Van Potter described the human being as "a cybernetic machine, a machine that 'hunts' for solutions; . . . a machine that can never be completely programmed . . . a machine with fantastic durability and adaptiveness yet amazingly delicate and fragile; a machine that can go without food for weeks but cannot survive without air for more than a few minutes . . ." (Van Potter, p.181, 1974).

A product of more than 3.5 billion years of evolution, this complex system started from primordial cells which evolved in the prehistoric seas. Our cells still exhibit fundamental characteristics of their primordial origins. The lymph which bathes cells in the human body, for example, is similar in salt content to the primeval sea water in which cells evolved. Like the primordial cells, our cells have a high water content (above 70%) and are enclosed by a selectively permeable membrane. Reflecting this primordial origin, our cells and tissues are optimized for claiming needed nutrients from a dilute solution. The cells of different organs have some basic similarities, yet they also differ significantly (Figure 1.1).

The history of the human body is far more complex than we might imagine. Its program of development is encoded in deoxyribonucleic acid (DNA). Genes, the biochemical units through which characteristics are transmitted from generation to generation (heredity), are made of DNA. Our ancestry can be traced back to primates and further to single-celled organisms that evolved from primordial cells. The complex system of the body machine operates according to the information encoded in the inherited genetic material.

This hereditary program, which dictates the anatomical structure, physiological functions, mental traits and even nutritional needs, is influenced to varying degrees by a second parameter, the environment. Environment refers not only to the physical surroundings—air, water, soil—but also to the environment within the body (substances dissolved in blood and lymph, colonic microbes and the products they generate in the lumen of the gastrointestinal tract etc.) In this book we are concerned with nutrition as an aspect of this internal environment and its influence on human development, physiology, and behavior.

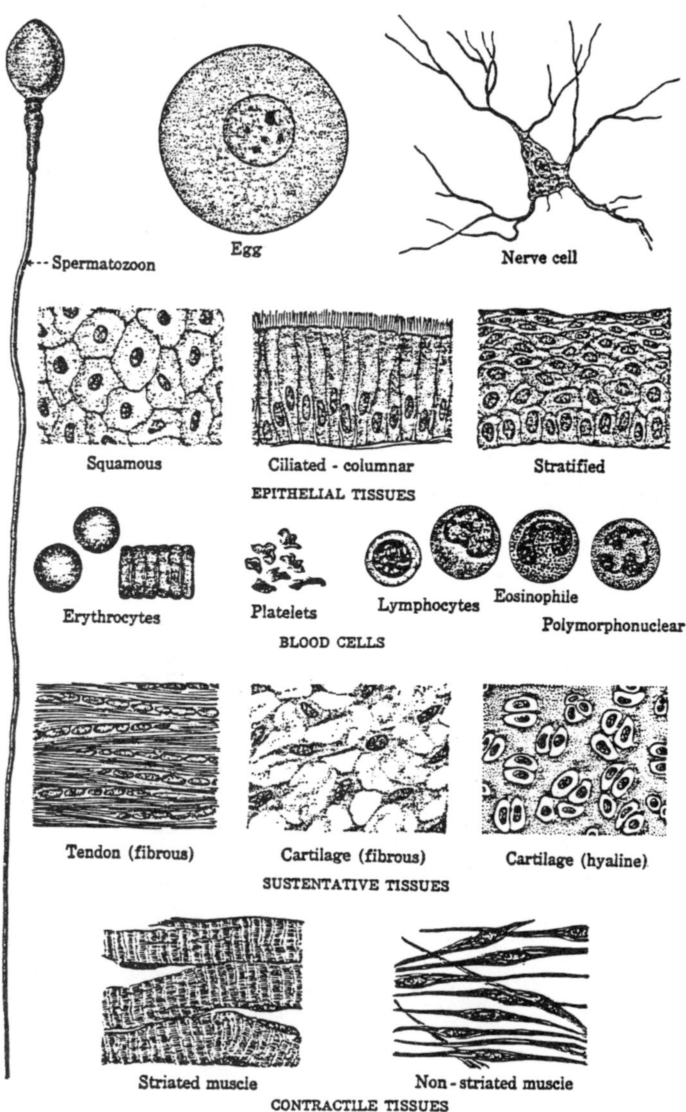

Figure 1.1. Various types of animal cells (R. W. Hegner, 1936)

Review of some features of cell and organ physiology

Just as a city is a community of different groups of people, the human body is a complex community of trillions of cells. The cells are the basic units of life. Just as people in a city are organized to perform various functions, the cells in the body are also specialized for particular tasks. The body has many kinds of cells such as muscle, bone, blood and nerve cells. Most of these cells are further specialized. The blood system, for example, consists of several types of cells including red blood cells, white blood cells, platelets and their progenitors. Some body cells such as red blood cells are so small even when they are magnified 200 times they would look like dried peas while some nerve cells on similar magnification would appear as a 600 foot long rope with a "frayed knot" at one end or as a branching tree. Some cells are specialized for storage (e.g. of fat or carbohydrate) whereas other cells perform communication functions (e.g. secretion of hormones) and so forth. Whatever their functions may be, healthy cells of the body communicate with one another and respond to signals from other cells. In contrast, cancer cells often lose the ability to communicate properly with other cells.

A special covering, the plasma membrane, separates the interior of the cell (cytoplasm) from the outside environment. The plasma membrane plays several very important roles such as controlling what is allowed in and out of the cell. In the cytoplasm of the cells are suspended many important structures (Figure 1.2). One of these structures is the nucleus that contains the genetic material (DNA). More than a dozen other minute structures that perform specialized functions may be found inside cells.

Cells of similar structure and function make up a tissue. Different kinds of tissues, organized to perform physiologic functions, constitute organs (e.g. the heart, liver and kidneys). The organs of the body function together as nine elaborate and complex systems (see below). These systems are structurally and functionally interconnected and constantly communicate with each other. Just as the prosperity of a city is dependent upon the degree of cooperation and efficiency of transactions among different segments of the community, so also, the well-being of the body depends upon integration among the body's systems. All systems of the body are organized to interact constantly among themselves and with the environment to maintain a dynamic balance of the entire body. Even a little damage to one system, or to one organ, or even to one type of cells, may upset this balance so as to affect the entire body's performance in the long run.

It has taken more than 3.5 billion years for the single-celled organism's simple housekeeping activities to evolve into the complex operation of the human body. The body is under the direct control of the central nervous system (CNS) which includes the brain and spinal cord. The CNS controls bodily functions through chemical messengers, neurotransmitters, peptides and hormones, with the help of other organs and systems. In the skin of a single person, for example, there are 45 miles of nerves that communicate activities of the

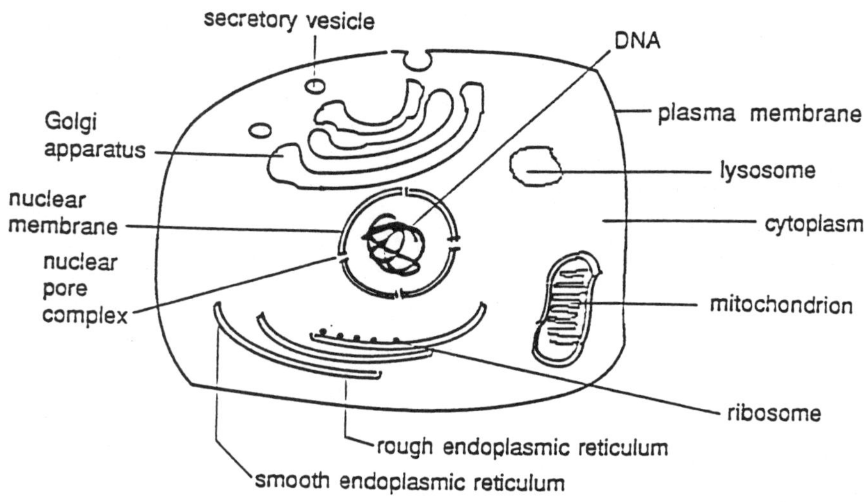

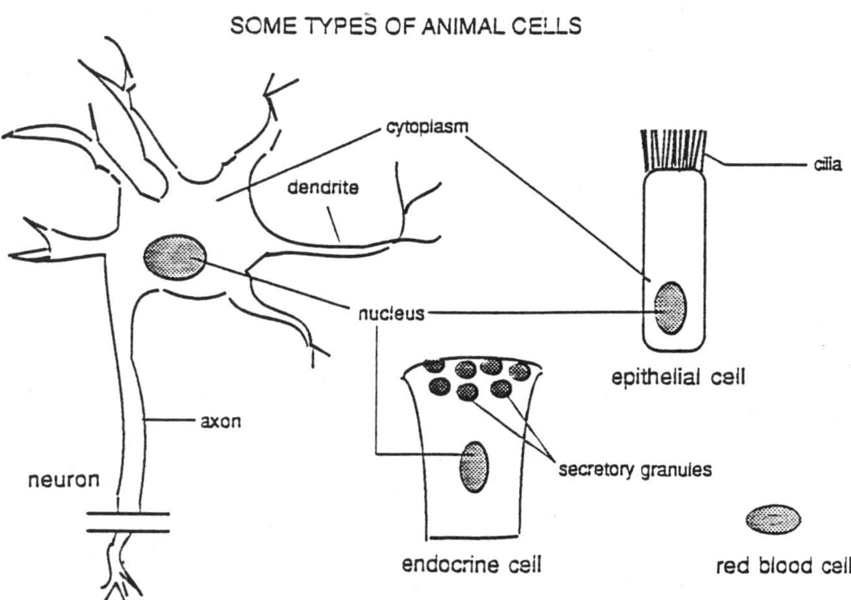

Figure 1.2. Schematic drawing to show characteristic subcellular compartments. A typical cell has one nucleus but may have a number of mitochondria, Golgi apparati etc. Also note extreme variation in morphology of cells; mature red blood cell has no nucleus and that the axon of a neuron can be many feet in length.

body to centers in the brain. When necessary the brain may stimulate other systems (e.g. to function faster or slower) using the hormones produced in the endocrine system.

The body fluids, lymph and blood (circulatory system), bathe all cells and organs, creating one internal environment. They also deliver nutrients absorbed from the G.I. tract or secreted into the bloodstream from storage tissues such as liver, fat and muscle. The body fluids also transport the wastes of cells and tissues to the lungs, liver and kidney, where they are detoxified or disposed of. One of the most complex and essential functions of the body is to keep these body fluids appropriately replenished with nutrients and free of waste products. Adverse changes in this environment may influence the performance of all systems of the body.

The cells, organs and systems in the body function at two levels. They take care of the housekeeping needs for their own survival and they perform certain specialized functions that contribute to the needs of other bodily systems. Thus, each cell and organ has to maintain its own self-regulated internal environment as well as cooperate with other systems in order to maintain the internal equilibrium of the body. Which of these goals gets priority is in large measure decided by coordinated, self-regulatory mechanisms that can be termed the body wisdom" (see Chapter 2). The decisions rendered by the body wisdom can be different at different periods of life (e.g. childhood vs. pregnancy vs old age) and depending on the individuals' lifestyle (e.g. active versus sedentary, well-fed vs starved). During pregnancy and lactation, for example, the body supplies nutrients to the developing fetus or infant even at the expense of the mother. Similarly, under starvation conditions, nutrients are provided to the vital organs that maintain life at the expense of nourishment of the muscles and bones. These are accomplished by the self-regulating and balancing mechanisms of the body wisdom.

The survival of the human species itself is proof of the success of these internal mechanisms. However, when this internal balance fails for any reason, the demise of the body may not be far off. The destruction may come in the form of degenerative or autoimmune diseases or cancers, or as failure of key organs such as the kidneys, liver or heart, or in the form of loss of resistance to infectious agents.

In this book, we would like to organize the component parts of the human body into three entities whose interactions are essential for the proper operation of body wisdom and maintenance of the internal environment: (1) the brain, (2) the body, and (3) the normal intestinal microflora.

The brain

The brain, a component of the central nervous system (CNS), is only a small part of the total mass of the human body, yet it controls all the other organs. It is intimately involved with important regulatory functions such as control of appetite, body weight, regulation of body temperature, fluid control, breathing rate and heart beat. These functions are so vital that if one of them fails, the whole body may be incapacitated and ultimately, succumb. Unlike the rest of the body whose rapid growth may continue even beyond the 1st decade of life, the brain's growth spurt starts from 12-14 weeks of fetal life and ends by eighteen months after birth. The neurons that make up the CNS are highly specialized. If some cells of an organ such as the liver are removed surgically, the remaining cells multiply and replace those cells. Such regeneration does not occur among the neurons; with these specialized cells any loss is permanent.

The number of neurons in the brain is established in the late embryonic period and by the first year of life. At maturity the brain contains approximately 20 billion neurons. Normally, neurons begin to die off at a constant rate after the age of 30. Losing brain cells at a rate faster than normal is a common feature of premature aging manifested by atrophy and weight loss of the brain. Such a physical deterioration of the brain is often correlated with a decline in mental vigor, stamina and agility.

The blood sugar, glucose, is an obligatory food for both the brain and the body. However, the brain gets preference in receiving blood sugar and other nutrients relative to most of the rest of the body. Even though the brain is only 2% of the body weight, it may utilize as much as 15% of the total body energy at rest.

The body

The body consists of nine broad generally recognized systems, named below. Each one of these systems consist of a number of organs. Generally, the organs in a system are essential for the function of that system. Failure of any one component organ may upset the function of a system as a whole or even of the entire body. The consequence of such a disturbance may be chronic minor complaints or serious long-term ill health sometimes leading to a reduced life span. The body's overall health depends upon its coordinated function with the other two entities, the brain and the intestinal microflora. With this in mind, we will briefly describe the nine systems through which the body is maintained.

1. The musculo-skeletal system consisting of approximately 600 muscles of several kinds which move joints and various parts of the body and approximately 200 bones, which are both a framework for soft tissues and a reservoir for valuable minerals such as calcium and phosphorus.

2. The respiratory system, which includes the trachea (windpipe) and lungs, brings air in close contact with blood allowing extraction of oxygen which binds to the hemoglobin in red blood cells. The respiratory system also disposes of carbon dioxide, one of the body's primary wastes, and thereby plays an important role in maintaining normal blood acid-base balance.

3. The circulatory system consists of the heart, arteries, veins and blood.

The circulating blood distributes oxygen and nutrients to all cells of the body and removes substances including wastes that they produce.

4. The digestive system (the gut or gastrointestinal tract) includes the mouth, stomach, intestines and associated glands. It digests the food into absorbable nutrients, excretes the undigested and unabsorbed residues as wastes, and provides a home for the intestinal microflora in the large intestine or colon.

5. The excretory system refers to those organs involved in removal of wastes from the body, including the kidney (which filters the blood to make urine), the lungs (which releases carbon dioxide during exhalation) and the GI tract (which excretes non-absorbed matter in the form of feces).

6. The lymphatic system consists of the lymph fluid, vessels and nodes as well as white blood cells. It recycles the lymph fluid that bathes all cells. The organs of the lymphatic system and the cells within them, comprise part of the body's immune defenses which protect against invasion of pathogens.

7. The endocrine system consists of glands such as the pituitary, the pancreas, the thyroid and the adrenals which are located in different parts of the body. Their secretions aid the brain in communicating swiftly with all kinds of cells and tissues throughout the body. These secretions are hormones such as growth hormone, glucagon, insulin, thyroid hormone and cortisol. The hormones act as messages to various organs, tissues or cells via the blood stream and control vital activities such as specific as heart rate and as general as the rate of metabolism itself.

8. The reproductive system consists of organs that produce the germ cells, sperm and eggs, as well as associated organs of reproduction such as the ovaries and uterus in women and testes in men.

9. The nervous system consists of vast network of nerves composed of cells called neurons. The network of neurons monitor both the internal and external environments and coordinate organ function accordingly. The nervous system shares this task with the endocrine system, although in general the nervous system's actions are more immediate, direct and circumscribed than the actions of the endocrine system. The nervous system also composes the brain-body interface.

Normal intestinal microflora

The normal intestinal microflora refers to the microorganisms which populate the normal colon. The development of the brain and the body in the fetus is coordinated in the womb by the nourishment provided by the mother and the fetal genetic program. However, the intestinal microflora which becomes an integrated part of the body, develops only after birth. It is introduced from the birth canal during the delivery of the infant and from the environment subsequently. The microbes thus introduced are selectively fostered by different parts of the infant's body including the large intestine, or colon. A characteristic microflora that is present in the mother's vagina during pregnancy populates the child's colon after birth. Other beneficial microbial types colonize the skin as well as the mucus membranes of most parts of the body. An adult may have as many as one hundred trillion microbes in the colon alone.

Continuously flowing nutrients, constant warm temperature and abundant moisture make the colon an ideal residence for the microorganisms. What specific organisms make up the colonic microflora, and what activities they carry out, depends upon the kind of nutrient environment provided by the body. Depending upon the diet, the microflora may consume essential nutrients and generate toxins and carcinogens instead of playing a normal beneficial (symbiotic) role in the body. Thus, nutrition is a decisive factor in tailoring the intestinal microflora to perform beneficial rather than harmful roles for human health (see Chapter 13).

Interaction of the entities

In nature, animals flourish by following their instincts. In the case of human beings, accumulated experience and reasoning ability play decisive roles in how we take care of ourselves. In various cultures, the ancient healers had an intuitive sense of the body's self-regulating mechanisms. They believed that the root causes of illnesses could be remedied by improving the internal environment of the body. Towards this end they used fasting, diet, exercise, and medicinal herbs and spices as preventive therapies. Although these traditions were established for different reasons and were interpreted differently from time to time, we can now see that ancient remedies helped the body's self-regulating mechanisms when the body needed assistance in excretion, dilution, or neutralization of foreign substances that were upsetting the internal environment as we understand it today.

Many cultures acknowledged that diet was the most important of the environmental factors which could be manipulated to achieve the optimal functioning of the body. They also believed behavior is influenced by diet. Consequently, they gave priority to maintaining health of the mind and the body through dietary management. That tradition has been followed by many scientists and physicians as well. Russell Chittenden, Christian Herter, Vernon McCollum, Leo Rettger, Henry Sherman, Roger Williams, René Dubos and Dennis Burkitt are just a few of the scientists during the past 100 years who attempted to understand the human body through holistic analyses. They were careful not to neglect the importance of internal environment when it concerned the function of the whole human being. Their guiding principle was to provide balanced nutrition to the entire body.

This attention to the internal environment has not been maintained in our modern affluent society. As a result, the incidence of diseases which are a consequence of a disturbed internal environment (e.g. including cancer and degenerative diseases), are rising. This disturbance of the internal environment is contributing to the burgeoning health problems of our time in other ways as well: stress and behavioral abnormalities, metabolic derangements, and diminished host defenses. As Alexander Leaf, Professor of Medicine at Harvard Medical School, pointed out, there are people in other parts of the world who lead a more active life in old age than do well-fed Americans. Why have people without sophisticated technologies been able to achieve an index of good health not seen with our "superior" science and technology? The following chapters, we hope, will help to answer this question.

We believe that the lacto-vegetarian diet described in this book evolved in harmony with the body and its amazing mechanisms. Reductionistic science fails to fully appreciate the holistic nature of the human organism and its evolutionary heritage, having lost the "forest" for the "trees" of isolated functions and systems. The time has come for us to correctly interpret the marvelous new knowledge of biochemistry and molecular biology in the context of the entire human being.

Selected Sources and Suggested Readings

Anonymous, 1992. Nutrition of the elderly. *Nutrition Today,* January/Feb. 33

Anonymous, 1988. Sex and violence in neuroscience. *Science,* 242, 1509

Anonymous, 1984. Human milk as a source of long-chain polyunsaturated fatty acids for preterm human infant neural tissues. *Nutrition Reviews,* 42, 247-248

Yoshimi Benno, et al., 1989. Comparison of fecal microflora of elderly persons in rural and urban areas of Japan. *Applied and Environmental Microbiology,* 55, 1100-1105

W.R. Bloor, 1916. The distribution of the lipoids ("fat") in human blood. *J. Biological Chemistry,* 25, 577-599

Mary A.B. Brazier. Challenges from the philosophers to the neuroscientists. *Brain and Mind,* 5-43, Ciba foundation Symposium 69 (new series), Excerpta Medica 1979

D.P. Burkitt, A.R.P. Walker and N.S. Painter, 1972. Effect of dietary fibre on stools and transit-times, and its role in the causation of disease. *Lancet,* 2, 1408-1412

Russell H. Chittenden. *Physiological Economy In Nutrition.* Frederick A Strokes, New York. 1904

John H. Cummings, 1983. Fermentation in the human large intestine: Evidence and implications for health. *Lancet,* 1, 1206-1208

R.J. Dubos, D.C. savage and R.W. Schaedler, 1967. The Indigenous flora of the gastrointestinal tract. *Diseases of the Colon & Rectum,* 10: 23-34

John C. Eccles, *Evolution of the brain: Creation of the self*. Routledge, London, 1989

John D. Fernstrom and Richard J. Wurtman, 1974. Nutrition and the brain. *Scientific American,* 230, 84-91

Stephen Jay Gould. *Ever Since Darwin.* W.W. Norton, New York, 1977

H. Haenel, 1961. Some rules in the ecology of the intestinal microflora of man. *J. Applied Bacteriology,* 24, 242-251

C.A. Herter, and A.I.Kendall, 1909-10. The influence of dietary alterations on the types of intestinal flora. *J. Biological Chemistry,* 7, 203-217

P. Hill and L. Garbaczewski, 1987. Gut-CNS peptide hormones, digestive dysfunction, and colon cancer. *Nutrition and Cancer,* 10, 11-22

William B. Kannel, 1971. Current status of the epidemiology of brain infarction associated with occlusive arterial disease. *Stroke,* 2, 295-318

Dorothy T. Krieger, 1983. Brain peptides: what, where, and why ? *Science,* 222, 975-985

L.L. Langley, *Homeostasis.* Van Nostrand Reinhold, New York. 1965

Alexander Leaf *Youth In Old Age.* McGraw-Hill, New York, 1975

Henrik Lund-Andersen, 1979. Transport of glucose from blood to brain. *Physiological Reviews,* 59, 305-352

Frank D. Mann, 1990. The dynamics of free cholesterol exchange may be critical for endothelial cell membranes in the brain. *Perspectives in Biology and Medicine,* 33, 531-534

Lynn Margulis, David Chase, and Ricardo Guerrero, 1986. Microbial Communities. *BioScience,* 36, 160-170

E. V. McCollum and Nina Simmonds. *The Newer Knowledge Of Nutrition.* MacMillan, New York, 1929

Linus Pauling, 1968. Orthomolecular psychiatry. *Science,* 160, 265-271

Van R. Potter, 1974. Probabalistic aspects of the human cybernetic machine. *Perspectives in Biology and Medicine,* 17, 164-183

Leo F. Rettger, 1906. Studies on putrefaction. *J. Biological Chemistry,* 2, 71-86

Edward Rubenstein, 1980. Diseases caused by impaired communication among cells. *Scientific American,* 242, 102-121

Henry C. Sherman. *Chemistry of Food and Nutrition.* 4th.ed. Macmillan, New York, 1935

David S. Sobel, edited. *Ways of Health.* Harcourt Brace Jovanovich, New York. 1979

Bernard Towers. *Consciousness and the Brain: Evolutionary Aspects.* Ciba Foundation Symposium 69 (New Science). Excerpta Medica, 1979

Kerstin Uvnas-Moberg, 1989. The gastrointestinal tract in growth and reproduction. *Scientific American,* 261, 78-83

Roger J. Williams. *Nutrition In a Nutshell.* Dolphin Books, Doubleday, New York, 1962

Melvin T. Yokoyama and James R. Carlson, 1979. Microbial metabolites of tryptophan in the intestinal tract with special reference to skatole. *American J. Clinical Nutrition,* 32, 173-178

Gordon Young, 1977. Salt-the essence of life. *National Geographic,* 152, 381-401

2

Homeostasis, Holism and Holistic Nutrition

Abstract: The concept of homeostasis is that dynamic mechanisms operate to maintain constancy of the internal environment. Small or large perturbations in the internal environment trigger compensatory mechanisms to a corresponding degree. The net result is a tendency to return to "normal." In this chapter, the historical origins of this concept are traced. Some examples are given of how homeostasis works, how its loss results in disease, and how its reestablishment is crucial to restoring good health. Adaptation and evolution are then discussed. The development of homeostatic mechanisms are seen to be a means by which adaptation allows organisms to thrive in diverse environmental niches. Holism is the concept that complex systems cannot be understood solely by the study of their individual parts. Rather, features unique to complex systems are lost when subjected to such reductionist analyses. The interactions between the three entities (brain, rest of the body organs and intestinal microflora) discussed in the first chapter are examples of holistic systems. Likewise the nutritional requirements that reinforce homeostatic mechanisms display features that are lost when individual nutrients are studied in isolation. Nutrition modification in support of homeostasis is developed as an important holistic approach to health care. Plant staples in the diet aid the operation of these homeostatic mechanisms for reasons to be considered in the next chapter.

The best way to introduce the concept of homeostasis is to paraphrase the observations of the originator of the term, the great American physiologist, Walter B. Cannon. Our bodies are made of highly unstable material, material that suffer constant wear and tear. The body is very readily affected by changing environmental conditions and yet, it readjusts and returns to normal when the affecting conditions are removed. The body has ability to quickly respond to external stimuli and regain balance by self-regulatory powers. The idea goes back to Hippocrates (460-377 B.C.) that disease is cured by natural powers. It is a common knowledge that the body very rapidly responds to changes in heat, cold, oxygen pressure in air or drying. The body naturally resists change and, at the same time, it quickly adapts to changes. The successful result is stability. This ability was developed in organisms in the eons of time during the course of evolution. The physiological processes that coordinate bringing about stability are highly complex and they involve the coordinated working of brain, nerves, heart, lungs, kidneys and spleen. Cannon designated for these states of the body a special term, homeostasis.

Awareness of homeostasis is evident in the writings and practices of ancient cultures from over four thousand years ago. For example, Yogic therapy of ancient India recognized that mind and body should work together to maintain the health of the whole body. Similarly, Hippocrates, in early Greece, believed that a lack of balance in the body was at the root of illness, and therefore, that treating tissues and organs would not cure the disease unless the fluids which integrate the whole body were stabilized. However, it wasn't until much later that these concepts were clearly enunciated by experimental scientists. In the early part of the 19th century, the French scientist Claude Bernard, concluded that human health was too complex to be understood in terms of individual organs, based on his experience in medicine and human physiology.

Bernard believed that to maintain health, higher organisms have to maintain their internal environment. He came to this conclusion not only because the different organs are nourished and bathed by common body fluids (blood and lymph), but also because the organs are intimately interrelated with each other in function. In nature, all animals strive to achieve this condition and when they reach equilibrium they put an enormous effort into maintaining the stability of their internal environment. A mild disturbance that alters the internal environment will act as a stimulus that induces a reaction by the body in order to neutralize, compensate for, or otherwise remedy the disturbance.

In his book, *The Wisdom of the Body,* Cannon paid tribute to Claude Bernard, to many European physiologists and to Hippocrates for generating the concept of homeostasis. He emphasized the important role of the internal environment in establishing and maintaining an equilibrium or steady state in the body. Homeostasis was originally applied to steady state acting as a self-regulating mechanism, in higher animals. An American physiologist L.L. Langley later expanded the application of the term homeostasis to self-regulatory controls in every living cell of both plants and animals. Examples of this broader view of homeostasis are numerous and diverse, and are manifest at the molecular, subcellular and cellular levels, in the tissues, organs and the organism as a whole. Let us look at some examples of regulatory mechanisms at each level.

At the molecular level, many enzymes, including those that are involved in the biochemical pathways of glucose utilization and energy generation, are subject to feedback inhibition. That is, the very products that are generated by an enzyme's action, block its function. In this way the enzyme is held in check, its further action prevented until the amount of product falls below a certain level, at which time the enzyme's action is "needed" again by the body.

Similarly, homeostatic mechanisms are at work at the subcellular level of organelles, the specialized particles and compartments within cells. For example, oxidation of fatty acids occurs only within mitochondria, the membrane bound subcellular structures within which energy generation occurs. For such energy generation to occur, fatty acids must be brought into the mitochondria using a specialized transport system. Those conditions which lead to a build up of free fatty acids in the liver (the main organ of energy metabolism) also activate fatty acid transport systems allowing enhanced rates of fatty acid oxidation. Conversely, those conditions in which free fatty acids or their byproducts are needed by the body, result in a decreased activity of the mitochondrial transport system, thereby releasing fatty acids into the blood stream where it can be taken up and used by tissues rather than oxidized in the liver mitochondria. Thus, we see homeostasis operating not only at the level of specific enzymes, but also in the function of subcellular structures within the living cells.

Turning to higher levels we see homeostasis at work in the interactions of tissues and organs. For example, within the endocrine portion of the pancreas are cells that secrete insulin (beta cells) and those that secrete glucagon (alpha cells). Each of these two hormones have opposing effects on glucose metabolism: insulin stimulates those enzymes involved in glucose breakdown and utilization while glucagon inhibits many of the same enzymes, stimulating instead the enzymes involved in glucose production. Not only does each of the hormones oppose the other's action, but, in addition, each inhibits the release of the other from the cells of the pancreas. For example, after a complex carbohydrate-rich meal, which produces high levels of glucose in the bloodstream, insulin secretion is stimulated.

Insulin secretion inhibits glucagon secretion while stimulating the utilization of glucose. No wonder homeostasis is called "body wisdom:" Glucagon secretion is not "needed" when glucose levels are already high—the very conditions which stimulate insulin secretion. When blood glucose levels start to fall as a result of the action of insulin, the stimulus for insulin release diminishes and its level falls, removing the inhibition on glucagon release. This results in higher levels of glucagon in the bloodstream, which then inhibits insulin release further and causes release of newly formed glucose into the bloodstream, and so on. These fine-tuned responses are further coordinated with behavioral ones which lead the body to feel hunger and satiety in response to the complicated biochemical changes. How these homeostatic mechanisms operate to maintain a normal blood glucose concentration through feeding, fasting, activity and rest is truly one of the most remarkable aspects of biochemical evolution.

A remarkable feature of homeostasis is that its actions, while operating at many different levels, have been tailored through evolution to bring about a desired physiologic result. Like so many ripples from a handful of pebbles thrown into a quiet pond, these responses merge and separate, reinforce and oppose one another operating at various ranges and time scales. The final outcome is complex, and at times seems paradoxical and bewildering to the casual observer. Yet the net effect on the organism is to promote well being and survival. Moreover, as we have mentioned, without homeostatic mechanisms, organisms would succumb to continually occurring deleterious alterations in both the internal and external environments.

Long-standing cultural practices have evolved to accommodate the demands of homeostasis. Breakfast, by whatever name, is served in all cultures to restore the energy reserve of liver glycogen (a storage form of glucose) depleted during the previous night's sleep. Complex carbohydrate dishes such as gruel, porridge, pancakes or other whole grains, eaten with milk and fruit dishes, admirably served this need. The traditional remedy of a bowl of hot soup and bed rest for mild illnesses served to prevent dehydration, reduce stress and thereby make the body's task of restoring homeostatic balance easier.

Understanding homeostasis is a task which is only in its infancy and for which many of our experimental approaches are not well suited. Modern experimental science proceeds from studies on isolated components or systems, and in the process of understanding the details, often loses sight of the complex interactions with other systems, the sum total of which makes up homeostasis. Thus, we must approach the study of homeostasis, as a complex puzzle that makes sense because it has been selected through evolution for its survival value for organisms. One challenge is to glean insight into the patterns and processes of homeostasis by studying the hieroglyphics and riddles of evolution. With this insight we can hope to apply specific details of our new knowledge about enzymes, hormones, cells and organ systems, in meaningful ways to the problem of adapting the human diet to our changing lifestyles and activities.

Survival is the primary accomplishment of evolution. This is achieved by either fine-tuning a specific response to a given situation or increasing the range of responses possible. Certain species of insects have chosen the former approach to survival and exist in the most specialized of ecological niches. However, human beings have thrived by the latter approach. We have adapted to an extraordinary variety of ecological niches, and have evolved varied cultures and life styles and, correspondingly, varied diets.

If nutrients are provided in a fashion that allows full advantage to be taken of the many levels of homeostatic controls built into the human organism, the outcome will be a balance that optimizes organ functions and leads to optimal health and longevity. However, if nutrients are provided in a non-physiological manner, the result may be malfunction of homeostatic mechanisms manifest as disorders as diverse as obesity or anorexia, with long-term consequences to the human being. (see Chapters 3 and 9).

Adaptation and homeostasis

According to Professor Richard Lewontin of Harvard University, adaptation is the evolutionary process which provides the organism a better and better solution to the problem it faces. Thus, it should not be surprising that humans have a tremendous potential for adaptation. Humans have the unique ability to adapt by making rational decisions and are able to augment the process with discoveries and inventions. Perhaps as a consequence, we have achieved the most complex regulatory mechanisms for maintaining homeostasis, and hence can survive in the widest range of environmental niches. The extent and diversity of the regulatory mechanisms are very hard to express with simple facts and figures and, indeed, remain to a large measure poorly understood. Let us consider evolutionary adaptations of homeostasis as they apply to nutrition. Primates and human beings have evolved a very high level of brain function and longevity. The utilization of predominantly complex carbohydrates as the primary energy source in the human diet rather than rich animal proteins and fats may be an evolutionary adaptation to achieve optimum growth of the brain, body and its microflora without disturbing the body's homeostasis through production and accumulation of toxic metabolic products (see Chapter 12). In this way, homeostasis would be maintained over the long term and contribute to longevity.

Messages from the brain by way of the nerves control the activities of most of the organs and tissues of the body. A muscle, for example, carries out voluntary movements of a bone only when it receives the appropriate signal from the brain. Involuntary functions such as the regulation of breathing, body temperature, the heart rate, are controlled by other regions of the brain. Given this crucial role of the brain in directing both voluntary and involuntary activity, it is not surprising that top priority in the allocation of nutrients is reserved for the brain. When this priority breaks down, so does proper bodily functions. A stroke, for example, may paralyze parts of the body by depriving blood supply to certain parts of the brain.

Similarly, pathogenic microbes, upon gaining entry into the gut can disturb the functions of both the body and the brain. Often small numbers of potentially pathogenic microorganisms inhabit the body, but they are held in check, in part, by the priority of distribution of nutrient resources, the innate resistance of the body and the antagonistic interactions among the microbes. Alterations in these relationship lead to a disturbed homeostasis and, if uncorrected, will lead to further disruptions and illness.

Biological clocks and rhythms of the body are examples of evolutionary adaptations that initiate and maintain new sets of homeostatic mechanisms.

Many cyclical events such as sleep and bowl movements integrate physiological functions in daily, monthly, or seasonal cycles. The daily cycles often depend on the duration, quality, or quantity of light or darkness, temperature and humidity and are known as circadian rhythms. Some of these are timing devices assisting in starting and ending many bodily events such as hunger, elimination, synthesis of hormones, and metabolic demands. Young animals and human infants are born relatively arrhythmic. They gradually become rhythmic in their general physiology, eating, sleeping, and elimination. How quickly human infants become rhythmic depends to certain extent upon the maturity of the body's systems and repeated punctual performance.

Some scientists are of the opinion that these bodily rhythms, which are sensitive to changes in the environment, are potential tools for maintaining good health. These internal rhythms integrate the external and internal environmental changes for the benefit of the body. If these rhythms are not maintained, their usefulness in promoting health will be lost. For example, bowel movement normally takes place rhythmically. However, a lack of fiber in the diet or failure to be punctual in using the toilet will upset this rhythmic function of the bowel. The resulting irregularity and constipation provide another stress on the body, ultimately to the detriment of homeostasis and the individual's health.

The cyclical rhythms, such as the daily sleep cycle and monthly menstrual cycle are genetically determined, but their expressions are profoundly influenced by factors in the external and internal environment. For example, many young women who diet excessively and remain underweight lose their menstrual cycles (amenorrhea). Untreated, such disorders have severe long-term health consequences (e.g. in this case, development of osteoporosis).

Holism

In addition to adaptation, we must introduce another concept in order to better understand homeostatic mechanisms as they apply to human behavior and nutrition. This is holism, the notion that the whole is more than the sum of its parts. The concept has its roots in many cultures, but the term holism was introduced in 1926 by Jan Christiaan Smuts in his book Holism and Evolution. He believed that an organism was not merely an aggregate of organs and tissues. He noted that the organ systems of a complex living organism are so well coordinated and regulated that they seem to function as a single entity. Smuts believed that the facts obtained by studying parts of a complex organism in isolation from each other will not be an adequate representation of the complex state. The evolution of the complex state enables the organism to work harmoniously with the environment. Smuts believed that this whole-making or holistic tendency is a fundamental part of nature.

Holistic nutrition

The concept of holism also applies in the utilization of nutrients. In the 1900s the English scientist Gowland Hopkins discovered that foodstuffs separated into component nutrients (proteins, carbohydrates and fats) did not maintain the health and longevity of experimental animals. However, the health and longevity were restored upon the addition of whole milk to the diet. For example, universal energy material, glucose, when made available to the body as a natural component of fruits along with "non-nutrient" roughage has a different effect on the body than when it is presented in its pure form as sugar or even as juice. Similarly, whole grains which contain glucose in complex form along with fiber, affect the body differently than white flour devoid of germ and bran (see Chapter 9 & 10). These are the sorts of holistic observations that lead Vernon McCollum to recognize fresh fruits, vegetables, whole grains and milk as "protective foods" more than half a century ago (see Chapter 15). The knowledge gained from such holistic studies became a stepping stone for the discovery of vitamins and nutritionally important minerals through reductionistic experimental science (see Chapter 7 and 8).

From prehistoric hunter-gatherer times to developed traditional cultures, people did not eat foods that were 'boiled and drained' or that were homogeneous in composition. Traditionally, even when foods were processed to neutralize toxins or to enhance taste, the unique features and complex nutrients of each food was maintained. In contrast, the reductionist enthusiasm for "pure and concentrated" nutrients has lead to such extensive processing and refining of foods in our modern society that the holistic, healthful and unique qualities of food ingredients are often lost (see Chapter 4).

In nature, primates such as gorillas and chimpanzees obtain their nutrients from various parts of hundreds of different plants. Such diets are rich in complex carbohydrates, fiber and a variety of micronutrients. They also help to maintain fermentative microflora in the gastrointestinal tract. Human beings evolved from earlier primates nourished by such high roughage diets and have adapted uniquely to meet the demand for energy with the least disruption of homeostasis. For example, human milk which is rich in diverse natural sugars is adapted to serve the whole developing human infant: its brain, body and its intestinal microflora (see Chapter 16). Similarly, the development of taste buds, a sharp sense of flavor and variety, teeth adapted for chewing, and a long gut that is designed to process a high roughage diet may all be part of the adaptation to a diet of plant staple. Obtaining needed amino acids by a variety of plant products may be another evolutionary adaptation not only to provide minimal amount of essential amino acids but also to avoid proliferation of putrefactive intestinal microbes that are detrimental to the general well-being of the body (see Chapter 3 and 13).

A strong argument can be made for the use of plant products as dietary staples to aid the operation of our homeostatic mechanisms. Digestion of high roughage foods has been evolutionarily tailored to favor beneficial rather than pathologic dispositions of nutrients. By depending on plant products as dietary staples, humans may take full advantage of the potential for homeostatic regulation of nutrient absorption, assimilation, storage and elimination that have evolved.

A diet of plant products provides both the needed nutrients for basic bodily requirements and a built-in mechanism to prevent saturation of any one nutrient. The fiber content of plant foods, for example, which promotes dilution of nutrients, also aids in frequent evacuation of the gastrointestinal (G.I.) system (see Chapter 12). In the chapters of section III we make the argument that the optimal operation of homeostatic mechanisms take place when the internal environment is not saturated with nutrients. When nutrients are limiting, feedback mechanisms operate efficiently to regulate the body's systems. In the presence of excess of nutrients, however, the homeostatic mechanisms may be overwhelmed by secondary problems such as the disposal of excess nutrients. These cause stress (see Chapter 17). Take for example, the range of the body's responses to cholesterol present in food. A small amount of cholesterol is necessary for the synthesis of bile, steroid hormones, and constructing cellular membranes. The body makes its own cholesterol and it has mechanisms to dispose of some dietary cholesterol. An excess intake of cholesterol, however, may result in deposition of cholesterol in blood vessel walls causing atherosclerotic plaques, formation of painful gallstones, or conversion by certain microbes into cancer-causing compounds. The extent to which cholesterol is used for each of these purposes depends in part upon the amount of cholesterol present, on the amount of "anti-cholesterolemic ingredients" in food, and other features of the internal environment (see Chapter 6 and 11).

Similar principles operate both in the storage as well as in the disposal of almost all nutrients including protein, carbohydrate, fats and minerals. (see chapters 5 through 10). The healthy body also has the ability to store or dispose of end products of metabolism (wastes). However, this ability is not unlimited. The limitation varies with the kind of nutrients as well as the particular organs (see Chapter 12). Body fluids such as blood and lymph are very sensitive to nutrient load. The nutrients they carry are rapidly stored or eliminated unless they are used immediately. Minerals such as iron and copper are stored in small quantities in healthy human beings. Over supplying of such nutrients, however, upsets the balance and burdens the organs of storage and excretion (see Chapter 12).

Often the body displays a great capacity to adapt to the nutrient imbalance at the cost of long-term consequences which may greatly curtail the longevity of the whole body or one of its parts. Many ailments such as hypercholesterolemia (excess cholesterol in the blood), gouty arthritis (excess uric acid in the blood), uremia (accumulation of nitrogenous urinary wastes in blood) and certain forms of hypertension (imbalanced minerals such as sodium, calcium and potassium) may occur as a consequence of homeostasis disturbed by the burden of excessive nutrients or their by-products.

Obesity is another example of an immediate homeostatic adjustment to excess nutrient intake. However, the long-term outcome of uncontrolled obesity may include a variety of diseases (e.g. diabetes mellitus, hypertension and coronary artery disease), which eventually damages other critical organs. Indigestion and constipation are yet other examples of immediate adjustments of the body to improper diets. Continuation of such defective diets by suppressing physiological responses with the aid of antacids and laxatives may only predispose the body to the more profound long-term consequences (e.g. esophageal disorders and colonic diverticular disease).

Holistic nutrition

Many successful cultures have put homeostasis and holism into practice to maintain their health and longevity. These are reflected in ancient social customs, religious, and healing practices. Whether it is the ancient wisdom of Ayurveda or those of Hippocrates, holistic diets formed the basis of preventive medicine.

We believe that this approach is a framework in which the data from physical and chemical reductionistic studies must be placed and interpreted, if it is to be understood. According to some thinkers, many human health and nutrition problems are exacerbated by drawing unwarranted conclusions from results of reductionistic analysis and applying less efforts towards holistic synthesis relevant to the organism. An enzyme or a hormone taken out of the body and isolated from other components of its system, for example, may function very differently than when it is in its complex environment, because of the absence of opposing and modifying influences of other components. Similarly, the effects of processed and refined nutrients are not comparable to those of complex nutrient substances that affect human behavior and growth.

Homeostasis can be disrupted at any level, involving the brain, body or intestinal microflora. When a localized disturbance is not corrected by either internal mechanisms or external ones (e.g. dietary manipulation or medicine), it can spread and involve more systems. Even a minor disturbance of the body homeostasis such as those resulting in constipation may lead to chronic ailments such as headaches and nausea. An individual whose internal environment is disturbed may become susceptible to internal or external forces such as cancer or pathogenic organisms (see Chapter 11 and 12).

Iago Goldston of the New York Academy of Medicine, in an address to The American Dietetic Association (1950), drew attention to nutrition from the psychiatrist's point of view. He pointed out that the physician should look into the emotional and motivational factors of the person in relation to his or her diets. Further he pointed out that the scientists became so preoccupied with the generation of much needed knowledge by analysis of food that they forgot the complex nature of the human being to whose needs it must be applied. In essence we cannot forget the fact that the human organism has evolved and adapted to certain nutrients that have aided in attaining a long-lasting healthy life. In the opinion of René Dubos "the relation of food to human existence involves factors that go above and beyond the relation of biochemical nutrition to physical life."

Selected Sources and Suggested Readings

Clifton A. Baile, Mary Anne Della-Fera and Deena Krestel-Rickert, 1985. Brain pepetides controlling behavior and metabolism. *BioScience,* 35, 101-105

Bernard Beck and Christian Villaume, 1987. Nutrient homeostasis: Long-term interrelations between pancreatic hormones, blood glucose and dietary wheat bran in men. *J. Nutrition,* 117, 153-158

Claude Bernard. *An Introduction to the Study of Experimental Medicine.* Dover Publications, New York, 1957.

Howard L. Bleich and Emily S. Boro, 1978. Fasting, feeding and regulation of the sympathetic nervous system. *New England J. Medicine, 298, 1295-1301*

W.R. Bloor and Arthur Knudson, 1917. Cholesterol and cholesterol ester in human blood. *J. Biological Chemistry,* 29, 7-13

Walter B. Cannon. *The Wisdom of the Body.* W.W. Norton, New York, 1963

David Cuthbertson, 1967. The influence of feeding patterns on nutrient utilization. *Proc. Nutrition Society* 26, 143-144

C.L. Hamilton, 1973. Physiologic control of food intake. *J. American Dietetic Association,* 62, 35-40

J. Henriksson, 1990. The possible role of skeletal muscle in the adaptation to periods of energy deficiency. *European J. Clinical Nutrition* 44, 55-64

Mathew J. Kluger and Barbara A. Rothenburg, 1979. Fever and reduced iron: Their interaction as a host defense response to bacterial infection. *Science,* 203, 374-376

H.A. Krebs, 1971. How the whole becomes more than the sum of the parts. *Perspectives in Biology and Medicine,* 14, 448-457

l. Michael Lerner. *Genetic Homeostasis.* Dover Publication, New York, 1954

Richard Lewontin, 1978. Adaptation. *Scientific American,* 239, 212-227

Jean Mayer, 1970. Challenge! The White House conference on Food, Nutrition and Health. *J. American Dietetic Association,* 56, 234-239

G.L.S. Pawan, 1974. Drugs and appetite. *Proc. Nutrition Society,* 33, 239-243

Kamala S. Jaya Rao, 1974. Evolution of Kwashiorkor and Marasmus. *Lancet,* 1, 709-711

Hans Selye, 1973. Homeostasis and heterostasis. *Perspectives in Biology and Medicine,* 16, 441-445

P.S. Shetty and A.V. Kurpad, 1990. Role of the sympathetic nervous system in adaptation to seasonal energy deficiency. *European J. Clinical Nutrition,* 44, 47-53

Jan Christiaan Smuts. *Holism and Evolution.* Viking, New York, 1926

James W. Valentine, 1978. The evolution of multicellular plants and animals. *Scientific American,* 239, 140-159

Jessica Wade, J.Milner and M.Krondl, 1981. Evidence for a Physiological regulation of food selection and nutrient intake in twins. *American J. Clinical Nutrition,* 34, 143-147

Roger J. Williams, et al., 1973. A Renaissance of nutritional science is imminent. *Perspectives in Biology and Medicine* 17, 1-15

Edward O. Wilson, 1991. Hoiism and reduction in sociobiology: Lessons from the ants and human culture. *Biology and Philosophy,* 6, 401-412

In conclusion, it may be said that carbohydrates are the most economical of the food-stuffs, both physiologically and financially. They are the greatest sparers of protein . . . .

– Graham Lusk, *The Elements of the Science of Nutrition*. 1928

3

Physiological Economy: Complex Carbohydrates are Special

Abstract: Energy can be supplied to the body in many ways, only some of which are conducive to good health. Even though energy can be generated from proteins and lipids, complex carbohydrates are the most efficient energy source. The use of protein or fat as the primary energy source results in undesirable long-term consequences including generation of an excess of potentially toxic metabolic wastes (see Chapter 5) and disturbance of intestinal microbial ecology (see Chapter 13). The homeostatic mechanisms that govern our physiology have intricate controls which interconnect the three entities (brain, other organs of the body and our intestinal microflora) of the human body. Some of these controls are manifest through nutrition, and therein lies the special role of complex carbohydrates which cater to the nutritional needs of all three entities. Glucose, the major metabolic breakdown product of complex carbohydrates, is the preferred energy source for the brain. Glucose is also the fuel most readily stored after meals (as liver glycogen which is broken down to release glucose in times of stress). Thus, liver glycogen is a special adaptation for the rapid and efficient use of complex carbohydrates as an energy source. Undigested complex carbohydrates, which enter the colon, support the establishment and maintenance of normal fermentative intestinal bacteria (see Chapter 13). Because complex carbohydrates are digested slowly, they function in a slow-release fashion that allows optimal homeostatic responses. These features of energy metabolism have some profound practical implications. For one, simple "calorie counting" as a means of dietary management misses a crucial nutritional point: How you get calories is more important than how many calories you get. The value of nutrients depends not so much on the abstract number of calories they contain, but more on their biological roles in meeting the existing homeostatic needs of the body. Nearly a century ago, Russell Chittenden, a pioneering American physiologist, demonstrated the practical application of these concepts. Chittenden concluded that both the protein and the total caloric recommendations of that time had been greatly exaggerated, not only for those with a sedentary lifestyle, but also for those engaged in vigorous physical labor. His arguments, and those of other early nutrition scientists, that a consideration of the role of physiologic economy in nutrition leads to better health, are summarized. The concept of physiologic economy remains elusive to mainstream reductionist nutrition science. The full benefits of nutrition modification on health will not be realized until the validity of holistic concepts such as physiological economy and its practical implications are recognized.

In order to better comprehend the physiological economy of the body, we will compare the human body to a city. A city's overall economy operates around the availability of labor and flow of capital. These operations involve bringing in materials for building new structures, repairing and renovating the existing ones, employing people, attending to their needs and promptly disposing of wastes. The intensity of all of these activities depends upon whether the city is in a growing steady state or declining economy. Whatever the state of the economy, the city has to have a thrifty and a judicious management. Similar situations exists in the human body. The body cells supply labor. Food provides both capital and material resources. A healthy body maintains a sound economy by generating and allotting energy for various activities, storing part of it in short and long-term depots and recycling or disposing of the by-products of bodily activities.

Glucose and the body's energy economy

All organisms, from minute microbes to humans are involved in continuous transfer and transformation of energy that they obtain from the environment in the form of nutrients. However, the kind of materials used to obtain energy differ from organism to organism. Animals such as cattle and sheep (herbivores), derive energy from plant materials while tigers and wolves (carnivores) by eating flesh. Primates and humans (omnivores) generally obtain energy from a mixed diet containing both plant and animal products (see Chapter 5).

Human beings need energy for all activities such as growth, recuperation, maintenance of body temperature, breathing, blood circulation, physical work and brain functions. Energy is expended by the body at all times, even while asleep. When energy transactions cease, indeed, life comes to an end! The physiological economy of the body refers to a thrifty management of all those activities that involve energy metabolism, its generation, utilization, storage, and disposal of its by-products. Irrespective of the initial food source, it is the simple sugar glucose which is the major fuel for most of the body's energy needs, used by tissues either directly from the bloodstream or after storage as glycogen. Energy can be generated from proteins and fats as well as from complex carbohydrates because all of them can be broken down or converted into metabolites that can be used to generate glucose. However, the efficiency with which glucose is generated varies considerably from one food source to another, as does the nature of the by-products produced during these transformations. Thus, in spite of the fact that glucose can be generated from fats and proteins, these are not the body's preferred sources for this common currency for generation of energy.

By analogy, various fuels may be used in a city, such as firewood, coal, natural gas, or fuel oil as sources of energy. However, which fuel is preferred for extensive and prolonged use not only depends upon its immediate convenience and cost but also on the long-term effect that it inflicts on the city environment. Well-known examples are the ill-effects of coal burning and automobile exhaust in large cities.

A similar situation applies to the human body's use of different food components for its energy needs. For example, both carbohydrate as well as protein produce approximately 4 Calories per gram. However, carbohydrate produces only carbon dioxide and water as by-products both of which are readily recycled or excreted without harm to the body. On the other hand, when protein is the primary energy source, high levels of by-products (such as ammonia and urea) result. When generated at high levels these products place an increased burden on excretory mechanisms (see Chapter 11). Moreover, under certain conditions their concentration may exceed the amount that could be safely recycled or excreted by the body (see Chapter 7 and 8).

Whatever the food source, the blood glucose level represents a balance between the input and the output, formation, storage and utilization of food energy. When blood glucose reaches a certain level (normally 80-140 mg per 100 ml blood), it will be removed from the bloodstream. This glucose may be utilized for current activities, stored for short-term general use as liver glycogen, as muscle glycogen for specialized use, transformed into protein for long-term use, or stored as fat in various tissues. Normally, the homeostasis of the body maintains blood glucose thorough the action of various body hormones. The hormones regulate the available blood glucose to meet the demand without drastic fluctuations. Maintaining a constant level of blood glucose at all times and supplying it with priority to specific tissues and organs is an important responsibility of the physiological economy of the body. The complex factors involved in these operations play key roles in the maintenance of health and well-being.

After a complex carbohydrate-rich meal, the blood glucose rises. Cells in the pancreas that produce the hormone insulin are activated to increase the rate of insulin production and secretion into the bloodstream. The increased level of insulin communicates to the brain to bring about the feeling of satiety and halts food consumption. As a result, less blood glucose is generated and more is consumed by tissues or stored as liver glycogen. These processes slow down the source of blood glucose. Consequently, within 3-4 hours after a meal, the blood glucose level goes back to its minimal threshold. At this point, the body homeostasis, working through other hormones such as glucagon and epinephrine, inhibits the production of insulin and prevents further depletion of blood glucose. These hormones also initiate conversion of liver glycogen to blood glucose in order to maintain blood glucose at the minimal threshold until the next meal when a new supply of glucose becomes available (Figure 3.1).

As the blood glucose level is lowered, hormones are released which stimulate the central nervous system to initiate the responses we know as hunger , demanding food and thereby paving the way to replenish blood glucose. Thus, interlocking homeostatic mechanisms, those that regulate the blood glucose level and others which regulate the intake of food, maintain a constant blood glucose level of the body. Short-term stores of liver glycogen directly and muscle glycogen indirectly are used to maintain the blood glucose balance during temporary fasting or during strenuous activity such as exercise. Excretion of blood glucose in the urine (glucosuria) or converting glucose into fat normally either a temporary stop-gap mechanism or a secondary and minor metabolic adjustment (see Chapter 4 and 8). However, with disordered glucose homeostasis syndrome characterized by significant glucosuria or obesity may develop.

The rate at which glucose enters the blood from the digested food not only varies from food component to food component but also with the quality and quantity of dietary fiber they contain (see Chapter 6). Many studies have shown that unrefined plant staples (complex carbohydrates) and milk furnish blood glucose at a slow and steady rate. On the other hand, refined food such as white sugar and candy bars provide glucose at a much faster rate. Under those conditions insulin may fail to fully keep pace with the regulation of blood glucose. In the case of protein and fat serving as sources of glucose, their metabolic products need to be processed extensively in the liver before they can enter the blood stream as glucose. For these reasons, refined sugars, fat and protein-rich foods are not the appropriate sources from which to generate blood glucose, except in times of stress (see Chapter 14 and 16).

Liver glycogen and blood glucose

Among the energy reserves of the body, liver glycogen is the preferred source of blood glucose because the back and forth conversion of glucose to liver glycogen is rapid, direct and does not involve the production of toxic waste products. After a complex carbohydrate-rich meal, excess blood glucose is rapidly converted to liver glycogen until 4 g or more of glycogen is stored in every 100 g of liver tissue. Between needs, the amount of glycogen in the liver

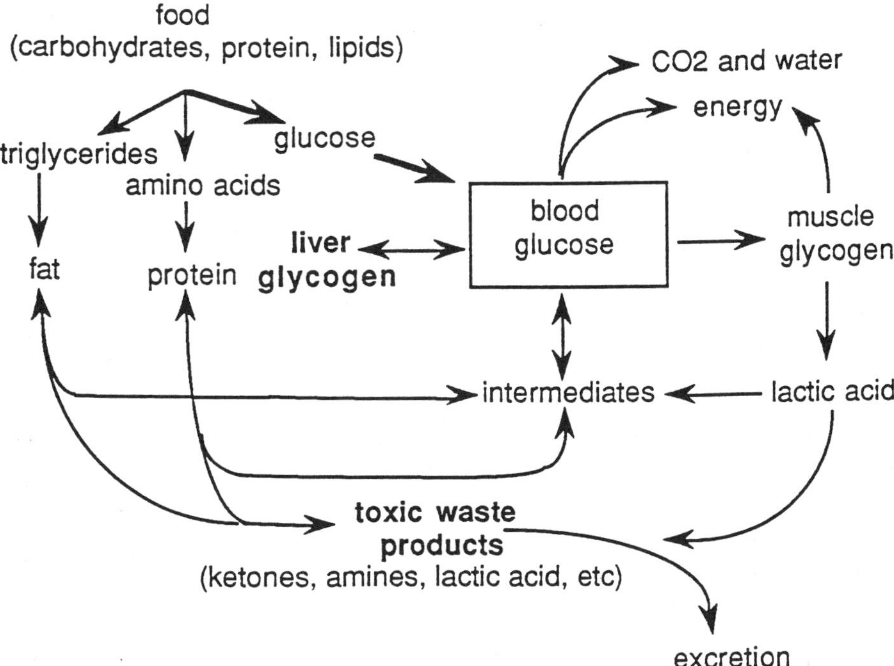

FIGURE 3.1. Glucose homeostasis. Outline of pathways by which ingested food is absorbed as triglycerides, amino acids, glucose, and converted to either blood glucose, the major fuel currency of the body or to liver glycogen, the major short-term storage reservoir for replenishing blood glucose under normal circumstances, or to fat or protein in adipose tissue and muscle. Note that muscle glycogen is for use by muscle and can be converted to blood glucose only by an indirect rout which involves generation of lactic acid. Note that utilization of fat and protein to generate blood glocose generates potentially toxic wasts in the form of ketones, amine etc. Only liver glycogn is rapidly and directly converted to blood glucose without generation of potentially toxic metabolic

progressively decreases due to reverse conversion into blood glucose. this conversion of glycogen to glucose maintains the blood glucose level during the 4-8 hours gap that may exist between two meals. If food is not taken in for 24-48 hours, depending upon the activities of the body, the liver loses practically all of its glycogen and severe hunger pangs set in.

Muscle glycogen, on the other hand, cannot be converted directly to blood glucose without going through a cycle producing a secondary by-product, lactic acid. The lactic acid generated during muscular activity is carried to the liver by the bloodstream where only a part of it is converted to supply blood glucose. The plant kingdom in general, also operates on a glucose based economy. However, it stores glucose mainly in the form of starch, whereas, animals store it as glycogen. Experiments have shown that the amount of glycogen stored in various parts of the body not only differs with species of animals but also with the type of diet. In the case of human beings, the liver glycogen storage is dependent on the nature of the diet as well as the physiological condition of the body. After a complex carbohydrate-rich meal, the liver may store from 10-40% of its weight as glycogen whereas muscles may contain up to 2% of their weight as glycogen. Even though, the liver has a higher concentration of glycogen than muscles, the total amount stored in the muscles is more because a person weighing about 70 kg will have about 28 kg of skeletal muscles and 1.6 kg of liver. Nevertheless, the amount of glycogen stored in the liver may not last more than 2 days if food is not taken in. The process of storing liver glycogen and using it with incredible efficiency are unique evolutionary features that are particularly well developed in primates and especially humans.

Even though liver glycogen is chemically the same as muscle glycogen, the former has a special significance to the body. Exercise depletes glycogen from the muscle while hunger and stress and more general metabolic needs deplete liver glycogen. Liver glycogen not only maintains the blood glucose level directly but also favorably influences the rhythmic functions of the body such as hunger, satiety, various brain functions and behavior. The stressful situations that deplete liver glycogen include anger, sorrow and disappointment. Individuals who have a low or inadequate supply of blood glucose (hypoglycemic) are prone to be irritable and even become violent and destructive. Some anthropologists even believe that adequate reserves of liver glycogen were necessary for the survival of primitive peoples (see Chapter 5).

Chittenden's practical application of physiologic economy

By 1900 scientists had come to considerable agreement on the food calories required for human basal and active metabolism. However, they had great disagreement over three issues: i) what should be the total number of food calories set as a dietary standard ii) how best to supply those food calories (e.g.

A sample of Dr. Russell Chittenden's nutritional experiments on Dr. Lafayette Mendel, Professor of Physiological Chemistry at Yale University. Mendel was 32 years old and weighed 76 kg. During the experiment he reduced intake of protein by giving up meat and undertaking a vegetarian diet with some milk. During nearly seven months of experiments, he consumed 40 g protein, nearly one-third the amount recommended by Voit and consumed 1900 to 3200 kcal food (average 2400 kcal) and was very active throughout. After initial losses body weight and N-loss remained stable at 70 kg and 6.53 g nitrogen. Notice the pattern of stabilization of weight, urinary excretion of nitrogen and uric acid over the extended period.[1]

		Urinary	
Date	**Body weight (kg)**	**Nitrogen (g)**	**Uric acid (g)**
10-26-1903	76.2	10.53	...
10-27-	75.0	13.46	0.580
10-28-	74.5	11.03	...
10-29-	74.5	11.48	...
10-31-	74.5	12.37	...
11-01-	74.5	10.38	0.602
11-07-	74.6	8.18	...
11-14-	74.0	8.04	0.494
11-26-	74.0	7.00	0.410
12-02-	74.5	7.28	0.480
12-10-	73.0	7.62	0.438
12-21-	73.0	6.37	0.259
01-01-1904	73.0	7.64	0.438
01-11-	72.0	6.17	0.443
01-30-	70.6	6.53	0.429
02-15-	69.5	7.50	0.420
03-02-	70.5	7.20	0.462
03-30-	70.3	6.26	0.389
04-04-	70.0	6.44	0.356
05-01-	70.0	5.95	0.373
06-16-1904	70.0	6.55	0.419
Daily Av.[2]		6.53	0.419

1. Randomly selected from daily records from October 26, 1903 to June 23, 1904.
2. Daily Average from November 10, 1903.

percentage as carbohydrate, protein and fat) and iii) what kind of foodstuffs to recommend as a source of calories (e.g. animal versus plant products). Some prominent scientists of the early 1900's such as Carl Voit and Max Rubner of Germany and Wilbur Atwater of the USA, agreed on a standard of 3,000 food Calories daily for an average man of 70 kg supplied as 118 g of protein, 56 g of fat and 500 g of carbohydrate.

However, Russell Chittenden of Yale University, a pioneer of physiological chemistry and human nutrition in the U.S. did not feel comfortable with that standard for the following reasons:

1. The standard was based on the prevailing belief that high food intake and increased body mass conferred better health, a notion with which Chittenden did not agree.

2. The experimental data used to formulate the standard came from short-term experiments and, thereby did not necessarily reflect life-long adapted dietary patterns.

3. Their recommendations did not give priority to carbohydrate as an energy source. Chittenden felt that, since carbohydrates would supply the same amount of calories as protein, but without the potentially toxic byproducts of protein metabolism, it should have been recommended as the preferred source of energy. Moreover, it has been the food staple of the majority of people in the world and hence would be more easily adapted to traditional diets.

4. If health and bodily strength can be maintained with a lower caloric intake of food, especially of protein, then, why should the human dietary standard be set at such a high calorie level?

In 1902 Chittenden carried out long-term experiments on human volunteers. Begining at 47 years of age, starting with himself he conducted one of the longest human nutrition experiments that has ever been done in nutrition history. As pointed out in his book, *Physiological Economy* in Nutrition, he adhered neither to fad diets nor to diets that completely forbade meat and other sources of animal protein. He gradually reduced intake of meat, egg and total protein from 118 to about 40 g and reduced daily food calories from 3,000 to approximately 1,600 Calories in a year's period. After the loss of 8 kg, his body weight stabilized. Maintaining that amount of food intake not only kept his weight almost constant but also made him feel more active at work. He experienced better physical strength, while maintaining mental vigor, endurance and resistance to disease.

Chittenden noted that increased plant staple in the diet resulted in an increase in the bulk and consistency of feces. He observed a decrease in headaches as well as in painful symptoms of arthritis, which he correlated to decreased uric acid excretion. Furthermore he noticed improvement in his sense of taste and appetite. As a result of these experiments which suggested that an individual could improve or maintain physical health, stamina and mental vigor on a reduced food intake Chittenden raised these questions about the recommendations of Atwater and others:

- Won't an excessive dietary standard encourage people to over eat?
- In the long run will it not load their systems with three times the amount of protein than they actually need as well as with an excess of food calories?
- Might the overall effect not be to worsen rather than improve health?

In 1903, following his belief that nutrition experiments should be broad based in order to be generally valid, he repeated similar experiments with three distinct groups of individuals: 1) A group of University faculty and administrators who represented a sedentary population. 2) A group from the U.S. Army made up of individuals of different ethnic backgrounds who represented moderately active workers and, 3) a group of young Yale University athletes some of whom were highly accomplished sportsmen.

Among the first group he included his colleagues of the department of physiological chemistry who were 25, 26, 32 and 38 years of age respectively. The results showed that in spite of broad differences in their age, their requirement of protein remained less than 50 g per day (0.947 g/kg) and that they required only 28 Calories/kg body weight. He concluded that young men engaged in sedentary work need not burden their bodies with either excessive protein nor food calories.

His next investigation was on groups of youths, 13 of whom were from the U.S. Army and 8 student athletes of the University. Some of them were consuming as much as 243 g of protein and excreting as much as 37 g of nitrogen in the urine, daily. He subjected them to similar moderation in intake of meat and total food calories. At the end of 5–6 months they all showed decided improvement in their muscular strength in spite of losing significant body weight, mainly adipose tissue. They performed better not only in their physical activity but also in their intellectual performance.

As a result of those studies Professor Chittenden concluded that physiological economy in nutrition brings about better mental and physical health and bodily endurance. He concluded that without any kind of strict dietary regimen, mere moderation in food intake brings about physiological economy in nutrition. He concluded that increased food calories, especially in the form of high protein, alters the body's energy economy in a homeostatically undesirable fashion. He hypothesized that intake of food, especially as protein, beyond the physiological need may affect composition of the blood and lymph which in turn brings about change in sensitive part of the brain, the central and peripheral nervous system. Together, these changes affect mental vigor, and physical strength. High protein diets also overload organs such as the liver and kidneys and curtails their longevity. Consequently, Chittenden emphasized that both rich and poor need to pay attention to the implications of their dietary selections for their body's physiological economy.

Chittenden's thesis raised many questions in the scientific community regarding the validity of the standards of human diet (see Chapter 4). Around 1920's professor Vernon McCollum of Johns Hopkins University who sympathized with Chittenden's views conducted his own investigations. McCollum studied dietary practices of various communities and advocated consuming most food calories in the form of whole grains, leafy vegetables and milk which he called "protective foods" (see Chapter 15). Around the 1930's Henry C. Sherman of Columbia University, a distinguished professor of nutrition, after extensive research not only suggested that the top priority of nutrition should be to supply energy to the body but also recommended that food calories should be supplied from plant products and milk (see Chapter 5). Professor Sherman argued that if such a diet is cultivated from childhood, nutrition becomes a simple art, and the taste for the right food becomes a habit.

The fallacy of calorie counting

The term "food calorie" (K calorie, or Calorie), refers to the amount of heat required to raise the temperature of one kilogram of water one degree Celsius. Using this unit of measurement, scientists determined that the carbohydrate and protein food components yield approximately 4 Calories per gram whereas fat will yield approximately 9 Calories. Based on these values scientists in the 1800's calculated the amount of food calories an individual requires in a day. However, the experimental calculation (physical heat calories) differed from the actual caloric benefit gained by the body from digesting food; the latter is distinguished as physiological fuel value. Thus, it must be emphasized here that physical caloric determination does not take into consideration many specific costs and benefits that the body experiences while obtaining the food calories through the process of digestion and assimilation (see Chapter 6).

There are considerable discrepancies between the actual food consumed and the amount of nutrients digested and absorbed. They vary with the composition of food, with the age and the physiological condition of an individual. Furthermore, scientific determinations are based on experiments in which very simple and isolated food components are used. Experiments have shown that by mixing various foods, the physiologic value of the diet can be dramatically modified. This is because the physiological values of foods involve complex processes of digestion, absorption and intermediary metabolism of nutrients and microbial interactions in the colon (see Chapter 11 and 13). Consequently, the value of Calorie counting remains controversial and the overall benefits of specific foods to the individual are still debated even after a century of investigation.

Scientists recognize that the energy requirements of the human body fall into two categories: 1) Basal Metabolism (Basal Metabolic Rate, BMR) and ii) energy needs of specific physiological activities. The BMR refers to the bodily functions such as respiration, blood circulation, temperature regulation and nerve functions that the body automatically carries out even at complete rest. It may amount to about 15% of the energy needs of the body. In addition, the body engages in a variety of daily activities which utilize energy above and beyond the BMR. An average person weighing 70 kg, for example, requires approximately 2400 Calories per day. Depending upon age and sex, an adult daily Caloric needs may, however, vary by about 400 Calories. Special condition such as pregnancy requires an additional 300 Calories, lactation 500 Calories and so on. Depending upon how soundly one sleeps, 25% of the BMR may be spent while sleeping. The BMR is high in the young but slows down and stabilizes during middle age and decreases during old age. After the age of 21 the BMR falls at a rate of about 2% per decade (see Chapter 17).

The BMR may also vary with heredity, environment and endocrinal adaptation. Certain individuals gain weight easily, while others on the same diet do not. This is mainly due to differences in hormonal profiles of different individuals. Similarly, the BMR of women is 12-15% lower than men. In other words, women eating the same quantity and quality of food as men gain more weight than men. Repeated fasting, starvation or overfeeding also changes BMR to a certain extent (behavioral adaptation). A poorly fed infant, for example, may adapt to a lower BMR and an overfed infant to higher BMR. However, it has also been found that, to a certain extent, adjustment of the BMR may not distort growth and development during short periods of starvation or overfeeding.

The amount of energy expended by the body for daily physical and physiological activities varies greatly with individuals: doing very light work requires 2-5 Calories per minute and heavy work 7-12 Calories. A woman will spend less Calories under similar situations than a man (see Table 3.1).

In a healthy individual the complex homeostatic mechanism that maintains the energy economy coordinates many of these varying factors through bodily rhythms. Appetite and hunger, for example, are experienced differently in warmer and colder climate; and by younger versus older persons. The dominant factor leading to variability in energy needs is the proportion of time an individual devotes to moderate to heavy physical activities. In general, daily energy expenditures of adult males is about 1.7 times and of women is about 1.6 times that of the BMR.

The value of nutrients depends not only on the calories they contain but also on the biological roles they play, the existing needs of the body and its homeostatic condition (see Chapter 18). This applies to proteins, cholesterol, sugar, salt, and other nutrients. For example, the total number of calories provided by a candy bar or a serving of meat may be equivalent to those obtained from a given amount of fruits and whole grains. However, the sum total of nutrients they contribute and their effects on homeostasis are very different, especially when consumed repeatedly over a long period of time. The calories obtained by repeated intake of candies for example, may promote diabetes or even, paradoxically, hypoglycemia; the calories obtained by excess meat consumption may result in constipation, hypercholesterolemia, mineral deficiencies and imbalanced microbial systems (see Chapter 14). An equal number of calories obtained through fruit, vegetables and whole grains, on the other hand, prevent those problems by contributing both glucose for the generation of energy and storage of glycogen, bulk to remedy constipation and

TABLE 3.1. Energy Allowance for Moderate Activity for Men and Women of Different Ages. (World Health Organization, 1985)

	Energy Allowances in kcal/day	
Age in years	**Males (kg)**	**Females (kg)**
11–14	2,500 (45)	2,200 (46)
15–18	3,000 (66)	2,200 (55)
19–24	2,900 (72)	2,200 (58)
25–50	2,900 (79)	2,200 (63)
51 above	2,300 (77)	1,900 (65)
Pregnancy		300
Lactation		500

appropriate varieties of minor nutrients to sustain our normal fermentative colonic microflora.

The popularity of counting Calories and of obtaining energy with utter disregard to the dietary components have brought chaos to the energy economy of the brain, the body and the intestinal microflora. The resulting ill-health has inspired a large number of "Reducing Diets" and numerous dietetic foods on the supermarket shelves. Unfortunately, these have failed to communicate the underlying delicate physiological economy in nutrition to the general public. People have resorted to quick solutions such as obtaining relief through frequent uses of laxatives, pain-killers, antacids and tranquilizers, rather than resolving the underlying disturbance in homeostatic mechanisms and physiologic economy. Perhaps as a result, health problems such as obesity, hypoglycemia, anorexia and bulimia are on the increase. As Chittenden suggested early in the century, the majority of the diseases of mankind today are due to, or connected with, perversion of nutrition. Unless judicious application of scientific truth is applied to the art of living, maintaining health may remain elusive and expensive. Lasting health is not possible without good nutrition. We have to reorient our life-style to the promotion of physiological economy in nutrition that leads to "preventive health care" rather than continuing the current expansion of "disease care."

Selected Sources and Suggested Readings

Herman Adlercreeutz, et al., 1989. Diet and plasma androgens in postmenopausal vegetarian and omnivorous women and postmenopausal women with breast cancer. *American J. Clinical Nutrition,* 49, 433-442

Demetrius Albanes, 1987. Caloric intake, body weight, and cancer: A Review. *Nutrition and Cancer,* 9, 199-217

Thomas A. Anderson, 1982. Recent trends in carbohydrate consumption. *Annual Review of Nutrition* 2, 113-132

Anonymous, 1988. Surgeon General's Report on Nutrition and Health. *Nutrition Today,* 23, 22-30

Anonymous, 1976. Treatment of massive obesity: Rice/reduction diet. *Nutrition Reviewws,* 34, 176-178

Anonymous, 1970. Cholesterol absorption versus cholesterol synthesis in man. *Nutrition Reviews,* 28, 11-15

Vivienne C. Aries, et.al., 1970. The effect of a strict vegetarian diet on the faecal flora and faecal steroid concentration. *J. Pathology* 103, 54-59

Wilbur O. Atwater and A.P. Bryant, 1889. The availability and fuel value of food materials. *Conn. (Storrs) Agr. Expt. Sta. 12th An. Rpt.* 73-110.

W.R. Bloor, 1916. Fat assimilation. *J. Biological Chemistry,* 24, 447-460

A.P. Boyar, et al., 1988. Response to a diet low in total fat in women with postmenopausal breast cancer: A pilot study. *Nutrition and Cancer,* 11, 93-99

Marian Burros, 1988. Cholesterol is not the only culprit. *New York Times,* January 13, 16

Russell H. Chittenden, *Physiological Economy in Nutrition.* Frederic A. Strokes, New York, 1904

J.V.G.A. Durnin, 1990. Low energy expenditures in free-living populations. *European J. Clinical Nutrition,* 44, 95-102

J.V.G. A. Durnin, 1978. Indirect calorimetry in man: a critique of practical problems. *Proc. Nutrition society,* 37, 5-11

P.J. Garlick and M.A. McNurlan, 1988. Factors controlling the disposition of primary nutrients. *Proc. Nutrition Society,* 47, 169-176

A.M. Greco, et al., 1984. Effects of an overload of animal protein on the rat: Brain DNA alterations and tissue morphological modifications during fetal and post-natal stage. *International J. Vitamin and Nutrition,* 55, 107-112.

Peter Greenwald, 1989. Strengths and limitations of methodological approaches to the study of diet and cancer: Summary and future perspectives with emphasis on dietary fat and breast cancer. *Preventive Medicine,* 18, 163- 166

B. Van Itallie, 1978. Dietary fiber and obesity. *American J. Clinical Nutrition,* 31, S43-S52

Eric Jequier, kevin Acheson, and Yves Schutz, 1987. Assessment of Energy expenditure and fuel utilization in man. *Annual Review of Nutrition,* 7, 187-208

Philippa, M. Lyons and A. Stewart Truswell, 1988. Serotonin precursor influenced by type of carbohydrate meal in healthy adults. *American J. Clinical Nutrition,* 47, 433-39

Ni McNeil, 1984. The contribution of the large intestine to energy supplies in man. *American J. Clinical Nutrition,* 39, 338-342

E.S. Nasset and Jin Soon Ju, 1961. Structure of endogenous and exogenous protein in the alimentary tract. *J. Nutrition,* 74, 461-465

Frank Q. Nuttall, 1987. Diet and diabetes, a brief overview: Personal perspective. *J. American College of Nutrition,* 6, 5-9

Morris H. Ross and Gerrit Bras, 1971. Lasting influence of early caloric restriction on prevalence of neoplasms in the rat. *National Cancer Institute,* 47, 1095-1113

Susan W. Ross, et al., 1987. Glycemic index of processed wheat products. American J. Clinical Nutrition, 46, 631-635

Abigail A. Salyers, 1979. Energy sources of major intestinal fermentative anaerobes, *American J. Clinical Nutrition,* 32, 158-163

S. Samman and D.C. K. Roberts, 1987. The importance of the non-protein compounds of the diet in the plasma cholesterol response of rabbits to casein zinc and copper. *British J. Nutrition,* 57, 27-33

W.J. Schultink, et al., 1990. Body weight changes and basal metabolic rates of rural Beninese women during seasons with different energy intakes. *European J. Clinical Nutrition,* 44, (Suppl. 1) 31-40

D.A. T. Southgate, 1981. Role of carbohydrates in the diet of industrialised countries. *Bibliethca Nutritio et Dieta,* 30, 124-130

J.P. Stammers, et al., 1989. High arachidonic acid levels in the cord blood of infants of mothers on vegetarian diets. *British J. Nutrition,* 61, 89-97

R. Thornton, P.M. Emmett and K.W. Heaton, 1983. Diet and gall stones: effects of refined and unrefined carbohydrate diets on bile cholesterol saturation and bile acid metabolism. *Gut,* 24, 2-6

Joan A. Treichel, 1973. The great medical debate over low blood sugar, *Science News,* 103, 172-174

Robert, J. Trotter, 1973. Aggression: A way of life for the Qolla. *Science News,* 103, 76-77

Roger H. Unger and Lelio Orci, 1981. Glucagon and the A Cell. *New England J. Medicine,* 304, 1518-1580

H.S. Wiggins, 1984. Nutritional value of sugars and related compounds undigested in the small gut. *Proc. Nutrition Society,* 43, 69-75

Francis C. Wood, Jr. and Edwin L. Bierman, 1986. Is diet the cornerstone in management of diabetes? *New England J. Medicine,* 315, 1224-1227

Pierre Wursch, Simone Del Vedovo, and Brigitte Koellreutter, 1986. Cell structure and starch nature as key determinants of the digestion rate of starch in legume. *American J. Clinical Nutrition,* 43, 25-29

Richard J. Wurtman, 1982. Nutrients that modify brain function. *Scientific American,* 246, 50-60.

John Yudkin, 1967. Evolutionary and historical changes in dietary carbohydrates. *American J. Clinical Nutrition,* 20, 108 115

Milk and leaves of plants occupy unique positions among available food-stuffs, in that they are so constituted as to correct, when suitable amounts are included in the diet, the defects of cereals, tubers, roots, and meats. For this reason it was suggested eleven years ago that they be distinguished by the term "protective foods."

– E. V. McCollum and Nina Simonds, *The Newer Knowledge of Nutrition*, 1929

4

What is Wrong with Our Nutrition?

Abstract: The affluent American diet is not based on sound principles of nutritional science. In this chapter the history of nutrition is surveyed. Plant products are high in complex carbohydrates and fiber and contain small amounts of all other necessary nutrients, making them superior dietary staples. Animal products are high in protein and fat but essentially devoid of complex carbohydrates and fiber making them a poor choice of dietary staple. Yet the affluent American diet emphasizes meat and protein at the expense of plant products and complex carbohydrates. This exaggerated importance of protein in nutrition is traced as an example of how recommendations, not necessarily based on sound scientific thought, can take on a life of their own, with the help of aggressive marketing by industry. Similarly, the role of market forces in popularizing highly processed foods which are generally rich in protein over unprocessed plant products rich in fiber and complex carbohydrates, is described. The rise in incidence of diseases of affluence which has accompanied this detrimental change in the popular diet is documented. Sound holistic nutritional concepts have been ignored for the last 50 years in favor of commercial interests and reductionist thinking. The current sorry state of Western nutrition is likely to continue or get worse until this situation is changed. Even as Americans suffer the effects of overnutrition, over-processing of foods and excess protein, the developing world, ravaged by undernutrition and deficiency diseases, is anxious to adopt our nutritional standards. Ironically, as will be developed in subsequent chapters, the only viable solution to both our nutritional problems and theirs lies in universal adoption of a predominantly lacto-vegetarian diet.

Food is used for more than just satisfying hunger. It is used to feed the growing young, maintain physical and emotional health, and prevent sickness. Food also serves interpersonal relations and promotes social well-being. From prehistoric times, various schools of cultural medicine such as Ayurvedic, Oriental and Native American used dietary regimens as remedies for illnesses. Traditionally, food consists of complex mixtures of natural ingredients rather than isolated and purified components. All traditional cultures, for example, consumed dietary fiber but it was not separated from the complex mixture of food nor evaluated for its precise dietary roles. With the advent of reductionist scientific approaches as applied to nutrition, scientists began analyzing foods into its components in order to understand their role in metabolism. Industries put this information to commercial use by processing food ingredients to serve marketing goals.

Origins of the mistaken emphasis on protein in nutrition

Scientific investigations of nutrition started with the studies on the production of body heat and respiration by the great French chemist Antoine Lavoisier in 1780. Around 1816, Francois Megandie, a French physician, noticed the difference in the growth of dogs fed separately with meat, oil and sugar. The higher the percentage of meat in the diet the faster and bigger the dogs grew whereas those that got oil or sugar only, eventually became sick and died. Such studies lead William Prout, an English scientist, to classify foods into three groups: animal foods, plant foods and fatty or oily foods. Justus Liebig, a well-known 19th century German chemist concluded that protein was the primary source of energy. Liebig's concept of protein as an energy source was later found to be incorrect and carbohydrate was established as the primary energy source of the human diet (see Chapter 3 and 5). Nevertheless, because of this early misconception, the food value of animal protein was exaggerated and contributed greatly to erroneous notions throughout the subsequent history of nutrition including the present.

Around the 1850s the celebrated French physiologist Claude Bernard carried out the first elaborate study of energy metabolism in human beings. His work on liver glycogen and its relation to homeostasis of the body captured the attention of all scientists and, even to-day, remains a classic in physiology.

At about the same time, German scientists including Carl Voit were engaged in studying the role of protein in human nutrition. Voit recommended 118 grams (g) of animal protein per day for an average man. A survey around 1907 showed that German workers were eating on the average 137 g of protein per day. Many U.S. scientists were getting their scientific training in Germany at that time, and their ideas on nutrition were significantly influenced by those associations.

Wilbur Atwater, a student of Voit, analyzed nearly 4,000 American foods of animal and plant origin for their nutrient values at the U.S. Department of

Agriculture Experiment Station in Connecticut. He also studied protein and energy requirements of humans in different types of activities and in various age groups. As a result, around 1900, the Atwater Standard Diet was established at 100 g of protein per day and with sufficient carbohydrate and fat to make the total food Calories 2,700 for light work and at 150 g of protein with 4,150 Calories for hard work. Currently, for a man of 70 kg body weight the 1990 RDA (Recommended Dietary Allowance) of protein is 55 g per day. Nevertheless, the higher protein standard is often assumed to be desirable by lay persons, scientists and the influential public alike (see Chapter 5).

Rise and fall of a low-protein school of nutritional thought

Around 1900, nutrition science as an aspect of human physiology was started in the U.S. at Yale University by professor Russell Chittenden, who also was German educated. His interest in studying protein requirements in human nutrition was influenced by the pain he was suffering from a form of arthritis. He was advised anecdotally by a fellow scientist to reduce his meat consumption, to alleviate his arthritis pain. The relief he obtained as a result of reducing meat in his diet prompted him to conduct dietary experiments on himself and on a large number of volunteers. He conducted one of the first long-term experiments on human subjects and concluded that consuming more than 35 g of protein per day by an average person was not only unnecessary but also harmful to health.

In the meantime, in response to a meat shortage during World War I, European scientists undertook experiments with meatless and low meat diets. The Danish Government supported a research laboratory in Copenhagen under the direction of the physician Mikkel Hindhede for the sole purpose of investigating the health implications of low protein diets. He conducted long-term dietary experiments on animals and on people including himself and his family members. He maintained adults in a healthy condition for 167 days in nitrogen equilibrium with potatoes as the sole source of protein (see Chapter 7). In the course of his investigations he lost faith in the value of the high-protein feeding of children that he, as a physician, had believed in for 30 years. He raised his 4 children into healthy academically accomplished individuals on low protein foods. Hindhede believed that 30 g of protein per person per day was adequate and that eating 118 g protein per day as recommended by Voit would severely tax the liver and the kidneys and cause various ailments. He concluded that meat as a source of protein was not necessary to maintain health.

By the 1920s the efforts of Chittenden, Hindhede and others provided convincing evidence that a high protein diet was unnecessary, wasteful and in the long run injurious to health; and that plant products could serve as healthful human dietary staples. Other prominent American scientists also began evaluating the effect of combinations of plant and animal proteins in the diet. Thomas Osborne and Lafayette Mendel of Yale University, Vernon McCollum of Johns Hopkins University and many others were engaged in studying the nutritional role of plant staples. McCollum and associates found that all the amino acids necessary for animal nutrition were contained in the proteins of wheat, maize and oat kernels. Low levels of some of the amino acids in certain cereals were complemented by the different nutrient and amino acid composition of other plant foods. McCollum's principle of nutrition was that the young should get adequate food but the protein content of food should be the minimum required for the physiological needs of the body.

McCollum found that leafy vegetables differ entirely in their nutrients from cereals, legumes and root crops. Even though greens are generally lower in protein, their mineral contents are 2-5 times higher than both cereals and legumes. Osborne and Mendel found that asparagus, lettuce and celery contain more B vitamins than apples, pears or grapes. Other scientists found that leaves complement the diet with those nutrients in which grains are poor. They found the protein content of leaves vary from 1.3% in cabbage to 3% in turnip leaves. Similarly, fruits as a class of food, provided nutritional benefits that meats, cereals, legumes and leaves all lacked. They not only compensate for the acidic residue of meat, eggs and other animal products by providing alkaline elements to maintain acid-base balance of body fluids but also add mild laxative properties to foods (see Chapter 10). In addition, they supply vitamins, minerals and fibers (see Chapter 5 and 9).

Thomas Osborne who extensively investigated protein qualities of various plant staples between 1891 and 1920 found that unlike animal proteins, plant proteins provide nutritional variety and bulk. Each variety complements the excesses and deficiencies of the other. Nuts for example, which contained 10-20% protein and 40-60% fat, complements fruits (0.5% to 2.5% protein, 0.1 to 1.5% fat) and leafy vegetables (1 to 9% protein, 0.2 to 2% fat). Fiber rich fruit and leafy vegetables in turn served to dilute the concentrated protein and fat of rich foods such as nuts. The carbohydrate, protein, fat and other nutrient contents of plant staples in general, complement each other and do not saturate the body's mechanisms of nutrient selection. In contrast, animal products, especially meat, are rich in nutrients such as protein (including all 20 amino acids), saturated fat, sodium and phosphate. As a result, they overwhelm the body's mechanisms of nutrient selection. Many prominent scientists of the 1920's realized the importance of mixing plant foods to dilute and balance the nutritional needs of the human body.

Professor Henry Sherman raised 30 generations of rats on whole grains supplemented with milk and found that such a diet contributed to their health, vitality, resistance to disease, fertility and longevity of members of the colony. Study after study during the 1930's showed that humans of all ages could benefit from diets rich in whole grains, fresh vegetables, fruits and milk. Surveys of traditional cultural diets and repeated long-term human nutritional studies showed that such diets played a prominent role in improving the performance of students in colleges and the efficiency of workers in the factories. Those diets reduced children's visits to doctors and lowered the incidence of chronic diseases of the middle-aged and the elderly. During the early 1900's researchers also reported a variety of other benefits of a plant staple diet on aspects of body physiology. These include acid-base balance, mineral balance, cholesterol, triglyceride and glucose levels in blood.

These researchers were also impressed by a variety of other influences that plant staples exerted on aspects of body physiology including i) acid-base balance and mineral balance, ii) reduction of cholesterol, triglyceride and glucose levels in blood, iii) lowering of blood pressure and iv) promoting regularity of bowel movements. In addition to their physiological benefits to the body, professors Christian Herter of New York, Leo Rettger of Yale University and others reported that a plant staple-rich diet was also essential to maintain beneficial intestinal microflora which play a very important role in human health and well-being (see Chapter 3 and 13). Thus, during the 1920s and 30s many scientists supported a diet based on plant staples with enthusiasm. They called such a diet one of "protective foods" and felt it was necessary to maintain the overall health of the body (see Chapter 15).

The depression years of the 1930s influenced both industries and the politicians to support the views held by these scientists. This consensus was reflected in the enactment of the School Luncheon and the Food Stamp programs to distribute such food to a larger portion of the population. This influence on diet continued during the 1940s. Scientists recommended the use of grain directly for human consumption or to increase milk production rather than to increase meat production, because they believed per capita meat consumption already had reached the desirable maximum. A communication published in the 1939 Yearbook of Agriculture, by the U.S. Secretary of Agriculture Henry Wallace, gives a glimpse of how receptive politicians were to those scientific nutrition ideas. He wrote, ". . . Fifty percent of the people of the United States do not get enough in the way of dairy products, fruits and vegetables to enable them to enjoy full vigor and health . . . ."

All through the 1940s the emphasis remained on obtaining at least two-thirds of food calories from unrefined plant staples and the remaining one-third mainly from milk, with a relatively small contribution from meat, poultry, eggs, cheese and sugar. As the depression years and World War II passed, Americans generally became more prosperous and more sedentary. Gradually, food industries once again elevated the animal foods such as meat, poultry, eggs and cheese to the level of food staples. The result was a diet reduced in dietary fiber, complex carbohydrate and minor nutrients. By the 1950s as meat, fat and sugar consumption increased, milk and bulky plant food consumption began decreasing. The per capita consumption of sugar, for example, increased from approximately 22 pounds per year in the 1850's to 110 pounds by 1930; it remained at 110 lb for 20 years and started going up again around the 1950s. Consumption of meat and refined products also increased in similar proportions.

As the 1950s passed, nutrition research was directed increasingly towards cellular, subcellular and molecular levels which led scientists away from focus on the whole human being. The reductionist approach that helped to better understand the parts failed to grasp the whole (see Chapter 2). The refined and high protein diet was recommended to achieve maximal body growth, without regard to long-term consequences on intellectual performance, behavior, resistance to diseases, etc. It led people to believe that red meat protein provided all the nutritional components for good health. It also contributed to drastic reduction in fluid milk consumption.

After World War II, a spectacular development of the free market economy began to take place in the U.S. All aspects of life began changing. The shattered economies of Europe gave additional incentives for the rapid expansion of agricultural industries. By the 1950s a marked change began in agricultural business and marketing techniques and in patterns of food consumption. The statistics clearly point out that a great surge in consumption of meat, poultry and sugar began during this period; This has continued for nearly 40 years. As people paid attention to increasing the amount of protein in the diet, they ignored the importance of other nutrients such as complex carbohydrates and fiber (whole grains, fruits and vegetables).

In the 1950s, the food and pharmaceutical industries began playing a decisive role in influencing the popular diet. As a result, the traditional diets were abandoned for a diet higher in fat, protein and refined foods. People were led to believe that high protein foods were energy foods, and that the bulk and fiber in unrefined plant staples were nonessential since they did not directly contribute calories. Even the U.S. Department of Agriculture Extension Service began encouraging people to aspire to eat more red meat. They suggested soybeans and cottage cheese as a second class substitute for those who could not afford meat. Physicians began expressing concern for the well-being of people who did not eat meat and eggs, while ignoring the negative health implications of not eating whole grains, vegetables and fruits. Beef was portrayed by advertising as "real food for real people." An impression was created that only vegetarians need be concerned about balancing their food intake to comprise a healthy diet. Under these influences it was not surprising that people began believing that the more meat they consumed, the better their health would be.

Per capita consumption of caloric sweets increased to 123 pounds per year in 1984 compared to 65 pounds in 1900's. Cakes and cookies accounted for approximately 11% of youngsters' dietary calories. By contrast, cereals accounted for only 3.3%. Even traditional desserts such as milk puddings and fresh and stewed fruits were replaced with pastries made of refined flour, white sugar and saturated fat. Not only the caloric need of the body but also other nutritional needs were wrongly served as milk and whole grain consumption began dropping sharply while consumption of meat and refined products increased rapidly. Never disproven, the views of Chittenden and other nutritional holists were simply ignored.

Processed foods and the affluent diet

The adjectives "refined" and "pure" reflected a view that foods such as whole grains, raw sugar, sea salt and other unprocessed items were unclean, inferior and undesirable. The postwar generation of the 1950s and beyond regarded whole grains as suitable only for cattle feed and never developed a taste for unprocessed plant products and milk. The thriving food industries of the 1970s added one more hazard to health by popularizing protein-rich fast foods and snacks of refined food products. Snacking became a national pastime. Fast-food establishments offering neatly packaged pure ground meat hamburgers, hot-dogs and uniformly peeled and sliced potatoes fried in saturated fats replaced traditional street corner hand carts selling nuts and fruits. Often ketchup represented the "vegetable" and soft drinks were substituted for milk in the school luncheon. Such a life-style became a hallmark of affluent America.

In fact, the surveys made in the 1970s indicated that a majority of school children consumed only the meat, snacks, soft drinks and desserts, dumping the remaining items of food on their school lunch trays into the garbage. With the acceptance of these substitutes, whole grains, fresh vegetables, fruits and milk were looked down upon as bulky, starchy and fattening. Ironically, as we shall see, it was the processed and fiber-depleted foods which made the major contribution to the modern-day epidemic of obesity. Thus the popular diet overwhelmed the homeostatic mechanisms of the body by over-nutrition. As plant staples became optional items on the dinner menu, the metabolic problems caused by excessive nutrients such as saturated fats, cholesterol, phosphate and sodium as well as the deficiencies due to lack of dietary complex carbohydrates, fiber, essential fatty acids and calcium, began to develop.

The rise of affluent diseases

The incidence of chronic ailments of heart, liver kidneys, and other internal organs, previously associated with old-age, has been noted to be increasing among members of the middle-aged generation in the United States today. Gastrointestinal problems ranging from constipation to colorectal cancers have become so common in the U.S. and other affluent countries, that these diseases have collectively come to be known as "affluent diseases."

Why has degenerative disease begun to affect individuals at younger ages? One compelling explanation is that the long-established cultural role for nutrition as preventive medicine was replaced in the last century with a reliance on readily available drugs and medicines. Together with other changes in science (e.g. the rise of reductionism) and the economy (e.g. the rise of food processing and marketing industries) this resulted in a dramatic change in popular nutrition towards an imbalanced diet not geared to homeostasis. The imbalanced diet began affecting not only individual organs and systems but also the health and well-being of the whole body. As time passed, isolated factors were cor-

factors were correlated with, and hence blamed for, affluent diseases (e.g. elevated serum cholesterol for atherosclerosis and sodium intake for hypertension) without recognizing that these factors and their associated disorders are most likely a result of a wider mismanagement of human nutrition.

It has been suggested that many medical problems including behavioral disorders, depression, insomnia and allergies may in some cases be caused by the effects of imbalanced diet and/or artificial food additives. Yet, because of their multicausal nature and the intricacy of homeostatic controls, the crucial common features of the affluent diseases of our time (e.g. their effects on homeostasis) are not as easy to appreciate as were, for example, the pathogenesis of infectious diseases in the past century.

Similarly, some scientists have suspected that disorders such as obesity and diabetes might be directly connected to the loss of homeostatic control of carbohydrate metabolism. It is possible that diseases as diverse as milk allergies in the young and osteoporosis in the elderly, are caused not only by the genetic makeup but also by adaptation of affected individuals to diets that are devoid of milk and plant staples from a very early age. The exact cause of a number of common medical problems, some minor (e.g. hemorrhoids and hernias) and some life-threatening (e.g. colorectal, bladder and breast cancers) remain controversial. Yet all of these diverse clinical conditions are associated with a preceding lifestyle characterized by one of the following: i) a lack of dietary fiber, ii) excessive dietary consumption of fat and chemical additives, iii) the indirect activities of undesirable intestinal microflora brought about by dietary alterations (see Chapter 13). Nearly thirty-five affluent diseases of the 1970's were linked by Dennis Burkitt to excessive consumption of meat and refined food which lack dietary fiber (see Chapter 6).

The affluent diseases were rare in the U.S. earlier in this century. They are rare, even now, among discrete groups: the vegetarians, lacto- vegetarians, the Seventh-Day Adventists and Trappist Monks who have maintained their traditional diets of plant staples. These affluent diseases are also not common among those ethnic groups who have retained their cultural diets of plant staples even when they emigrated to the U.S. Conversely, irrespective of their national origin, the affluent diseases have increased among the ethnic groups who adopted the so called Western or affluent diet. Similarly, while many people in the third world suffer from infectious and deficiency diseases, the affluent diseases are rare in those parts of the world where unrefined plant staples still dominate the diet.

What is wrong with our nutrition?

The nutritional concerns of the late 1960s lead to the formation of the U.S. Senate Select Committee On Nutrition and Human Needs under the Chairmanship of Senator George McGovern. The committee took testimonies from many prominent scientists, consumer advocates and business groups. The committee concluded that the consumption of a diet devoid of plant staples and oversupplied with meat, poultry and refined food products was the major cause for the increase in affluent diseases among Americans. Mark Hegsted, a professor of Harvard School of Public Health, while testifying to the Senate Committee said "... death and disability in the U.S. are related to the diet we eat." W. Farquhar, professor at Stanford University Medical Center supported the conclusion by saying that the elimination of a disease such as obesity may also reduce cardiovascular disease saving half of the 24 billion dollars, spent at that time, on its treatment.

The U.S. population has been eating significantly less grains, potatoes, fresh fruits and vegetables since the 1950s. It has been consuming less milk and more soft drinks; soft drink consumption doubled between 1950 and 1975. Per capita consumption of processed fruits and vegetables, however, nearly doubled and most of the increases in the dairy products are due to cheese. Cheese consumption is now about 4 times as great as it was in 1909. All these increases in consumption of processed products are largely attributable to the explosive development of fast food industries.

Concomitantly, consumption of fresh fruits declined by more than 35%, of fresh vegetables by more than 22%, of potatoes/sweet potatoes by more than 70% and of cereals by more than 52%. As pointed out by USDA scientists Louis Page and Berta Friend, some of these changes are due to people getting away from "starchy" foods and going towards "protein" foods. What does it all mean in terms of nutrition? Sugars now constitute nearly 70% of carbohydrates consumed; 80 years ago nearly 70% of carbohydrates came from starches which supplied 56% of the total Calories while vegetable fats provided 32%. Fiber consumption has gone down from about 6 g to less than 4 g/day.

The New York Times in a report on an extensive nationwide survey quoted Bonnie Liebman of the Center for Science in the Public Interest in Washington D.C., to the effect that most people have gotten the message that excess sodium, fat and cholesterol are harmful but they don't want to, or don't know how to, translate that information into changes in their daily meals. The NYT survey pointed out that there really hasn't been any improvement towards eating healthful food in spite of the changes in scientific opinion and recommendations from governmental agencies. Perhaps this is because the focus on specific food components (e.g. cholesterol or sodium) misses the nutritional point that these components are associated with certain foods (high protein and fat-containing animal products) which should be replaced by unprocessed high fiber plant products.

More Americans are overweight today than ever before. People are eating less and gaining more weight. As Jane Brody pointed out (NYT, 1988), it is not just the calories that people consume that matter but where those calories are coming from. in spite of the concern about butter and avoiding drinking milk, Americans are eating nearly 30% more fat than they should. It takes only 3% of the calories consumed as fat to put dietary fat into storage in the body. However, 23% of the calories consumed as carbohydrates must be expended for storage of carbohydrate as body fat. A recent survey in China showed that the Chinese obtain 20% more calories from complex carbohydrates than the Americans, yet there is a much lower incidence of obesity in China. Thus the relationship between obesity and consumption of dietary fat versus complex carbohydrate is apparent.

The United States population gets nearly 100 g protein per person per day (mostly from animal sources) which is far in excess of the recommended 60 g/day. An even lower amount, about 40 g protein would suffice if other ingredients are adequate in the diet. People are not eating enough fiber-rich complex carbohydrates.

Professor Beverly Winikoff of Rockfeller University pointed out in 1975, to the U.S. Senate Select Committee, that the American marketplace bears a responsibility for health problems because it provides easy access to sweetened soft drinks, sugar coated cereals, candies, cakes and high-fat beef and promotes many things that are not healthy. Sugar has been implicated in many diseases and one of them is tooth decay. In the U.S. it has been estimated that 98% of American children suffer from tooth decay; by age 55 about half of the population of the country has no teeth.

Professor William Connor of the Department of Internal Medicine of the University of Iowa pointed out that a few simple changes in the American diet and lifestyle could greatly reduce the number of people who suffer from affluent diseases. The expenditure in health has escalated dramatically from 4.6% of the Gross National Product (GNP) in 1950 to over 13% of the GNP (some $700 billion) by 1990, without a proportional improvement in the health status of the people. At present less than 3% of our national health care expenditure is for preventive measures, the rest going for "disease care" much of it due to the lack of readily applied preventive measures, including nutrition modification.

After hearing lengthy testimonies of experts, the U.S. Senate Select Committee drafted seven recommendations in 1977 to improve the nation's nutrition and health:

1. Consume as much food as you need to replace the energy you expend and not more.
2. Increase consumption of complex carbohydrates (natural plant staples) to 48% of food intake.
3. Reduce the consumption of refined and processed sugars by about 45%.
4. Reduce overall fat consumption from approximately 40% to about 30% of energy intake.
5. Reduce saturated fat consumption to about 10% of total energy by balancing with unsaturated fats (vegetable oils).
6. Reduce cholesterol consumption to about 300 mg a day.
7. Limit the intake of salt to about 5 g daily.

Resolving the American nutritional debacle

All these recommendations could be accomplished by consumption of wholesome food as advocated by Chittenden, McCollum and others in the 1930s. The current sad state of our nation's nutrition continue to attract attention. One study was conducted by the Committee on "Diet, Nutrition, and Cancer" of the National Research Council in 1982. The study was conducted by experts from diverse disciplines such as biochemistry, microbiology, genetics, embryology, epidemiology, nutrition and public health and reviewed by the prestigious Committee consisting of members from the National Academy of Sciences. They concluded that most cancers are influenced by dietary patterns. The Council issued interim guidelines to reduce consumption of fat and increase fruits, vegetables and whole grains in the diet. Other studies in the United States as well as in other countries have come to similar conclusions.

In spite of the progress demonstrated by these recommendations for correcting American nutritional practices, some fundamental questions remain which no one with political power seems to want to raise explicitly:

Where does the excess saturated fat, cholesterol and sodium come from?
Answer: Meat and other animal products.

What is happening to Americans despite epidemic weight-watching?
Answer: The prevalence of obesity is increasing.

What is happening to per capita consumption of fresh fruits, vegetables and whole grains?
Answer: It continues to go down per capita in the United States.

Why is it that fresh produce is not marketed in ways that lure people as is done for meat and junk foods?
Answer: It is not as profitable.

In spite of dietary guidelines from prominent committees, the yearly per capita meat consumption rose to a record level of 210 pounds per person per year in 1983, 6 pounds more than in 1982. The consumption of sugar jumped from 100 pounds per capita in the 1960's to 123 pounds in the 80's. As pointed out by the New York Times survey, consumption of sweets and snacks have become a way of life and the young people are the worst culprits.

What went wrong with our nutrition? Scientific nutrition of today, rather than providing insight into the basis for age-old traditional diets emphasizing bulk and variety, in fact has played a key role in elimination of those items from the affluent diet. The healthful plant staples were replaced by high protein meat which is potentially 10 times as expensive; especially if the meat producers pay the real environmental cost of production. People ignore the fact that instead of feeding ten pounds of grain to animals to produce one pound meat, that grain could be directly fed to people. In this way hunger would be prevented in the poor and a more healthful nutrition would be provided to the rich. Human beings like all other omnivores could use the primary products, plants, to obtain as much as 80% of their total food calories with only the remaining 20% derived from animal sources, primarily as milk.

Today, in spite of our economic woes, whatever Americans fancy is aspired for by the whole world. Whatever Americans eat and drink and the lifestyle we lead is imitated and copied by the rich and poor alike, especially in the developing countries. Politicians of the world find it easier to succeed by encouraging the popular aspirations for the American lifestyle rather than by cogently arguing for a more healthy alternative. Consequently, developing countries are trying hard to replace their plant staple and milk-rich diet for one notable for meat and soft drinks.

The dietary changes promoted following the 1950s gave not only false prestige to a diet rich in meat, poultry and fish but also attached a stigma to those who consumed plant staples! The irony is, at present, that people in the developing countries are aspiring for precisely the affluent diet which has brought ill health to Western populations. They want formula instead of breast milk for their infants, and hotdogs and hamburgers for everyone else. These processed foods are neither affordable nor good for their health and will only contribute to the degradation of their internal and external environments!

It is our contention that the burgeoning problem of health in the U.S. is rooted in its misplaced dietary modifications that have taken place during the past decades. As Alexander Leaf, a professor of medicine at Harvard Medical School put it "We Americans dig our graves with a fork." America's wrong food habits must change not only for our well-being but also for the sake of the world.

The public needs to be educated to understand that wholesome nutrition means nourishing the entire human being, the mind, the body and the normal intestinal microflora. People need better access to, and appreciation of, healthy foods. The society should have easy access to protective foods. The situation, however, cannot be altered without a major effort on nutrition education as was done in the 1920's. In the words of George McGovern ". . . unless we can do a better job of getting elementary knowledge about nutrition into the heads of people, then, everything else is lost."

Protein consumption and world hunger

Undernutrition used to exist in the world only among the poor who could not afford to obtain whole grains, vegetables, fruits and milk. Now, according to the Citizen's Commission on Hunger In New England (Harvard University School of Public Health), hunger is a grim reality for a growing number of people in America. Consequently, the nutrition gap keeps widening rather than shrinking. It takes approximately 10 pounds of grains to produce one pound of meat; the more meat the affluent people consume the larger the amount of whole grains and milk that are shortchanged from the masses. According to Frances M. Lappé, even in 1968, the U.S. imported 332 million pounds of meat from Latin America. Currently, there is an outcry that the rain forests of South America are being destroyed to raise meat animals for lucrative North American and European markets. An acre of land devoted to growing plant protein rather than to raising meat can produce 5 times more protein, 10 times more legumes or 15 times more vegetables. Jean Mayer, President of Tufts University, pointed out that nearly 400 million people in the world live on the edge of starvation and 10 million children were so undernourished that their very existence was at risk. No wonder in 1984 that Citizens Commission on Hunger in New England, headed by J. Larry Brown of the Harvard School of Public Health came to the conclusion that hunger and malnutrition had returned to America.

Newer knowledge of nutrition shows that animals and humans can become susceptible to various diseases not only with undernourishment but also with overnourishment of protein. Nearly 70% of the world population gaps in the world suffer from undernourishment and 30% from overnourishment. North Americans who comprise only 7% of the worlds population and utilize approximately 30% of the worlds resources are suffering from excessive protein consumption, especially, meat. According to the USDA, the meat consumption that started steadily increasing in the 1950s is still rising. Consumption of poultry has tripled. As pointed out by Francis Lappé, an average American consumed 212 pounds of meat per year in the 1980s which is 75 times the amount eaten by an Asian Indian. Even by the USDA account the average American eats 10-12% more protein than his body can use. Directly and indirectly, excess meat and protein consumption is contributing to the overnutrition of the majority of people in developed countries and to the malnutrition and near starvation of the majority in many parts of the developing world.

In conclusion, we would like to emphasize that decades of research in nutrition and epidemiological studies of healthy people have clearly indicated that a diet built around whole grains and milk along with variety of fruits and vegetables provides adequate dietary protein. Also, such a diet is rich in complex carbohydrates and low in fat. The majority of healthy centenarians in any part of the world have been found to consume no more than 20% of their food Calories from animal sources and mostly as milk or yogurt rather than as meat or eggs. It is also a prudent way to obtain the dietary requirement of calcium. Unless one gets nearly 80% of the dietary Calories as complex carbohydrates (whole grains, leafy vegetables and fruits) both balancing protein and other nutrients will become extremely difficult, but not impossible.

Since the 1940s, in the U.S., in spite of tripling meat consumption, people's health has not improved because their diet is insufficient in whole grains (complex carbohydrate) and milk. Failing to provide a prudent diet has escalated the nation's health costs continuously without any added benefit to general health. Now, as Geo. Borgstrom, a Michigan State University professor pointed out meat consumption in the U.S. is straining not only our food resource but also the land and water resources. A lacto-vegetarian diet or a mixed diet of similar composition, is very close to the diet with which our bodies evolved. Returning to this diet will not only help to close the gap that exists between traditional cultural diet and misapplied reductionist "scientific" nutrition, but also the gap that exists between the "haves" and the "have nots." Whether one looks at the narrow interest of the individual or at the broad well-being of the society and ecology, the lactovegetarian diet makes an important contribution to correcting what is wrong with our nutrition.

Selected Sources and Suggested Readings

Philip H. Abelson, 1992. Diet and cancer in humans and rodents. *Science,* 255, 141

Anonymous, 1991. Diet, nutrition and the prevention of chronic diseases. A report of the WHO Study Group on Diet, Nutrition and Prevention of Noncommunicable Diseases. *Nutrition Reviews,* 49, 291-301

Anonymous, 1990. Effects of calorically restricted diets on health and aging in animals. *Nutrition Today,* July/August, 4-5

Anonymous, 1982. Dietary Recommendations for Diabetics for the 1980s- A policy statement by the British Diabetic Association. *Human Nutrition: Applied Nutrition,* 36A, 378-394

Anonymous, *Eating in America. Dietary Goals for the United States.* Report of the Select Committee on Nutrition and Human Needs, U.S. Senate. Cambridge, M.I.T. Press, 1977

Anonymous, 1975. Diet, intestinal flora, and colon cancer. *Nutrition Reviews,* 33, 136-137

Anonymous, 1946. The present knowledge of calories in human nutrition. *Nutrition Reviews,* 4, 34-37

Lloyd Arnold, 1928. The passage of living bacteria through the wall of the intestine and the influence of the diet and climate upon intestinal auto-infection. *American J. Hygiene,* 8, 604-629

H.R. Attebery, V.L. Sutter and S.M. Finegold, 1972. Effect of a partially chemically defined diet on normal human fecal flora. *American J. Clinical Nutrition,* 25, 1391-1398

John C. Bailar III and Elaine M. Smith, 1986. Progress against cancer. *New England J. Medicine,* 114, 1226-1232

Rodney D. Berg, M.A. and Dwayne C. Savage, 1972. Immunological responses and microorganisms indigenous to the gastrointestinal tract. *American J. Clinical Nutrition,* 25, 1364-1371

Paul C. Billings, et al., 1990. Protease inhibitor content of human dietary samples. *Nutrition and Cancer,* 14, 85-93

Sheila A. Bingham, N.I. McNeil and J.H. Cummings, 1981. The diet of individuals: a study of a randomly-chosen cross section of British adults in a Cambridgeshire village. *British J. Nutrition,* 45, 23-35

Jane E. Brody, 1988. It's not just the calories, it's their source. *New York Times,* July 12, B-7

Norman F. Boyd, et al., 1990. Quantitative changes in dietary fat intake and serum cholesterol in women: results from a randomized, controlled trial. *American J. Clinical Nutrition,* 52, 470-476

Denis P. Burkitt. *Eat Right to Stay Healthy and Enjoy Life More.* Arco Publishing, New York, 1979

Denis P. Burkitt, 1971. Epidemiology of cancer of the colon and rectum. *Cancer,* 28, 3-13

Beth L. Carlson and Mary H. Tabacchi, 1986. Meeting consumer nutrition information needs in restaurants. *J. Nutrition Education,* 18, 211-213

Kenneth J. Carpenter, 1992. Perspective: Comparative aspects of protein requirements. Protein requirement of adults from an evolutionary perspective. *American J. Clinical Nutrition,* 55, 913-917

Russell H, Chittenden. *The Development of Physiological Chemistry in the United States.* Chemical Catalog, New York, 1930

Peter Cruse, Michael Levin and Charles G. Clark, 1979. Dietary cholesterol is co-carcinogenic for human colon cancer. *Lancet,* 1, 752-755

Guillermo L. DeRomana, 1980. Utilization of the protein and energy of the white potato by human infants. *J. Nutrition*, 110, 1849-1857

B. S. Draser and M.J. Hill, 1972. Intestinal bacteria and cancer. *American J. Clinical Nutrition,* 25, 1399-1404

Jonathan Fielding, James N. Hyde Jr., and Pearl K. Russo, 1978. A program for prevention in Massachusetts. *Preventive Medicine,* 7, 564-640

S.E. Fleming, A.U. O'Donnell and J.A. Perman, 1985. Influence of frequent and long-term bean consumption on colonic function and fermentation. *American J. Clinical Nutrition,* 41, 909-918

Otto Folin, 1905. Laws Governing the chemical composition of urine. *American J. Physiology,* 13, 66-116

Lago Galdston, 1952. Nutrition from the Psychiatric viewpoint. *J. American Dietetic Association,* 28, 405-409

C. Gopalan, 1987. *Nutrition Problems and Programmes in South-East Asia.* World Health Organization, Regional Office for South-East Asia, New Delhi

Louis E. Grivetti, 1991. Nutrition past-Nutrition today. Prescientific origins of nutrition and dietetics. *Nutrition Today,* January/February, 13-24

Scott M. Grundy, 1986. Comparison of monosaturated fatty acids and carbohydrates for lowering plasma cholesterol. *New England J. Medicine,* 314, 745-747

Ellas Halac, Jr., 1961. Effects of stress on animals fed high protein diets. In symposium on overnutrition. *American J. Clinical Nutrition.* 9, 557-564

Alfred E. Harper, 1991. 1990 Atwater Lecture. The science and the practice of nutrition reflections and directions. *American J. Clinical Nutrition,* 53, 413-420

D.M. Hegsted, 1992. Point of view: Defining a nutritious diet: Need for new Dietary Standards. *J. American College of Nutrition,* 11, 241-245

Mark Hegsted, 1985. Nutrition: The changing scene. The 1985 W.O. Atwater Memorial Lecture. *Nutrition To-day,* July/Aug, 16-25

C.A. Herter and A.I Kendall, 1909-1910. The influence of dietary alterations on the types of intestinal flora. *J. Biological Chemistry,* 7, 203-236

M. Hindhede, *Protein and Nutrition. An Investigation.* Ewart, Seymour, London, 1913

Peter B. Hill, Guy Daynes and K.S. Gaire, 1986. Gonadotrophin release and meat consumption in vegetarian women. *American J. Clinical Nutrition,* 43, 37-41

Takashi Hirayama, 1978. Epidemiology of breast cancer with special reference to the role of diet. *Preventive Medicine,* 7, 173-195

Yasuo Kagawa, 1978. Impact of westernization on the nutrition of Japanese: Changes in physique, cancer, longevity and centenarians. *Preventive Medicine,* 7, 205-217

Saulo Klahr and Mabel L. Purkerson, 1988. Effects of dietary protein on renal function and on the progression of renal disease. *American J. Clinical Nutrition,* 47, 146-152

Walter Kempner, Ruth L. Peschel, and Clotilde Schlayer, 1958. Effect of rice diet on diabetes mellitus associated with vascular disease. *Postgraduate Medicine,* 24, 359-371

Kempner Foundation, 1956. Why rice? *Bul. Walter Kempner Foundation,* 2, 1-16

Gina Kolata, 1982. Food affects human behavior. *Science,* 218, 1209-1210

H.A. Lee and S.T. Talbot, 1989. Nutrition in renal failure. *Nutrition Research Reviews,* 2, 1-16

Carl Lamanna, 1972. Needs for illuminating the microbiology of the lumen. *American J. Clinical Nutrition,* 25, 1488-1494

E.M. Leeper, 1978. Senator McGovern on dietary goals: Without nutrition education, "Everything else is lost", BioScience, 28, 161-164

Bonnie Liebman, 1983. Are Vegetarians healthier than the rest of us? *Nutrition Action.* Center for Science in the Public Interest, Washington D.C. June 8-11

Yamuna Lingappa, 1977. Diet versus degenerative diseases. *Worcester Medical News,* 42, 18

Yamuna Lingappa, 1973. Some of the advantages of not eating meat. *The Evening Gazette,* Worcester, April 28

William C. MacLean, Jr. and George G. Graham, 1979. The effect of level of protein intake in isoenergetic diets on energy utilization. *American J. Clinical Nutrition,* 32, 1381-1387

Patricia B. Mutch, and Patricia K. Johnston, 1988. Foreword and dedication. *American J. Clinical Nutrition,* 48, 707

Louis Page and Berta Friend, 1978. The Changing United States Diet. *Bio-Science,* 28, 192-197

G. Neale, et al., 1972. The metabolic and nutritional consequenves of bacterial overgrowth in the small intestine. *American J. Clinical Nutrition,* 25,1409-1417

Betty B. Peterkin, 1990. Dietary Guidelines for Americans, 1990 edition. *J. American Dietetic Association,* 90, 1725-1727

Roland L. Philllips, 1975. Role of life-style and dietary habits in risk of cancer among Seventh-Day Adventists. *Cancer Research,* 35, 3513-3522

H. C. Sherman. *Selected Works of Henry Clapp Sherman.* Macmillan, New York, 1948

H.C. Sherman and H.L. Campbell, 1924. Growth and reproduction upon simplified food supply. 1V. Improvement in nutrition resulting from an increased proportion of milk in the diet. *J. Biological Chemistry,* 60, 5-15

Selma E. Snyderman, et al., 1962. "Unessential" nitrogen: A limiting factor for human growth. *J. Nutrition,* 78, 57- 72

Alison M. Stephen and Nicholas J. Wald, 1990. Trends in individual consumption of dietary fat in the United States, 1920-1984. *American J. Clinical Nutrition,* 52, 457-469

D.A.T. Southgate, and J.V.G.A Durnin, 1970. Calorie conversion factors. an experimental reassessment of the factors used in the calculation of the energy value of human diets. *British J. Nutrition,* 24, 517-535

Emile F. Terroine, 1936. The protein component in the human diet. *Qurterly Bullatin of the Health Organization of the League of Nations,* Geneva, 5, 419-491

Michael V. Tracey, 1978. Human nutrition. What one authority knows about what we don't know about nutrition. An optimistic view from The Encyclopedia of ignorance. *Nutrition Today,* November/December, 17-20

J.C. Waterlow, 1986. Metabolic adaptation to low intakes of energy and protein. *Annual Review of Nutrition,* 6, 495-526

J.C. Waterlow, 1970. Total protein turnover in animals and man. *Nutrition Reviews,* 28, 115-118

Janet H. Weinberg, 1974. Roughing it. Decrease in cereal fiber intake is being linked to a long list of modern western diseases. *Science News,* 105, 379

Richard J. Wurtman, 1983. Neurochemical changes following high-dose aspartame with dietary carbohydrates. *New England J. Medicine,* 309, 429-430

Ernst, L. Wynder, 1976. Nutrition and Cancer. *Federation Proceedings,* 35, 1309-1315

Earnst Wynder, 1975. Introductory remarks. *Cancer Research,* 35, 3238-3239

Vernon R.Young, et al., 1973. Protein requirements of man: Efficiency of egg protein utilization at maintenance and sub-maintenance levels in young men. *J. Nutrition,* 103, 1164- 1174

PART B

The Dietary Constituents: Subsaturation Is Optimal

5

Protein: Essential in Moderation, Harmful in Excess

Abstract: Proteins are a major structural component of our bodies and hence adequate intake of the amino acids from which proteins are built is a crucial part of a healthy diet. On the other hand, as currently over-consumed by most Americans, protein often does more harm than good. An excess of protein in the diet can be viewed as any amount greater than that necessary to provide adequate amino acids for the purpose of allowing the body to synthesize the proteins it needs. Thus, the consumption of calories in the form of protein to be expended for energy, is an example of excess protein consumption. Under conditions of limited protein and adequate carbohydrate intake, the body has "protein sparing" mechanisms to utilize the latter for energy generation. Protein excess results in a range of metabolic aberrations. For example, elevation of the levels of amino acids available for absorption in the intestine and subsequently after absorption in the bloodstream, saturates the normal mechanisms of nutrient selection and utilization. Such excesses of aminoacids supply the needs of pathogens and established or potential cancer cells which would be unable to compete with normal cells for these nutrients if they were present at appropriately subsaturating levels. A second consequence of protein excess is its effects on the kidneys predisposing individuals to degenerative diseases. Increased generation of products of amino acid metabolism, which are toxic to the kidney, ultimately may contribute to kidney failure. Likewise, the effects of a high protein diet on calcium absorption from the gut and excretion by the kidney may contribute significantly to the development of osteoporosis. A third consequence of protein excess is alteration of the character of the intestinal microflora from a fermentative to putrefactive species with resulting negative health consequences (see Chapter 13). The products of microbial metabolism of dietary protein can include toxic amines which can affect the brain. These have been implicated in the development or exacerbation of some cases of disorders such as schizophrenia and depression. Finally, foods that are high in protein such as meat, are typically high in nucleic acids. As a result, a diet high in animal protein diet results in ingestion of high levels of nucleic acids rich in phosphate. Excess phosphate exacerbates calcium deficiency (see Chapter 16) by interfering with its assimilation into the skeleton. Taken together, a consideration of the role of protein in the diet underscores an often neglected concept of nutrition: just because a small amount of something is good for you does NOT mean that an excess is even better.

"Protein" is actually a general term which describes a diverse class of substances themselves individually called "proteins", which are made of different numbers of, and combinations of, the 20 naturally occurring amino acids (AA) linked together chemically. Milk, for example, contains two major proteins, lactalbumin and casein; corn contains large amounts of the protein zein, while the major protein in wheat is gluten. In addition to major proteins, all organisms contain an enormous variety of different minor proteins. The proteins present differ from species to species and from tissue to tissue; different tissues of the same animal or plant and even different cells from the same tissue contain different proteins.

Protein is a very important component of all organisms. Without protein, life as we know it would not be possible. Almost all foods whether of plant or of animal origin, contain protein along with other components such as carbohydrates and fats. Animal tissues in general are much richer in proteins than are plants; In contrast, plants are richer in carbohydrates than are animal tissues. Growing organisms contain a higher concentration of protein than mature ones. Young leaves, for example, may contain as much as 4% of their fresh weight as protein, while older leaves are typically composed of 2%

protein or less. Milk of humans and animals contain more protein in the first few days after parturition than later. The seeds, nuts and eggs which serve as the sole sources of nutrients to their respective embryos also contain relatively large amounts of protein. Whole grain cereals contain as much as 13% protein, whereas legumes such as beans and peas contain approximately 40% protein. On the other hand, green vegetables such as cabbage, lettuce and spinach contain only 2% protein.

The AAs function in a manner similar to the alphabet of a language in building proteins. This language of life (molecular genetics) conveys messages from the genes which are the hereditary materials of all organisms. Understanding molecular genetics has become the primary concern of modern life sciences. One implications of such an alphabet is that, like the many entries in a dictionary, an enormous number of different proteins can be made by changing the order in which the specific AA "letters" are linked together to make a protein. Thus, even if there were only 12 different amino acids and a limit of 288 total AAs in a protein molecule, using various combinations it is theoretically possible to create as many as 10 to the 300 power different proteins!

The bonds that link the AAs to make a protein are called peptide bonds (see Figure 5.1). Structures termed ribosomes, located in the cytoplasm of cells, are the factories in which proteins are made according to blueprints termed messenger ribonucleic acid (mRNA) which are copied from genes. The number, kind, sequence and consequent folding patterns of these AA chains determine the physical and chemical properties of proteins. Such specificities distinguish proteins not only from species to species and individual to individual but also from cell to cell. This complexity is due to the great diversity of proteins. The hormone insulin, for example, is a relatively small protein with a molecular weight of 6,000. It contains two peptide chains, one of 17 AAs and the other of 34 AAs. for a total of 51 AAs. Some of the largest proteins may have as many as 5,000 AAs, yet they are still too small to be seen under a light microscope.

The efforts to study the nature of proteins started when scientists began the inquiry into human and animal nutrients. In 1838, Dutch physiologist G. J. Mulder, noticed that all animal tissues contained an important chemical that was different from carbohydrates and fats. He called it protein meaning "to take first place." Later on, it was recognized that protein is not a single substance but a large class of compounds. Further analysis established that in addition to the elements carbon (C), hydrogen (H) and oxygen (O) that all carbohydrates and fats contain, proteins contain the additional element, nitrogen (N).

Early research showed that all proteins contain nitrogen (N) but all N containing compounds are not proteins. Both human milk and plant materials are rich in non-protein N compounds such as taurine in milk and alkaloids in plants. On the average, most proteins contain 16% of their weight as N. The N content of a substance, therefore, gives a measure of its protein content. On this basis, it has been estimated that the human body contains approximately

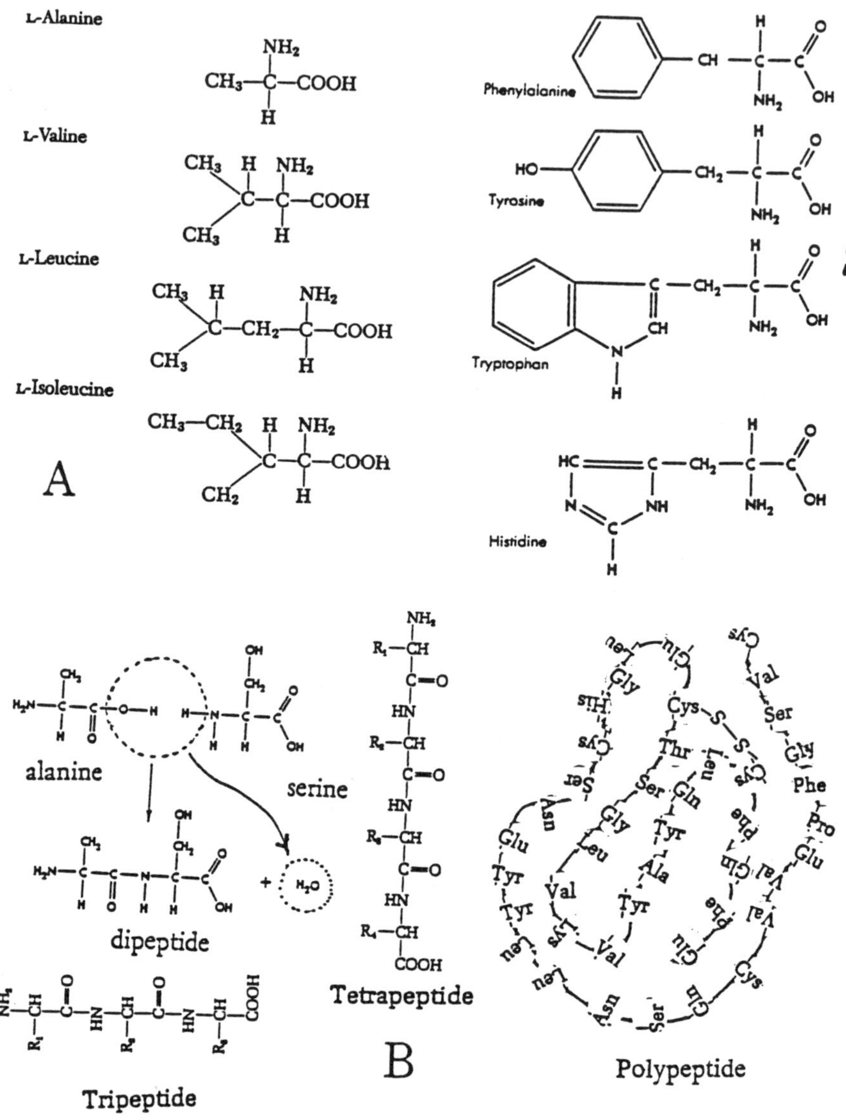

FIGURE 5.1. Examples of amino acids in A and how they make bond in B. The bond so established is the peptide bond.

20% of its weight as proteins. In addition to the elements C,H,O and N, many proteins contain sulfur (S) and phosphorus (P). A few proteins also contain metallic components such as iron and copper. Hemoglobin, the oxygen carrier in red blood cells, for example, consists of an iron containing pigment bound to the protein globin.

Amino acids (AA) were discovered as constituents of natural products even before they were recognized as components of proteins. The AA asparagine, for example, was discovered in 1806 in the juice of the asparagus plant. Cystine was isolated from urinary stones in 1810. In 1820 the first AA glycine was derived from a protein.

Amino acid and protein metabolism

Almost all food proteins, whether they are of plant or animal origin, break down in the gastrointestinal (G.I.) tract into peptides and amino acids; they become part of a complex mixture along with carbohydrate, fat and dietary fiber. The human body and its intestinal microflora are able to obtain the AAs required to make all of our necessary proteins from dietary nutrients (exogenous sources); AAs may also be obtained by catabolizing and recycling dead and damaged body cells and their products (endogenous sources). The body can use salvaged AAs either by incorporating them into proteins or by converting them into other molecules. The amino group, the part of the molecule containing N, can be removed (deamination), metabolized and discarded as waste. Alternatively the amino group can be transferred to other molecules (transamination). The carboxyl group, acidic protions of the AAs, can be removed and metabolized (decarboxylation). Certain AAs can be metabolized in multiple ways and some only within restricted paths. Some AAs may be generated by conversion of carbohydrate derivatives (intermediates) and nonprotein-compounds through transamination processes (Figure 5.2).

The G.I. tract alone can generate as much as 100-200 g of endogenous protein from the body's own shed cells and secretions. How much of it is reused along the with other digested mixture varies with many factors and with each individual. Most of the digested protein is absorbed in the small intestine and transported as amino acids and small peptides to various organs and cells. The complex processes of absorption, transport and assimilation are influenced not only by other nutrients in the mixture but also by the genetic makeup and physiology of the body. Whatever food material that are not absorbed move into the colon. Thus, in calculating the amount of protein that should be included in the diet, it is important to take into consideration protein generated from endogenous sources.

Unlike carbohydrates which can be stored in large amounts as glycogen in the liver or fats which are in adipose tissues, there are no special organs or tissues in the body that store AAs or proteins in large quantities. All tissues including liver and blood hold small amounts of pooled amino acids. Any

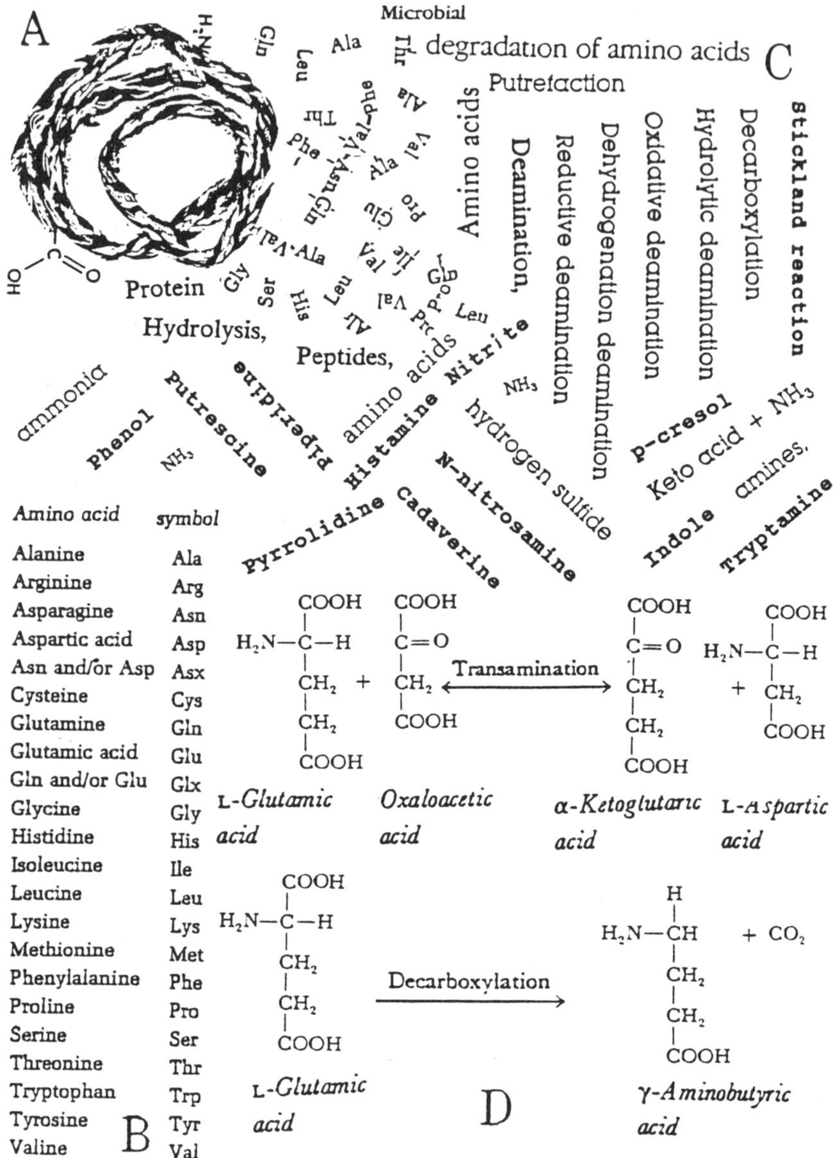

FIGURE 5.2. Amino acid transformations. A protein is braking down releasing amino acids. At B. important amino acids and their symbols are shown. At C a variety of processes that the amino acids undergo through the colon bacteria. Notice the variety of products some of which are toxic. D. Two specific examples of amino acid transformation.

excess AAs supplied to the body that are not used in the synthesis of proteins are metabolized through deamination, mainly in the liver. Approximately 60% of excess AAs can be transformed into carbohydrates through this mechanism. Amino acids that can be converted to carbohydrates are known as glycogenic and those AAs that are convertible into fats are called ketogenic. During these conversions of AAs, by-products such as phosphate, sulphate, urea, ammonia and creatinine are produced. A limited amount of these compounds may be excreted in the sweat, urine and feces (see Chapter 12).

Only certain bacteria and plants can synthesize all the AAs to build their proteins directly from inorganic chemicals contained in soil, water and air. This is part of the Nitrogen Cycle in nature (see Figure 5.3). However, animals cannot do this. Herbivores such as cattle, horses and rabbits obtain their AAs by consuming plant materials whereas the carnivores such as tigers and wolves obtain their AAs by preying on animals; omnivores such as mice, dogs, monkeys and humans use both plant and animal resources directly. The proportion of the required AAs an omnivore obtains from plants and how much from animals origin are influenced by the availability

When protein intake was raised from 7 to 20% of dietary calories in infants suffering from Kwashiorkor (the protein deficiency disease of children in the developing countries), rather than improving nitrogen retention and growth, the result was an elevation in blood urea nitrogen. The urea level subsided when the amount of carbohydrate in the diet was increased. It has been found that milk, a low protein and high carbohydrate food, provided a more positive nitrogen balance than higher protein foods such as eggs, meat or fish, in malnourished children.

As early as the 1900s professor Graham Lusk and others found that nitrogen equilibrium can be achieved at a much lower dietary protein intake than was generally believed at the time, provided that the carbohydrate content of the diet was adequate. These workers called this phenomenon the "protein sparing" action of carbohydrates. Since then, many experiments done with humans and other animals have demonstrated this phenomenon. In 1973, G.Y Inoue and others found that the mean requirement of protein, 0.56 g/kg body weight needed for young Japanese men could be reduced to 0.429 g if the dietary carbohydrate were increased from 45 Calories/kg to 57 Calories/kg. In 1976 Scrimshaw and associates of the Massachusetts Institutes of Technology also reported that an increased energy intake increased the assimilation of dietary protein.

A study conducted in India where approximately 40% of preschool children are malnourished and 15% suffer from protein-calorie malnutrition, demonstrated that merely increasing the protein allowance for malnourished children did not bring about positive nitrogen balance. It became positive, however, when their energy needs were met with adequate carbohydrates, in the form of plant staples. Similarly, a recent study of U.S. women showed that in spite of providing them 50-62 g of protein per day they remained in negative nitrogen balance as long as their diet contained less than 1500-1800 Calories

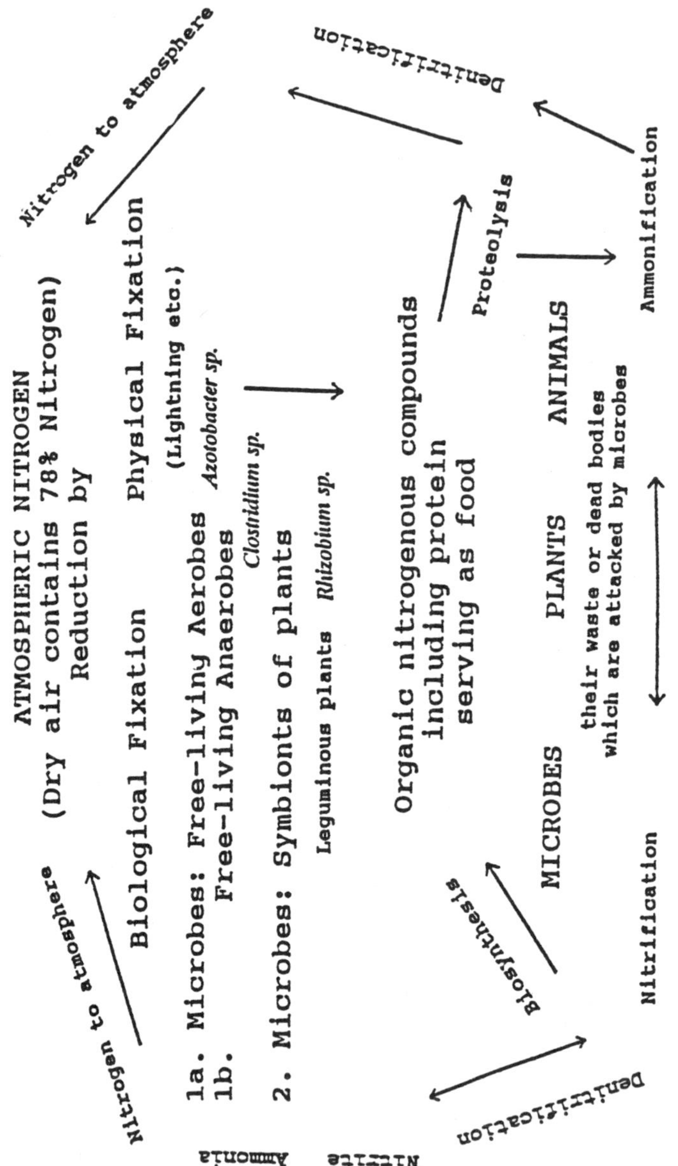

FIGURE 5.3. A simplified nitrogen cycle in nature.

daily. Continued studies on human volunteers have shown that increasing the protein content of the diet beyond 9% of the total dietary calories does not improve overall growth. Similarly, nitrogen retention in the body has been found to be better with low protein and high complex carbohydrate diets than with high protein and low complex carbohydrate diets. In the opinion of John C. Waterlow, a British nutrition scientist who studied malnourished children of Jamaica, the protein gap was a myth. What really existed was a food and energy gap. These and other studies lead to the conclusion that the amount of protein required in the diet is that necessary to provide AAs for protein synthetic purposes. Moreover, as is argued in Chapters 3 and 9, calories for energy expenditure should be consumed as carbohydrate, not protein. Hence protein intake above the level that provides the AAs necessary for protein synthesis is excessive.

Important milestones in the study of protein metabolism

In the 1880s Carl Voit, a German scientist, and his associates hypothesized that the amount of amino acids (AA) circulating in blood and tissues is related to the exogenous protein supplied in the diet. They were also convinced, that human beings require a certain amount of meat protein in their daily diet to be healthy. They established a way of measuring protein breakdown (catabolism) of the body by calculating protein nitrogen (N) consumed as food (intake) and N excreted as urea, ammonia and other waste products in urine and feces (output). By these measurements they determined the net N assimilation which came to be known as Nitrogen Balance.

When intake of N exceeds output, protein deposition in the tissues occurs and the body is in a positive nitrogen balance. When N output exceeds intake, body loses N and that results in a negative nitrogen balance. When N intake equals output, the body is in nitrogen equilibrium. Max Rubner in Germany, Wilbur Atwater in the U.S. and other scientists supported Voit's lead in advocating diets that result in positive nitrogen balance by providing generous amounts of protein. However, Carl Voit in 1838 recommended 118 g of protein per day for a man weighing 70 kg as a standard diet. In 1900 Wilbur Atwater of the U.S. Department of Agriculture (USDA), increased that allowance to 125-150 g as a factor of safety to the American population.

In 1904 Russel Chittenden of Yale University concluded from his studies (see chapter 3 and 4) that consuming more than 35 g of animal protein was not only unnecessary to achieve nitrogen balance but also deleterious to various organs and to the health of the body. Several of Chittenden's colleagues confirmed his findings by conducting nutritional experiments on animals as well as on humans. Other scientists who studied the effects of high meat consumption in animals reported that the animals developed chronic renal disease. During the early 1900's, Francis Benedict, Director of the Nutrition Laboratory of the Carnegie Institution of Washington, studied protein and energy metabolism in healthy, fasting and diabetic people. Repeated experiments clearly indicated that high protein diets caused kidney disease. The severity of kidney damage varied with different meats. At the end of his prolonged experiments, Benedict abandoned his earlier view that a liberal protein allowance was necessary for the promotion of health and became a supporter of the low-protein diet advocated by Chittenden.

In 1905, Otto Folin of Harvard University carried out classical studies on nitrogen metabolism by analyzing a large number of urine samples of his own and of his colleagues who were fed with specified diets. In addition to obtaining valuable information on the nitrogenous constituents of human urine, Folin discovered that the amount of urea excreted varied directly with the amount of protein consumed whereas the amount of creatinine, a product of AA transformations in the muscles, excreted in urine was unaffected. Creatinine excretion, however, varied directly with the individual's body mass which reflected the turnover of body protein. From these studies, Folin concluded that the body carries out two kinds of protein metabolism, endogenous and exogenous.

The body tissue proteins are constantly being broken down and remade (turnover). The quantity of creatinine excreted is a direct measure of this tissue protein turnover. Based on these discoveries, Folin argued that the physiological needs of the body for protein be satisfied and a reasonable supply of reserve protein be provided. In view of the fact that even strenuous muscular work does not normally increase endogenous protein breakdown, Folin argued that it was neither necessary nor desirable to supply excessive amounts of protein food which in turn would create large quantities of nitrogenous by-products in the body. Today it is quite well known that the process of protein metabolism is dynamic and that the endogenous and exogenous metabolism of protein are not compartmentalized. However the distinction between these components of protein metabolism was historically useful in establishing that a high protein diet was unnecessary.

Like Chittenden, Folin also believed that supplying protein beyond growth and repair needs adapts the body to a high protein economy, generates excessive protein by-products and causes unnecessary stress on organs of the body (see Chapter 12).

In contrast to the high protein diets advocated by Voit and Atwater, V.O. Siven, a Swedish physiologist and later Mikkel Hindhede, a Danish physician, demonstrated that nitrogen equilibrium could be attained in adults with as little as 20 g of protein per day, without meat as a dietary ingredient, if the diet were balanced with adequate amount of carbohydrates (see Chapter 3).

Essential and non-essential amino acids for a balanced diet

Around the 1920s Thomas Osborne and Lafayette Mendel of Yale University, demonstrated that amino acid deficiencies that occur when animals are fed with a single purified protein such as gelatin from animals or zein from corn, could be avoided by complementing the diet with other dietary protein sources (a mixed diet) that provide complementing amino acids (AA). Any AA deficiency that may arise when an animal is fed with zein, for example, could be avoided by complementing its diet with another protein such as casein of milk, gluten of wheat or by providing a mixed diet of bread and milk. Around the 1930s William Rose, a student of Lafayette Mendel conducted experiments which involved substituting mixtures of pure AA in place of proteins or mixed food. By feeding mice with various AA mixtures he hypothesized that growing animals (including human infants) cannot maintain adequate growth if their diet lacked any one of certain amino acids such as histidine, isoleucine, leucine, lysine, methionine, phenylalanine, threonine, tryptophan and valine for long periods in their diet. These amino acids were found to be absolutely necessary and that they have to be supplied through food (exogenous source) because the human body has lost the capacity to synthesize them endogenously. Only plants and some bacteria can synthesize them. Thus they are known as indispensable or essential amino acids (EAA).

The number and the amount of EAAs required varies between different species of animals as well as between human infants and adults. The remaining AAs, alanine, arginine, asparagine, cysteine, glutamine, glycine, proline, serine and tyrosine are known as non-essential amino acids (NEAA) because the human body can make them. Based on EAA and NEAA content, individual proteins can be classified into two main categories. Those that contain all required EAAs to support growth of young animals and human infants are designated as complete proteins. Examples are lactalbumin of milk, ovalbumin of egg and gliadin of soybean. Those proteins that lack some EAA and need to be complemented with another protein are designated as incomplete proteins or partially incomplete proteins depending upon how many EAAs they lack and whether they are used for growth of the young or for maintenance of adults. Examples are gluten of wheat, hordein of barley, zein of corn and gelatin of animal tissues.

Further research in this direction lead to the evaluation of food stuffs on the basis of both their AA contents and their digestibility; those foods that not only contained complete proteins such as lactalbumin and ovalbumin, but also could be readily digested and assimilated were grouped as superior foods of high biological value (BV) proteins. Those foods that contained lesser proteins of lesser BV were lower on the ladder of food value. In general, the more fiber or roughage a food contains the lower the BV of its proteins (see Table). Using BV as the indicator of the protein value of foods, scientists made further distinctions even among biologically superior foods; egg was rated above milk because of its higher BV. Since plant foods contained proteins of lower BV than animal foods the acceptance of BV as a standard, contributed to plants being viewed as an inferior food source compared to meat, poultry, fish and cheese. Such comparative evaluations lead to the shifting of status among different food groups. Whole grains and milk which had been the top rated food groups were replaced in that position by meat, poultry and fish (see Chapter 15).

Even while these notions were on the rise, thoughtful scientists questioned their logic. Professor Vincent du Vigneaud of Cornell University Medical School pointed out that the so-called NEAA might be more properly regarded as being so essential to the body that the ability to synthesize them has been retained. Similarly, according to professor H.N. Munro of the Massachusetts Institute of Technology EAAs have special metabolic importance only when they are in short supply. The BV of proteins, which is determined by short-term experiments on short-lived animals may not apply to longer-living and more complex humans who engage in many other activities and for whom quality of life is more important than physical size in the short term. They felt that foods which are superior in BV are not necessarily superior in providing several other essential dietary components such as bulk, complex carbohydrates, minerals and vitamins which are also necessary for human health (see Chapter 14).

A diet based on foods with superior BV protein, such as eggs and meat, significantly lacks dietary fiber and complex carbohydrates. Professors Thomas Osborne, Lafayette Mendel, Henry Sherman, E. V. McCollum and other scientists emphasized mixed diets in which priority was assigned to whole grains rather than to meat or eggs. They emphasized the value of balancing the diet with variety, rather than enriching it with foods of high BV proteins (see Chapter 15). The consensus of the scientists up to the late 1940s was that the human diet should give priority to mixing or balancing a variety of foods rather than to reducing the bulk with increased intake of foods of high BV proteins.

Henry Sherman and associates, found that the most efficient way of supplying a full complements of proteins is by milk and bread (whole grains) rather than by meat, poultry and cheese. They were convinced that grains, fruits, vegetables and milk were the most effective means supplying all nutrients including protein. During the depression years of the 1930s, a dietary survey of 224 families made by the USDA in cooperation with New York City Associates of Improving the Condition of the Poor, revealed that people consumed approximately 3256 total food calories per person per day; 35-40% as meat, fish, cheese and egg (106 g of protein), 30-40% as whole grain cereals, vegetables, bread and fruits and 8-10% as milk (700 mg of calcium per person). According to Sherman such a diet supplied "a liberal surplus of protein."

Sherman believed that the American population was over-nourished in protein intake and under-nourished in calcium. He even felt that such a diet might lead to calcium deficiency not only because of its insufficient amount of milk but also because it contained excess meat, since a high meat diet adversely affects calcium balance (see Chapter 10). He strongly encouraged the public to increase the amount of milk, rather than meat or eggs, in their diet. Other scientists who subscribed to this view felt that milk protein should be made the reference standard even though they were of lower BV than protein from foods such as eggs or meat.

The human milk which feeds an infant at its time of fastest growth is a low protein and high carbohydrate food (see Chapter 16). Plant staple-rich cultural foods that feed the world community are also rich in complex carbohydrate and low in protein. Studying these facts lead many scientists such as Henry Sherman and E. V. McCollum not only to emphasize a mixed diet rich in whole grains but also de-emphasize the role of meat in the diet. In 1943, Sherman, who was a Chief of the Bureau of Human Nutrition in the USDA remarked that milk was by far the most efficient source of protein. He was convinced that grain turned into milk yielded much greater nutritional return than grains turned into meat, and that milk was much more efficient in supplementing and balancing the human nutritional needs.

Amino acids, peptides and the brain

In 1921 Otto Loewi of Austria showed for the first time that chemicals mediate the transmission of nerve impulses. The chemical he demonstrated was acetylcholine. Since that time, a variety of neurotransmitter substances have been isolated which affect a wide range of bodily functions as well as the behavior and mood of animals and human beings. Several amino acids also have been implicated in affecting nerve functions. In 1964, T.V. Hodge showed that the amino acid tryptophan was essential for neurological functions in animals and humans. A tryptophan imbalance produces neurological disturbances. Also, other amino acids such as tyrosine in the synthesis of dopamine, and tryptophan in the synthesis of serotonin play important roles in brain function and behavior.

In the 1970s Richard Wurtman and John Fernstorm of Massachusetts Institute of Technology investigated the relationship of brain neurotransmitters to behavior and disease. They found that the release of neurotransmitters is controlled by various amino acids (AAs) supplied by the blood to the active sites of the brain. They found that the supply of AAs reaching the bloodstream is also influenced by the competition among the various AAs during transport from the gut. The transport of tryptophan to the brain, for example, was found to be faster and greater when the diet was rich in complex carbohydrates and low in proteins, and slower and less in quantity when it was rich in protein. An adequate supply of tryptophan has been found to be very essential to coordinate many neurological functions such as sleep, appetite and learning. The transport of other AAs such as phenylalanine and tyrosine which serve as precursors to the hormones thyroxine and epinephrine respectively, which affect a range of neural and metabolic functions. The relationship of amino acid absorption to homeostasis and health is complex and will be discussed in Chapters 12 and 13.

Recent knowledge of peptides show that they are involved in many crucial physiological and neurobiological functions of the body. Currently, more than 400 dipeptides (two AAs joined in one molecule) and 8,000 tripeptides (three AAs joined in one molecule) of dietary origin have been identified. Many small peptides have been found to be involved in carrying out normal biological functions such as maintenance of blood pressure, contraction of the uterus during labor, regulation of cholesterol in the blood and facilitation of cell mediated communications.

Membranes surrounding the cells contain many receptors which act as mediators of communication. Scientists around the globe are engaged in studying peptide hormones. A large number of hypothalamic (a portion of the human brain) neurons respond with hunger to the taste and sight of foods. The hypothalamus produces several neurochemicals which are amines or peptides. Some of them inhibit appetite whereas others promote it. Recently brain peptides such as endorphins and enkephelins have been discovered. They are known to resemble drugs such as morphine in their functions. They involve in a wide range of brain functions such as sleep and behavior.

The body's own cellular debris and products, and the dietary proteins, peptides and AAs that are not absorbed by the body are attacked by the bacteria in the colon before they are eliminated in the feces. Depending upon the colon environment and the length of time the residue stays in the colon, the bacteria may hydrolyze proteinaceous residue, and deaminate, transaminate or decarboxylate the AA to various pharmacologically active compounds such as bioamines, urea and ammonia. Some of these are absorbed by the body and produce physiological effects (see Chapters 12 & 13).

Protein consumption and cancer

According to a 1986 publication by Bailer and Smith of the Harvard School of Public Health, death in the U.S. due to cancers increased dramatically from 1952 to 1982: approximately 280,000 persons died of cancers in 1952 and 435,000 in 1982, a 56% increase. According to Ernst Winder of Naylor Dana Institute of American Health, cancers of the colon, pancreas, kidney, breast, ovary, endometrium and prostate are all related to the diet, especially to the consumption of animal products. Likewise, 50% of all female and one-third of all male cancers are related to nutritional factors.

In an environment of abundant protein supply, the voracious EAA needs of cancerous cells are fulfilled. As early as in 1915 R.A. Kocher of the University of California at San Francisco, concluded that amino acids such as lysine which are necessary to promote growth but cannot be synthesized by the body may provide a necessary check against malignant growth. Further work showed that the ability of malignant cells to metastasize diminished when deprived of essential amino acids, whereas the growth of malignant cells advanced when the supply of amino acids was abundant. Some cancer cells have been shown to require eleven amino acids from exogenous sources in contrast to the nine or ten essential amino acids required by the normal body.

In 1968 Ernst Wynder reported a close correlation between breast cancer and meat consumption. Since then many national and international studies have shown that meat consumption may affect the endocrine system by increasing prolactin production, a hormone found in high levels in the blood of breast cancer patients. Conversely both lactovegetarian and vegan women showed reduced level of prolactin in the blood and they have a reduced risk of breast cancer. According to Yasuo Kagawa a biochemist at the Jichi Medical School, Tokyo, the traditional Japanese diet changed between 1950 and 1975 from low to high protein. During that period cancers of colon, breast and prostate increased 2 to 3 fold among the Japanese. Other scientists who experimented with animals have shown that diets high in protein produced spontaneous tumors while low protein diets promoted regression of existing tumors.

In the opinion of microbiologists M.J. Hill, B.S. Draser, and B.S. Reddy, 80% of the cancers attributed to environmental factors relate to metabolism that takes place in the colon where the food residue accumulates. It can be argued that the colon is the crucial internal environment of the body with respect to carcinogenesis because of the intense activities of the microbial flora in the prolonged presence of certain food residues. According to them, many toxic products such as pharmacologically active bioamines, phenols, phenolic acids and ammonia that exist in the gut are mainly derived from bacterial action on the residue of meat protein. Those products of protein decomposition have been shown to cause tumors in experimental animals.

In 1978, Abigail Salyers, a microbiologist at the University of Illinois at Urbana, reported that the colon bacteria which play a major role in determining the chemical environment of the colon prefer the polysaccharide fractions of dietary fibers as their energy source. When deprived of a carbohydrate source they are capable of readaptation to proteolytic action and thereby altering the colon environment. V.C. Aries of St. Mary's Hospital Medical School, London, implicates the changed colonic environment provided by a rich diet of animal protein and fat to environmental cancers that are common in Europe and North America and rare in Asia, Africa and South America. In 1926, scientists reported that an excessive intake of food calories increased tumor growth in experimental animals. Further investigations by scientists such as A.Tannenbaum, Morris Ross, and others confirmed that excess food calories supplied through rich nutrients increased the number and extent of tumors in the laboratory animals. Conversely, restriction in total food calories, especially in the form of animal protein and fat, reduced tumor size and delayed tumor growth. Since then, many scientists have reported that high caloric intake, especially as meat, promotes cancers of the breast, colon, kidneys and gall bladder in the humans.

Protein consumption and degenerative diseases

Other scientists have reported excessive excretion of indole, skatole and other tryptophan metabolites in the urine of patients suffering from ailments as diverse as bladder cancer, rheumatoid arthritis and schizophrenia. Bacteria capable of synthesizing these chemicals have also been isolated from the colons of these patients. When rabbits were injected with indole and skatole their joints exhibited signs of arthritis. Other ill effects caused by residue of high protein diets and colon bacterial interactions also have been reported (see Chapter 13).

In 1941, a syndrome characterized by back pain and fractures of the vertebrae was described (Osteoporosis). It was attributed to the loss of bone density and was characteristic of old age. It is caused by insufficient calcium (Ca) assimilation in bones of the body due to low intake, low assimilation or excessive loss. In recent years an increased incidence of osteoporosis has been reported in younger age groups, especially in women. According to reports, high protein diets induce negative Ca balance in the adults and, thereby, increase the risk of age-related osteoporosis. Doubling protein intake has been found to result in a 50% rise in urinary calcium (Ca) loss.

Studies show that with a high protein diet an individual might lose as much as 84 mg of Ca daily. Even daily loss of only 50 mg of Ca over a 20 year period could cause significant osteoporosis and other ill effects on the skeleton. Each year 6 million Americans, especially postmenopausal women, suffer from bone fractures as a result of osteoporosis. Osteoporosis afflicts 1 in 4 elderly women and 1 in 8 elderly men. Hip fracture alone costs the nation one billion dollars per year. As reported by Jane Brody of the New York Times, osteoporosis is largely a preventable disease. A quart of milk per day (1,200 mg of Ca) provides an individual not only Ca but also the necessary factors for its absorption (see Chapter 9).

Even at the beginning of this century meat consumption was known to cause serious ailments. In 1923 Vernon McCollum and associates of Johns Hopkins University reported that a high protein diet caused deterioration of normal kidneys. Since then, many investigators have reported that a high protein diet increases loss of renal function in patients with some degree of renal failure and that a low protein diet attenuates further loss. Chronic Renal Failure (CRF) is the terminal event of many kidney diseases. It has been found that when protein consumption is restricted in kidney patients approximately 40% of the urea generated from dietary protein is reused to synthesize the needed protein. Consequently, the kidneys are spared the work of eliminating urea and other protein breakdown products.

According to professor A.E. Harper of the University of Wisconsin, the increase in cardiovascular diseases which accounted for about 14% deaths in 1900, 37% in 1940 and 40% by 1975, correlated with the increase in refined sugar, animal fat and protein in the diet of the U.S. population over that time.

Elias Halac of New York University School of Medicine studied a large colony of rats fed high protein diets (HPD) did poorly when compared to those receiving normal protein diets (NPD). Although the NPD rats were heavier, internal organs, especially, the adrenal and kidneys, were significantly larger in the HPD rats. The overall mortality rate of the HPD rats at the end of 169 days of experimental feeding was nearly 3 times higher than the NPD rats. Halac came to a modest conclusion that with respect to dietary protein, more is not necessarily better.

Thus, consumption of excessive food calories in general, and of protein in particular, damages vital organs and predisposes individuals to a variety of degenerative diseases and cancer. The degenerative diseases which are common in the industrialized world are still rare in many countries where people depend on unrefined plant staples as their energy source.

Protein metabolism and the intestinal microflora

In 1909 Professor Christian Herter of Columbia University and Arthur Kendall of Rockefeller Institute demonstrated that changing the composition of the diet from low to high protein altered the intestinal microflora of animals from carbohydrate-dependent fermentative metabolism to protein-centered proteolytic metabolism. They found that the altered microflora bring about adverse changes both in the colon environment and in the body physiology (see Chapter 13). They demonstrated that monkeys fed with a high protein diet produced putrefactive substances such as indole and skatole in the colon which affect the animal's physiology and behavior. They were also able to prevent or reduce such effects by adapting the animals to low protein diets. In 1929 Harold Mitchell and T.S. Hamilton showed that animals fed with a variety of plant diets were able to maintain a stable fermentative microflora without producing putrefactive substances.

In 1940, Professor Ernest F. Gale of Cambridge University showed that intestinal bacteria were capable of decarboxylating amino acids such as arginine, lysine, ornithine, histidine, glutamic acid and tyrosine to form the corresponding bioamines agmatine, cadaverine, putrescine, histamine, gama aminobutyric acid, and tyrosine respectively. Other investigators showed that altered intestinal microbes utilize residues of undigested meat or eggs to produce pharmacologically toxic by-products which can be absorbed by the body. The British microbiologists, B.S. Draser and M.J. Hill have described the kind of products that our intestinal microbes are capable of producing and the implications for human nutrition and health in their book "Human Intestinal Microflora." The intimate biological relationship that exist between intestinal microflora and the human body will be described in more detail later (see Chapter 13).

Selected Sources and Suggested Readings

Aaron M. Altschul*Proteins. Their Chemistry and Politics.* Basic Books, New York, 1965

Carl F. Anderson, et al., 1973. Nutritional therapy for adults with renal disease. *J. American Medical Association,* 223, 68-72

Anonymous, 1990. Protein restriction and the progress of renal insufficiency. 48, 320-323

Anonymous, 1976. Interrelationships of diet, gut microflora, nutrition and health. *Dairy Council Digest,* 47, 19-24

Anonymous, 1974. Endogenous nitrogen excretion in man and the utilization of egg protein. *Nutrition Reviews,* 32, 115-117

Anonymous, 1971. Urea metabolism in man. *Lancet,* 2, 1407-1408

Anonymous, 1968. Endogenous nitrogen requirement. *Nutrition Reviews,* 26, 277-27?

Anonymous, 1963. Unessential nitrogen, an essential dietary factor. *Nutrition Reviews,* 21, 68-71

F.J. Ballard, 1978. Restricted nutrition and protein turnover. *J. Human Nutrition,* 32, 245-252

N.J. Benevenga and R.D. Steele, 1984. Adverse effects of excessive consumption of amino acids. *Annual Review of Nutrition,* 4, 157-181

Floyd E. Bloom, 1981. Neuropeptides. *Scientific American,* 245, 148-168

Jean Bowering, et al., 1970. Dietary protein level and uric acid metabolism in normal man. *J. Nutrition,* 100, 249-261

Doris H. Calloway and Harry Spector, 1954. Nitrogen balance as related to calorie and protein intake in active young men. *American J. Clinical Nutrition,* 2, 405-412.

Kenneth J. Carpenter, 1986. The history of enthusiasm for protein. *J. Nutrition,* 116, 1364-1370

An-Na Chiang, and Po-Chao Huang, 1988. Excess energy and nitrogen balance at protein intakes above the requirement level in young men. *American J. Clinical Nutrition,* 48, 1015-1022

J.C.B. Fenton, E.J. Knight and P.L. Humpherson, 1966. Milk-and-cheese diet in portal-systemic encephalopathy. *Lancet,* 1, 164-166

Sydney, M. Finegold, 1978. Fecal flora in different populations, with special reference to diet. *American J. Clinical Nutrition,* 31, S116-S122

Otto Folin and Hilding Berglund, 1922. The retention and distribution of amino-acids with especial reference to the urea formation. *J. Biological Chemistry,* 51, 395-418

Daniel L. Gallina and Jose M. Dominguez, 1971. Human utilization of urea nitrogen in low calorie diets. *J, Nutrition,* 101, 1029-1036

Michael L. G. Gardner, 1984. Intestinal assimilation of intact peptides and proteins from the diet-A neglected field ? *Biological Reviews,* 59, 289-331

Milton T. Hanke and Karl K. Koessler, 1924. Studies on proteinogenous amines. xx. On the presence of histamine in the mammalian organism. *J. Biological Chemistry* 59, 879-888

C.A. Herter and A.I. Kendall, 1909-1909. The influence of dietary alterations on the types of intestinal flora. *J. Biological Chemistry,* 7, 203-236

Takeshi Hirayama, 1978. Epidemiology of breast cancer with special reference to the role of diet. *Preventive medicine,* 7, 173-195

L. Emmett Holt, Jr., Elias Halac, Jr., and Charlotte N. Kajdi, 1962. The concept of protein stores and its implications in diet. *J. American Medical Association,* 181, 699-705

David M. Ingram, 1981. Trends in diet and breast cancer mortality in England and Wales 1928-1977. *Nutrition and Cancer,* 3, 75-80

W.T. Irvine, H.L. Duthie and N.G. Waton, 1959. Urinary output of free histamine after a meat meal. *Lancet,* 1, 1-12

M. Isabel Irwin and D. Mark Hegsted, 1971. A conspectus of research on protein requirements of man. *J. Nutrition*, 101, 385-430

Ashok K. Iyengar and B.S.Narasinga Rao, 1983. Long-term nitrogen balance in preschool children fed the safe level of protein from a cereal-legume-milk diet and adequate energy. *Human Nutrition: Clinical Nutrition,* 37c, 43-51

A. Iyengar, and B.S. Narasinga Rao, 1979. Effect of varying energy and protein intake on nitrogen balance in adults engaged in heavy manual labour. *British J. Nutrition,* 41, 19-25

Alan A. Jackson, 1983. Amino acids: Essential and non-essential. *Lancet,* 1, 1034-1037

Nancy E. Johnson, Emerita N. Alcantara and Hellen Linkswiler, 1970. Effect of level of protein intake on urinary and fecal calcium and calcium retention of young adult males. *J Nutrition,* 100, 1425-1430

R.A. Kocher, 1915. The hexone bases of malignant tumors. *J. Biological Chemistry,* 22, 295-303

Refael N. Levi and Samuel Waxman, 1975. Schizophrenia, epilepsy, cancer, methionine, and folate metabolism. Pathogenesis of schizophrenia. *Lancet,* 2, 11-13

Graham Lusk. *The Elements of the Science of Nutrition.* Saunders, Philadelphia and London, 1906

Bruce R. Maier, et al., 1974. Effects of a high-beef diet on bowel flora: A preliminary report. *American J. Clinical Nutrition,* 27, 1470-1474

D.M. Mathews, 1972. Symposium on protein metabolism and Hormones. Intestinal absorption of amino acids and peptides. *Proc. Nutrition Society,* 31, 171-177

Lafayette B. Mendel and Morris S. Fine, 1911-1912. Studies in Nutrition. 1V. The utilization of the proteins of the legumes. *J. Biological Chemistry,* 10, 433-478

Peter Merry, Bruce Kidd and David Blake, 1989. Modification of rheumatic symptoms by diet and drugs. *Proc. Nutrition Society,* 48, 363-369

D.J. Millward, et al., 1991. Symposium on 'Clinical aspects of protein and energy metabolism'. Whole-body protein and amino acid turnover in man: what can we measure with confidence? *Proc. Nutrition Society,* 50, 197-216

D.J. Milward, et al., 1989. Human amino acid and protein requirements: Current dilemmas and uncertainties. *Nutrition Research Reviews,* 2, 109-132

Hamish N. Munro, 1986. Back to Basics: An evolutionary odyssey with reflections on the nutrition research of tomorrow. *Annual Review of Nutrition,* 6, 1-12

Donna Murphy, 1979. Update: Cost of protein in foods. *National Food Review,* USDA, Consumer Research, 31

Dieter Muting, Wolfgang Eschrich, and Johann-Baptiste Mayer, 1968. The effect of Bacterium Bifidum on intestinal bacterial flora and toxic protein metabolites in chronic liver disease. *American J. Proctology,* 19, 336-342

E.S. Nasset and Jin Soon Ju, 1961. Nature of endogenous and exogenous protein in the alimentary tract. *J. Nutrition,* 74, 461-465

M.C. Nesheim, R.E. Austic and Shu-Heh, 1972. 4. Dietary factors influencing amino acid degradation. *Poultry Science,* 51, 28-35

Thomas B. Osborne and Lafayette B. Mendel, 1911-1912. The role of gliadin in nutrition. *J. Biological Chemistry,* 12, 473-487

Vinayak N. Patwardhan, 1970. Dietary allowences- An international point of view. 56, 191-194

V. N. Patwardhan, 1961. Biochemistry of human protein metabolism. *Federation Proceedings (suppl.7),* 20, 73-79

Peter L. Pellett and Vernon R. Young, 1988. Commentary: Protein and amino acid for adults. *Ecology of Food and Nutrition,* 21, 321-330

Julia Polak and S.R. Bloom, 1983. Regulatory peptides: Key factors in the control of bodily functions. *British Medical J.,* 286, 1461-1466

Peter, Richards, et al., 1971. Synthesis of phenylalanine and valine by healthy and uremic men. *Lancet,* 2, 128-134

Morris H. Ross, Gerrit Bras and M.S. Ragbeer, 1970. Influence of protein and caloric intake upon spontaneous tumor incidence of the anterior pituitary gland of the rat. *J. Nutrition,* 100, 177-189

Morris Ross and Gerrit Bras, 1965. Tumor incidence patterns and nutrition in the rat. *J. Nutrition,* 87, 245-260

Sally A. Schuette, et al., 1981. Renal acid, urinary cyclic AMP, and hydroxyproline excretion as affected by level of protein, sulfur amino acid, and phosphorus intake. *J. Nutrition,* 111, 2106-2116

Nevin S. Scrimshaw, 1978. Through a glass darkly. *Nutrition Today,* January/February, 14-34

H.C. Sherman and Jet C. Winters, 1918. Efficiency of Maize protein in adult human nutrition. *J. Biological Chemistry,* 35, 301-311

Charles J. Smith, and M.P. Bryant, 1979. Introduction to metabolic activities of intestinal bacteria. *American J. Clinical Nutrition,* 32, 149-157

Selma E. Snyderman, et al., 1962. "Unessential" nitrogen: A limiting factor for human growth. *J. Nutrition,* 78, 57-72

J.C. Somoygi, 1979. Nutritional problems in developing and industrial countries and possibilities for their solution. *Bibliothaca Nutritio et Dieta,* 28, 1-11

Harry Spiera, 1963. Excretion of a tryptophan metabolite in Rheumatoid arthritis. *Arthitis and Rheumatism,* 6, 364-371

R.L.M. Synge, 1977. The probelm of assessing the safety of novel protein-rich foods. *Proc. Nutrition Society,* 36, 107-111

Ruth M. Walker and Helen M. Linkswiler, 1972. Calcium retention in the adult human male as affected by protein intake. *J. Nutrition,* 102, 1297-1302

Roy E. Weiss, et al., 1981. Influence of high protein diets on cartilage and bone formation in rats. *J. Nutrition,* 111, 804- 816

A.M.J. Woolfson, 1983. Amino acids- their role as an energy source. *Proc. Nutrition Society,* 42, 489-495

The same material conditions which make the brain of a healthy body a relatively well-protected tissue make it less easy to demonstrate the effect of diet upon mental than upon muscular work. But we have just seen examples in which a more scientific guidance of nutrition resulted in higher mental as well as physical efficiency, even in people who were already healthy and efficient; and the present-day science of nutrition shows that this is logically to be expected.

Our bodies have wonderful self-regulating mechanisms, yet our food does influence our bodily internal environment. Here the blood is the great mediator and the same blood circulates through every part of the body, carrying the influence of the food (whether for better or for worse) to muscles and brain alike.

– Henry C. Sherman, *Selected Works of Henry Clapp Sherman*, 1948.

6

Fats Are Also Essential

Abstract: In addition to carbohydrates and proteins, fats represent a third class of chemical compounds that are major components of our diets. It is well recognized that consumption of excess dietary fat—especially animal fats (e.g. in meat, poultry, eggs and cheese) which are largely so-called "saturated" fats—is an important cause of cardiovascular disease. What is less commonly appreciated however, is the crucial role small amounts of certain fats play in normal development and in maintaining health. This chapter outlines some aspects of the nutritional biochemistry of fats and highlights some of the less commonly appreciated roles they play in body physiology. The essential fatty acids are discussed as an example of valuable fats which are often lacking from the typical Western diet. Cholesterol is discussed as an example of a fat consumed in excess in the Western diet. The types of disorders that can develop as a result of dietary excess or deficiency of fats are also considered. In excess, certain fats can contribute to obesity and cancer (e.g. of the breast and colon), in addition to cardiovascular disease. Deficiency of certain fats can also cause disease. For example, lack of essential fatty acids is believed to be a cause of learning disabilities. Taken together, a consideration of the role of fats in the diet underscores another often neglected concept of nutrition: just because an excess of something is bad for you does NOT mean that a small amount is not essential.

Vegetable oils, butter, lard and waxes belong to a large class of naturally occurring organic substances called lipids. The word "lipid" means greasy or fat-like. Lipids occur in all plant, animal and microbial cells. Insoluble in water, they dissolve readily in organic solvents such as ether and chloroform. Lipids may exist complexed with proteins and carbohydrates in cells. The chemical composition of lipids differ from species to species and from organ to organ. In general, animal products have higher total lipid contents than plant products. An adult human body contains about 12-20% lipids whereas a mature corn plant contains less than 1%. However, specific parts of both plants and animals may be very lipid-rich. Thus, adipose (fat) tissues may contain 43% lipids and many nuts and oil seeds may contain up to 60% lipids.

Chemically, lipids resemble carbohydrates and proteins in many respects; their molecules are made of the elements carbon (C), hydrogen (H) and oxygen (O). However, the ratio of the O to C is greater in carbohydrates than in lipids; lipid molecules are richer in H atoms. These chemical differences makes lipids an excellent reserve energy source for the body.

Lipids are classified in 4 groups. First, there are simple lipids which are esters of fatty acids and glycerol (an alcohol); examples are the common fats and oils. Second, derived lipids are substances that are derived from larger lipid molecules; examples are various fatty acids. Third, Compound lipids are those that contain other substances in their molecules in addition to fatty acids and glycerol. They include phospholipids which contain phosphoric acid and nitrogen. Fourth are sterols which have a characteristic ring structure; examples are cholesterol and vitamin D (see Figure 6.1).

Essential oils are a class of plant constituents which are not included in lipid classification. They are made of volatile alcohols and aldehydes. They are pungent and characteristic of plant species such as clove and cinnamon, herbs such as mint and thyme and flowers and fruits such as lemon and orange. The oils they contain are known not only for their characteristic aromas and tastes but also for their medicinal and culinary uses (see Chapter 19).

Fatty acids (FA) are components of most lipids. More than 70 different FA have been found in nature. They vary in their structures and number of double bonds in the molecules. The FA which contain less than 10 carbon atom chains are volatile and water soluble (volatile fatty acids, VFAs); examples are acetic, butyric and capric acids. The intestinal and other normal microflora of animals including humans produce many VFAs (see Chapter 13). FA which contain more than 10 carbon atoms are non- volatile and insoluble in water (non-volatile fatty acids, NVFAs).

The NVFAs are further sub-divided: those with carbon atoms linked by single bonds are saturated fatty acids (SFAs). Their molecules cannot accept any more H atoms or equivalents in chemical reactions; most animal fats contain them in high ratios. In contrast, the FA which contain double bonds are unsaturated fatty acids (USFAs); their molecules have room to take more H atoms. Some of the USFAs have more than one double bond in their molecules. The oleic acid molecule has one double bond, linoleic has two, linolenic has three and arachidonic has four double bonds. Those oils that contain USFAs with more than one double bond are polyunsaturated fatty acids (PUFAs). Most vegetable oils contain USFAs and PUFAs. The USFAs and PUFAs play a variety of roles in many biochemical reactions of the body.

FATS, OILS AND WAXES ARE LIPIDS MADE-UP OF
GLYCEROL and FATTY ACIDS

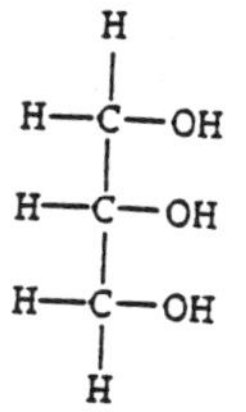

$$H-\overset{H}{\underset{}{C}}-OH,\quad H-C-OH,\quad H-\underset{H}{C}-OH$$

$$CH_3(CH_2)_7CH{=}CH(CH_2)_7-\overset{O}{\overset{\|}{C}}-OH)$$

oleic acid

CH_2—O—oleic acid
CH—O—palmitic acid
CH_2—O—oleic acid

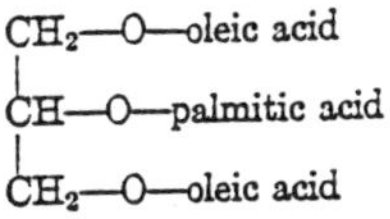

An Oil molecule
containing 2 different fatty acids

FATTY ACIDS MAY BE SATURATED or UNSATURATED

Stearic	$CH_3(CH_2)_7-CH_2-CH_2-(CH_2)_7COOH$
Oleic	$CH_3(CH_2)_7-CH{=}CH(CH_2)_7COOH$
Linoleic	$CH_3(CH_2)_4-CH{=}CHCH_2CH{=}CH(CH_2)_7COOH$
Linolenic	$CH_3CH_2CH{=}CHCH_2CH{=}CHCH_2CH{=}CH(CH_2)_7COOH$
Ricinoleic	$CH_3(CH_2)_5CHOHCH_2CH{=}CH(CH_2)_7COOH$

CHOLESTEROL and VITAMIN D ARE ALSO LIPIDS
(of a very different structure)

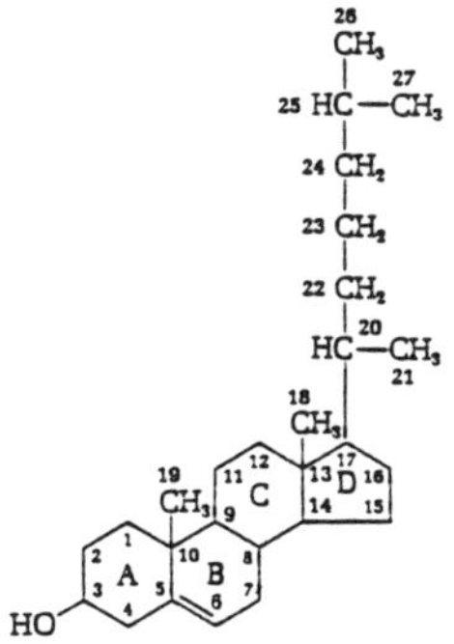

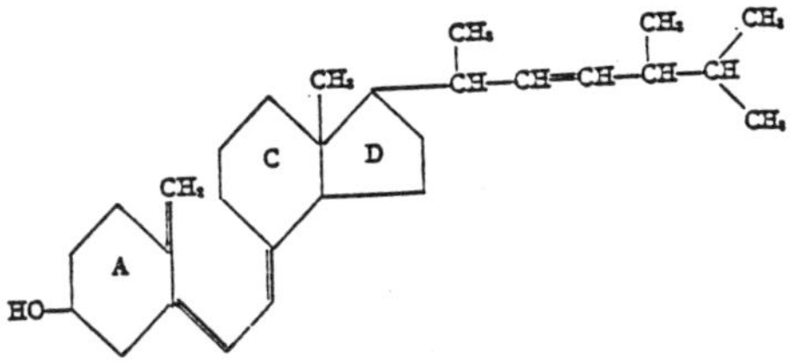

FIGURE 6.1. Examples of lipids: showing molecular structures of glycerol, oleic acid, a glyceride. saturated and unsaturated fatty acids, cholesterol and vitamin D.

Consequently, the nutritional value of food fats and oils depend upon the amount and ratio of SFAs and PUFAs they contain.

Fats may contain both SFAs and USFAs; their ratios vary from one food to another. Animal fats such as lard (beef fat) and tallow (mutton fat) are rich in stearic and palmitic acids (SFAs) and poor in oleic acid (USFA). They remain solid at room temperatures. Butter fat contains not only SFAs and USFAs but also some VFAs (butyric and caproic acids). The butyric acid content is responsible for the flavor and softness of butter at room temperatures. Most plant oils such as olive, corn and safflower oils are rich in PUFAs. However, the palm oils such as coconut oil are exceptions because they contain a high ratio of SFAs. Thus coconut oil solidifies at cool temperatures (20°C), a property of saturated fats. The nutritional value of oils depends upon the quality and quantity of PUFA and SFA they contain.

By evolution humans, like other animals, have adapted to store excess nutrients as lipids in the tissues. Fats and oils represent such stored lipids. Fats and oils are used by the body as essential reserve fuel, as a source of essential nutrients and as insulating materials. They also play important roles in the formation of membranes and in the synthesis of hormones and hormone-like substances. They transport many essential nutrients such as fat soluble vitamins and give mechanical protection for organs such as the brain, kidneys and heart.

During the course of evolution monkeys and humans have retained fats that resemble those of plants and fishes rather than those of other higher mammals. Unlike the majority of animal fats, they remain liquid at body temperature because they contain high concentrations of USFAs; to a large extent, animal fat composition depends upon the food the animals consume. The body fat of vegetarians, for example, is known to contain more PUFAs than the fat of people who have a meat staple diet; similarly, fish, which feed on lower plants (planktons) also contain relatively more PUFAs. The plant oils in general are richer in PUFAs than the fat of most animals. Unrefined edible oils are the least expensive sources of PUFA (see Table 6.1).

Storage of fats

Animals store fat as adipose tissue. Adipose tissue development begins in fetal life; an infant weighing 3–5 kg may have as much as 560 g of adipose tissue. In addition to adipose tissue, there are other fat depots in the body that surround nerve endings and organs such as the heart and the kidneys. These fat deposits provide mechanical protection and unless the body is subjected to catastrophic hunger, they are not used for energy. Even the fat stored in the adipose tissue is used only after the exhaustion of glycogen, the primary carbohydrate reserve of the body. Thus, fats stored in the adipose tissue are available as a secondary rather than primary energy source. However, fat in adipose tissue does not remain static: it is subject to constant turnover even when energy needs are supplied from carbohydrates in the diet.

TABLE 6.1. Total Fat and Polyunsaturated Fatty acids in 100 g edible portions of selected Foods . The water content of ingredients vary widely. Therefore, values are also derived for 100 g dry weight for comparison.

Items	Water (g)	Fat (g)	PUFA (g)	Fat (g*)	%PUFA
Broccoli	86	0.3	0.2	2.1	66
Cowpeas	77	0.4	0.2	1.7	50
Tomato	94	0.3	0.1	5.0	33
Peanuts	07	49	16	53	33
Rice, brown	10	2.3	1.0	2.6	44
Wheat, hard	13	1.9	0.8	2.2	42
Beef, raw	57	24.4	0.9	57.0	04
Fish, Halibut	78	02.3	.84	10.4	37
Egg, Chicken	75	10.0	1.4	40.0	14
Turkey	72	07.5	1.9	27.0	25

* Calculated on dry weight basis.

Both animals and humans undergo special adaptations before storing fat in the body even temporarily. Hibernating animals, for example, undergo metabolic adaptations to store fat which sustains them during hibernation. Infants store fat prior to walking and use it in the beginning of the walking period; similarly, adolescent males and females gain a certain amount of weight prior to puberty and lose it soon after. Fat accumulation in the body takes place during cold season more than in hot weather. Inhabitants of cold regions, the Eskimos, for example, have more fat than people of tropical regions. When the body is supplied with excess food calories, it may deposit them in various tissues as fat.

Generally, the fat content of tissues is inversely proportional to water content. As fat content increases water content decreases. In young people, approximately 13% of the body weight is fat, but around the age of fifty it may have increased to nearly 20%. The skin tissue contains more water (moist skin) and less fat in the young than in the old. The body of lean people contains less fat and more water than the body of overweight people.

A normal adult may digest 90% of their dietary lipids in the small intestine. Aided by bile and pancreatic juice, dietary lipids are digested (hydrolyzed) to yield fatty acids, glycerol and other compounds. The glycerol portions of the lipids follow mainly the path of carbohydrate metabolism whereas the fatty acid portions become droplets of triglycerides (chylomicrons) during passage through the intestinal wall. Chylomicrons enter the circulatory system through the lymph vessels (lacteals) (see Figure 6.2).

The fat that enters the cells, especially of the liver, is hydrolysed and the fatty acid molecules so generated are oxidized into 2 carbon molecules of acetyl CoA, a key intermediate, generated not only from fatty acids but also from carbohydrates and proteins (see Figure 6.3). Acetyl CoA is involved in the endogenous synthesis of the building blocks of not only fats, carbohydrates and proteins, but also of a variety of other important compounds such as hormones.

Normally, the bile that goes to the colon is eliminated before intestinal bacteria transform it into coprosterol, coprostenone and other by-products some of which can cause cancer (see Chapter 13). The bile in the feces gives the characteristic brown color to it. Chalky or grayish feces indicates gallbladder or liver disorders. The proportion of the various lipids and bile in the intestines that goes out with the feces depends upon the diet, the condition of the liver and the environment of the G.I. tract.

Various factors such as excessive lipids in the diet, overeating, depression, old age and sickness may interfere with digestion and cause malabsorption. Under those conditions the unabsorbed lipids pass into the colon where some of it is transformed by resident bacteria and the rest is eliminated in the feces.

In disorders such as ketoacidosis, as can occur in patients with insulin dependent diabetes, the body generates an excess of acetyl CoA as a by-product of fatty acid oxidation. Since acetyl Co A is generated faster than it can be eliminated as carbon dioxide and water, the excess is converted to "ketone bodies" which can build up to high levels in the bloodstream, lowering

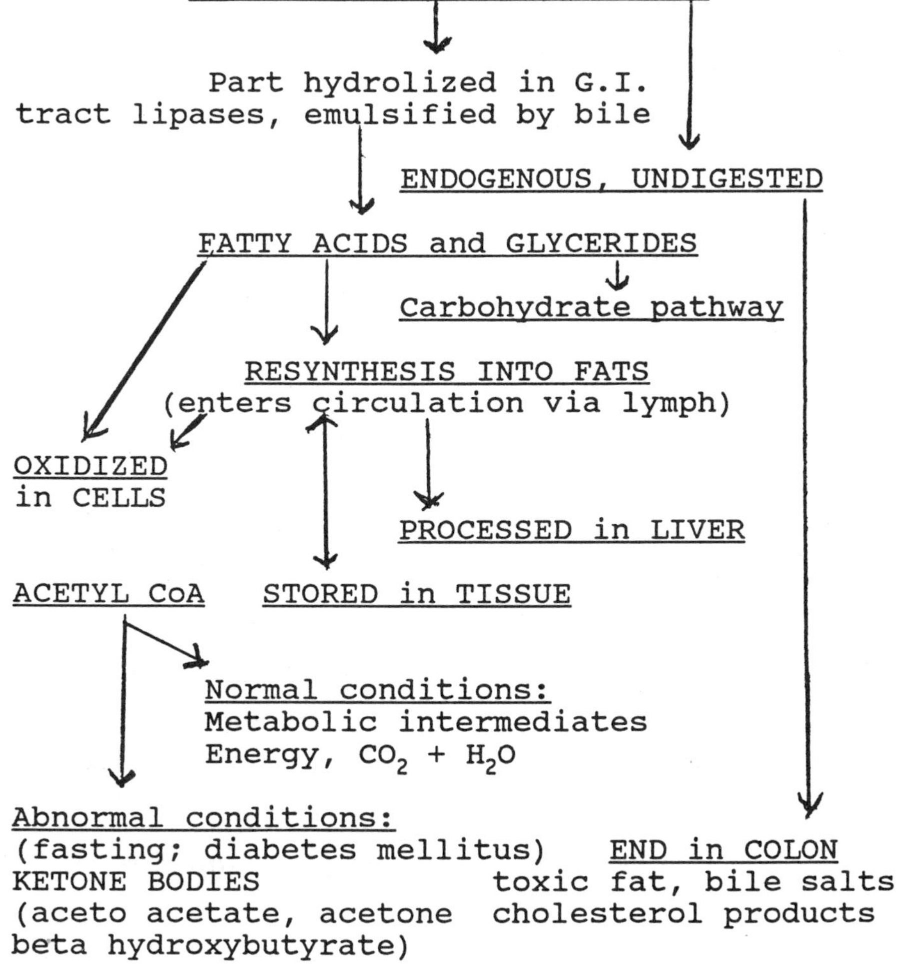

FIGURE 6.2. Digestion of lipids and beyond. Normally fats are stored and used for generating energy and building blocks. Physical abnormalities and bacterial actions in the colon generate toxic products.

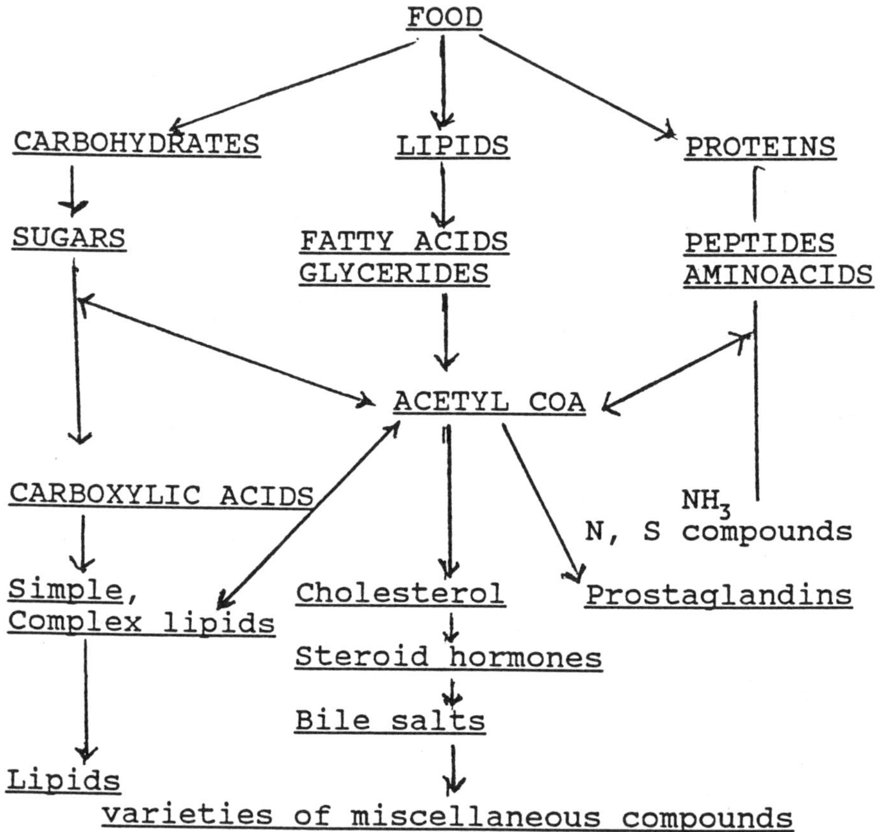

FIGURE 6.3. Key role of Acetyl CoA in the cells. Acetyl CoA is produced in large quantities from fats. Some of it also can come from sugars or amino acids. The diagram shoes how it is involved in the synthesis of many different valuable compounds.

the blood pH. The resulting "acidosis" can cause coma and death. This is an example of loss of lipid homeostasis.

When the diet is low in animal fats, the acetyl CoA generated undergoes complex changes in the liver where its chain length may be extended to as long as 22 carbon atoms with up to 6 double bonds. The required cholesterol is also synthesized by the body and stored in the gallbladder as bile. The bile is used for the digestion of fats and is recycled in the body.

In 1988 Amos Norman and associates of the University of California, noticed that malignant tumors were very rare in the small intestine; further animal experiments lead them to conclude that it is the high concentration of PUFAs, especially linoleic acid which is responsible for preventing the development of small intestinal cancer. Scientists have also related deficiency of PUFAs to other diseases. Some cases of infant sudden death syndrome (SDS) has been attributed to the deficiency of PUFAs in the diet. According to published reports, when fatty acid analysis of the liver of some infants who died of SDS were examined, significant deficiencies of PUFAs were found in them.

Essential fatty acids

In 1929, G.O. and M.M. Blurr of the University of Minnesota, working with animals and human volunteers found that the body can synthesize all the SFAs as well as part of the oleic acid needed but not linoleic, linolenic and arachidonic acids (USFAs); they found that these USFAs which are essential to many biochemical reactions of the body need to be acquired from exogenous sources just as were essential amino acids, described in the previous chapter. Thus they termed these USFAs essential fatty acids (EFAs). While the EFA linoleic acid occurs abundantly in many natural foods, linolenic and arachidonic are not as prevalent. Safflower seeds which are rich EFAs may contain as much as 75% EFAs, corn 58%, coconut oil 8% and pork 7%.

Researchers have shown that EFAs are involved in many functions, such as membrane synthesis, cholesterol metabolism and in the synthesis of prostaglandins (PG), a group of remarkable biologically active substances produced by the human body. They were first discovered in the human semen which is still the richest known source. There are as many as 14 different PGs which are synthesized from PUFAs, especially arachidonic acid. They are effective in extremely small concentrations. They bring about a variety of cellular and physiological reactions. Some of them promote blood platelet aggregation. Some of them cause the smooth muscle of the uterus to contract and others cause it to relax.

A deficiency of EFAs in experimental animals has been found to cause growth failure, skin lesions, kidney deterioration, red blood cell fragility, impaired fertility and learning disabilities. Patients with diseases such as multiple sclerosis and cystic fibrosis have been found to be deficient in EFAs. It has been reported that feeding sunflower seed oil, which is rich in EFAs, to cystic fibrosis patients reduced their symptoms.

The human body fat is not only rich in USFAs, but also humans have an absolute requirement of EFAs to support growth and to maintain health. Teleologically speaking, it is no wonder that human breast milk, which is known to maintain infant health better than any formula is rich in EFAs. EFA requirements for adults are not known to diminish radically with age. The best sources of all the EFAs are plant staples. The popular reports that fish provides beneficial fatty acids do not explain that fish derive those fatty acids from plants, phytoplankton, which serve as their dietary staple! A plant staple rich diet not only supplies needed lipids but also other lipid associated nutrients such as antioxidants, vitamin E, carotenes, lecithins and dietary fiber which are necessary for the regulation of body lipids, especially cholesterol.

The EFAs which influence brain development and other crucial biological functions in infancy also play roles in later body functions such as the timing of puberty, the onset of menstrual periods and starting and carrying pregnancy to term. The EFAs are also basic ingredients in synthesizing prostaglandins which play important roles even in old age. The homeostatic mechanisms of the body regulate a variety of bodily functions, provided the diet is supportive.

In healthy persons, lipid biosynthesis is regulated according to the changing needs of the body and to dietary intake. It has been shown that the body's own synthesis of FAs such as palmitic and oleic acids are high when the fat content of the diet is low. When the diet is rich in animal fat more of the dietary fatty acids are incorporated into the body fat. A balanced diet is recommended to contain 3% of its food calories as EFAs. However, the western diet is generally very poor in EFAs. Substituting corn oil alone for other fats in the Western diet is known to contribute a four-fold increase in linoleic acid consumption.

Artemis Simopoulos in a review in 1988, drew attention to the observation that human milk contains approximately 8.5% of its total energy in the form of EFAs and that infant brain growth is most rapid during the breast feeding stage. He interpreted this correlation to suggest an important role for EFAs in brain development. Breast milk contains 3.4% linoleic acid compared to 1.3% in cow's milk. The fact that growth of brain tissue is faster during the first trimester of pregnancy than after birth, further emphasizes the need for the EFAs in the diet of pregnant and nursing women. Simopoulos recommended supplying as much as 1.5% of the dietary energy of pregnant women in the form of EFAs.

A group of lipids that contain phosphorus (phospholipids) plays several important roles in all cells. In 1930, Bloor found that the brain contained the highest percentage of phospholipids; 54% of the brain is lipid by dry weight. Approximately 28% of this lipid is in the form of phospholipids. One category of phospholipid are the lecithins. They are constituents of plant and animal cells and they take part in several important metabolic reactions. Lecithins contain different kinds and amounts of PUFAs. They are abundant in many leafy greens and in oil seeds such as sesame and sunflower.

According to scientists from the University of Ottawa, hypertension assumed to be caused by sodium (Na) excess or deficiency of calcium (Ca) or both may be caused indirectly by the deficiency of EFAs. EFAs modify membrane uptake of Na and Ca and their deficiency may raise systolic blood pressure (hypertension).

According to H.M. Sinclair of the International Institute of Human Nutrition of Sutton Courenay, Oxon, in the U.K., people who consume Western diets rich in SFAs may have relative deficiency of EFAs. This deficiency has been suspected to have a role in a wide range of ailments including atherosclerosis, coronary thrombosis, multiple sclerosis, hypertension and certain types of malignancies. In the U.S. the dramatic 25% decrease in deaths attributed to coronary heart disease since 1968, coincides with the rise noticed in the amount of linoleic acid in the adipose tissue of healthy subjects. Similarly, in a community of the United Kingdom, where the death rate due to coronary heart diseases has remained constant, the population also showed unchanged high linoleic acid content in their adipose tissues.

Many reports show that PUFAs and phospholipids such as lecithins, which are abundant in plant staples such as leaves, seeds and grain germs are interconvertible and play a prominent role in cholesterol metabolism. Lack of PUFAs in the diet has been suggested to lead to hypertension, cardiac enlargement and acute kidney disease, among other ailments. Many reports published in the 1980s, revealed that increased PUFAs and decreased SFA in the diet reduces ailments such as high blood pressure and cardiovascular disease. Reducing the consumption of animal fats from 39 g to 24 g caused significant improvements in the health of the participants.

The lipid metabolism of the fetus is influenced by the nutrients derived from the mother. At the stage when brain development is rapid, long chain PUFAs are very essential for the brain growth and fetal metabolic processes. The human infant derives its lipids from the breast milk which provides more than 50% of its energy content in the form of lipids. The lipid content of breast milk is strongly influenced by the mothers diet.

Among nutritionally important sterols, cholesterol has received the most publicity. The Greek term cholesterol means alcohol derived from bile. Cholesterol is the precursor of bile acids which are important components of the digestive juice, bile. Bile synthesized by the liver is stored in gallbladder. Cholesterol is a primary constituent of almost all animal cells. Approximately 10% of the brain lipid is cholesterol. However, the amount of cholesterol present varies from individual to individual and from organ to organ. Plant cells also have sterols, called phytosterols.

The human body synthesizes its own cholesterol and obtains it from dietary sources of animal origin such as meat, egg and sea food. Among foods of animal origin milk has the least cholesterol and egg the most (see Table 6.2). Blood cholesterol is present in both a free form and an ester form. The total

TABLE 6.2. Cholesterol Content in milligrams/100 g edible portion of Dietary Ingredients. Notice the absence of Cholesterol in plant ingredients and relatively low levels in milk, yogurt and buttermilk.

Item (100 g)	Cholesterol (mg)
Beef	68
Chicken	98
Clams	50
Fish, Cod	50
Fish, Haddock	60
Fish, Herring	85
Crab	100
Egg, Chicken	1,480
Lamb	71
Liver, Chicken	555
Lobster	182
Milk, Whole	14
Milk, Lowfat	06
Milk, Nonfat	02
Yogurt, Nonfat	08
Buttermilk	02
Fruits	0
Vegetables	0
Cereals	0

cholesterol level of normal blood may very from 110-390 mg or more per 100 ml blood; two-thirds of it may be present as esters. Some of this cholesterol is synthesized by the body itself but most of it comes from foods of animal origin because plant sterol are not absorbed in our G.I. system. Certain animals such as dogs and rats posses mechanisms that shut off cholesterol synthesis when it is plentiful in the diet. Such self-regulation does not exist in humans. The body which synthesizes cholesterol for its needs, suffers greatly when the diet supplies additional large quantities of cholesterol. A diet with a high fat content increases the blood cholesterol content. When lipemia was controlled through diet, the blood cholesterol also diminishes.

Bloor and associates, who extensively studied lipid metabolism, concluded that the increased blood cholesterol level was the consequence of the body using protein and lipid as energy sources, instead of carbohydrates (see Chapter 5). In 1950 L.W. Kinsell working with a group of diabetic patients found that consuming vegetable fat consistently reduced serum cholesterol levels. Since then, arteriosclerosis and other cardiovascular diseases have been identified as partially caused by the intake of excessive saturated fats. In the U.S. cardiovascular diseases alone are now responsible for more deaths than all forms of cancers combined. More than 900,000 deaths are caused by them; approximately 5.4 million people have been diagnosed to have these diseases. Cardiovascular diseases cost more than $50 billion a year in direct and indirect costs. Most scientists agree that the major cause of these diseases is excessive intake of animal food (see Table 6.3).

In 1973, J.J. Groen of the University of Leiden in the Netherlands, supported by organizations such as the National Heart Institute, examined the relationship between diet and serum cholesterol in the development of atherosclerosis and ischemic heart disease. Several investigators had shown that consumption of a diet rich in saturated fat, cholesterol and sucrose increased the serum cholesterol level and that polyunsaturated fat in diet reduced the cholesterol level. Groen examined food intake and serum cholesterol in individuals 40 to 70 years old among Trappist monks in Holland, Yemenite Jews and Arab Bedouin in Israel, and compared them with those of individuals on the Western diet. He found that all three groups had lower serum cholesterol levels than westerners. All three groups consumed much more carbohydrates, especially starches, and much less fat than those in the West. The diet of Western group was also higher in sugar.

By examining the diets of those groups, Groen hypothesized that replacement of dietary fat by bread and legumes lowered the cholesterol level. The hypothesis was tested on Western volunteers and their serum cholesterol level came down to the Yemenite level after 5 weeks. When the volunteers returned to the Western diets, their cholesterol returned to their previous high level (2.3 g/L). A group that went on diets with animal protein (meat and milk) and sugar showed high cholesterol levels. From these studies, which went on for over 10 years, Groen recommended that bread be recognized as an important component of a healthful diet.

TABLE 6.3. Death Rates from Coronary Heart Disease Compared with Mean Daily Intake of Cholesterol in Diet. Approximate rate in deaths per 100,000 in men aged 55-59; 1955-56. Cholesterol intake in milligrams per day per person. Selected from *Nutrition and Health,* Select Committee on Nutrition and Human Needs, U.S. Senate, 1975.

Cholesterol intake (mg/day)	Death Rate per 100,000 males	Country
575	720	U.S.A.
520	630	Australia
500	610	Canada
450	450	U.K.
450	520	New Zealand
420	325	Sweden
320	350	Germany
300	350	Austria
200	220	Italy
150	70	Greece
130	70	Yugoslovia

Many scientific studies of the 1960s demonstrated that not only reducing animal fat but also reducing animal protein in the diet lowered the serum cholesterol level. Experiments conducted with animals and human volunteers in the 1980s showed that triglyceride and cholesterol levels not only were increased by consuming excessive animal protein but that they could be lowered by substituting the animal protein in the diet with plant protein. Rabbits develop atherosclerosis on a diet high in cholesterol. This outcome can be prevented by feeding the rabbits with a diet rich in alfalfa. Alfalfa appears not only to enhance metabolism of endogenous cholesterol, but also sequesters cholesterol in the stool, preventing its absorption in the gut. Dietary studies showed that when animal proteins are replaced with plant proteins such as soybean and chickpea, serum cholesterol levels decreased 20-22% in a short period.

A study of the Tarahumara Indians of Mexico showed that as long as the amount of animal products in their diet remained low, consuming as much as 400 mg/day phytosterols in their staples of beans and corn did not increase their serum cholesterol levels. According to Robert Wissler of the University of Chicago, middle-aged monkeys that consumed a typical U.S. diet rich in animal fat for 2 years had developed 4 times more arteriosclerotic deposits than monkeys that received lower quantities of fats, cholesterol and refined sugar. Unfortunately, 200,000 Americans undergo coronary bypass surgery every year to treat coronary artery disease and 44% of them need an another one within 10 years! Dietary modification may be a better solution.

In the 1980s, an elaborate study of the relationship between diet and cardiovascular diseases conducted in Framingham, Massachusetts, found that vegetarians had approximately 130 mg cholesterol per 100 ml of blood compared to the 250-600 mg levels found in most other Americans. A cholesterol level in the vicinity of 150 mg/100 ml of blood is considered normal. In general, the blood cholesterol level starts to increase in the U.S. population around the age of 35, depending upon various conditions such as the life style, the dietary intake of animal and plant foods, the ratio of SFAs and USFAs in the diet, the capacity of the intestine to absorb dietary fat and the ability to eliminate the excess in the feces.

Many studies found that the higher the dietary content of SFAs, the higher the cholesterol content as well. An average American, eating meat as a dietary staple, has approximately 250 mg serum cholesterol/100 ml serum. The Trappist monks, Seventh-day Adventists and other Americans who do not consume meat as a staple show cholesterol levels close to 150 mg/100 ml serum. Nearly 73% of a sample of Americans tested in 1986 showed cholesterol levels higher than 180 mg. According to the RDA the cholesterol intake should not exceed 300 mg per day. However, many Americans may be getting as much as 600 mg cholesterol every day in their diet. A single egg contributes as much as 270 mg of cholesterol. In addition, the human body itself makes more than 600 mg cholesterol daily.

Nearly 80-85% of gallstones found in the people of industrialized countries are made of cholesterol. These gallstones occur when bile is supersaturated with cholesterol which happens when the diet is rich in animal lipids and low in PUFAs. Although the causal relationship is unclear, there is a strong correlation between a meat staple diet and a high prevalence of gallstones.

The cholesterol present in the blood stream may vary in its content of Low Density Lipoproteins (LDLs) in proportion to High Density Lipoproteins (HDLs), depending upon a variety of factors including the diet. The HDL may play a role of "scavenger" to reduce the amount of cholesterol in the blood. The body can recycle HDL and use it to control the cholesterol level in the plasma. As much as 55% of HDLs may contain linoleic acid which needs to be supplied from plant staples. Consistent with this view, linoleic acid lowers the cholesterol level in the blood, when it is provided in the diet. Likewise, the cholesterol-lowering and other beneficial effects of the phospholipid lecithin has been shown to be due to the linoleic acid component of lecithin.

James Gamble of Johns Hopkins University reported that in normal healthy infants, excretion of cholesterol is always greater than intake; according to him the body not only adapts to synthesize cholesterol, but also to excrete it provided the diet consumed is appropriate. According to a 1988 report published in the New York Times, 25% of Americans surveyed said that they are watching their cholesterol. According to Alexander Leaf, the Chief of Medicine in Harvard Medical School, members of the communities in several remote areas of the world that have a high population of relatively old individuals who have a blood cholesterol of not more than 150 mg/100 ml blood. Their diets are rich in plant staples, milk and milk products. In our opinion, the only animal product that shold not be de-emphasized in the diet is milk.

The chemical composition of fecal lipids may differ greatly from that of dietary lipids. Fecal lipids resemble blood lipids more than they do than dietary lipids. Fecal lipids may vary with the dietary intake, the stagnation period of food residue in the colon and the kind of bacteria that act upon this residue. Symptoms such as malaise, headache and irritability that are associated with constipation may be due to microbiologically transformed lipid by- products. Generally, physicians and physiologists have ignored this role of the colonic bacteria and have failed to recognize their role in causing such symptoms.

Studies have shown that obese persons carry a higher risk of some cancers than the under-weight. One of the reasons for this is that obesity alters the fat metabolism and hormone production of the body. Cancers of the colon, ovaries, rectum and leukemia have been associated with the abnormal metabolism of fat and related compounds. Undigested lipids and bile acids that stagnate in the colon, alter the resident bacterial population and have been implicated in the etiology of breast and colorectal cancers. Many colorectal cancer patients have abnormally high percentages of Clostridium species of bacteria in the colon which are capable of transforming bile acids, cholesterol and other lipids into carcinogens (see Chapter 13).

According to Ernst Winder and colleagues of the American Health Foundation in New York City, a close correlation exists in the population between high meat and high animal fat consumption and the incidence of breast cancer. The high dietary animal fat consumption may increase the secretion of the hormone prolactin. Prolactin, which may be involved in the development of breast cancer, is a normal hormone in lactating women and it often rises significantly in the blood prior to the clinical onset of breast cancer. Frequently, this happens in women whose diet is high in meat. When a group of American women were put on a vegetarian diet for six weeks, their prolactin secretion decreased 40-60%; conversely, when a western-type meat diet was introduced to predominantly vegetarian Bantu women, prolactin levels increased in their blood. Seventh-Day Adventist women and members of other vegetarian groups are known to have an incidence of breast cancer that is 80% less than that of women who consume a high meat diet.

Studies have shown that the nature of dietary fat influences the composition of the body fat. Excess food, especially from animal sources and refined plant products, contribute to lipid storage and cholesterol deposits. According to Bruce Armstrong of Perth Medical Center in Australia, obesity, late onset of menopause, mild cases of diabetes mellitus and high blood pressure may all be in part attributable to the fat in high meat diets. As pointed out by Professor A. E. Needham of Oxford University, there is a strong tendency for stored fat to resemble in composition the food source of an animal. Unrelated animals living under the same conditions store more or less similar fats in their bodies than do their biological near relatives living under different conditions. In other words, the nature of body fat depends on dietary fat.

Just as breast milk supplies the infants requirements of EFAs, cultural diets rich in unrefined plant staples supply variety of food factors including lipids, which in moderation are nourishing and protective. When the affluent Western diet replaced the traditionally mixed cultural diets with more foods of animal origin, the intake of some lipids such as cholesterol increased to the point of causing harm. Consequent to those increases in certain fats, hormone profiles and fat storage patterns were altered (see Chapter 14).

A prudent lacto-vegetarian diet is high in roughage, regulates body cholesterol, provides protection against degenerative ailments and, thereby prolongs a vigorous and productive life.

Selected Sources and Suggested Readings

Roslyn B. Alfin-Slater, 1960. Relation of vitamin E to lipid metabolism. American *J. Clinical Nutrition,* 8, 445-460

James W. Anderson and Wen-Ju Lin Chen, 1979. Plant fiber, carbohydrate and lipid metabolism. *American J. Clinical Nutrition,* 32, 346-363

Anonymous, 1975. Effects of diet on biliary lipid secretion and bile composition. *Nutrition Reviews,* 33, 72-74

Anonymous, 1973. Overfeeding in the first year of life. *Nutrition Reviews,* 31, 116-118

Elliot M. Berry and Jules Hirsch, 1986. Does dietary linolenic acid influence blood pressure? *American J. Clinical Nutrition,* 44, 336-340

W.R. Bloor, 1916. The distribution of the lipids ("Fat") in human blood. *J. Biological Chemistry,* 25, 577-597

Joan M. Bulfer and C. Eugene Allen, 1979. Fat cells and obesity. *BioSciencice,* 29, 736-741

Kenneth K. Carroll and Heli I. Parenteau, 1991. A proposed mechanism for effects of diet on mammary cancer. *Nutrition and Cancer,* 16, 79-83

D.G. Cramp, J.F. Moorehead and M.R. Wills, 1975. Disorders of blood-lipids in renal disease. *Lancet,* 1, 672-673

Michael A. Crawford, 1992. The role of dietary fatty acids in biology: Their place in the evolution of the human brain. *Nutrition Reviews,* 50, 3-11

Ahmed Eid and Elliot M Berry, 1988. The relationship between dietary fat, adipose tissue composition, and neoplasms of the breast. *Nutrition and Cancer,* 11, 173-177

I. S. Fentiman, et al., 1988. The binding of blood-borne estrogens in normal vegetarin and omnivorous women and the risk of breast cancer. *Nutrition and Cancer,* 11, 101-106

Martin H. Floch, Edited, 1976. Symposium on Diet, Bacteria and the Colon. *Clinical Nutrition,* 29, 1409-1484

Alan C. Fogerty, et al., 1984. Liver fatty acids and the sudden infant death syndrome. *American J. Clinical Nutrition,* 39, 201-208

William A. Forsythe, Manfred S. Green and John J.B. Anderson, 1986. Dietary protein effects on cholesterol and lipoprotein concentrations: A review. *J. American College of Nutrition,* 5, 533-549

David Gambal and F.W. Quckenbush, 1960. Effects of cholesterol and other substances on essential fatty acid deficiencies. *J. Nutrition,* 70, 497-501

Christopher J. Georges, 1990. Studies find a link between aggressiveness and cholesterol. *New York Times,* Medical Science, September 11, 1990

J.J. Groen, 1973. Why bread in the diet lowers serum cholesterol. *Proc. Nutrition Society,* 32, 159-167

D.C. Hewson, et al., 1984. Food intake in multiple sclerosis. *Human Nutrition: Applied Nutrition,* 38A, 355-357

G.A. Higgs, 1985. The effects of dietary intake of essential fatty acids on prostaglandin and leukotriene synthesis. *Proc. Nutrition Society,* 44, 181-187

M. J. Hill and Vivienne C. Aries, 1971. Faecal steroid composition and its relationship to cancer of the large bowel. *J. Pathology,* 104, 129-139

Jules Hirsch, 1972. "Can we modify the number of adipose cells?" *Postgraduate Medicine,* 51, 83-86

Ralph T. Holman and James J. Peifer, 1960. Acceleration of essential fatty acid deficiency by dietary cholesterol. *J. Nutrition,* 70, 410-417

David J.A. Jenkins, et al., 1983. Leguminous seeds in the dietary management of hyperlipidemia. *American J. Clinical Nutrition,* 38, 567-573

Jan T. Knuiman, Anton C. Beyman and Martijn B. Katan, 1989. Lecithin intake and serum cholesterol. *American J. Clinical Nutrition,* 49, 266-268

David Kritchevsky, 1978. Fiber, lipids and atherosclerosis. *American J. Clinical Nutrition,* 31, S65-S74

Michael Liebman and Terry L. Bazzare 1983. Plasma lipids of vegetarian and nonvegetarian males: effects of egg consumption. *J. Clinical Nutrition,* 38, 612-619

John D. Lloyd-Still, Susan B. Johnson and Ralph T. Holman, 1981. Essential fatty acid status in cystic fibrosis and the effects of safflower oil supplementation. *American J. Clinical Nutrition,* 34, 1-7

Frank D. Mann, 1990. The dynamics of free cholesterol exchange may be critical for endothelial cell membranes in the brain. *Perspective in Biology and Medicine,* 33, 531-533

Edward C. Naber, 1980. The cholesterol dilemma. *BioScience,* 30, 571

Amos Norman et al., 1988. Antitumor activity of sodium linoleate. *Nutrition and Cancer,* 11, 107-115

A. Nouvelot, et al., 1983. Changes in the fatty acid patterns of brain phospholipids during development of rats fed peanut or rapeseed oil, taking into account differences between milk and maternal food. *Ann. Nutrition Metabolism,* 27, 173-181

Robert E. Olson, 1963, The two-carbon chain in metabolism. *J. American Medical Association,* 183, 471-474

Robert W. Owen, et al., 1987. Fecal steroids and colorectal cancer. *Nutrition and Cancer,* 9, 73-80

J.P.D. Reckless, 1987. Can nutrition favourably affect serum lipids? *Proc. Nutrition Society,* 46, 361- 366

Farah Roshanai and T.A.B. Sanders, 1984. Assessment of fatty acid intakes in vegans and omnivores. *Human Nutrition: Applied Nutrition,* 38A, 345-354

HansRuppin, et al., 1980. Absorption of short-chain fatty acids by the colon. *Gastroenterology,* 78, 1500-1507

Frank M. Sacks and Walter W. Willett, 1991. More on chewing the fat. The good fat and the good cholesterol. *New England J. Medicine,* 325, 1740-1742

T.A.B. Sanders and S. Reddy, 1992. The influence of rice bran on plasma lipids and lipoproteins in human volunteers. *European J. Clinical Nutrition* 46, 167-172

Milton G. Schmitt Jr.et al., 1977. Absorption of short-chain fatty acids from the human ileum. *Digestive Diseases,* 22, 340-347

David A Snowdon, Roland L. Phillips and Warren Choi, 1984. Diet, obesity, and risk of fatal prostate cancer. *American J. Epidemiology,* 120, 244-250

Warren M. Sperry and W.R. Bloor, 1924. Fat excretion.II. The quantitative relations of the fecal lipoids. *J. Biological Chemistry,* 40, 261-287

Timo E. Strandberg, et al, 1991. Long-term mortality after 5-year multifactorial primary prevention of cardiovascular diseases in middle-aged men. *J. American Medical Association,* 266, 1225-1229

Roy L. Swank and Aagot Grimsgaard, 1988. Multiple sclerosis: the lipid relationship. *American J. Clinical Nutrition,* 48, 1387- 1393

J.E. Sweet, Ellen P. Corson-White, and G.J. Saxon, 1915. Further studies on the relation of diet to transmissible tumors. *J. Biological Chemistry,* 21, 309-318

Emanuela Taioli, Alfredo Nicolosi, and Ernst Wynder, 1991. Dietary habits and breast cancer: A comparative study of United States and Italian Data. *Nutrition and Cancer,* 16, 259-265

Reijo S. Tilvis, and Tatu A. Miettinen, 1986. Serum plant sterols and their relation to cholesterol absorption. *American J. Clinical Nutrition,* 43, 92-97

V. Utermohlen and M.A.M. Tucker, 1986. Possible effects of dietary n-6 series polyunsaturated fatty acids on the development of immune dysfunction and infection. *Proc. Nutrition Society,* 45, 327-331

Nicholas Wade, 1972. DES: A case study of regulatory abdication. *Science,* 177, 335-337

Alexander R.P. Walker, 1976. Colon cancer and diet, with special reference to intakes of fat and fiber. *American J. Clinical Nutrition,* 29, 1417-1426

7

The Value of Vitamins and Antioxidants

Abstract: In addition to carbohydrates, proteins and fats, the three major constituents of a healthy diet, additional substances, the vitamins, the antioxidants and minerals are needed to maintain health – but some in very small amounts. Vitamins are those nutrients needed, typically in very small amounts, e.g. as cofactors for enzymes, for optimal organ system function and homeostasis. Antioxidants are substances that neutralize (quench) harmful substances that would otherwise engage in chemical reactions with delicate and sensitive cellular components. Many antioxidants are vitamins, others are minerals. This chapter reviews the history of vitamins and antioxidants in nutrition and explains their role in maintaining good health. Some vitamins and antioxidants display a degree of overlap in their actions which allows them to substitute for one another in certain circumstances, but not in others. Perhaps due to differences in levels of particular enzymes and hence, activities of pathways of intermediary metabolism, different individuals may have dramatically different needs for particular vitamins. The full range of overlap in vitamin and antioxidant functions, and the basis for the differences in individual dietary requirements, remains poorly understood. Thus it is important that the dietary intake of vitamins and antioxidants be both varied and plentiful. Plants are the primary source of vitamins and antioxidants. An excess of certain vitamins (e.g. fat soluble vitamins) may be as harmful as their deficiency.

Vitamins are organic substances that are required for proper functioning of animals and humans. Vitamins or their precursors need to be supplied through various foods, or as synthetic products, because the body either does not make them or makes them in insufficient amounts. They do not yield energy or provide building blocks for the body, but rather, are catalysts or mediators of chemical reactions. Therefore, unlike the major nutrients such as carbohydrates, proteins and lipids, vitamins are needed in extremely small quantities. Nevertheless, they are absolutely necessary to maintain the health and well-being of humans of all ages.

History and significance of vitamins

The history of vitamins and their deficiency diseases can be traced back over 4000 years. Traditionally, people of all cultures satisfied the need for nutritional supplements by consuming many varieties of leaves, barks, roots, fruits and seeds of many plant foods, herbs and spices, in their diets (see Chapter 14). Traditional systems of medicine in both Eastern and Western countries utilized a variety of plant materials and their extracts and ashes. When variety of food sources became scarce deficiency ailments began appearing; the mystery of deficiency diseases was solved by providing missing ingredients initially in the form of crude natural substances and later on as purified or synthetic vitamins.

As early as 1536, scurvy was recognized to be a deficiency disease. In one voyage by Jacques Cartier on the St. Lawrence river, 26 sailors died of scurvy. Those who survived did so by drinking extracts of pine needles, which are rich in vitamin C. James Lind, an English navy surgeon, discovered that fruits and vegetables, especially citrus fruits, prevent scurvy (antiscorbutic). He recommended Sea Captains to carry plenty of limes and lemons in the ships. Scurvy used to be so common among soldiers and sailors that it came to be known as "the calamity of soldiers". It took a heavy toll of Crusaders in the 13th century. According to reports, the vitamin B deficiency disease of beriberi existed in China as early as in 2600 B.C. In 1878 nearly 2,000 Japanese navy men became sick with beriberi. Takaki, a medical officer of the Japanese navy cured them by decreasing white rice consumption and increasing other foods.

Eijkman, a Dutch physician in the East Indies noticed that only the fowl that ate white rice became afflicted with an ailment similar to beriberi, but not the ones that ate unpolished rice. In Kuala Lumpur, Malaysia, Horace Fletcher found that people who ate "cured" (parboiled) rice did not have symptoms of beriberi but those who ate milled and polished rice frequently developed the disease. He conducted feeding experiments on people and confirmed these conclusions. The vitamin D deficiency disease Rickets was known as "wrikken" which means bend or twist in old English. The disease was noticeable with obvious sign of bone deformation. It was more common among infants and children fed with condensed or sterilized milk than in breast-fed children. It was more common during winter time when fresh vegetable consumption was low. The affected children suffered from anemia, bleeding gums, internal pain and bowlegs (external bone deformities).

These and similar observations lead scientists world-wide to look for substances that occur in natural foods which are necessary to maintain health. This idea was strengthened by noticing that certain diseases were not common among people who ate varied traditional diets. World-wide, the deficiency diseases were common among people who were deprived of variety in their diet or who consumed only refined, processed and preserved foods. The deficiency diseases also followed a common course of starting with specific organs with specific symptoms, gradually becoming generalized so as to debilitate the victims and even cause death.

Remedies to those diseases were developed gradually during the past 100 years. During 1906-1912 Gowland Hopkins, an English biochemist, observed that feeding laboratory animals with purified dietary ingredients (carbohydrate, protein and fat) caused growth retardation, sickness and death. Addition of even a small proportion of whole milk into the experimental diets enabled the animals to grow. From such nutrition studies Hopkins referred to those nutrients supplied by milk as accessory food factors. Around 1913, Thomas Osborne, Lafayette Mendel, Vernon McCollum and other physiological chemists in the U.S., proved the existence of such accessory food factors beyond any doubt. Thus, the scientific concept of vitamins developed by observing the deficiency diseases that ravaged the world as a consequence of "advances" in food technology.

In spite of their great contributions to the knowledge of vitamins, nutrition scientists of the 1920s such as Robert McCarrison, E. V. McCollum and Henry Sherman were strong advocates of a mixed diet because they believed that, although synthetic vitamins can supplement certain obvious dietary necessities, the many beneficial factors supplied by a diet rich in bulk and variety could not be reliably substituted with synthetic vitamins. McCollum fervently prevailed on that theme to popularize "protective food," a diet rich in vegetables and milk. It served the U.S. population well for almost 3 decades until the post-war economic prosperity led to the promotion and widespread acceptance of a diet rich in meat and refined food rather than protective and bulky food (see Chapter 15).

In 1911 Casimir Funk, the Polish scientist used the term "vitamine" to describe the unknown accessory food factors that he and other scientists had found that prevents the disease beriberi. However, further reserch revealed that not all of these food factors (vitamins) belonged to one group of chemicals, the amines. The name "vitamine" was then changed to vitamin. In general, vitamins function as components of certain essential enzymes (coenzymes) which play crucial roles in the utilization of nutrients (intermediary metabolism). The optimal quantity of individual vitamins required depends to some extent upon variables such as age, sex, diet, the use of drugs and other factors. Taking oral contraceptives, smoking cigarettes or drinking alcohol, for example, increases the body's need for certain vitamins.

Symptoms of vitamin deficiency

The symptoms of vitamin deficiencies are often difficult to recognize because they overlap with symptoms of many other ailments. Pellagra, for example, has been found to arise in deficiency of nicotinic acid (a B complex vitamin), zinc (a mineral) or tryptophan (an essential amino acid). It also occurs in the presence of excess of an another amino acid, leucine, in the diet. All of these nutrients are involved with tryptophan metabolism. This kind of inter-relationship of nutrients makes diagnosing vitamin deficiency diseases quite complicated.

Classes of vitamins and their sources

The common sources of most vitamins, or their precursors, are natural foods such as whole grains, leafy vegetables and fruits. Carrot, for example, is a rich source of carotene, a precursor of vitamin A. Certain vitamins are supplied by converting chemicals that exist in the body. 7-Dihydroxy cholesterol present in the skin, for example, can be transformed into vitamin D in the presence of sun light. The intestinal microflora in animals and humans are also a good source of several vitamins. Much of the human needs of both vitamin B12 and of K, for example, can be met from this endogenous source (see Chapter 13). Finally, vitamins may be taken in pill form or in foods fortified by their addition. Processed milk, for example, is fortified with added vitamin D.

Classification of vitamins

The vitamins are grouped as fat-soluble and water soluble. The vitamins A, D, E, and K are fat soluble. Vitamins B and C are water soluble. In general, foods of animal origin are rich in fat soluble vitamins and poor in water soluble ones whereas plant sources supply both in moderate amounts either as vitamins or as precursors. Supplementing the diet with synthetic water soluble vitamins in moderate amounts is not harmful because the body can eliminate any excess easily in urine. However, fat soluble vitamins are not easily eliminated. The body accumulates them in various tissues, especially in the liver, and thus they must be provided cautiously. Sometimes provitamins (precursors to the most active vitamin metabolites) have functions different from the most active vitamins. Provitamin carotenes, found in yellow and green vegetables and fruits, for example, are known to fulfill different functions from synthetic vitamin A. Vitamin supplements typically contain only the most active, purified synthetic forms of the vitamins rather than the mix of metabolites serving different and overlapping functions that are found naturally in plant products.

Fat-soluble vitamins

Carotene was first isolated from the orange pigments of carrots. It exists in several forms: alpha, beta and gamma carotenes. Among them, beta carotene is the most effective in the formation of vitamin A in the body. Animals and humans synthesize their vitamin A from plant carotenes. Carotene contains mixture of A1 and A2 whereas the synthetic form may have only A1. Carotenes are abundant in all dark-green and yellow vegetables and fruits whereas vitamin A occurs only in the bodies of animals.

Both carotenes and vitamin A influence aspects of many organ systems. One important role is in promoting growth of epithelial tissues that cover the gastrointestinal, respiratory and genitourinary tracts. Vitamin A also enhances resistance to bacterial infections, improve the general health of the skin, and enhance fertility and longevity in animals. Deficiency of vitamin A may cause Xerophthalmia, dryness of the eyes, night blindness and other problems. Recent reports indicate that nearly 10 million children around the world suffer from Xerophthalmia. Another common effect of vitamin A deficiency is keratinization, the formation of scales on the skin and mucous membranes, especially in young children. Other deficiency symptoms may include a general increased susceptibility to infections, especially of the respiratory and G.I. tracts. Recently it has been reported that carotenes inhibit malignant growth and their deficiency encourages malignancy. Vitamin A on the other hand, inhibits malignancy in some cases and stimulates it in others. Excess intake of vitamin A has been implicated in other adverse effects ranging from mild headache, fatigue, and hair loss to psychoneurosis and schizophrenia, in some cases.

Even though provitamin D is known to exist in nature in as many as 16 forms only D3 is synthesized in the body. It is very important for the health of bones and teeth. It is known as the sunshine vitamin because in addition to dietary sources humans can generate it when sunlight converts the 7-dehydrocholesterol that exists in the human skin into vitamin D. The presence of glistening and strong teeth in healthy children in tropical countries has been credited to their exposure to abundant sunshine. Recently a team of researchers have shown that in Boston, Massachusetts, synthesis of D3 can take place in the body between March and October but not from November to February. A sunny climate such as that found in Southern California and Puerto Rico allows the synthesis of this vitamin to take place even in the mid-winter months.

Vitamin D is vital for the absorption of calcium (Ca) and phosphorus (P) and its deficiency can imbalance not only Ca and P but also other minerals such as potassium (K), sodium (Na) and magnesium (Mg) (see Chapter 10). The deficiency of vitamin D may cause problems ranging from minor bone and teeth deformities to serious life-threatening rickets, especially in fetuses, infants and young children. The vitamin was discovered in 1920s when rickets was epidemic around the globe; it came to be known as the antirachitic vitamin.

Yet, excess consumption of vitamin D is toxic. The toxic effects may vary from loss of appetite to extensive calcification of soft tissues. Vitamin D is absorbed from food through the gastrointestinal tract and is carried to the liver and other tissues throughout the body. However, the process of intestinal absorption and assimilation of vitamin D is very complex because it is influenced not only by variables such as Ca, P, fat and roughage but also by thyroid and parathyroid hormones. Milk, yogurt and yeast are also good sources of vitamin D.

The group of substances known as tocopherols are collectively called vitamin E. Vitamin E was discovered in the 1920s as a fertility factor; animals raised on vitamin E deficient diets did not reproduce. Even though it is present in vegetables it is stored mostly in oil rich structures such as wheat germ, sunflower seeds and nuts. Even though vitamin E was considered as a single substance in the beginning, later on the existence of alpha, beta and gamma tocopherols was recognized. Among them alpha tocopherol has been identified as the most significant one. The important natural source of this vitamin are oil seeds such as peanuts, sesame and sunflower, or unrefined oils from those seeds and leafy vegetables.

A diet deficient in nuts, seeds and vegetable oil may not only deprive the body of not only vitamin E but also of essential fatty acids (see Chapter 6). It has been found that the early human milk, colostrum, is much richer (1.3–3.6 mg/ 100 ml) in vitamin E than mature milk (0.1–0.48 mg/100 ml). Healthy nursing infants therefore, have a better balance of this vitamin than bottle-fed infants. It is also found in animal products such as milk.

Vitamin E and its precursors take part in the metabolism of lipids in general and cholesterol in particular. The demand of the body for both vitamin E and essential fatty acids are known to increase with the supply of saturated fats and cholesterol in the food (see Chapter 8). According to some reports animals deprived of vitamin E and essential fatty acids developed a form of muscular dystrophy.

Vitamin K, the last of the fat soluble vitamins isolated, was discovered in the 1930s as antihemorrhagic factor. Vitamin K prevents hemorrhage by initiating synthesis of blood clotting factors. Vitamin K also plays a significant role in maintaining the structure of skeletal, cardiac, and vascular tissues. It is essential to maintaining the normal reproductive functions of the body. In nature it occurs as vitamin K1, K2, and K3. Menadione is a synthetic version. Animals including human beings obtain this vitamin from their own intestinal microflora; consequently, its supplementation is rarely required. Often the disorder sprue, in which vitamin K deficiency occurs, is traced to an abnormal intestinal microbial population.

Water soluble vitamins

Water soluble vitamins include the components of vitamin B complex and of vitamin C (ascorbic acid). Vitamin B complex is a conglomerate of chemically different substances whose functions may overlap. B complex vitamins include Thiamine(B1), Riboflavin (B2), Niacin (nicotinic acid), Pyridoxine (B6), Pantothenic acid (B5), Folic acid, Cyanocobalamin (B12), Biotin and miscellaneous compounds such as Choline and Inositol.

Vitamin B1, thiamine, was the first vitamin that was isolated as antiberiberi or antineuritic vitamin by Casimir Funk. Mild deficiency of this vitamin may cause loss of appetite, nausea, apathy and numbness in the legs. Advanced deficiency may result in high output cardiac failure and serious nervous system disorders. Various forms of beriberi, especially in the developing countries, have been attributed to deficiency of this vitamin.

Vitamin B2 (riboflavin) deficiency causes skin disorders ranging from local inflammation to severe dermatitis. Deficiency of niacin (nicotinic acid) may cause diarrhea and inflammation of the mucous membranes, especially of the G.I tract. Severe deficiency may lead to pellagra (a syndrome characterized by dermatitis, diarrhea and dementia), mental disorders, depression, and anxiety. Tryptophan, an essential amino acid, which plays an important role in brain function, is a precursor of this vitamin.

Vitamin B6 (pyridoxine), is a compound of three closely related substances. It is involved in essential fatty acid metabolism, hormone functions and in the activities of central nervous system. Deficiency of B6 is associated with some cases of insomnia, depression, convulsion, pigmented dermatitis, reduced reproductive performance and infection of the genitourinary tract.

Pantothenic acid is one of the B complex vitamins that is most widely distributed in nature; the name means "everywhere" in Greek. According to Roger Williams, the discoverer of this vitamin, Royal Jelly, which is fed to the queen bee by worker bees to prolong the queen's life, is enriched in this vitamin. Feeding pantothenic acid to experimental animals improves their reproductive performance. It is very essential for the overall health of the skin, hair, G.I. tract and nervous system. It is produced by the normal intestinal bacteria of healthy people. Among the dietary sources, yeast is rich in this vitamin. Kale, broccoli, oranges, legumes, peanuts, whole wheat and wheat germ are other rich sources of B complex vitamins.

Biotin, sometimes called vitamin B7, is another B complex vitamin that is produced by our own intestinal microflora. Deficiency of biotin may result in anemia, dryness of the skin and loss of hair.

Folic acid and vitamin B12 (cobalamin), are two vitamins involved in the building of blood cells. They are remarkable catalysts of essential cell functions such as the biosynthesis of genetic material (DNA). Folate is a coenzyme in many critical metabolic reactions in the body. Deficiency of these vitamins causes pernicious anemia. It is becoming increasingly evident, however, that pernicious anemia may be due to malabsorption of these vitamins and not just their inadequacy in the diet. The intestinal microflora of healthy persons supply both B12 and folate.

The activities of lecithin, choline and inositol which are regarded as part of B complex often overlap one another. They are involved in the metabolism of fatty acids, essential fatty acids and cholesterol, and in the biosynthesis of prostaglandins, a family of hormone-like substances with varied roles in animal and human physiology (see Chapter 8). Fatty liver and abnormal cholesterol and triglyceride metabolism can occur due to imbalance or deficiency of these vitamins. Recent reports indicate that choline deficiency may lead to excess synthesis of triglycerides from sugars such as sucrose.

Deficiency of the B complex vitamins can have effects on emotions and behavior as well as causing specific ailments (e.g. pellagra, beriberi and anemia). Thus, feelings of inadequacy, depression, irritability, apathy, loss of appetite and insomnia can occur. Milder deficiency may lead to G.I. tract abnormalities such as disorders of motility and absorption of nutrients. Reports also suggest that deficiency of B complex may predispose an individual to the development of certain cancers. The nutrients of vitamin B complex have overlapping functions. Any one metabolic function may need the participation of more than one vitamin of the B complex or its precursors; deficiency of any one of them may impair the functions of the whole body. To prevent development of such a situation, some scientists recommend supplementation with vitamin B complex rather than a single B vitamin. Normal intestinal microflora is a good internal source. Almost all plant products such as whole grains, lentils, fresh vegetables, fruits, nuts, seeds, sprouts and brans all provide various B complex vitamins. Foods such as milk, yogurt and food yeast are also excellent source of many B complex vitamins.

It has been reported that thiamin deficiency, which has been found to cause various symptoms of metabolic acidosis and cardiac failure, may be quite common among Western populations who consume an excessive amount of meat. Excessive intake of lipids and generation of ketogenic amino acids from a high meat diet increases the body's requirement of vitamin B complex.

Vitamin C and the antioxidants

Vitamin C, abundant in many plant products, is one of the best known antioxidants. Many functions of vitamin C, which appear obscure, according to the nutrition biochemist, Roger Williams, are due to its function as an antioxidant; its biological effects have not been duplicated by any other chemicals. Many scientists feel that it is the antioxidant property of vitamin C that has made it a preventive as well as curative medicine to numerous ailments.

Chemically, vitamin C, also known as ascorbic acid, is a derivative of glucose. It is sensitive to heat and oxygen. Soaking and cooking of natural food, therefore, reduces vitamin C content. Fresh fruits and vegetables are rich dietary vitamin C sources (see Table 7.1). The requirement of vitamin C varies significantly from species to species. Vitamin C, for example, is required in the diet of bats, guinea pigs, monkeys and humans but not of most mammals including dogs and cats. According to one theory, during the evolutionary

TABLE 7.1. Vitamins in Fruits and Vegetables. Selected from Nutritive Value of Indian Foods, National Institute of Nutrition, India, 1984; and Composition of Foods, Handbook No.8, U.S.Department of Agriculture, 1989.

Item	Vitamin A (I.U.)	Thiamine (mg)	Riboflavin (mg)	Niacin (mg)	Vitamin C (mg)
Amaranth	3564	—	—	—	33.0
Apricots	2160	0.04	1.3	0.6	6.0
Bananas	190	0.05	0.08	0.5	7.0
Beans (green)	600	0.1	0.1	0.5	19.0
Beans (Lima)	290	0.24	0.12	1.40	290.0
Cabbage	130	0.05	0.09	0.04	124.0
Carrot	1,100	.04	.04	0.6	8.0
Mustard greens	7000	0.1	0.22	0.8	97.0
Oranges	1106	0.1	0.04	0.4	30.0
Peas	680	0.28	0.12	3.0	21.0
Peppers	21,,600	0.20		3.0	369.0
Sweet potatoes	5520	0.1	0.1	1.2	99.0

process both primates and humans who adapted to a predominately plant staple diet might have lost the capacity to synthesize this vitamin.

Individuals whose diet is richer in plant products than in meat and other animal products, may require much less vitamin C, not only because their diet contributes more, but also because less vitamin C (and vitamin B complex) is required to metabolize food poor in saturated fat. Among the milk of various animals, human milk is the richest source of vitamin C; it has 2–3 times more vitamin C than cow's milk. Zalani and associates of Baroda, India, who studied the development of fetuses reported that the vitamin C level of the brain remains greater than that of the adrenal at all gestational ages; the vitamin C level declines in organs such as liver, lung and kidney after 24 weeks whereas it remains high up to 32 weeks of gestation in the brain. Brain retardation was found to be associated with decreased vitamin C. Animal studies also show that placental vitamin C remains constant throughout pregnancy.

Other studies have shown that vitamin C is stored unevenly in the body. The adrenal gland and the aqueous humor of the eye are rich in vitamin C but its content in muscle is low. It is one of the most physiologically active compounds which is transferred back and forth among the leukocytes (white blood cells), plasma and the tissues. Deficiency of this vitamin causes anemia, weakness, shortness of breath, loss of weight, bleeding of gums, edema, nervous disorders, personality and emotional changes and affects practically every function of the body. The body's requirement of vitamin C increases with age and in pathological conditions such as Hodgkin's disease, rheumatic heart disease and certain cancers.

In 1954 Denham Herman of the University of Nebraska, College of Medicine, proposed a "free radical" theory of aging. According to this theory, free radicals are constantly produced by the body and their production increases with age and in sickness. Free radicals are extremely reactive molecules which can damage or destroy essential cellular components and structures. Unless free radicals are constantly removed or inactivated, the body may deteriorate structurally and functionally, age prematurely and succumb to degenerative diseases and cancers. Further research revealed that a high degree of lipid peroxidation found in many chronic diseases is an oxidative consequence of the activities of free radicals. Excessive free radicles are generated even in healthy conditions such as pregnancy when there is increased cellular oxidations and metabolism. Scientists have found that naturally occurring chemicals called antioxidants supplied by food act as scavengers of free radicals in the body and render them harmless. Antioxidants, therefore, retard or prevent common oxidative changes brought about by free radicals. Even the undesirable flavor, color and odor found in roasted and overcooked food are linked to activity of free radicles. Plant materials in general supply a variety of antioxidants such as vitamin C and E and others.

In recent years many synthetic compounds such as sodium sulfite, bisulfite, metabisulfite, propylene glycol and butylated compounds (BHA, BHT) have been used in the food industries as antioxidants to prevent undesirable flavor, color and increase shelf life of marketable foods. However, some of them, such as sulfites and bisulfites, used in some restaurants to enhance the appearance of fresh salad, have been found to cause undesirable side effects in some individuals.

The tocopherols, especially alpha tocopherol, which is widespread in plant products, also function as strong antioxidants in the body. Vitamin C alone or in association with vitamins A, E and B complex, is known to play a vital role in growth and repair of cells as well as in scavenging and eliminating free radicals from the body. When guinea pigs were administered various xenobiotics (synthetic chemicals) such as polychlorinated byphenols (PCB) and various synthetic pesticides, cholesterol levels in the serum rose and growth was retarded; the addition of large amounts of vitamin C to the diet, however, reduced lipid peroxidation and serum cholesterol accumulation, while improving growth. Further research revealed that peroxidation of fatty acids in the plasma membranes is one of the mechanisms exhibited by some chemicals such as carbon tetrachloride, ethanol and orotic acid which destroy plasma membranes via free radical action.

Other xenobiotics such as the dangerous herbicide TCDD (2,3,6,7, tetrachlorodibenzodioxin) and the sedative pehnobarbitol also increased lipid peroxidation; the addition of antioxidants such as vitamin C and vitamin E to the diet prevented lipid peroxidation. According to Akida Yoshida of Nagoya University, Japan, both vitamin C and E enriched diets lowered lipid peroxidation in the liver more effectively than either one of them alone.

Vitamin C participates in vital bodily functions such as maintaining the structural integrity of bones, teeth, connective tissues, skin, cartilage and capillary walls. It hastens wound healing and iron absorption. Vitamin C participates in so many diverse functions of the body that its role has become confusing. It is such a "panacea" of popular health maintenance that it has provoked considerable controversy.

In Great Britain, N. J. Wald and associates found an inverse relationship between plasma vitamin E concentration and the incidence of breast cancer. According to Robert S.London and associates of Department of Obstetrics and Gynecology of Johns Hopkins University School of Medicine at Baltimore, MD, vitamin E has been found to relieve some of the symptoms of the Premenstrual Syndrome (PMS) a complex of symptoms seen in many women during their reproductive lives. Studies also have shown a reduced risk of colon and other cancers in populations receiving adequate vitamin E in the diets. Kneket and associates studied over 21,000 men from 15-99 years of age from 6 geographic regions of Finland and found that the risk of cancer was reduced with higher vitamin E intake.

Vitamin C and E have been found to function synergistically in assisting with detoxification functions (see Chapter 12). In many cases supplementation of vitamin C has been found to increase the plasma level of vitamin E. Conversely, the body's demand for vitamin E has been found to increase with increased lipid consumption in the diet and cigarette smoking. Vitamin C has been shown to be utilized in the body to detoxify histamine which is produced under a variety of stressful conditions.

Bioavailability

The extent to which the body can utilize ingested vitamins is termed bioavailability and includes parameters such as absorption, distribution, extent and rate of metabolism (assimilation) and excretion. Both stressful situations as well as a diet rich in meat are known to reduce the vitamin pool of the body drastically. In the U.S. serum vitamin C levels have been reported to be higher in high income individuals. It has been speculated that this is due to inadequate consumption of fresh fruits by the poor. The ability of the body to absorb and use many vitamins including vitamin C to the body varies with many factors such as the overall composition of the diet, age and the amount of stress the individual is being subjected to (see Chapter 10).

Biochemical individuality

According to Roger Williams, the discoverer of pantothenic acid (vitamin B5), bioavailability is not the only determinant of differences between the daily vitamin requirements of individuals. His view is that the actual amount of vitamins required for health maintenance may vary from person to person depending upon the activity of metabolic pathways in which the vitamins participate. Thus, a person's heredity, general health status and lifestyle such as smoking and the use of drugs, can influence their daily needs of vitamins.

The concept of biochemical individuality has the intriguing implication that, even apart from differences in bioavailability, the vitamins that one person requires may be inadequate for another person or excessive for a third. Individuals differ in their genetic, physiological and psychological makeup which in turn influences their endocrine activity, metabolic efficiency and nutritional status. In general, the ancient saying "what is one man's food is another's poison" applies to any nutrients, but more so to minerals and vitamins, especially as related to large dosages. Roger Williams believed that an individual who has an average need of vitamins, may have special need of certain vitamins at certain times in life. According to him serious diseases such as heart diseases, muscular dystrophy, arthritis, mental diseases, alcoholism and even cancer may benefit by nutritional supplements.

Megavitamin therapy

The concept of Megavitamin Therapy involves the consumption of large quantities of vitamins (from 100 mg to 5 g a day) to overcome a wide range of physiological or psychological problems. It became popular in the 1970s, due in part to the efforts of Linus Pauling, the two-time Nobel Laureate who developed a strong interest in the beneficial value of vitamin C. Pauling applied his ideas to modify his own nutrition and that of his family members to prevent various ailments. Research on the benefits of this approach has continued at the Linus Pauling Institute in Palo Alto, California. The data of Pauling and his associates suggests that vitamin C in large (gram) quantities may be effective against a range of viruses including those causing the common cold, influenza and certain forms of hepatitis. They also believe that vitamin C is effective as a treatment of certain cancers. Vitamin C has also been claimed to be effective in treatment of many other ailments including some cases of schizophrenia and depression. Megavitamin therapy with vitamin C remains a subject of considerable controversy, opposed by much of the medical establishment. However, reporting on a National Cancer Institute (NCI) Conference held in September 1990 at the National Institutes of Health, in Bethesda, Maryland, Dr. Donald Herbison of NCI stated that "... the take home message was that vitamin C has multiple complex effects on a variety of biologic activities, perhaps wider than any other nutrient. Many of these effects seem related to its chemical properties and not to its role as a vitamin. What seems needed is a unifying principle that can provide a common explanation for the diverse observations . . . ."

Among the well-known non-medical specialists, Norman Cousins who was a distinguished editor of Saturday Review, championed megavitamin therapy with vitamin C. He was suddenly afflicted with a debilitating ailment (ankylosing spondylitis). After various medications failed to relieve his pain and suffering, he embarked on a therapy including megadoses of vitamin C, which he believes helped him to recover. According to him, megadoses of vitamin C did not "cure" his ailment but gave enough relief that he was able to return to his daily work. In his widely acclaimed book, *Anatomy of an Illness,* Cousins most eloquently discusses the philosophy of illness and pain, its prevention and cure, as perceived by the patient. Among scientists, Roger williams was a notable supporter of megavitamin therapy for chronic ailments ranging from migraine headaches to depression and schizophrenia. Recently it has been reported that megavitamin therapy with vitamin B6 significantly improved the IQ of many Down's syndrome children. The controversy regarding the beneficial effect versus the risks involved in megavitamin therapy still continues.

Plants are rich source of antioxidants including vitamin C and E. Photosynthesis, the process by which green plants generate glucose and oxygen from carbon dioxide and water, involves extremely destructive oxidative reactions. However, the capacity of plants to produce abundant antioxidants (powerful reducing substances) protects them from potential damage by these oxidative processes. Consequently, all parts of plants, leaves, buds, fruits and seeds serve as storehouse of antioxidants. Many spices and herbs such as ginger, mint, rosemary and oregano are rich in several kinds of antioxidants (see Chapter 20). Some of them have been found to contain as much as 10% of their dry weight as antioxidants.

In addition to vitamins and antioxidants, plants also contain other chemicals that are beneficial in small quantities. Vegetables of the cruciferous family such as broccoli, brussels sprouts and cabbage, which contain small amounts of isothiocyanates, for example, are found to reduce the incidence of tumors in experimental animals treated with carcinogens. In 1936 Albert Szent-Györgyi, who was isolating vitamin C, found that the samples of provitamin preparations obtained from paprika and citrus fruits gave better results than synthetic vitamin C in reducing capillary bleeding in human subjects. Further research by Szent-Georgyi lead him to isolate an associated substance which was then called vitamin P; it increased the beneficial effects of Ascorbic acid. Such instances of crude products having superior biologic effects than purified or synthetic vitamins has lead many scientists to believe that natural substances contain more than what is known; this indeed is the case with substances such as the bioflavonoids which are widely distributed in the plant kingdom.

According to R.E. Hughs of the University of Wales, U.K. nearly 2,000 plants have been recorded that contain general groups of organic chemicals such as polyphenols, glycosides and alkaloids which are rich in bioflavonoids. Citrus fruits alone contain several similar unknown food factors. Roger Williams was of the opinion that vitamins and those unknown substances may effectively work in the body as a team. According to Hughes, a frequent consumers of fruits may obtain as much as 1-2 g of bioflavonoids per day. They are known to increase vitamin C absorption in the G.I. tract and spare it metabolically by retarding the chemicals that break it down. The bioflavonoids are known to reduce the concentration of lipids in the blood and tissues, detoxify many chemicals and scavenge free radicals in the body. Thus, they are known to slow down the aging process and prolong health and longevity in general.

Indiscriminate use of foods, food technology and marketing innovations lead to the removal of basic accessory food factors that are needed to maintain health. Technological innovations and mass production not only stripped natural food of important ingredients such as germ, bran and dietary fiber but also reduced the range of species used as food crops from hundreds to twenties. As the emphasis on a diet of diverse whole grains and fresh vegetables has decreased, nutritional deficiencies and degenerative diseases have risen around the globe (see Chapter 4). According to one estimate, just substituting whole-wheat bread for white bread, for example, could raise the vitamin B1 content of an average American diet from more than 20% below to almost 30% above the RDA.

Meanwhile, the public is using synthetic vitamins in ever increasing amounts; sale of vitamins increased from $500 million in 1972 to 1.2 billion in 1980 and it is predicted to exceed $3.5 billion in the 1990s. Can synthetic vitamins compensate for missing food factors? Can people around the globe afford them? Will people use them appropriately? How will the population get food factors such as antioxidants and bioflavonoids that are necessary to counteract the free radicles generated in the body? These questions which have not been adequately discussed by nutrition scientists, are important ones which we wish to raise in this book. In spite of the knowledge that vitamin A cannot completely replace carotenes, a recent nutritional controversy is more concerned with establishing the RDA for vitamin A rather than making foods rich in carotenes available to all people. This applies to all vitamins: no amount of synthetic vitamin will substitute for protective foods.

Supplementing the diet insufficient in protective food leads to nutritional imbalance. With adequate protective food in the diet, food supplements may not be necessary and small amounts will not harm. Decreasing fresh fruits containing vitamin C and complex carbohydrates in the diet while increasing consumption of foods rich in artificial sweeteners such as nutrasweet may exacerbate health problems rather than solve them. As professor R. K. Robson of the Department of Medicine of the University of South Carolina points out, our hunter-gatherer ancestors survived by adapting to hundreds of varieties of fruits, vegetables and whole grains. The early agriculturists of 10,000 years also flourished on many varieties of fruits, vegetables and other plant staples rather than depending on meat animals or seafood.

Various cultures that followed the prehistoric agricultural development not only created a mixed diet of dishes rich in plant varieties but also cultivated the habit to derive most nutrients from plant staples (see Chapter 14). However, with the rise of the processed food industry, priority was placed on mass producing those foods on which profits could be maximized. This meant emphasizing those products with increased shelf-life and which were more easily marketed – which tended to be highly processed rather than natural products. In such a system of values, preserving accessory food factors such as vitamins, minerals and natural antioxidants became a secondary consideration. We believe that the rise of "affluent diseases" in the industrial world is a direct consequence of these trends (see Chapter 4). As René Dubos pointed out, "In practice, diets are made up of natural products containing many substances other than those listed in textbooks of nutrition. Some of these substances have biological activities that do not necessarily express themselves in growth rates; but may nevertheless result in important physiological effects . . . . The relationship of food to human existence involves factors that go above and beyond the relationship of biochemical nutrition to physical life."

Selected Sources and Suggested Readings

T. W. Anderson, 1973. Nutritional muscular dystrophy and human myocardial infarction. *Lancet,* 2, 298-302

Anonymous, 1990. Buriti: A rich natural source of provitamin A for the treatment of xerophthalmia in Brazil. *Nutrition Reviews,* 48, 155-156

Anonymous, 1989. Season, latitude, and ability of sunlight to promote synthesis of vitamin D_3 in skin. *Nutrition Reviews,*47, 252-253

Anonymous, 1989. Vitamin A and iron deficiency. Nutrition Reviews, 47, 119-121

Anon. 1988. Infant vitamin B_6 deficiency and preconvulsant activity in brain. *Nutrition Reviews,* 46, 358-360

Anonymous, 1987. Beriberi can complicate TPN. *Nutrition Reviews,* 45, 239-243

Anonymous, 1979. Vitamin A deficiency and anemia. *Nutrition Reviews,* 37, 38-40

Anonymous, 1979. Vitamin B_{12} analogues and intestinal bacteria. *Nutrition Reviews,* 37, 45-46

Anonymous, 1975. Central Nervous System changes in deficiency of vitamin B_6 and other B-complex vitamins. *Nutrition Reviews,* 33, 21-23

Anonymous, 1955. Importance of vitamin D milk. *J. American Medical Association,* 159, 1018-1019

Anonymous, 1946. Present knowledge of vitamins E and K in nutrition. *Nutrition Reviews,* 4, 324-326

Anonymous, 1943. Protein metabolism and the vitamin B-complex. *Nutrition Reviews,* 1, 397-400

Anonymous, 1942. Thiamine in American diets. *Nutrition Reviews,* 1, 54-55

Anonymous, 1943. Thiamine in stone milled flour. *Nutrition Reviews,* 1, 72

Anonymous, 1943. Vitamin synthesis by intestinal bacteria. *Nutrition Reviews,* 1, 175-176

G. Block, D.E. Henson, and M. Levine, 1991. Vitamin C: Biologic functions and relation to cancer. Sponsored by National Cancer Institute and National Institute of Diabetes and Digestive and Kidney Diseases. *Nutrition and Cancer,* 15, 249-250

Montrose T. Burrows, 1926. The effect of vitamin feeding on the growth of cancer. Proc. *Society for Experimental Biology and Medicine,* 24, 88-90

Norman Cousins. *Anatomy of an Illness as Perceived by the Patient. Reflection on Healing and Regeneration.* Norton, New York. 1979

Rodger Doyle, 1986. On the disease trail. Dietary causes of diseases are notoriously difficult to test. *Science 86,* May, 16-17

G.G. Duthie, K.W.J. Wahle and W.P.T. James, 1989. Oxidants, antioxidants and cardiovascular diseases. *Nutrition Research Reviews,* 2, 51-62

Betty A. Eipper and Richard E. Mains, 1991. The role of ascorbate in the biosynthesis of neuroendocrine peptides. *American J. Clinical Nutrition,* 54, 1153S-1156S

Millicent C. Goldschmidt, 1991. Reduced bacterial activity in neurophils from scorbutic animals and the effect of ascorbic acid on these target bacteria in vivo and in vitro. *American J. Clinical Nutrition,* 54, 1214S-1220S

H. Gerster, 1991. Review: Antioxidant protection of the ageing macula. *Age and Ageing,* 20, 60-69

Denham Harman, 1968. Free radical theory of aging: effect of free radical reaction inhibitors on the mortality rate of male LAF mice. *J. Gerontology,* 23, 476-482

Michael F.Holic, 1986. Vitamin D requirements for the elderly. *Clinical Nutrition,* 5, 121-129

Max K. Horwitt, 1986. The promotion of vitamin E. *J. Nutrition, 116, 1371-1377*

Lyn J. Howard, 1990. The neurologic syndrome of vitamin E deficiency: Laboratory and electrophysiologic assessment. *Nutrition Reviews,* 48, 169-177

R.E. Hughes, 1978. Fruit flavonoids: Some nutritional implications. *J. Human Nutrition,* 32, 47-52

P.F.Jacques and Leo T. Chylack Jr., 1991. Epidemiologic evidence of a role for the antioxidant vitamins and carotinoids in cataract prevention. *American J. Clinical Nutrition,* 53, 352S-355S

Thomas H. Jukes, 1992. Historical perspective. Antioxidants, nutrition, and evolution. *Preventive Medicine,* 21, 270-276

Kyoko Kawai-Kobayashi and Akira Yoshida, 1986. Effect of dietary ascorbic acid and vitamin E on Metabolic changes in rats and guinea pigs exposed to PCB. *J. Nutrition,* 116,98-106

Ingeborg Krieger and Marian Statter, 1987. Tryptophan deficiency and picolinic acid: effect on zinc metabolism and clinical manifestations of pellagra. *American J. Clinical Nutrition,* 46, 511-517

David Kritchevsky, 1992. Antioxidant vitamins in the prevention of cardiovascular disease. *Nutrition Today,* January/February, 30-32

Robert S. London et al,. 1984. The effect of alpha-tocopherol on premenstrual symptomatology: A double blind study. II. Endocrine correlates. *J. American College of Nutrition,* 3, 351-356

George V. Mann, 1974. Hypothesis: The role of vitamin C in diabetic angiopathy. Perspective in Biology and Medicine, 17, 210-217

Kiwao Nakano and Seiji Suzuki, 1984. Stress-induced change in tissue levels of ascorbic acid and histamine in rats. *J. Nutrition,* 114, 1602-1608

James A. Olson, 1986. Carotenoids, vitamin A and cancer. *J.Nutrition,* 116, 1127-1130

Prabhudas R. Palan, Magdy S. Mikhail and Jayasri Basu, 1991. Plasma levels of antioxidant B-carotene and alpha-tocopherol in uterine cervix dysplasias and cancer. *Nutrition and Cancer,* 15, 13-20

A. Pirie, 1983. Vitamin A deficiency and child blindness in the developing world. *Proc. Nutrition Society,* 42, 53-64

J.W.G. Porter, 1978. Milk as a source of lactose, vitamins and minerals. *Proc. Nutrition Society,* 37, 225-230

A. Pronczuk, Y. kipervarg and K.C. Hayes, 1992. Vegetarians have higher plasma alpha-tocopherol relative to cholesterol than do nonvegetarians. *J. American College of Nutrition,* 11, 50-55

Etsuo Niki, 1991. Action of ascorbic acid as a scavenger of active stable oxygen radicals. *American J. Clinical Nutrition,* 54, 1119S 1124S

Rudolph A. Riemerma et al., 1990. Plasma antioxidants and coronary heart disease: Vitamin C and E, and selenium. *European J.* Clinical Nutrition 44, 143-150

James M. Robertson, A.P. Donner and J.R. Trevithick, 1991. A possible role for vitamin C and E in cataract prevention. *American J. Clinical Nutrition,* 53, 346S-351S

Alex Sevanian, Kelvin J.A. Davies, and Paul Hochstein, 1991. Serum urate as an antioxidant for ascorbic acid. *American J. Clinical Nutrition,* 54, 1129S-1134S

Earl R. Stadtman, 1991. Ascorbic acid and oxidative inactivation of proteins. *American J. Clinical Nutrition*, 54, 1125S-1128S

K. Suboticanec et al., 1986. Plasma levels and urinary vitamin C excretion in schizophrenic patients. *Human Nutrition: Clinical Nutrition,* 40C, 421-428

Shambhu D. Varma, 1991. Scientific basis for medical therapy of cataracts by antioxidants. *American J. Clinical Nutrition,* 53, 335S-345S

C. W. M. Wilson, 1974. Vitamins and drug metabolism with particular reference to vitamin C. *Proc. Nutrition Society,* 33, 231-237

Victor Wynn, 1975. Vitamins and oral contraceptive use. *Lancet,* 1, 561-564

Sunita Zalani, R. Rajalakshmi and L.J. Parekh, 1989. Ascorbic acid concentration of human fetal tissues in relation to fetal size and gestational age. *British J. Nutrition,* 61, 601-606

8

The Role of Minerals

Abstract: Minerals are the inorganic substances in the body. They are a crucial determinant of acid-base balance and play a variety of roles from composing the skeleton to serving as cofactors necessary for proteins that carry out cellular functions. The precise role of each mineral within the body is not fully understood. A number of stereotyped behaviors are observed in individuals deficient in certain minerals, suggesting that mechanisms exist to adapt behavior in response to mineral deficiency or excess. The dietary requirements for different minerals differ tremendously. Some minerals are needed at such low concentrations that they are termed "trace" – and others even "ultra-trace" – minerals. Yet, their deficiency causes disease. Moreover, equally important, their supplementation in more than trace or ultra-trace amounts also causes disease. Unprocessed plant products contain these substances in the trace or ultra-trace amounts in which they are needed. A problem with modern processed foods is that some of these substances have been removed while others have been replaced in excess. Because our knowledge of mineral metabolism is incomplete, it is difficult to manage mineral nutrition through supplementation without significant risk of excess or deficiency. Thus, the best approach to adequate mineral nutrition is to consume a mixed diet of plant products supplemented with milk (see Chapter 16).

When any organic matter is burned to completion in air, carbon dioxide and water are released. The remaining residue is termed ash and consists of the inorganic or mineral components. The mineral component of a human body includes some that are present in large amounts, such as the calcium and phosphate in bones, the sulfur in certain amino acids, phosphorus in the nucleic acid double helix backbone and in certain proteins and metabolites. All of these are present in relatively large amounts. In addition, a number of minerals are found in the body in extremely small amounts. These include copper, zinc, cobalt and a number of others. The mineral components of our food are responsible for the acidic, basic or neutral influences (pH) of different foods on blood and other body fluids. Likewise, the body uses its reservoir of minerals as a means of preventing changes in pH that would otherwise be harmful. Minerals themselves make up approximately 4% of total body weight.

Definition of pH

pH is a mathematical symbol denoting the concentration of hydrogen ion which is expressed as the negative logarithm of exponential power of concentration of hydrogen ions. In simple terms, pH is expressed in a scale of 1 to 14; a pH of 7 is neutral, anything below 7 is acidic and above 7 is basic or alkaline. On that scale the pH of pure water is 7, of saliva is 6.4- 7, of gastric juice is 2 and of lime juice is 2.3. There are substances called buffers which prevent or retard sudden changes in pH. Maintenance of pH is extremely important for well-being of all living organisms. A small departure from the normal pH of blood can be fatal. Blood pH is maintained between 7.35 and 7.45. Deviation in blood pH beyond this range results in progressive symptoms from muscle spasms to mental confusion and ultimately, coma and death as pH falls below 7 or rises above 8.

Effect of the diet on pH

In the 1900s Russell Chittenden and later M. Hindhede argued that eating potatoes reduced the acidity of urine whereas consumption of meat increased urinary acidity. Later on, other scientists confirmed and extended the findings for potatoes to foods such as oranges, raisins, apples and bananas which also reduced the acidity of urine. They concluded that the mineral residue left behind by the majority of fruits is basic, whereas the residue of protein-rich foods and cereals is acidic. In general, fruits and vegetables, except a few such as cranberries, plums and rhubarb leave behind calcium, potassium and other basic mineral residues whereas most protein-rich foods such as meat, cheese, and egg increase sulphur, phosphorus and other acidic residues. Milk, however, promotes a neutral pH.

What is the significance of the inorganic mineral residue of the food we eat? Inorganic minerals present in foods are derived from rocks, soil and water. Nearly 30 minerals are incorporated in the structure and function of living organisms. Animals and human beings get various minerals by drinking water or consuming foods. Natural water is a good source of many minerals depending upon the kind of rocks and soil it flows through. Plants also accumulate minerals depending upon the kind of soil they grow in. Herbivores get minerals from plants and carnivores obtain minerals from the herbivores and omnivores they prey upon. Disintegration of plants and animals refurbish the minerals of the soil and water through a continuous cyclic process in nature known as mineralization. Mineralization is carried out by a variety of soil microbes (Figure 8.1).

Plants grown in some soils are poorer in certain elements and richer in others. The iodine content of potatoes grown in eastern Minnesota, for example, is 85 parts per billion whereas it is 226 parts per billion in potatoes grown in the western part of the state. The iodine in sea water, for example, not only enriches the iodine content of the seaweed which grows in it, but also the air, and the plants in the vicinity. The mineral content of natural water also varies with the locality.

Minerals that are important in human nutrition may be grouped into three groups; major minerals, trace minerals and ultra trace minerals. Those that are present in relatively large amounts are major minerals or macronutrients. They are calcium (Ca), chlorine (Cl), magnesium (Mg) potassium (K), phosphorus (P), sodium (Na) and sulfur (S). Ca and P, the major inorganic constituents of bone, compose nearly 75% of the body's mineral store.

Those minerals which are present in minute quantities of less than 5 mg in the body of an average person are called minor or trace minerals. They include; chromium (Cr), copper (Cu), cobalt (Co) fluorine (Fl) iron (Fe), iodine (I), manganese (Mn), molybdenum (Mo), selenium (Se) and zinc (Zn) and they participate in many important biochemical reactions of the body. Serious, sometimes irreparable damage to organ systems can occur when these minerals are deficient or present in excess.

During the 1970s, 17 minerals including arsenic (As), boron (Bo), bromine (Br), cadmium (Cd), lithium (Li), nickel (Ni), silicon (Si), tin (Tn) and vanadium (Vd) were claimed to be required by the body in quantities of as little as 50 ng (10^{-9} gm). These were proposed as Ultra Trace Minerals, a concept that remains controversial.

Beneficial and toxic minerals find their way into the human body mainly through food and water. Water itself is the single largest inorganic component taken into the body. Water is the medium in which chemical reactions that are essential for life function take place. Humans survive much longer when deprived of food than when deprived of water; death will result if the body loses 20% of its water. The lower organisms and plants, however, have a greater ability to withstand prolonged periods of desiccation. Research done in Michigan State University has shown that dry seeds have remained viable even after 90 years of storage. Mature dry seeds contain less than 6% water. Approximately 62% of the weight of the average human body is water. The water content of a lean person may be up to 70% of body weight while that of an obese person may be only 56%. Various tissues of the body differ in their water content depending upon the body type and age of an individual.

The sources of body water include the fluids consumed, the water component of solid foods consumed and the water produced by the chemical reactions that go on in the tissues of the body. Even the solid food components

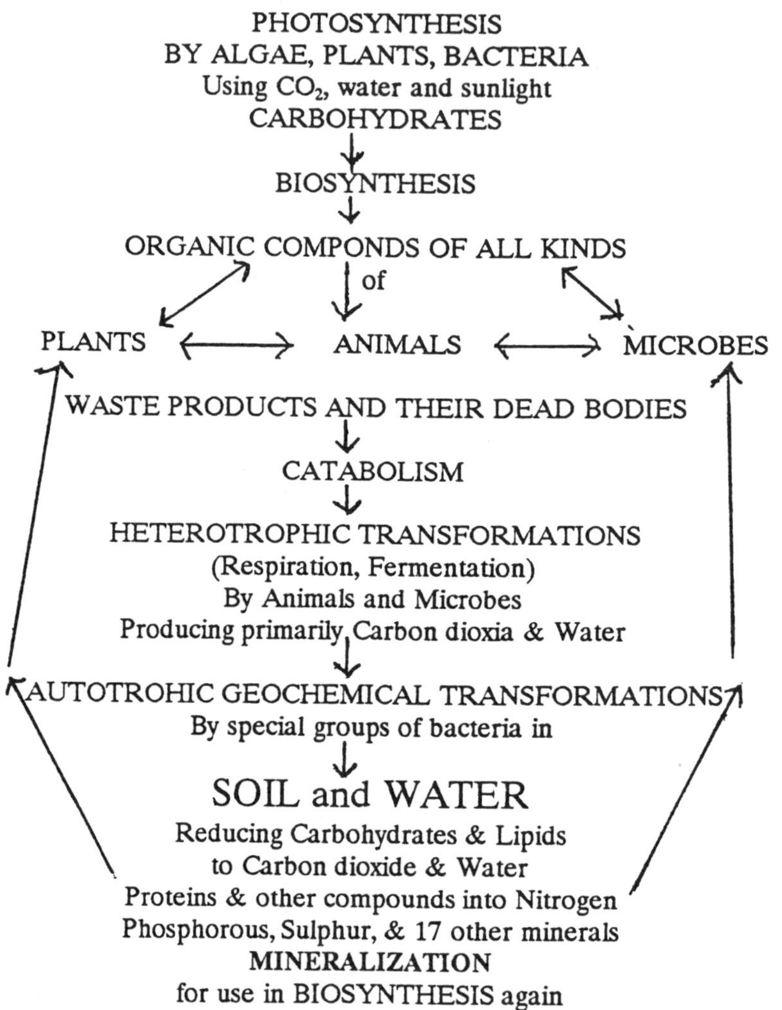

FIGURE 8.1. Shows the interrelationship of synthesis and breakdown of organic compounds in nature. Carbon dioxide and minerals are taken from the environment and returned back. Bacteria play a crucial role.

(carbohydrate, protein and fat) yield upon complete oxidation nearly 50% of their weight as water. Vegetables such as cucumber, tomatoes and watermelons may contain over 90% water by weight. All these sources provide the body 2 or 3 liters of water daily.

When the body loses water it also loses minerals, mainly sodium (Na), potassium (K) and chloride (Cl) ions. These ionizable minerals of body fluids are termed electrolytes. They participate in crucial functions such as transmission of nerve impulses, maintenance of water balance, pH and osmotic pressure. The homeostasis of the body helps restore water and mineral losses by causing thirst or hunger for certain mineral rich foods or non-food items (craving).

An individual is in water equilibrium when the water gain of the body equals the water loss. Water lost through sweating will be restored by thirst and excess water will be eliminated from the body through increased urination. During these processes if electrolytes (mineral salts) are not restored along with the fluid, muscle spasms and other disorders may occur. The natural water supply is an important source of minerals for the body.

Not all minerals are beneficial. Some can be viewed as toxic contaminants in the environment. Among the toxic contaminants are minerals such as lead, mercury and chromium. They are harmful when they accumulate in the blood or tissues. Lead, for example, which is not toxic when present in hair, teeth and bones becomes toxic even in minute quantities, especially for children and pregnant women, when present in the blood. In Japan, a neurological disorder termed Minamata disease, was traced to consumption of mercury contaminated fish. Lead, mercury, arsenic and cadmium poisoning remains a serious world-wide problem.

The major minerals, calcium (Ca), phosphorus (P) and magnesium (Mg) are responsible for the structure and rigidity of the skeletal system and the teeth. Approximately 99% of the total Ca in the body and 90% of the P, serves this purpose. The remaining 1% of the Ca and 10% of the P are soft tissues and participate in many critical physiological reactions such as endocrine functions, nerve stimulation, enzyme activation, blood clotting and muscle contractions including heart beat.

The mineral composition of the body and it's fluids are not always constant. The requirement of minerals may change with changing age, environmental conditions and physiological states of the body. For example, the requirement of iron goes up during pregnancy, the sodium and chloride requirement increases in hot weather and the calcium requirement is high during childhood, pregnancy and menopause. Fluoride (F) is beneficial to the health of teeth and bone. There is ample evidence that the resistance of teeth to caries is related to an adequate supply of F during the pre-eruptive phase of teeth development.

Minerals of the bone may remain in the matrix of the skeleton without participating in any functions. Nevertheless, bones are constantly absorbing and depositing minerals (mineralization) or sharing them with soft tissue (demineralization). Both processes have important roles in maintaining mineral homeostasis. Constant levels of minerals in the soft tissue are maintained even at the expense of demineralizing the bone (osteoporosis). Both diet and physiological factors such as hormones play crucial roles in maintaining mineral homeostasis.

The availability of certain trace minerals, such as iron and zinc, need to be safeguarded. They are crucial not only for the growth and development of the body but also for the growth and proliferation of pathogenic microbes and cancer cells. The mineral homeostasis of the body is involved not only in meeting the body's minimal needs for minerals, but also in making these essential minerals unavailable to pathogens. A slight deficiency of iron, for example, may cause an inconsequential mild anemia whereas the presence of excess iron may promote infections and cancerous growths. Thus, in a healthy body, homeostasis works to avoid both deficiency as well as excesses. Excessive intake of mineral supplements may over-ride homeostatic control and become a cause for ill health.

Iron utilization in the body is coordinated not only with its supply but also with the availability of other minerals such as zinc or copper in the milieu. Most of the iron from the billions of red blood cells that are broken down in the body daily, is recovered and recycled. A complex recycling mechanism of the body also aids in maintaining certain crucial minerals at minimal levels in soft tissues. Thus, the availability of iron in breast milk and in the blood of an infant is maintained at minimal levels. This is probably an evolutionary adaptation to protect the infant from infections by restricting iron available to the pathogen. Thus, a several month supply of iron is deposited in the fetal liver to serve the needs of the infant.

There are other minerals whose functions are not clear but they occur in the body in trace amounts. They are believed to be beneficial under special situations. Lithium, for example, gives temporary relief to people suffering from manic-depressive illness but is not known to have any special beneficial role in healthy people. Prolonged lithium intake can to cause uremia and serious kidney problems; its adverse effects are known to increase with calcium deficiency. Many minerals such as lead and chromium that enter the body as environmental contaminants are either eliminated or held harmless by the homeostatic mechanism of the body, provided a balance of other minerals such as calcium and iron are maintained at adequate levels. When calcium, for example, is deficient, lead assimilation may accelerate and interfere in the body's metabolism and cause lead poisoning especially in young children and pregnant women.

Several published reports reveal that the deficiency of many trace and ultra trace minerals may arise because of other inter-elemental imbalances. Iodine deficiency, for example, was rare among people as long as they used natural sea salt. Its deficiency increased and became endemic when purified and re-crystallized salt was supplied without supplementing it with iodine (fortification). Calcium loss, for example, may be accelerated by the presence of excessive phosphorus or to the lack of potassium in the diet.

Humans have evolved the ability to maintain specific amounts, and also specific ratios, of different minerals in the body. Milk is an evolutionary food of all mammals. Its total ash content has an inverse relationship to the growth rate and life-span of the species. The crude ash content of cow's milk, for example, is 0.71 g while that of human milk is 0.21 g; not only is the growth rate of human beings slower but, the life-span is longer than that of the cow. The milk of the monkey is similar to that of the human. The efficiency of function also appears to the ratio of specific mineral. The Ca/P ratio of the human breast milk is approximately 1:1; the bioavailability (absorption and assimilation) of those minerals to infant is far superior from breast milk than from cow's milk or infant formulas which have different ratio of those minerals. The Ca/P ratio of cow's milk is approximately 1:2 and its bioavailability for human infants is lower than that of human breast milk; however, cow's milk is suitable for adults.

Many minerals of the body function best when paired with another component, such as another mineral, or a vitamin. Zinc (Zn) and copper (Cu), for example, play many roles in the body depending upon such variables. According to a report, a high dietary intake of Zn relative to Cu may increase cholesterol level in the blood and may even cause arteriosclerosis in human adults. Maternal deficiency of Zn may cause brain damage, cleft palate and deformities of the lungs and urogenital systems of fetuses of animals. Excess Zn may cause anemia and adversely affect reproductive function. Copper deficiency causes arterial fragility and defective connective tissue formation. Likewise, it has been reported that selenium acts as a cancer inhibitor in certain environments and becomes carcinogenic in others. Similarly, selenium and vitamin E have been reported to affect cancerous growth differently as a pair than when given alone.

Pairing minerals in certain ratios may be important for their metabolism. When the Na/K ratio is imbalanced the body will suffer from serious electrolyte and acid-base imbalance. According to Louis Tobian, a professor of medicine at the University of Minnesota, the K/Na ratio in humans may have been an adaptation made between 3 1/2 million to around 10,000 years ago when humans became agriculturists. According to him, even the hunter-gatherers diet provided as much as 200-285 mEq of K/day. The development of agriculture that increased the amount of whole grains in the diet did not upset the Na/K ratio because cereals have a very low Na content. The increase in consumption of meat and processed foods not only leads to K depletion but also increases Na in the diet. Many urban whites in the U.S. get as little as 65 mEq, of K/day and southern blacks may get as little as 25-30 mEq/day much less than our hunter gatherer ancestors. Various groups of people who consume continuously low K diet also have an increased incidence of cardiovascular problems, high blood pressure and certain renal diseases. According to Tobian, southern blacks who had a lower K intake than whites showed 18 times higher incidence of renal damage.

Minerals are concentrated in the germs of grains and in bran. Other plant parts such as leaves, stems, fruits, nuts and tubers also contain a variety of minerals. Nuts are rich in phosphorus whereas leaves and stems are rich in calcium. Green leaves are also excellent source of iron (Table 8.1). Historically, people obtained balanced amounts of minerals by consuming plant parts such as roots, stems, leaves, fruits and seeds in their diets. A traditional dinner of Udipi cuisine of India, for example, used to contain as many as 25 different food ingredients including grains, vegetables, fruits, lentils, nuts, raw sugar, herbs and spices. Together, such a mixed diet contributed all necessary dietary ingredients including minerals. Moreover, consumed as natural products, the minerals were provided in very small amounts, thereby avoiding the risks of mineral excess. Minerals are not destroyed by cooking. The water in which the vegetables are cooked contains 35% or more of the minerals. Therefore, the water drained from cooked vegetables should be added to soups or vegetables and never discarded.

Among animal products, milk and yogurt are the most readily available sources for minerals. The bioavailability of trace minerals from milk and yogurt is higher than in other animal products such as poultry, egg and meat, even though the latter are richer in total mineral content. The superior bioavailability of minerals in milk and yogurt has been attributed to their dilute concentration, appropriate ratio, and the presence of materials such as lactose that enhance mineral absorption in the G.I. tract. After milk and yogurt, a balanced vegetable rich diet is the best source of needed minerals (Table 8.2).

Disorders and adaptations of mineral deficiency

Normally, herbivores and omnivores balance minerals of their body by instinctively consuming a large variety of plants and plant parts as their food. Extreme deficiency of basic minerals has been documented to drive animals, including humans, to exibit particular mineral-consumption behaviors including eating or licking natural materials such as clay, charcoal, dirt and rocks that are rich in minerals (geophagia), picking and eating artificial products such as lead paint (pica), and even eating their own or other animal feces (coprophagy). Herbivores such as elephants have been found to travel many miles to lick rocks that contain salt (NaCl). Among humans geophagia is more common in the developing countries and among the lower socioeconomic groups in the industrialized countries, where incidence of deficiency of iron, zinc, and other trace minerals is common.

Lead pica is common in the industrialized countries of Europe and North America, among those who live near lead mines, and among children and women in low socioeconomic groups who lack the diversity of foods that supply calcium and iron in the diet. Chemically lead and calcium resemble each other

TABLE 8.1. Minerals in Cereals, Bran, Germ, Fruits and Leafy Vegetables in 100 edible portion. Selected from *Composition of Foods*, Handbook No.8, U.S.Department of Agriculture, 1989 Calcium (Ca), Iron (Fe), Potassium (K), Sodium (Na).

Items	Ash (g)	Ca (mg)	Fe (mg)	K (mg)	Na (mg)
Amaranth grain	3.0	153	8	366	21
Rice, brown	1.5	23	1.5	223	7
Rice bran	10	57	19	1485	5
Wheat, hard	1.9	25	3.6	340	2
Wheat bran	5.8	78	11	1,182	2
Wheat germ	4.2	39	6.3	892	12
Apples	0.3	7.0	0.3	1.0	110
Broccoli	1.4	42	1.4	389	25
Celary	0.82	40	0.4	287	87
Cowpeas	0.6	126	1.1	431	4
Onion	0.4	20.0	0.2	157	3
Peanuts	2.3	92	4.6	705	18
Peaches	0.5	09	0.5	1.0	202
Pears	0.4	8.0	0.3	2.0	130
Raisins	1.9	62	3.5	27	763
Strawberries	0.5	21	1.0	1.0	169
Potato	0.6	07	0.6	407	3
Tomato	2.3	92	4.6	705	18

TABLE 8.2. Nutritive Value of Milk and Yogurt Compared to Other Foods of Animal Origin (100 g of edible portion). Yogurt and buttermilk are cultured. Amaranth leves are somewhat comparable to most leaves; Salmon is fresh sample. Selected from Composition of Foods. Handbook No. 8 and Nutritive Value of American Foods. Handbook No. 456. U.S. Department of Agriculture, 1975.

Item	Water (g)	Ash (g)	Fat (g)	Carbohy. (g)	Protein (mg)	Energy (kcal)	Ca (mg)
Milk, whole	87	0.7	3.7	4.9	3.5	66	117
Milk, skim	90	0.7	0.1	5.1	3.6	36	121
Buttermilk	91	0.7	0.1	5.1	3.6	50	121
Yogurt	89	0.7	1.7	5.2	3.4	50	120
Milk, human	87	0.21	3.8	7.0	1.2	60	30
Amaranth	85	2.7	0.5	6.0	4.0	45	347
Beef	49	0.7	24	0.0	26	327	11
Eggs	73.7	1.0	11.5	0.8	12.9	163	54
Fish, Salmon	64	1.4	13.4	0.0	22.5	217	79

in that both are divalent elements. However lead cannot function in the range of biochemical reactions for which calcium is necessary. Lead pica is more prevalent on the East- coast of the U.S. than on the West-coast where fresh fruits and vegetables are more abundant and the people consume them more.

Coprophagy is a common phenomena among animals. Experimental rats and mice that are deficient in calcium (Ca) have been found to reingest 30–65% of their own feces. In developing countries coprophagy is a common behavior among stray dogs. Sometimes it is seen even among malnourished infants who have access to their feces.

The balancing of mineral intake was practiced by many ancient medicinal systems. Ayurveda, the ancient system of Indian medicine administers various kinds of ashes (bhasma), with milk or honey as remedies to many ailments. Nineteenth century scientists noticed that adding wood ash to cattle feed improved their health. In the 1880s Sidney Ringer, an English physiologist demonstrated that an isolated frog heart could beat rhythmically for a considerable period of time when it is placed in a balanced mineral solution rather than in a sugar solution. In 1915 Francis Benedict, an American biochemist, studied mineral metabolism in subjects who fasted for 31 days. He found that the urinary excretion of Na and Cl was reduced immediately and dramatically after the start of fasting compared to other elements measured. As early as 1912, Henry Sherman found that substituting rice (an acid producing food) for potato, (a base producing food) in the diet can effect the acid-base balance of the body. However, such imbalances are compensated in a mixed diet rich in vegetables and fruits.

During the early 1900's scientists discovered that a single cereal such as wheat or rice could not meet all the mineral requirement of experimental animals; however, they found that incorporating wood ash or milk improved their diets. Vernon McCollum and his associates found that many mineral deficiencies occur when minerals such as sodium, potassium, calcium and phosphorus become imbalanced. Such imbalances can be avoided by mixing whole grains with other plant products in the diet. The mineral balance of the body also could be improved by cultivating food crops in good quality soil and irrigation water. Many scientist found that refining of whole grains and some cooking procedures also depleted the mineral content of food. Copper for example, is lost when cereals are processed. The amount of minerals that leach into cooking water varies with type of cooking (boiled, steamed or pressure cooked) used. Boiling of food may cause up to 30% of the calcium and 75% of the magnesium to be lost unless that boiling water is utilized.

The consensus recommendation of many scientists of the 1930s was to improve the mineral content of soil and to encourage the consumption of a mixed diet rich in plant varieties. After World War II however, the emphasis on consuming whole grains and a mixed diet diminished as the popularity of refined products increased. The ailment goiter, for example, was rare when most communities used sea salt. When refined table salt replaced sea salt goiter became endemic in many parts of the world including the Great Lakes and the Northwest regions of the U.S. In the U.S. and other industrialized countries, it was remedied by the fortification of table salt with iodine. However, in very few developing countries can this be done. According to reports, as many as 800 million people around the globe may be afflicted with various forms of Iodine Deficiency Disorders (IDD). This manifests in various congenital anomalies, miscarriage, stillbirth, goiter, cretinism and hypothyroidism. The total iodine content of the body is as little as 25 mg and most of it is restricted to the thyroid gland. Yet its deficiency can influence the physiology of the whole body. Like deficiency, excess of iodine can also cause disturbances, such as hyperthyroidism in some individuals.

Rickets is another ailment that appeared in the 1920s during the popularization of refined foods. It is a complex manifestation of vitamin D deficiency involving the interaction of minerals such as calcium and phosphorus. It affects the structure and physiology of bones in many ways especially in young children. During the 1920s it spread in epidemic proportions in many parts of the world including Europe. It is still a common ailment in many developing countries.

Excessive processing and refining of foods have resulted in the loss of many minerals, especially trace and ultra trace minerals. Refining of sugar cane juice into crystalline sugar, for example, removes chromium (Cr) and other trace minerals. Animal experiments show that rats given refined sugar have a higher level of serum cholesterol than those fed with raw sugar that contain Cr and other trace minerals. However, supplementing foods with pure Cr may cause toxic effects. Similar deficiencies have been reported for other trace minerals such as zinc, iron and copper.

Trace minerals play an extremely valuable role in the antioxidant system of the body (see Chapter 9). Minerals such as Cu, Mn and Se are cofactors for enzymes which are involved in reducing the harmful effects of free radicals that are constantly generated in the body. Deficiencies of these minerals become more harmful when antioxidants such as vitamins E and C are also deficient. Zinc is involved in the metabolism of polyunsaturated fatty acid and the regulation of a number of cell functions.

Both in developing countries and in industrialized countries, health problems associated with the deficiency or imbalance of essential minerals appear to be on the increase, perhaps because the consumption of a variety of whole grains, vegetables, fruits and milk has decreased. According P.J. Aggett of the Department of Child Health, University of Aberdeen U.K., attempts to compensate such deficiencies with fortification may only precipitate other inter-element-imbalances, rather than remedy the problem. Moreover, the clinical manifestations of trace mineral excess or deficiency disorders are complex and hence difficult to diagnose. In 1918, scientists found that the intravenous injection of zinc caused hyperglycemia and glycosuria in rabbits. Children with learning and behaviour disorders show higher concentrations of toxic metals such as lead and cadmium in their hair. According to a British report 10% of 10 year olds have developmental dyslexia. When concentrations of minerals in sweat and hair of children were compared, the study clearly showed an association between low concentration of zinc in sweat and dyslexia.

Deficiency of essential minerals may also arise when they are not absorbed. The pH in the G.I. tract plays a role in the absorption of minerals. Regulation of the pH in the body fluids and in the G.I. tract is influenced by the homeostatic mechanism which utilizes certain by-products of the body such as carbonic acid (H2CO3), sodium bicarbonate (NaHCo3), phosphates, ammonia and organic acids and their salts, which act as buffers. Understanding the role of diet in relation to pH lead scientists to emphasize on mixed diet and protective foods (see Chapter 15).

According to F.M. Clydesdale, a professor of food science at the University of Massachusetts, Amherst, the role of pH in increasing solubility and consequent bioavailability of minerals is multifaceted. The presence of oxalic acid, which reduces calcium availability, for example, increases the availability of iron. Many dietary ingredients may act as enhancers or as inhibitors of the bioavailability of minerals. Cereals contain phytic acid which is known to inhibit the availability of calcium. In a mixed diet, the acidic components solubilize the phytate complex and enhance the availability of Ca as well as Zn. Clydesdale found that whole milk enhanced the availability of Ca 5-fold and of Zn 2-fold. Ca Zn-phytate complex of cereals is an excellent example which elucidates the beneficial role of a mixed diet.

Disorders of mineral excess

Eugene Weinberg of Indiana University and other scientists studying host-parasite relationships discovered new complexities in mineral homeostasis and dietary supplementation of minerals. They found that the body deters many pathogens by withholding crucial mineral elements such as iron (Fe) from them; it either deprives or minimizes the availability by various means such as decreased intestinal absorption, increased storage in the liver and binding the mineral with special proteins such as lactoferrin, transferrin, ferritin and hemosiderin. A single ferritin molecule may bind tightly 4,500 atoms of iron, thereby restricting their access to pathogens. Conversely, some virulent pathogens may produce different kinds of ligands such as sidrophores that snatch Fe molecules from the host. Whether the resistant host or the virulent pathogen wins the Fe battle depends on many factors such as the extent of mineral deficiency, the overall health of the host and the virulence of the pathogen. Given these complexities of mineral homeostasis, there is no easy way to determine whether supplementation of essential minerals in any given case will tip the scale in favor of the host or the pathogen. For example, children suffering from the debilitating protein deficiency disease of Kwashiorkor have been found to have adequate iron in their plasma but they may have insufficient transferrin, the carrier of iron and hence be unable to make the iron properly available to their tissues. Thus, since the 1940s, scientists have argued without reaching a definitive conclusion, whether supplementation of essential minerals such as iron contributes to improving the body's resistance or promoting the virulence of pathogens such as Salmonella, hepatitis virus and malarial parasites.

In 1988 Richard Stevens, an epidemiologist at Battele Pacific Northwest Laboratories in Washington, who studied over 14,000 human blood samples reported that the overall cancer risk was 37% higher in men with high iron levels than in those with low levels. According to Walter Mertz, director of the USDA Human Nutrition Research Center, the absolute amount of iron required daily is 1-2 mg and Americans get 10-12 mg. Therefore, the iron deficiency that exist in the U.S. may be more related to some feature of the bioavailability of iron in the American diet rather than to its outright deficiency.

Minerals and acid base balance

During the 1920s Henry Sherman and others showed that foods have very pronounced effects on the acid-base balance in the body. They grouped foods according to their acid or base forming properties (Table 8.3). All forms of animal products, meat, poultry, eggs and seafood are acid-forming whereas most fruits and vegetables are base-forming. Since the blood pH has to be maintained within narrow limits, the body has several mechanisms to compensate for dietary and metabolic generation of acidic and basic residues. Urine ultimately plays a prominent role in this process of balancing. Consequently, the urinary pH may vary from 4.5 to 8.4. It is an overall indicator of body's health.

The acidic conditions in the body promote bone dissolution, a process that among other causes leads to osteoporosis. The original Recommended Dietary Allowance of Ca was approximately 320 mg/day, the minimum amount required to replace endogenous losses of the body presuming a mixed diet was consumed. However, as animal product consumption increased and plant product and milk consumption decreased, Ca deficiency has increased in the U.S. population. The current recommendation is 800 mg Ca per day. Nevertheless, approximately 15 million Americans suffer from some degree of osteoporosis, including one out of one out of every 4 women over the age of 60. Osteoporosis is responsible for some 70% of the one million bone fractures that occur every year in the U.S.A. including approximately 190,000 hip fractures. According to Helen Linkswiler, the one reason Americans need more Ca is that they consume too much animal protein (meat).

People consuming a high protein diet have been found to suffer from early osteoporosis in spite of consuming as much as 1,000 mg of calcium/day. The bone mineralization of Eskimo women is poor compared to female Seventh-Day-Adventists. The people of a village community in Teharan, 90% of whose dietary calories were derived from bread and milk, were found to have no osteoporosis at all. The Bantu women whose lacto-vegetarian diet provided approximately 220–440mg of Ca/day were found to have highly calcified bones, in contrast to those of urban caucasian women whose protein-rich diet provide them over 800 mg Ca/day. After compiling such data Olaf Micklsen, Professor Emeritus of Michigan State University, suggested that it may be desirable to follow a vegetarian diet to maintain a neutral or alkaline urine that avoids calcium loss.

Mineral management through wholesome nutrition

The scientists of the 1920s recognized the role that whole grains, fresh fruits and vegetables and milk play in promoting balanced mineral nutrition. They identified them as protective foods and gave them high priority in the diet (see Chapter 15). According to a recent report, a 100 Calorie portion of potato may be needed to furnish enough base to neutralize the acid generated from an equal caloric portion of lean beef. According to epidemiological studies, the diet rich in meat and poor in plant products and milk promotes mineral imbalances such as increased sodium and deficiency of calcium and potassium. Such imbalances have recently been implicated in common ailments such as hypertension.

The total sodium (Na) content of the body is approximately 160 g. The body's homeostasis limits and regulates it within that range, provided the diet is rich in plant staple. Consuming more than 5 g Na/day is known to increase the workload of organs, especially of the kidneys. Vegetarians, or people with a plant staple diet consume as little as 0.1–0.6 g salt/day, compared to the 10-24 g salt/day of high meat consumers. Similarly, the infants and children on high protein diets receive as much as 15–65 times more sodium than those who are breast-fed or fed with milk and unprocessed plant staple.

Many cultures have evolved patterns of consuming foods in various combinations such as rice and curry, potatoes and meat, pasta and sauce, etc. where plant products, rather than animal products, play the major role. Such diets contribute major nutrients, growth substances, minerals and particularly, the dietary fiber which help to eliminate rapidly those substances that are in excess. Since the 1950s, the diet promoted in industrialized countries has been rich in meat, processed foods and soft drinks instead of whole grains, vegetables and fruits. This modern diet causes an imbalance of minerals such as sodium, calcium, potassium and phosphate. Compensating for deficiencies by supplementing or fortifying processed foods with minerals may precipitate yet other complications rather than remedying the initial problem of mineral deficiency. According to a 1986 report, Americans spent 166 million dollars on calcium (Ca) supplements. Yet all the needed Ca, along with various accessary factors necessary for its absorption and assimilation, could have been obtained by drinking 2-4 glasses of milk a day.

Irrigating food crops with water containing lead, nickel, chromium and other toxic metals also has created health problems. According to occupational safety studies, exposures to minerals such as cadmium in water and air may cause prostate cancer and kidney damage. Depletion of essential minerals and addition of potentially toxic contaminants have created unusual health risks.

Since 1970 more than a dozen minerals have been proposed as being required in ultra-trace amounts, but controversy exists on their roles. How much this is due to newer knowledge and how much to excessive processing of food ingredients can be debated. Nobody questions the need for adequate amounts of various minerals for maintaining good health. Unfortunately, the fact that a diet contains adequate amounts of minerals does not mean that the minerals will be absorbed and, that those minerals that are absorbed will be assimilated. Therefore, supplementing dietary ingredients with specific minerals may be futile or dangerous. Instead, the emphasis should be to encourage production, marketing and consumption of plant products which have been subjected to a minimum of the sorts of processing steps which remove constituents such as minerals and fiber. The reductionist approach to meeting human mineral requirements will have to be tempered with holistic concern for human nutrition, resulting in what may be called a prudent diet. A prudent diet is one that supplies all nutrients in optimal amounts through a variety of ingredients.

Selected Sources and Suggested Readings

P. J. Aggett, 1988. Trace element status of the human diet. *Proc. Nutrition Society,* 47, 21-25

Lindsay H. Allen, 1986. Calcium and osteoporosis. *Nutrition Today,* May/June, 6-10

Chander R. Anand and Hellen M. Linkswiler, 1974. Effect of protein intake on calcium balance of young men given 500 mg calcium daily. *J. Nutrition,* 104, 695-700

Anonymous, 1989. Iron nutriture and risk of cancer. *Nutrition Reviews,* 47, 176-178

Anonymous, 1988. Dietary calcium and the prevention of postmenopausal osteoporosis. Review from the National Nutrition Institute in Canada. *Nutrition Today,* May/June, 33-35

Anonymous, 1974. Iron and resistance to infection. *Lancet,* 2, 325-326

Anonymous, 1970. Potassium supplementation during fasting for obesity. *Nutrition Reviews,* 28, 177-178

Geoffrey D. Block, Richard J. Wood and Lindsay H. Allen, 1980. A comparison of the effects of feeding sulfur amino acids and protein on urine calcium in man. *American J. Clinical Nutrition,* 33, 2128-2136

F.M. Clydesdale, 1989. The relevance of mineral chemistry to bioavailbility. *Nutrition Today,* March/April, 23-30

Margaret D. Crawford, M.J. Gardner and J.N. Morris, 1971. Changes in water hardness and local death-rates. *Lancet,* 2, 327-329

William H. Crosby, 1969. Intestinal response to the body's requirement for iron. Control of iron absorption. *J. American Medical Association,* 208, 347-351

N.T. Davies, 1974. Recent studies of antagonistic interactions in the aetiology of trace element deficiency and excess. *Proc. Nutrition Society,* 33, 293-298

E. Druce, 1986. Salt technology and dietary intake. *Proc. Nutrition Society,* 45, 253-257

Roger Fernandez and S.F. Phillips, 1982. Components of fiber bind iron in vitro. *American J. Clinical Nutrition,* 35, 100-106

Lloyd J. Filer, Jr., 1971. Salt in infant foods. *Nutrition Reviews,* 29, 27-30

C.A. Finch, and H. Huebers, 1982. Perspectives in iron metabolism. *New England J. Medicine,* 306, 1520-1528

Steve Findlay and Bonnie Liebman, 1982. Brittle bones. *Nutrition Action,* June, 12-13

Ellen C. G. Grant, et al., 1988. Zinc deficiency in children with dyslexia: concentrations of zinc and other minerals in sweat and hair. *British Medical J.* 296, 607-609

R. Lorimer Grant, et al., 1938. The influence of calcium and phosphorus on the storage and toxicity of lead and arsenic. *Pharmacology and Experimental Therapeutics,* 64, 446-457

Yan-Shi Guo, et al., 1990. Differential effects of Ca^{2+} on proliferation of stomach, colonic, and pancreatic cancer cell lines in vitro. *Nutrition and Cancer,* 14, 149-157

H. Haenel, M. Kujawa, 1981. Problems of mineral supply in industrialized countries. *Bibliotheca Nutritio et Dieta,* 30, 100-110

L.Hallberg, 1982. Iron absorption and iron deficiency. *Human Nutrition: Clinical Nutrition,* 36C, 259-278

Leif Hallberg, 1981. Iron nutrition in women in industrialized countries. *Biblotheca Nutritio et Dieta,* 30, 111-123

K.M. Hambidge, 1974. The clinical significance of trace element deficiencies in man. *Proc. Nutrition Society,* 33, 249-255

Edward D. Harris and Susan S. Percival, 1991. A role for ascorbic acid in copper transport. *American J. Clinical Nutrition,* 54, 1193S-1197S

Claus Hasling, et al., 1992. Calcium metabolism in postmenopausal osteoporotic women is determined by dietary calcium and coffee intake. *J. Nutrition,* 122, 1119-1126

Robert P Heaney, 1991. Osteoporosis at the end of the Century. *Western J. Medicine,* 154, 106-107

D. Mark Hegsted, 1961. Some consequences of overnutrition with minerals. *American J. Clinical Nutrition,* 9, 548-552

Basil S. Hetzel and Mark T. Mano, 1989. A review of experimental studies of iodine deficiency during fetal development. *J. Nutrition,* 119, 145-151

Kim E. Hoffman, Kathy Yanelli, and Kenneth R.Bridges, 1991. Ascorbic acid and iron metabolism: alterations in lysosomal function.*American J. Clinical Nutrition, 54, 1188S-1192S*

B. Isaksson and B. Sjogren, 1967. A critical evaluation of the mineral and nitrogen balances in man. *Proc. Nutrition Society,* 26, 106-115

Timothy Johns and Martin Duquette, 1991. Detoxification and mineral supplementation as functions of geophagy. *American J. Clinical Nutrition,* 53, 448-456

June L. Kelsay and Elizabeth S. Prather, 1983. Mineral balances of human subjects consuming spinach in a low-fiber diet and in a diet containing fruits and vegetables.*American J. Clinical Nutrition,* 38, 12-19

Gina Kolata, Value of low-sodium diets questioned. *Science,* 216, 38-39

Ludwig G. Lederer and Franklin G. Bing, 1940. Effect of calcium and phosphorus on retention of lead by growing organisms*J. American Medical Association,* 114, 2457-2461

Yamuna Lingappa, Ann C. Wesolowski and Allan Jones, 1976. The relationship between calcium deficiency and lead poisoning in children. (*Unpublished data*).

Josaphine Lutz, 1984. Calcium balance and acid-base status of women as affected by increased protein intake and by sodium bicarbonate ingestion.*American J. Clinical Nutrition,* 39, 281-288

Alice G. Marsh, et al., 1983. Bone mineral mass in adult lcato-ovo-vegetarin and omnivorous males.*American J. Clinical Nutrition,* 37, 453-456

David A. McCarron, et al., 1984. Blood pressure and nutrient intake in the United States. *Science,* 224, 1392-1398

Olaf Mickelsen and Alice G. Marsh, 1989. Calcium requirement and diet. *Nutrition Today,* January/February, 28-32

Forrest H. Nielsen, 1988. Nutritional significance of the ultratrace elements. *Nutrition Reviews,* 46, 337-341

J. Pawlega, 1989. Does salt protect against breast cancer? *Nutrition and Cancer,* 12, 197-199

D.D. Ramdath and M.H.N. Golden, 1989. Non-haematological aspects of iron nutrition. *Nutrition Research Reviews,* 2, 29-49

Elizabeth Rosenthal, 1991. Hypertension research challenges role of salt. *New York Times,* December 31

Irving M. Shapiro, et al., 1991. Ascorbic acid regulates multiple metabolic activities of cartilage cells. *American J. Clinical Nutrition,* 54, 1209S-1213S

Richard G. Stevens, et al., 1988. Body iron stores and the risk of cancer. *New England J. Medicine,* 319, 1047-1052

Iain Thornton and Brian J. Alloway, 1974. Geochemical aspects of the soil-plant-animal relationship in the development of trace element deficiency and excess. *Proc. Nutrition Society,* 33, 257-266

Judith R. Turnlund, 1988. Copper nutriture, bioavailability, and the influence of dietary factors. *J. American Dietetic Association,* 88, 303-308

E.J.Underwood, 1978. Changes in trace metals in protein or energy restriction. *J. Human Nutrition,* 32, 253-257

Amnon Wachman and Daniel S Bernstein, 1968. Diet and osteoporosis. *Lancet,* i, 958-959

Eugene D. Weinberg, 1989. Cellular regulation of iron assimilation. *Quarterly Review of Biology,* 64, 261-290

Eugene D. Weinberg, 1975. Metal starvation of pathogens by hosts. *Bioscience,* 25, 314-318

Eugene D. Weinberg, 1974. Iron and susceptibility to infectious disease. *Science,* 184, 952-956

Eugene Weinberg, 1972. Infectious diseases influenced by trace element environment. *Annals N.Y. Academy of Sciences,* 199, 274-284

Elsie M. Widdowson, 1968. Minerals in the animal body. *Proc. Nutrition Society,* 27, 138-143

M.R. Wills, 1973. Intestinal absorption of calcium. *Lancet,* 1, 820-823

Gordon Young, 1977. Salt-the essence of life. *National Geogrphic,* 152, 381-401

Doris E. Yuen, Harold H. Draper and Geeta Trilok, 1984. Effect of dietary protein on calcium metabolism in man. *Nutrition Abstracts and Reviews in Clinical Nutrition,* 54, 447-459

TABLE 8.3. Selected Foods and their Acid- or Base-forming Potentials. Selected from *Chemistry of Food and Nutrition* by Henry C. Sherman, 1935. These are meant to indicate the extent of their contribution of minerals such as sulphur, chlorine and phosphoric acid (acid-forming) and calcium, potassium, magnesium etc (base-forming). Potential is expressed in milliliters of normal acid or normal base per 100 g food portion.

Food Item	Acid-forming	Base-forming
Beef	12	
Eggs	11	
Oysters	15	
Rice	9	
Wheat	12	
Apples	—	3.7
Bananas	—	5.6
Beans, dry	—	18.0
Cabbage	—	6.0
Carrots	—	10.8
Chard	—	15.8
Cucumbers	—	7.9
Dates	—	11.0
Onions	—	1.5
Oranges	—	
Peas, fresh	—	1.3
Peaches	—	5.0
Potatoes	—	7.0
Tomatoes	—	5.6

9

Complex Carbohydrates Provide Variety and Bulk

Abstract: One class of nutrients, termed complex carbohydrates, is of special importance in the dietary contribution to good health. These complex carbohydrates and their metabolites play this beneficial role because they provide i) glucose, the preferred energy source of the body (see Chapter 3), ii) small amounts of a variety of other nutrients and iii) bulk in the form of indigestible fiber. Yet, neither simple sugars nor fiber alone are nutritionally equivalent to complex carbohydrates (see Chapter 2 and 3). The variety contributed to the diet by complex carbohydrates also reflects the fact that the precise structure of the fiber and the precise mix of nutrients differs for complex carbohydrates from one plant source to another. Thus, eating different plant foods provides the best opportunity to insure neither nutritional excess nor deficiency. In contrast to complex carbohydrates, a meat staple diet lacks both bulk and variety from a nutritional perspective.

The sources of complex carbohydrates in nature are plants. This should not be surprising when you consider that plants along with a small proportion of microorganisms are the primary producers of food on this planet. They accomplish this by an extraordinary process termed photosynthesis by which carbon dioxide and water are converted into sugars (carbohydrates), by use of the energy in sunlight (Figure 9.1). All animals, including human beings and most microorganisms depend upon plants for their nourishment either directly or indirectly. Herbivores are those animals that consume plants only; Carnivores consume herbivores and therefore, indirectly depend on plants as their food source. On a global scale, plants supply nearly 88% of food calories consumed by humans; the rest comes from animal products.

Unprocessed plant products consist mainly of complex carbohydrates.

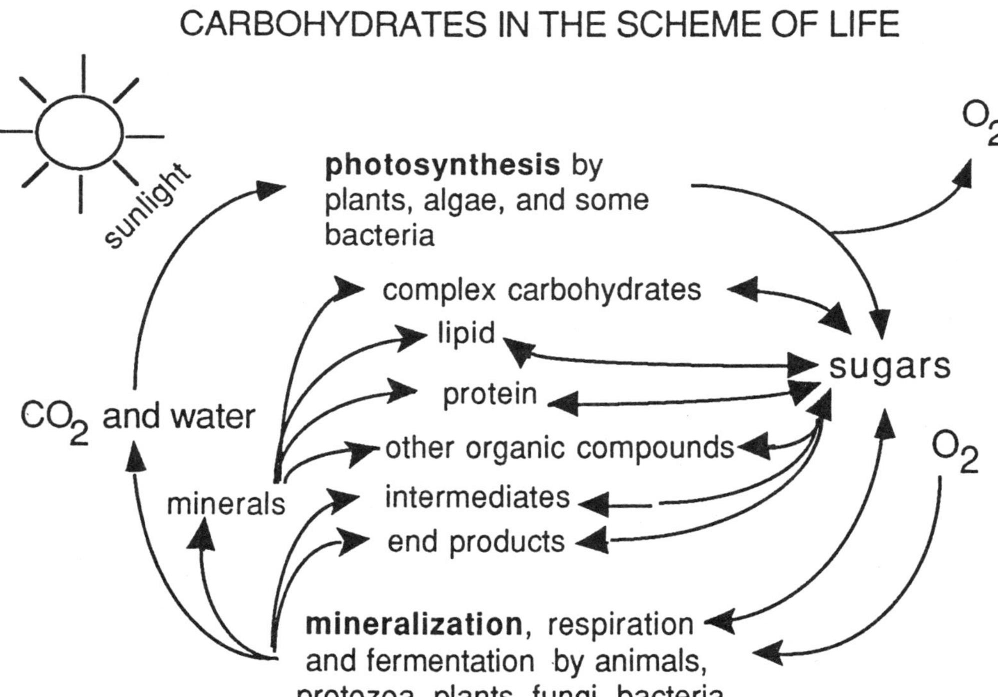

FIGURE 9.1. Cyclical nature of carbon compounds is made possible by crucial role of plants (Photosynthesis), animals (Respiration) and microorganisms (fermentation).

Plants store carbohydrates in various forms of celluloses, starches and sugars and their derivatives. The most important carbohydrate-rich food staples are cereals, such as rice, wheat, corn and millets. Tuber and root crops such as potatoes, sweet potatoes and cassava are other important sources of carbohydrate foods. In addition to these, a wide variety of plant parts such as leaves, buds, stems, fruits, nuts and seeds provide dietary carbohydrates. Among the processed foods, pasta products, breads, and breakfast cereals are rich in carbohydrates.

In the course of history, humans have used nearly 3,000 plant species as sources of food. In recent decades, especially in the industrialized countries, the selection of plants as food staples has been narrowed down to as few as twenty different plant species based upon their marketing qualities. Even these limited number of crop plants are not fully used for human consumption. The U.S., for example, leads the world in production of corn, but only 5% of it is directly used as human food; most corn goes to feed meat animals. Plant resources are shrinking for other reasons as well. Before the advent of modern plant breeding, farmers around the world were growing more than 1,000 varieties of rice; of various shapes, colors and flavors. Since 1966, most of these have been replaced by a few varieties of high yielding rice. While this has allowed the "green revolution"—mass production of a few select varieties of foodgrains—it has come at a potentially high price. The green revolution has contributed to a reduction in biodiversity of wheat and rice. This decrease in the diversity of food sources not only increases the risk of catastrophe in the event of new crop diseases, but also has implications for the range of nutrients obtained from a "single" dietary food source. A variety deficient in one nutrient could be complemented by another variety in which that nutrient is plentiful. A toxic compound present in one variety may be missing in another. Thus the nutritional significance of narrowing food plant resources as well as their diversities should be a topic of serious concern to thoughtful biologists everywhere.

But what are complex carbohydrates?

Chemically, carbohydrates are made up of carbon (C), hydrogen (H) and oxygen (O), elements which the plants obtain from air and water. Only green plants and certain microorganisms can synthesize carbohydrates directly from the elements by using sun light as a source of energy through the process of photosynthesis. All other organic compounds are derived from carbohydrates through the processes of biosynthesis (Figure 9.2).

Carbohydrates are broadly divided into three main categories. Simple sugars, oligosaccharides and polysaccharides. Simple sugars exist as single units called monosaccharides. Oligosaccharides occur in units of twos (disaccharides), or in units of threes (trisaccharides), and so on up to units of ten

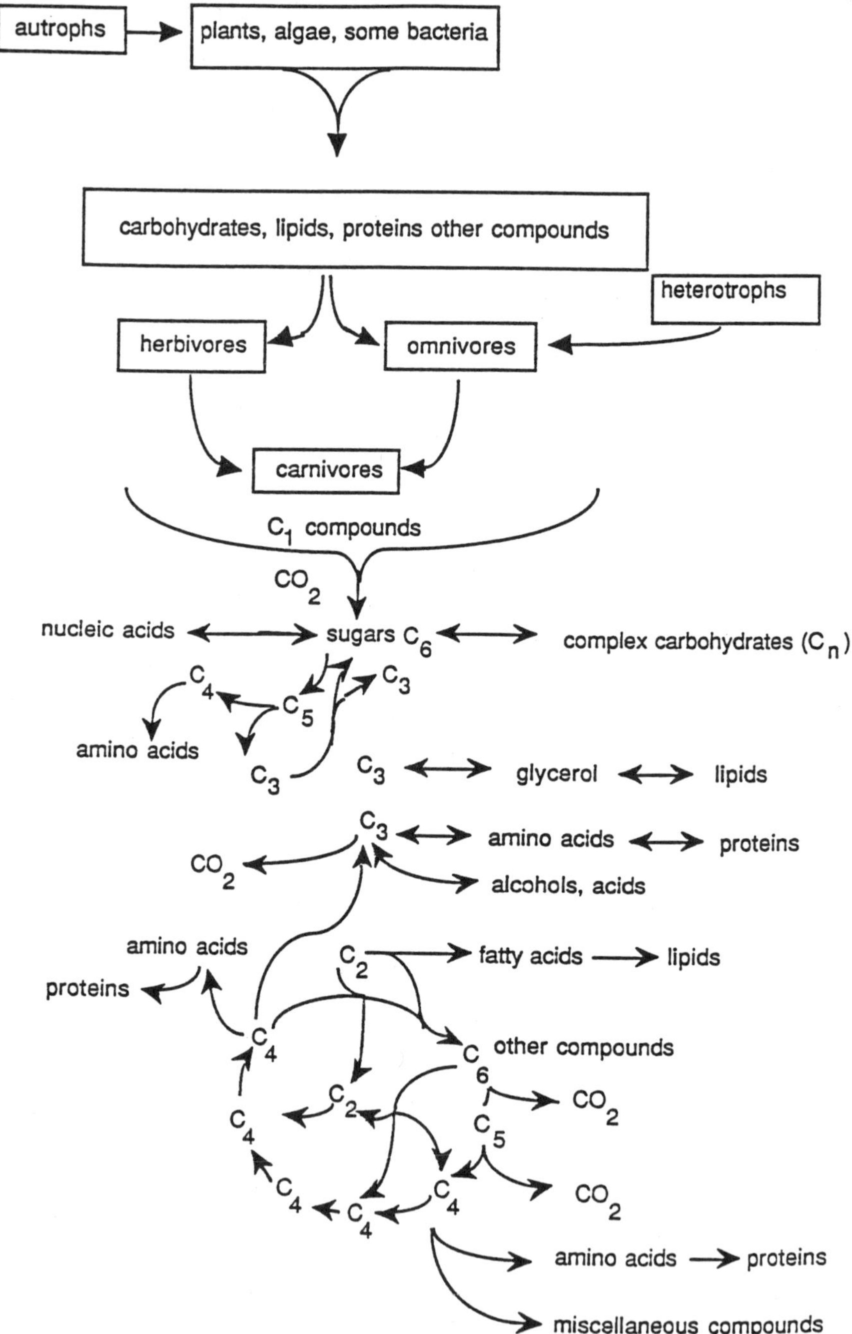

FIGURE 9.2. A simple outline of flow of carbon through various biological processes during biosynthesis and degradation.

sugars. The polysaccharides are high molecular weight carbohydrates that are made up of larger number of monosaccharides.

The nutritionally important monosaccharides are those that are made up of three carbons (trioses) as represented by glycerol, those that contain five carbons (pentoses) which are part of nucleic acids, and those that contain six carbons (hexoses) such as glucose (also known as blood sugar), fructose (fruit sugar) and galactose. Both glucose and fructose are abundant in fruits, honey and in plant saps either alone or in combinations. Monosaccharide molecules are the simplest forms of sugar whereas disaccharide molecules are made of two monosaccharides. Milk sugar, known as lactose, is made by joining a molecule of galactose with a molecule of glucose. Structurally, the molecules of monosaccharides glucose, fructose and galactose all have the same kinds and number of elements ($C_6H_{12}O_6$), yet they vary significantly in their physical, chemical and biological properties. Galactose, for example, is less sweet and more slowly absorbed in the human G.I. tract than either glucose or fructose. Likewise, fructose is sweeter than glucose.

Sucrose (white sugar or cane or beet sugar) is the most abundant disaccharide present in plants. Each molecule of sucrose is made up of one molecule each of glucose and fructose. Sugarcane juice may contain as much as 20% sucrose along with other ingredients. Cereals are rich sources of another disaccharide, Maltose (malt or grain sugar). It is made up of two glucose units. The oligosaccharides break down into their constituent simple sugars when acted upon by digestive juices in the GI. system, or when heated with dilute acids. This process is called hydrolysis.

Sugars are crystalline in their pure forms, highly soluble in water, sweet to the taste and rapidly digestible. Sweetness differs from sugar to sugar (see table 1). In general, unrefined sugars taste less sweet than their purified forms. Raw sugars, molasses and honey contain several sugars along with minerals such as iron and calcium as impurities. During the ripening of fruits, polysaccharides (starch) are slowly converted into oligosaccharides and monosaccharides. This is why ripe fruit is sweeter than unripe fruit.

Refined white sugar was rare until the time of Napoleon when the sugar beet was established as a major source. The consumption of white sugar which was approximately 4 pounds per person per year around the early part of the 18th century, gradually increased to 20 pounds by 1845, to 93 pounds by 1900s. White sugar consumption leveled off and even began declining during the time of the second world war. In America, the per capita sugar consumption picked up again in the 1950s reaching 120 pounds per person by the 1960s.

Since then, a number of synthetic substances have become popular as substitutes for white sugar. These artificial sweeteners such as saccharin, cyclamate and aspartame (Nutrasweet), are several hundred times sweeter than any sugars (see Table 9.1) and yield no food calories. After widespread use for decades, both saccharin and cyclamate were found to induce bladder cancer in experimental animals. They also affect body metabolism and the intestinal microbial population adversely. The new sweetener aspartame (trade

Relative Sweetness of Various Sugars[a]

Sucrose	100.0	Maltose	32.5
Fructose	173.3	Rhamnose	32.5
Invert sugar	130.0	Galactose	32.1
Glucose	74.3	Raffinose	22.6
Xylose	40.0	Lactose	16.0

TABLE 9.1. Notice that sucrose (table sugar) is a disaccharide made up of glucose and fructose. When sucrose is hydrolyzed into the component sugars the syrup (invert sugar) is sweeter than sucrose itself. The sweetness of honey is due to fructose it contains. Non-nutritive sweetener saccharin is 500 times and aspartame is 160 times sweeter than sucrose. a. Data of Biester, Wood, and Wahlin, 1935.

name nutrasweet) has been on the market since 1981. Nutrasweet has been incorporated into most soft drinks and diet foods. It has been suspected by some scientiststo be harmful in large quantities, especially for children and pregnant women.

The complex carbohydrates are polysaccharides, made of long, straight or branched chains of monosaccharide molecules (Figure 9.1). They are insoluble or sparingly soluble in water but hydrolyze and go into solution through the action of acids or enzymes. Polysaccharides are fermentable by microorganisms. When hydrolyzed, they release other components such as uranic acids, amino sugars and sugar alcohols in addition to monosaccharides. Although polysaccharides are made of long chains of simple monosaccharide molecules they do not taste sweet. Nutritionally the most important polysaccharides are starch, glycogen, cellulose, inulin and hemicelluloses.

Starch is widely distributed throughout the plant kingdom as amylose and amylopectin. On hydrolysis each starch molecule will yield more than 300 glucose molecules. The amylose molecules are made of straight chains of glucose whereas the molecules of amylopectin are made of branched chains of glucose molecules. Most plants store their excess nutrients in the form of starch. Nearly one-half of the solid matter of cereal grains and three-quarters of the solids of potatoes, are starch. During germination of grains, their starch reserves are converted to maltose which is used as a source of metabolic glucose. On the other hand, unripe corn kernels and green peas contain free sugars which condense into starch as they mature into grains and seeds. The starch granules are insoluble in cold water but, on warming (cooking), they absorb water, swell and finally, burst open the hard plant cells and become soft enough to make a paste, as in mashed potatoes. In this condition starch molecules are more accessible to digestive juices than those in raw and uncooked foods.

Glycogen (animal starch) is similar in some aspects to plant starch but is found exclusively in animals including human beings (see Chapter 3). It is found in the liver, kidneys, muscles and other tissues but notably absent or present in very small amounts in the brain. Like some starches, glycogen molecules are made of highly branched chains of glucose units and, on hydrolysis yield large number of glucose molecules. However, the number and structural arrangement of glucose units in starch and in glycogen differ significantly. Unlike starch, glycogen is soluble in cold water.

Cellulose is the most abundant polysaccharide found in the cell walls of plants. Each molecule of cellulose is made of 200–2,000 glucose units bundled into a straight chain. The closely aligned packing of these bundles gives enormous mechanical strength to plant structures. Unlike starch, cellulose is not digested by the G.I. secretions of humans. Approximately 25% of cellulose is digested by herbivores (cattle, sheep etc.). The intestinal bacteria of the herbivores transform cellulose into various organic acids which are absorbed by the animals. A small amount of cellulose is actually digested in this way by the intestinal microflora of humans.

Inulin is a polysaccharide which is found in some plants such as the tubers and roots of Jerusalem artichoke (girasole), roots of chicory and dandelion. It is a polymer of fructose sugar. On hydrolysis it yields fructose. Inulin resembles and tastes like starch, but human digestive enzymes cannot hydrolyze it. Thus it is a good source of bulk without calories. A native North American plant, girasole is, in our opinion, a much neglected crop that could contribute to weight-reducing diets.

Hemicelluloses are a conglomeration of compounds of pentoses (five carbon sugars), hexoses (six carbon sugars) and uranic acids. Vegetable gums and pectins are rich in hemicelluloses. Intestinal microbes of both animals and humans may partially utilize hemicelluloses. Pentosans, polymers of pentoses, are present in leaves, roots, seeds and stems of plants. They occur in intimate association with pectins (complex mixtures of galactose, galacturonic acid and other sugars and sugar derivatives that are an important fraction of water-soluble dietary fiber and provide the consistency to fruit jams and jellies). Gum arabic is a common pentosan. The human intestinal microbes are able to utilize 80% of the pentosans in food which therefore can play a significant role in human nutrition. Galactans are another widely distributed hemicellulose in the plant kingdom. Seaweed is a very rich source. On hydrolysis they yield galactose. Herbivores are known to utilize 50% of it and humans 8- 27%. Galactans and pentosans have been popular therapeutics in human health (see Chapter 10).

Complex carbohydrates are often found in intimate association with some non-carbohydrate compounds such as lignin or waxes. Lignin which is not digested even by herbivores, however, is a major component of dietary fiber (see chapter 10). The nature of complex carbohydrates varies in different plants and even in different parts of the same plant, depending upon the presence of the non-carbohydrate components. Nutritionally, complex carbohydrates are grouped into available and unavailable categories based on the extent of digestion and absorption. However in practice the separation is not clear cut and many food ingredients fall in between these two categories. Thus available carbohydrates include polysaccharides that may be digested and absorbed into the blood stream to various extents. The nutritionally important ones in this category are starch and glycogen. The unavailable carbohydrates such as cellulose and part of hemicelluloses are found in the undigestible matters of bran, fibers of vegetables and the skin of fruits and other unrefined plant products. Collectively they are known as dietary fiber, bulk or roughage. A large portion of their bulk may not be available as food calories because human beings lack enzymes to digest them. Some components associated with complex carbohydrates such as pectins and pentosans, however, are made available by the action of our intestinal microbes (see Chapter 6 & 13). Refined flours are devoid of these diverse fibrous components and hence their starch can be nearly completely digested and absorbed. Therefore white flour does not provide the nutritional benefits of most complex carbohydrates.

The role of complex carbohydrates in energy metabolism

Graham Lusk who was trained under Carl Voit was a professor of physiology at Cornell Medical School in the early 1900's. Lusk spent nearly 20 years experimenting on animals, as well as on himself and his colleagues, in order to better understand the role of carbohydrates in metabolism. In particular he and his associates studied the role of carbohydrates in low and high fat and protein diets. Using an apparatus large enough to study the respiratory metabolism of dogs and babies, they reached certain important conclusions: Under normal conditions, carbohydrate which has been absorbed into the body may be utilized for energy or stored as glycogen or fat. However, carbohydrate use is not restricted to these metabolic pathways. In addition, the body may use a portion of absorbed carbohydrates to synthesize so-called "nonessential" amino acids, and thereby contribute to protein stores. Indeed, carbohydrates are the primary feedstock from which all major ingredients of the body are derived.

Lusk called this phenomenon of carbohydrate-rich diet reducing the need of dietary protein as Protein Sparing Action of carbohydrate. Conversely, the body draws upon its protein resource or stored body protein for energy if the food is deficient in carbohydrate. Lusk found that depriving carbohydrate in the diet increased the nitrogenous waste of urine which is an indication of increased protein metabolism. Extensive knowledge gained on carbohydrate metabolism led scientists to recognize its primacy for energy generation in the human diet. Consequently, the plant staple rich mixed diet was raised to prominence (see Chapter 3 & 15). This was important because it related for the first time the carbohydrate metabolism to that of protein. Based in part on their early insight, it is clear that a wholesome diet should contain sufficient carbohydrate to exert the protective protein sparing effect.

The role of complex carbohydrates in absorption

Even though diabetes mellitus is an age-old disease, by 1900, scientists were aware that it was a disorder of carbohydrate metabolism. It involves the relationship between the concentration of glucose in blood, its storage as glycogen and fat and its loss in urine as glucose. These depend on the activities of hormones such as insulin, glucagon and epinephrine that aid in interconversion of blood glucose to glycogen, fat and protein. Lusk and other scientists studied diabetes mellitus to achieve important insights into the normal metabolism of carbohydrates.

As early as 1917, Lusk and other scientists recognized that a diet rich in certain foods (those containing large amounts of complex carbohydrates, such as oatmeal, milk, bread and rice), improved the "glucose tolerance" of some diabetic patients. These scientists hypothesized that the control of glucose metabolism was not the sole determinant for the control of diabetes mellitus. Rather, they suspected that the composition of the diet was also crucial. They found not only that the amount of starch but also the kind of carbohydrates significantly influenced glucose metabolism.

In the 1930's two scientists Lawrence and McCance tested over 60 different plant foods and created a special diet that contained various complex carbohydrates in different ratios to control blood glucose level. In the 1950's Walter Kempner a physician at Duke university, succeeded in controlling many cases of diabetes by using rice as a dietary staple and supplying nearly 90% of the food calories through this complex carbohydrate. He found the diet was also therapeutic to other ailments such as hypertension and hypercholesterolemia as well.

With the advent of injectable insulin in the 1940's, the importance of diet as an adjunct to therapy for diabetes has often been neglected. More recently scientists have once again "rediscovered" that complex carbohydrate diets slow down the rate of glucose absorption both in normal as well as in the diabetic people, depending upon the variety present in the foodstuffs. For example, they found legumes were better in slowing down glucose absorption than cereals and vegetables, and milk ranked top among foodstuffs of both plant and animal origin. These scientists have recommended complex carbohydrate-rich diets for diabetics. However, importance of diet as a therapy for diabetes was often obscured with the advent of insulin therapy for the treatment of diabetes around the 40's.

The enthusiasm for insulin as a "cure" for diabetes also lead to relaxation of dietary restrictions recommended to predisposed individuals. Since 1940 the consumption of refined sugar, flour and various animal foods that are devoid of diverse nutrients and roughage have consequently kept increasing (see Chapter 4 & 14). Even quite recently many physicians routinely advised diabetic patients to avoid carbohydrate-containing food in their diet because it seemed a logical approach to reducing blood glucose. Diets rich in protein, fat and artificial sweeteners (but poor in complex carbohydrates) became the choice diet of both diabetics and nondiabetics! Consequently, as the dietary surveys of the 1960s showed, in the U.S., the consumption of complex carbohydrates went down from 57% of the food calories in 1900 to 45% or less by the 1970s. Similar changes in the popular diet took place in other industrialized countries.

Studies in the 1970s indicated that over 10 million Americans were affected by diabetes mellitus and its incidence was not restricted to older people. It was increasing in all age and socioeconomic groups. According to some scientists, these dietary changes may have actually contributed to the increased incidence of overt diabetes. Moreover they are also likely to have contributed to the increased incidence of six of the top ten most prevalent diseases in Western societies, namely heart disease, cancer, cerebrovascular disease, arteriosclerosis and cirrhosis of the liver.

According to British scientists Hugh Trowell and Denis Burkitt, many ills including diabetes and obesity among people of industrialized countries are due to the elimination of complex carbohydrate foods, especially, those that contain unavailable carbohydrate components (i.e. fiber). They argued that the primitive human diet which was largely made up of complex carbohydrates not only supplied diverse nutrients but also supplied them in low concentrations. The high roughage diets released glucose from the foods at slow rates while passing through the small intestine (see Chapter 11). This slow and steady supply of glucose is vital to maintain the desirable blood glucose level and nourish the tissues of the body and especially that of the brain. Poorly controlled swings in blood glucose levels as a consequence of prolonged consumption of a complex carbohydrate-poor diet, will inevitably manifest as diabetes in some individuals.

The brain has a high metabolic rate and glucose is its source of energy. As the glycogen reserve of the brain is negligible, the brain is completely dependent on a steady supply of blood glucose from the body. The importance of this is illustrated by the fact that the brain which is only 2% of the body weight receives 15% of energy supply and that irreparable brain damage will occur if this supply (and oxygen) is interrupted even for a few minutes. Since the brain has very little stored glycogen, liver glycogen reserve is known to deplete rapidly under emotional stress and intellectual exertion. Conversely, emotional problems and stress increase when blood sugar level goes down. For this reason hypoglycemic individuals (those with a tendency to develop low blood glucose levels) become excessively irritable or tired either early in the morning before breakfast or late in the evening after a strenuous day.

John Fernstrom and Richard Wurtman of the Massachusetts Institute of Technology (MIT), have studied the influence of complex carbohydrate on brain metabolism. They found that the components of even a single meal influenced brain function, especially the level of neurotransmitters which are responsible for many vital functions of the body such as heart beat, appetite, satiety and sleep. Richard Wurtman and other scientists further found that the synthesis and turnover of serotonin, a neurotransmitter, depended directly on the uptake of precursor tryptophan, an amino acid, the brain uptake of which increased after a rich meal of complex carbohydrates and decreased after a high protein meal. Apparently, a high amino acid load in the bloodstream impedes brain uptake of tryptophan. Moreover, according to Wurtman, not only pure sugar but also the sweetener aspartame, can affect function of neurotransmitters in the brain and bring about behavioral changes.

Scientists have reported that students performed better in their scholastic tests when they were fed with high complex carbohydrate diets than with protein-rich diets. It is quite well-known that athletes perform better with complex carbohydrate-rich diets. Presently popular "carbohydrate loading" diet of athletes is based on that realization. This is not a new concept; in the 1900s, Professor Chittenden found that young athletes at Yale University maintained their stamina, alertness and endurance best on low protein and high carbohydrate diet.

Complex carbohydrates and maintenance of normal GI tract microflora

British scientists, Dennis Burkitt, M.J. Hill and B.S. Drasar, and American scientists Bandaru Reddy and Earnst Wynder and others have argued that deprivation of complex carbohydrates, especially, unavailable carbohydrates in the diet, can suppress the normal, beneficial, fermentative human intestinal microflora. The natural microflora is the first line of defense of the body. Anything that contributes to its weakening will, sooner or later, endanger the health and the well-being of the whole body (see Chapters 3 and 13).

Complex carbohydrates and cultural diets

The diet controversies of the 1970's promoted many studies on diets of people of different cultures. Among them was a study of the diet of Tarahumara Indians of Mexico. It was a community of 50,000 people who lived under primitive condition in the Occidental mountain area of Sierra Madre. The Indian community attracted attention because, in their community, diseases such as diabetes, obesity and hypertension and the usual age-rise of serum cholesterol in adults were found to be nonexistent. Deaths from cardiac and circulatory complications were unknown. Their diet was analyzed for more than 4 years; it showed that their chief caloric sources were beans, corn, squash, varied vegetables and fruits. It contained very little food from animal sources. Their diet supplied approximately 75% calories as carbohydrate, 13% as protein and 12% as fat in which 2% was saturated fat. The diet was high in fiber (30 mg/day) and low in cholesterol (7mg/day).

Many such cultural studies show, as a tradition, people balanced their diet unconsciously, with complex carbohydrate- rich diets. Such diets promote homeostasis as a constant function of the body. According to a 1988 report of Louis Tobian of the University of Minnesota, the diet of primitive human communities supplied minimal sodium and liberal amounts of potassium. He provided data from different sources to conclude that high potassium and low sodium diets contributed to health and that such diets, composed of unrefined plant staples, resemble those on which the human species evolved (see chapter 10 & 16). He gave an example of a diet of hunter-gatherers which provided approximately 200-285 mEq of potassium per day compared to urban whites in the U.S. who averaged 65 mEq per day. Tobian concluded that such natural diets may have been protective against hypertension and cardiovascular diseases.

While growing up in rural communities, in India, the authors saw their grandmothers and mothers obtain, literally a hundred different culinary greens and herbs from backyards and nearby fields. The elders of the community knew the culinary and medicinal as well as poisonous plants growing in their surroundings. So much so, we do not recollect a single episode of food poisoning either attributable to improper food handling or to mistaken plant identification! Furthermore, our grand parents strongly believed in providing variety in the family dietary through local plant staples. They believed in the dietary importance of varied vegetables, whole grains and fruits. If our generation was saved from malnutrition, the credit goes to mothers who took enormous trouble to provide variety in our diets.

The investigations on many well-known communities which have large population of centenarians have shown that they live on complex carbohydrate-rich diets. Frances Moore Lappé, the author of "Diet for a Small Planet", points out that 90% of the population outside the U.S. derive their energy and essential nutrients for growth and maintenance from complex carbohydrates. Even in the U.S. communities such as vegetarian groups, Trappist monks and Seventh-day Adventists who are known to suffer the least from affluent diseases, attribute their health to a diet rich in complex carbohydrates.

In contrast, according to many published reports the increasing violence, depression, anxiety, fatigue, sexual inadequacy and nervous breakdown among the people of industrial societies may be attributed to the widespread hypoglycemia (reduced blood sugar) as well as high fluctuation of blood glucose level caused by improper diets. Anthropologist Ralph Bolten of Pomona College in California, studied the Qolla, an Andean community for whom aggression was a way of life. He spent 5 years studying this community and according to him they were ill tempered, hostile and very aggressive people. Their community has a very high rate of homicides. The anthropologists who studied their behavior suggested many causes for their behavior, such as environment, poverty, drinking and drugs. However, Bolten convincingly argued that the cause was chronic hypoglycemia for which he received Sterling Award in Culture and Personality Studies in 1973.

An investigation of a prison population attributed frequent headache, exhaustion, irritability, agitation, frustration and explosive behavior to lack of complex carbohydrates in their diet. The study also found that such ailments could be successfully remedied by increasing complex carbohydrates in their diet.

Professors William and Sonja Connors of Iowa University, attribute health problems such as coronary heart disease, atherosclerosis, hyperlipidemia and diabetes to decreased consumption of complex carbohydrates. According to them, people with a low incidence of these diseases obtain nearly 85% of their total energy from complex carbohydrates. They also found that carbohydrate-rich diets reduced the risk of these diseases, improved glucose tolerance and reduced the requirement of insulin in diabetic people. Professor Jeremiah Stamler of Northwestern University reported that a carbohydrate-rich diet prevented elevation of triglyceride and cholesterol levels of blood. In fact, both the British and American Diabetic Associations have recommended increasing complex carbohydrates by 50-60% of the energy needs in their patients.

The evolutionary food of all human infants is breast milk (see Chapter 16).

It is one of the foods that exemplifies for its richness in variety of nutrients and diverse carbohydrates. Nearly 60% of human milk solids is made up of carbohydrates but human milk has a large number of different kinds of sugars, oligosaccharides and mucopolysaccharides such as sialic acids. One of them, a hetero-tetrasaccharide is an essential growth substance for intestinal lactobacilli, the prominent intestinal microorganism. For millions of years, the complex carbohydrate-rich diet has protected human beings. Since our primate ancestry, and even to-day milk merits as a dietary standard for all people. As adults, that standard may be maintained by a complex carbohydrate rich lacto-vegetarian diet.

Selected Sources and Suggested Readings

Richard A. Ahrens, 1974. Sucrose, hypertension, and heart disease: an historical perspective. *American J. Clinical Nutrition,* 27, 403-422

James W. Anderson, 1977. Effect of carbohydrate restriction and high carbohydrate diets on men with chemical diabetes. *American J. Clinical Nutrition,* 30, 402-408

Anonymous, 1988. Role of fat and fatty acids in modulation of energy exchange. *Nutrition Reviews,* 46, 382-384

Anonymous, 1954. Calorie requirements, *Lancet,* 1, 41-42

Joyce D. Baird, 1973. Diabetes mellitus and obesity. *Proc. Nutrition Society,* 32, 199-204

Michael Bergman, 1984. Diabetes more than sixty years since the discovery of insulin-An historical perspective. *New York Medical Quarterly,* 4, 110-111

Walter L. Bloom, 1967. Carbohydrates and water balance. *American J. Clinical Nutrition,* 20, 157-162

Robin P. Bolton, et al., 1981. The role of dietary fiber in satiety, glucose, and insulin: studies with fruit and fruit juice. *American J. Clinical Nutrition,* 34, 211-217

John H. Bond, et al., 1980. Colonic conservation of malabsorbed carbohydrate. *Gastroenterology,* 78, 444-447

John H. Bond, Jr., and Michael D. Levitt, 1976. Fate of soluble carbohydrate in the colon of rats and man. *J. Clinical Investigation,* 57, 1158-1164

George A. Bray, 1987. Obesity-A disease of nutrient or energy balance? *Nutrition Reviews,* 45, 33-43

George A. Bray, 1982. Regulation of energy balance: studies on genetic. hypothalamic and dietary obesity. *Proc. Nutrition Society,* 41, 95-108

John H. Cummings, 1984. Microbial digestion of complex carbohydrates in man. *Proc. Nutrition Society,* 43, 35-44

M.J. Dauncey and S.A. Bingham, 1983. Dependence of 24 h energy expenditure in man on the composition of the nutrient intake. *British, J. Nutrition,* 50, 1-13

B.S. Draser, et al.,1973. The relation between diet and the gut microflora in man. *Proc. Nutrition Society,* 32, 49-52

René Dubos, 1979. Intellectual basis of nutrition science and practice. *Nutrition Today,* July/August, 31-34

H.N. Englyst, G.T. Macfarlane and J.H. Cummings, 1988. New concepts in starch digestion in man. *Proc. Nutrition Society,* 47, 64A

John D. Fernstrom and Richard J. Wurtman, 1971. Brain serotonin content: Increase following ingestion of carbohydrate diet. *Science,* 174, 1023-1025

Elizabeth Forsum, Peter E. Hillman and Malden C. Nesheim, 1981. Effect of energy restriction on total heat production, basal metabolic rate, and specific dynamic action of food in rats. *J. Nutrition,* 111, 1691-1697

E. Goth, 1973. Aetiological factors in obesity. *Proc. Nutrition Society,* 32, 175-179

F. Grande, J.T. Anderson, and A. Keys, 1974. Sucrose and various carbohydrate-containing foods and serum lipids in man. *American J. Clinical Nutrition,* 27, 1043-1051

Gary M. Gray, 1973. Drugs, malnutrition and carbohydrate absorption. *American J. Clinical Nutrition,* 26, 121-124

O. Gregor, R. Toman, and F.Prusova, 1969. Gastrointestinal cancer and nutrition. *Gut,* 10, 1031-1034

G.R. Hervey and G.Tobin, 1982. The part played by variation of energy expenditure in the regulation of energy balance. *Proc. Nutrition Society,* 41, 137-153

W.P. T. James and P.S. Shetty, 1982. Metabolic adaptation and energy requirements in developing countries. *Human Nutrition: Clinical Nutrition,* 36C, 331-336

D.J.A. Jenkins, R.H. Taylor and T.M.S. Wolever, 1982. The diabetic diet, dietary carbohydrate and differences in digestibility. *Diabetologia,* 23, 477-484

David J. A. Jenkins and Thomas M.S. Wolever, 1981. Slow release carbohydrate and the treatment of diabetes. *Proc. Nutrition Society,* 40, 227-235

David J. A. Jenkins, et al., 1981. Glycemic index of foods: a physiological basis for carbohydrate exchange. *American J. Clinical Nutrition,* 34, 362-366

D.J.A. Jenkins, et al., 1979. Bioavailability to man of carbohydrate in foods. *Proc. Nutrition Society,* 39, 11A

D.J.A. Jenkins, et al, 1974. Bioavailability to man of carbohydrate in foods, *Proc. Nutrition Society,* 39, 11a

Ruth M. Kay, W. Grobin, and N.S. Track, 1981. Diet rich in natural fibre improve carbohydrate tolerance in maturity-onset, non-insulin dependent diabetes. *Diabetologia,* 20, 18-21

Arthur I. Kendall and Chester J. Farmer, 1912. Studies on bacterial metabolism. *J. Biological Chemistry,* 12, 13-17

Arthur I. Kendall, Alexander A. Day and Arthur W. Walker, 1926. Chemistry of the intestinal bacteria of the artificially fed infants. *J. Infectious Diseases,* 38, 205-210

R.A. Kocher, 1916. The mechanism of the sparing action of carbohydrates on protein metabolism. *J. Biological Chemistry,* 25, 571-576

Gina Kolata, 1982. Food affects human behavior. *Science,* 218, 1209-1210

W.A. Krehl et al., 1967. Some metabolic changes induced by low carbohydrate diets. *American J. Clinical Nutrition,* 20, 139-148

Frances M. Lappé, *Diet for a Small Planet.* Ballantine, New York, 1971

Charles G. Lewis, 1989. Sucrose: Is a reevaluation warranted? *J. Applied Nutrition,* 41, 1-2

A.G. Low, 1988. Gut transit and carbohydrate uptake. *Proc. Nutrition Society,* 47, 153-159

Philippa M. Lyons and A Stewart Truswell, 1988. Serotonin precursor influenced by type of carbohydrate meal in healthy adults. *American J. Clinical Nutrition,* 47, 433-439

Alice C. Maurer, 1979. The therapy of diabetes. *American Scientist,* 67, 422-431

L.M.Morgan, et al., 1979. Effect of unabsorbable carbohydrate on gut hormones. *Diabetologia,* 17, 85-89

W.E.C. Moore and L.V. Holdeman, 1975. Discussion of current bacteriological investigations of the relationships between intestinal flora, diet, and colon cancer. *Cancer Research,* 35, 3418-3420

R. Passmore, 1967. Nutrition balance techniques and their limitations. Energy balances in man. *Proc. Nutrition Society,* 26, 97-101

Simon J. Pilkis and M. Raafat El-Maghrabi, 1988. Hormonal regulation of hepatic gluconeogenesis and glycolysis. *Annual Review of Biochemistry,* 57, 755-783

M.H. Ross, 1972. Length of life and caloric intake. American *J. Clinical Nutrition,* 25, 834-838

I.R. Rowland, R.D. Robinson and R.A. Doherty, 1984. Effects of diet on mercury metabolism and excretion in mice given methylmercury: Role of gut flora. *Archives of Environmental Health,* 39, 401-408

A.A. Salyers, J.K. Palmer and T.D. Wilkins, 1978. Degradation of polysaccharides by intestinal bacterial enzymes. *American J. Clinical Nutrition,* 31, S128-S130

H.C.R. Simpson, et al., 1981. A high carbohydrate leguminous fibre diet improves all aspects of diabetic control. *Lancet,* 1, 1-5

Sudha Sud, et al., 1988. Nutrient composition is a poor determinant of the glycaemic response. *British J. Nutrition,* 59, 5-12

Deborah Thomas-Dobersen, 1989. Calculation of aspartame intake in children. *J. American Dietetic Association,* 89, 831-833

J.R. Vercellotti, A.A. Salyers and T.D. Wilkins,1978. Complex carbohydrate breakdown in the human colon. *American J. Clinical Nutrition,* 31, S86-S89

J.C. Waterlow and P.R. Payne, 1975. The protein gap. *Nature,* 258, 113-117

Pierre Wursch, Simone Del Vedovo and Brigitte Koellreutter, 1986. Cell structure and starch nature as key determinants of the digestion rate of starch in legume. *American J. Clinical Nutrition,* 43, 25-29

G.M. Wyatt, et al., 1988. Intestinal microflora and gastrointestinal adaptation in the rat in response to non-digetible dietary polysaccharides. *J. Nutrition,* 60, 197-207

CO_2 + $12H_2O$ + light energy **Photosynthesis** $C_6H_{12}O_6$ + $6O_2$ + $6H_2O$
carbon dioxide + water — glucose oxygen water

This highly complicated process makes 3, 4, 5, 6, 7 carbon sugars (**monosaccharides**).

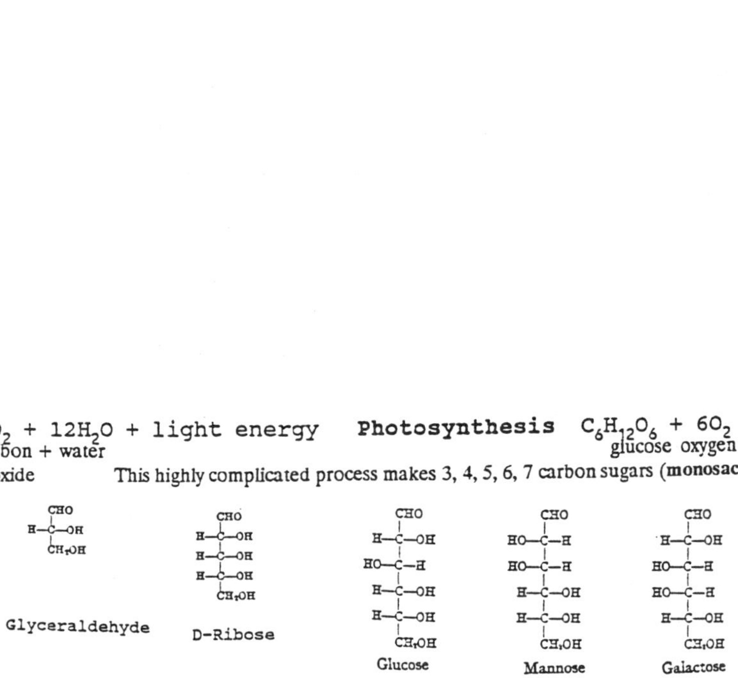

Glyceraldehyde D-Ribose Glucose Mannose Galactose

The simple sugars combine among themselves into larger and larger sugar units: 2 sugars: a **disaccharide**, 3 sugar: a **trisaccdaride**, etc.

$2C_6H_{12}O_6 \longrightarrow H_2O + C_{12}H_{22}O_{11}$ (disaccharide)
$3C_6H_{12}O_6 \longrightarrow 2H_2O + C_{18}H_{32}O_{16}$ (trisaccharide)
$4C_6H_{12}O_6 \longrightarrow 3H_2O + C_{24}H_{42}O_{21}$ (tetrasaccharide)

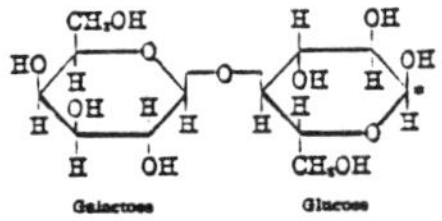

Lactose

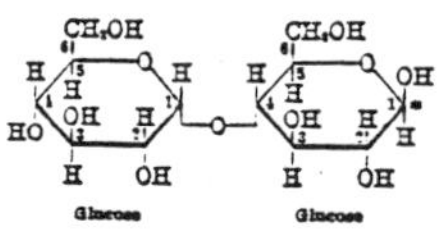

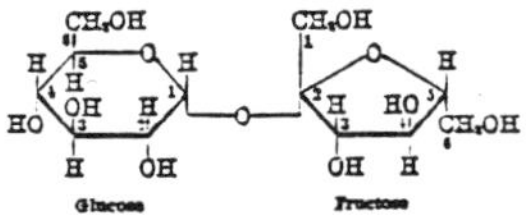

Sucrose

Maltose

When a large number of the sugar molecules are combined again and again it will be a **polysaccharide**.

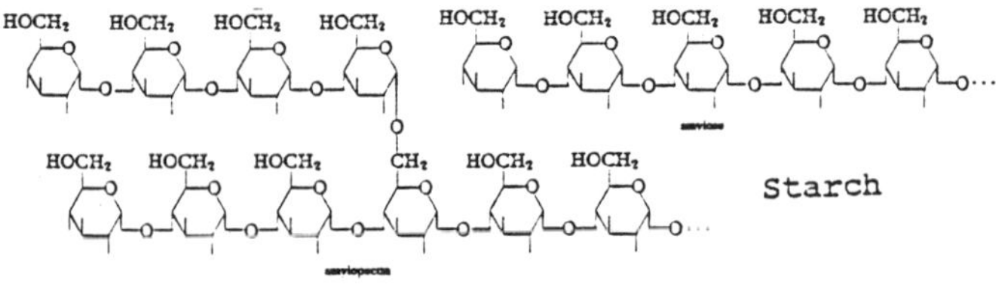

Starch

Figure 9.3. Shows the nature and complexity of carbohydrates. Showing structures of simple sugars, disaccharides and polysaccharides.

10

Dietary Fiber, Sedentary Life and Modern Disease

Abstract: The modern diet is nearly devoid of fiber. The modern lifestyle is largely sedentary. These recent historical trends have lead to an unprecedented rise in certain diseases. Fiber refers to various substances, generally of plant origin, which are partly or completely indigestible by the human G.I. tract. Fiber not only maintains regularity of bowel movements, it speeds transit, and slows absorption of substances from the G.I. tract. The lack of fiber is associated with important disorders including constipation, diverticular disease and colon cancer. Fiber used to be plentiful in the the diet of a century ago. However, today, most fiber is removed during preparation of processed foods that dominate the modern American diet. The combination of a sedentary lifestyle with a fiber-deficient diet has also lead to a dramatic increase in obesity. This is because satiety on a fiber-deficient diet typically requires consumption of an excess of calories, a situation exaccerbated by a sedentary lifestyle. Only through reform of American eating habits towards a diet based on unrefined plant products can these undesirable changes in our state of nutrition effectively be reversed. Examples of such dietary alternatives are discussed.

The terms bulk, roughage, residue, fiber or dietary fiber refers to the ingredients of food that are undigested by humans and hence are eliminated in the feces. Unlike foods of animal origin, unrefined plant products contain considerable amounts of residue. Moreover, even the small residue contained in foods of animal origin has entirely different effects on the body than does the residue left by plant products (see chapters 11 and 13).

Dietary fiber collectively includes chemically different materials such as cellulose, hemicelluloses, resins, waxes and lignin, pectin and mucilage. Cellulose is a polysaccharide. Hemicelluloses, which include gums, pectin and mucilage are also carbohydrate or derivatives. Waxes are lipids whereas lignin is made of complex aromatic compounds. Nutritionally, dietary fibers are subdivided into insoluble or crude fibers and soluble or fine fibers. Cellulose, resins, waxes and lignin are insoluble fibers (see Chapter 5). They are not digestible in the human gut and contribute to the bulk of feces. Such dietary fibers are also referred to as unavailable fiber. On the other hand, most or part of soluble or fine fibers such as gums, pectin and mucilage are digested in the human gut and, therefore, are also referred to as available fiber. They release nutrients such as pectic acid, phytic acid, pentoses, flavonoids and saponins.

Both kinds of fibers exist intermixed in all unrefined plant products. Irrespective of whether they are cereals, nuts, legumes, fruits or vegetables the ratio of available to unavailable fiber vary depending upon species, maturity and other features of particular foods. Most whole grains are rich in unavailable fiber, vegetables and fruits in available fiber and legumes may be rich in both. Leguminous seeds which may consist of as much as 4–7% fiber are considered the richest of all vegetable foods in dietary fiber. According to an analytical study, wheat bran, kale, green pepper and cucumber contain more unavailable fiber than do rice, corn, oats and beans. Dietary fiber may vary not only in the ratio of available to unavailable fiber, but also in the specific chemicals that compose the fiber. This can vary with plant species, plant parts and their maturity. Pectin and flavonoids, for example, present in intercellular regions of most plant tissues, are abundant in certain fruits such as apples and berries.

In a nutritional study of 30 different foods (including meat, eggs, rice, bread and fruit) meat was found to be lowest in fiber content, and prune and baked potato were among the highest. The laxative effect of prunes may be due to their high fiber content. Some vegetables and fruits may contain as much as 95% water and their fiber content may vary from 0.5 to 8%. Some nuts may have as much as 14% fiber. However, fruits and vegetables in general contribute more fiber to the diet than do nuts, because they are eaten in larger amounts.

The role of dietary fiber in human nutrition

Dietary fiber as such is not considered a nutrient in the same way that proteins, carbohydrates, fats, minerals and vitamins are, because it is not absorbed. The reason that grass, rich in cellulose, supplies needed nutrients to cows, but not to humans is that the microflora (the bacteria in the intestines) of herbivores have the necessary enzymes to digest cellulose. The majority of intestinal microflora of humans do not. However, the human intestinal microflora are endowed with the capacity to derive many nutrients from available fiber and some nutrients even from some forms of unavailable fiber.

Humans cannot maintain good health without consuming a certain amount of fiber. Fiber maintains regularity of bowel movements. It speeds transit through the colon, and slows absorption of substances from the GI tract. Moreover it promotes satiety at a lower level of caloric intake. The lack of fiber is associated with important disorders including constipation, diverticular disease and colon cancer.

The presence of dietary fiber delays gastric emptying and thereby increases satiety. It also delays and slows the rate of glucose absorption from small intestine. Adequate dietary fiber intake provides many health benefits to diabetic individuals. In 1974 James Anderson and associates developed a high carbohydrate and high fiber diet for diabetics which provided 70% of energy as carbohydrates and 70g fiber a day. This diet also lowered the serum cholesterol level by an average of 30%. Vegetables and fruits have also been found to improve glucose tolerance and decrease insulin requirements in diabetic patients. In an experiment, when overweight patients were provided with a fiber-rich diet, they lost an average of 8.2kg or 24% of their excess weight during the study. In addition, the patients developed healthy eating habits that helped them to maintain a lower body weight and improved overall health.

D.A.T. Southgate and other scientists reported that the lack of dietary fiber in the diet reduced the efficiency of the whole G.I. system; fiber-rich foods requires mastication which exercises the teeth and gum, increases the secretion of saliva and other digestive juices, stimulates the muscles of the intestines and maintains the required pH (acid-base balance). Cleave showed that whole grain maize meal maintained intragastric pH significantly lower during digestion than refined meal; the buffering capacity of the saliva was found to be reduced with fiber depleted non- masticatory foods. Some dietary fiber such as that in strawberries and cucumber have more water-holding capacity than others. Dried apple and celery powders have been reported to absorb as much as 12–19 times their weight of water and thus aid in increasing the mass of feces. Carrageen, a seaweed, forms a jelly that holds up to 99% water. Some vegetables are known to increase the water content of stool by 33% or more.

The water-holding and gel-forming capacity and the viscosity of dietary fiber play very influential roles in inducing peristalsis (the movement of food in the G.I. track) and improving digestion, absorption and assimilation of food. Dietary fiber helps to bind bile acids and other products as it sweeps the content of the G.I. tract. As described by the British scientist, Hugh Trowell, bulk (dietary fiber) operates as a physiochemical complex for the benefit of several functions of the G.I. system and contributes to maintaining the overall health of the body. Soluble fibers such as those contributed from guar gum, pectin and oat bran are known to be most effective in lowering plasma cholesterol. Plant staples such as soybeans, chickpeas and peanuts contain chemicals such as saponin, lecithin and others that reduce plasma cholesterol. Vegetables such as eggplant, gourds and alfalfa which are rich in pectin, mucilage and gum also have been found to be choice materials for lowering plasma cholesterol. When three hundred subjects were examined for plasma cholesterol, high density lipoprotein (HDL) and blood pressure, the 85 persons with the lower cholesterol, higher HDL and leaner body weight were either vegetarians or those who consumed a high fiber diet; an average of 37g of fiber per day as compared to those with higher serum cholesterol or lower HDL who consumed 25g.

A related role of dietary fiber is in preventing absorption of toxins. This may occur both by direct binding of toxins by fiber thereby decreasing absorption and as an indirect consequence of more rapid GI transit allowing less time for toxin absorption. When animals were fed with diets containing toxic chemicals they became sick unless their diet were supplemented with fiber. It was also found that the addition of fiber to the animal's diet eliminated or reduced mutagens and carcinogens in the bowel. Carcinogens such as afflatoxins that may come from moldy peanuts and grains, residual hormones and antibiotics from animal feed additives that are ingested with meat are more harmful if they remain in high concentrations in the G.I. tract for a long period of time. For the same reason, pollutants such as lead and mercury, may be more toxic to individuals who consume a diet poor in fiber.

Dietary bulk is essential for the intestinal microflora to maintain their fermentative activity; B.S. Drasar, M.S.Hill and Vivienne Aries compared the bacterial flora of stools from 3 areas where bowel cancer is low: Uganda, India and Japan, with that of 3 high risk areas: England, Scotland and the U.S. They found that not only the bacteria of the stools differed but also the chemicals such as bile salt, cholesterol and estrogens. Based on extensive studies they hypothesized that the diet which determined the type of feces and its composition also determined the type of intestinal microbial flora of an individual.

In contrast to the fermentative microbes that predominate in a high fiber diet, low- residue diets, typified by modern processed high-fat and high-protein foods, show more nonfermentative microbes. A diet with the least possible residue supplied to astronauts with the specific purpose of minimizing bowel action (fiber-free diet) delayed passing of stools 5-6 days. Even adding as little as 2g of cereal fiber improves bowel function. Scientists have found that people with colorectal and bowel cancers typically had a history of constipation and high concentrations of bile salts and cholesterol metabolites in their stools; and that their fecal bacterial population differed distinctly from that of healthy people. They hypothesized that carcinogens may arise from the interaction between bowel contents and the intestinal bacteria; the fecal content and its bacterial population may be the most important environmental factors that influence bowel behavior and mucosal changes (see Chapter 13).

In the colon the ingested dietary fiber is decomposed by fermentative microbes. The fermentation products of the microbes influence the colonic environment. The short-chain fatty acids, primarily acetic, propionic and butyric that are produced from the fiber by the microbial actions are absorbed into the blood stream and they exert favorable effects on the body physiology (see Chapter 5). The fecal arrest which is the consequence of a fiber-depleted diet provides the opportunity for proliferation of bacteria that act on bile acids and fats. Such an environment may promote environmental cancers.

According to a recent report, G.J. Leitch of Morehouse School of Medicine in Atlanta contended that a diet high in soluble fiber may protect even against infection from the intestinal giardiasis (parasites). In animal experiments nearly 80% of the laboratory animals receiving a low fiber diet developed giardiasis as compared to 35% of those receiving a high-fiber diet.

Historical origins of the modern fiber-deficient diet

In the U.S, the early settlers utilized greens such as dandelion, cowslips, pigweed, turnip tops and various berries which they felt were vital to maintaining the overall health of the body. However, lack of transportation restricted distribution of fresh produce from farms to cities and towns during growing seasons. Therefore, before 1900, city dwellers often lacked fresh farm produce in their diet. Consequently dyspepsia (a complex of symptoms like indigestion) became a household word. Constantin Volney, a French man who visited the U.S. around 1800 regarded the American diet to be a scheme that injured their stomach, teeth and their health in general. However, the introduction of railroads, and especially of refrigerated cars, increased the supply of fresh fruits and vegetables throughout the country.

Fruits such as grapes, for example, which were previously available only for a few months during the season became available throughout the year by 1865 due to better transportation and cold storage. Increased use of fresh vegetables and fruits improved the health and physique of the population. However, such developments benefitted mostly the upper and middle classes who were better informed and who could afford to buy better food products. A large segment of the population remained prejudiced against eating fresh fruits and vegetables as a result of a widespread misconception that the cholera epidemic of 1849 was caused by eating fresh produce. The belief that fresh fruits and vegetables cause ailments such as cholera, typhoid and diarrhea was ingrained in the minds of people. Even now, that belief exists in many parts of the world, even though poor sanitation is the true culprit.

Many people avoided eating fresh fruits and vegetables altogether because they mistook the soft and bulky feces of the high roughage diet for diarrhea caused by infection. The coincidence of the arrival of fresh fruits and vegetables with the increase in cholera in warm weather confused the issue of consuming fresh produce and diarrheal incidence. The industries took great advantage of people's apprehension of infectious diseases to promote refined products such as white flour, pure crystal sugar, meat and egg which contained little roughage. Processed food began gaining the respect of the intellectuals and the affluent.

Nevertheless, periodically health reformers began opposing the popularity of the highly processed low-fiber foods. Among them was Silvester Graham, an ardent member of Pennsylvania Temperance Society who believed in diet reforms and made history by defending natural vegetarian food during the

1840s. Graham condemned low residue food ingredients such as refined flour as health hazards and emphasized the importance of dietary bulk and its health benefits. He pointed out that bulk was a necessary nutrient and that if meat is used sparingly and "bolted" flour substituted with "unbolted" flour, the diet would sustain the highest and best physiological and psychological interest of human nature. Thus, whole-wheat flour came to be known as "graham flour."

Many academicians and politicians began supporting Graham's preference for unprocessed food. For example, the Boston Medical and Surgical Journal supported his views and the American Health Convention endorsed Graham's diet. Graham succeeded to some extent in convincing people to eat healthful fruits, vegetables and natural unprocessed food. However the processed food industry spokesmen called Graham, "a crank" and used the resources at their disposal to discredit his views on natural foods. Slowly, the popularity of fresh fruits, vegetables and whole grain products declined and refined and processed products such as white bread, white sugar, salted snacks and sugar-frosted desserts became popular. By 1900s, dangerous infectious diseases such as cholera and typhoid that prevented consuming fruits and vegetables were virtually eradicated from the U.S. by instituting better public health measures, improved sanitation and water supply. But the high fiber unprocessed ingredients that had been removed from the public's diet did not reappear!

As early as 1921 Robert McCarrison who was a British Medical Officer in India, noticed that people who ate whole grain cereals, milk and vegetables had better overall physique compared to those who ate polished rice and refined food products. Further research and personal experience as a physician convinced him that deficiency diseases were produced by the consumption of highly refined food products, especially when the diet is devoid of milk, vegetables and fruits. Many such observations around the world preceded the discoveries of the beneficial roles of vitamins and minerals (see Chapter 9 and 10).

In the U.S. E. V. McCollum and his colleagues summarized in 1929 their life-time work with a statement that the most satisfactory diet includes a quart of milk daily and the consumption of adequate leafy greens. They recommended the consumption of liberal amounts of vegetables not only to provide valuable nutrients but also to promote intestinal hygiene by regular elimination. They found that grazing animals which lived only on grass and green leaves (forage) maintained far superior health than those animals which were fed otherwise with everything but greens. Such studies impressed McCollum and his colleagues so much that they popularized a diet containing whole grains, milk, fruits, and vegetables, especially the greens, as "protective foods" (see Chapter 15).

The depression years of the 1930s provided the environment to popularize the diet rich in plant staples, i.e. protective foods. McCollum not only promoted diets rich in plant staples but also discouraged the industrial practices of promoting diets that contained excessive refinement of food ingredients. He upheld the value of old-fashioned dishes such as soups and stews that were rich in bulk and variety.

However, by the late 1940s, as the depression years passed, the emphasis on the protective food concept began declining. In industrialized countries, the intake of dietary fiber (DF) fell from an estimated 40-65g per person daily around 1870 to less than 23g in the 1960s. As refined products afforded the convenience of mass production, longer shelf-life and improved shipping quality, the industries began stripping more nutrient-rich fibrous layers from grains and other food ingredients. The improved low extraction flour, for example, contains only one-twentieth of the original fiber content and one-fifth of the nutrients such as B vitamins. The whole grain bread contains approximately 8.5% fiber, brown bread contains 4.5–5% while white bread contained 2.7% fiber. Bran, the outer coat of the wheat grain just underneath the husk, is one of the richest sources of dietary fiber. It contains more than 40% DF. If a conventional white bread were to be replaced by whole-wheat bread it would raise the average intake of thiamin (vitamin B1) from 0.78mg to 1.28mg per 2500 Calories intake.

Vegetables are also indiscriminately stripped of their nutrients and dietary fiber by removing their skins, rinds and seeds before they are cooked or processed for freezing or canning, and they are mixed with large amounts of sugar or salt which are devoid of natural nutrients. In Asia, for example, the introduction of polished white rice alone brought an epidemic of beri-beri and other vitamin deficiency diseases; in the U.S., purified salt which deprived the source of iodine lead to increased incidence of goiter (see Chapter 8).

According to the USDA, consumption of grain products, potatoes, sweet potatoes, fresh vegetables and fruits drastically declined since the beginning of this century, especially since the 1950s. The U.S. population consumed 50% less cereals in 1970 than they had consumed during 1909. Whatever potatoes were used in 1976, half of them were used as processed products. Unprocessed foods became strange to the younger generations of the postwar era! Combination dishes, such as stews and casseroles, and foods with herbs and spices gradually went out of circulation. Processed meats, potato chips and french fries, assorted breads and pastries made of white flour and sugar became popular among the affluent.

During the postwar era, most industrialized countries were able to eradicate infectious diseases with appropriate sanitary measures and medical services. The deficiency diseases such as beriberi, rickets and goiter were eradicated with supplements of newly discovered vitamins and minerals (fortified foods). However, the altered tastes and physiological cravings of younger generations caused by a steady increase in the consumption of refined foods were never remedied. Consequently, by the 1970s an epidemic of degenerative and non-infectious diseases began to increase among the population.

In relatively recent human history, sufficient fiber was readily obtained through the diet. However the intentional removal of dietary fiber by modern industrial food processing has transformed the consumption of fiber from a natural feature of most meals into a nutritional issue often not met by popular "fast food" based diets.

Dietary fiber, constipation, degenerative diseases and cancer

According to Ernest Wynder of the American Health Foundation, one-half of all female cancers and about one third of all male cancers in the Western world are related to nutritional factors; the interactions that go on between intestinal flora and the residue present in the colon may be responsible for many cancers. In the U.S. colorectal cancer accounts for about 50,000 deaths a year while breast and prostate cancers account for about 40,000 and 24,000 deaths respectively. Epidemiological studies show that there is a close correlation between a high fat intake and carcinogens and mutagens formed by interactions with microbes in the colon. The incidence of breast cancer was found to be estrogen dependent. It showed positive correlation with a high intake of meat and a negative correlation with high cereal and bean consumption. It was hypothesized that a higher intake of dietary fiber resulted in a lowered estrogen status.

Constipation, diverticular disease and colon cancer are common disorders associated with a lack of dietary fiber. Diverticular disease is due to degenerative defects in the muscular wall of the colon believed to be a consequence of a low fiber diet. They cause pain, bleeding, are a major risk of infection and potentially life-threatening perforation. Nearly half the American population over the age of 60 has diverticular disease. Carcinoma of the colon and rectum killed more people than any form of cancer except that of the lung.. Furthermore, nearly one-quarter of the adult population has benign tumors of the rectum.

Scientists found a high correlation between bowel diseases including colorectal cancer and the increased consumption of refined or dietary fiber-deficient food among the populations of the industrialized countries. Danish residents of Copenhagen with fiber intakes of 17g/day developed 3 times as much colon cancer as rural Finish residents with fiber intakes of 31g/day. Even in the U.S. colon cancer and bowel diseases were found to be significantly less common among Seventh-Day Adventists and the Mormons who consumed more unrefined plant products in their diets.

Among the people of Africa and of the Indian sub- continent, in contrast, diverticular diseases and bowel cancer or benign tumors remain rare occurances. This discrepancy disappeared, however, when natives of these countries settled in Britain or consumed a diet of excessively refined products in their native lands. The epidemiological evidence clearly indicated that environmental rather than genetic factors were involved. Based on such observations Dennis Burkitt and associates concluded that the dietary changes had influenced bowel contents and bowel behavior, and that they had a profound pathological effect.

Further studies showed that the African diet with a high fiber content resulted in rapid intestinal transit times (25–40 hours), and large (250g) soft stool. The Western Europeans and North Americans, on the other hand, had very slow bowl transit (70 hours or more), half as much stool (120g) and often they were hard and faceted. In one elaborate study, they examined the intestinal transit times of more than 1,000 ethnic people to confirm their conclusions regarding dietary fiber, bowel content and bowel function.

Extensive epidemiological studies of Burkitt and others led to the realization that lack of fiber in the diet is responsible for, or may directly and indirectly contribute to, many non-infectious diseases including constipation, diverticulosis, hiatus hernia, appendicitis, varicose veins, hemorrhoids, diabetes, coronary heart disease, gallstones and several cancers. They found convincing correlations between the low intake of dietary fiber and an increased incidence of these diseases which Burkitt and associates called "affluent diseases".

Traditional cultures have often loathed constipation. Orthodox Hindus forbade even worshipping in the morning, unless the individual had bowel movement and took a bath. They had promoted regular defecation by various techniques such as consuming fruits and drinking cold water in the morning or night, with psychological adaptation and yogic exercises of the abdominal muscles. Hippocrates recommended two or three bowel movement daily for a healthy person. Among primitive populations where colorectal cancers are virtually absent people are known to have more than one bowl movement a day. Among the industrialized people where colorectal cancers are common constipation is more prevalent. More than 100 million Americans, 6 out of 10, use laxatives or cathartics regularly. It has been said that constipation has become a natural "neurosis". It is a non-specific disease which can be prevented easily by consumption of high roughage diet.

Traditionally, physicians attributed many chronic diseases to long-lasting constipation. Constipation has been implicated in diseases such as large bowel carcinoma, adenomatous polyps, appendicitis, hemorrhoids and anal fissures. Epithelial tumors are 100 times more prevalent in the large bowel than in small bowel. It has been found that both benign polyps and cancerous tumors found on G.I. mucosal surfaces vary with the diet. In the U.S. 70,000 cases of bowel tumors are reported annually and two-thirds of them become fatal. The difficult passage of hard stool is known to be common among individuals who regularly eat highly refined and processed food and fiber-poor diets, especially among the elderly. The urge to move the bowels occurs when a sufficient volume of material from the intestinal tract reaches the rectum; the periodicity with which this occurs largely depends upon the quantity of indigestible material in the diet. In many geriatric wards where constipation is a common problem in recent years, bran and whole grain breads have been used to bring about some relief.

According to reports, where the mean fiber intake of vegetarians was 42 g/day and of non-vegetarians 21 g/day 33% of non- vegetarians and 12% of vegetarians were found to have diverticular disease. Those vegetarians who suffered from the disease had a lower intake of cereals. Diverticular diseases was a relative curiosities until after the first World War. Since then it has gradually increased for 30 years and reached endemic proportion in the 1970s. According to Neil Painter of London Manor Hospital, one in every five Western adults has some degree of diverticular diseases.

Some studies suggest that a deficiency of essential fatty acids and ultratrace minerals such as chromium and selenium in the western diet may be another outcome of the diet devoid of bulk and variety; the deficiencies may be contributing to ailments such as arteriosclerosis, hypertension and some of the malignancies (see Chapter 8).

During the 1940s, T.L. Cleave who treated many people for ischemic heart diseases, diabetes and obesity in the U.S. and in Britain felt that those diseases may be related to the excessive consumption of refined carbohydrates. Based on that assumption he called those ailments "noninfective saccharine diseases" (Cleave's hypothesis). Further work by Cleave, Alexander Walker and others suggested that non-infectious diseases were mainly due to the lack of fiber in the diet. During the 1960s, Trowell who was a physician for 30 years in East Africa divided these non-infectious diseases into two groups. The diseases of the colon such as diverticular diseases, ulcerative colitis, carcinoma, hemorrhoids and irritable bowel syndrome made up the colonic group. Diseases such as diabetes, ischemic heart diseases, obesity and gallstone were called the metabolic group.

Based on world-wide evaluations, Trowell held that there was direct evidence that the cause of the colonic group of diseases was the low fiber, high fat, sugar and salt diet common in industrialized countries, while there was indirect evidence the cause of the metabolic group was the same. In 1964, the British scientist, Neil Painter demonstrated that colon and diverticular diseases could be prevented or treated by merely adding wheat bran to the diet. In the 1970s Dennis Burkitt, a British physician, and his associates noticed a glaring contrast between the nature of non-infectious diseases in developing countries such as Africa and the industrialized western countries such as Britain and North America.

In 1986 James Anderson suggested the beneficial effects of high-carbohydrate high-fiber diets on development of coronary heart disease, hypertension, obesity, and colon and breast cancers. He cited studies on men in the state of Connecticut who have the highest colon cancer rates in the world; their cancer rate was positively correlated with animal protein intake and negatively correlated with cereal and potato intake.

In view of many such reports it is no surprise that since the1980s American Diabetic Association, the American Heart Association, the Food and Nutrition Board and the Committee on Diet, Nutrition and Cancer of the National Academy of Sciences of the U.S.; the U.S. Department of Agriculture and Health Education and Welfare (the U.S. dietary Guidelines for Americans), the American Cancer Society, The National Cancer Institute, The Canadian Diabetic Association and The British Diabetic Association among others have recommended diets high in complex carbohydrates which are also rich in dietary fiber.

Dietary fiber, the sedentary lifestyle and obesity

A sedentary lifestyle has become common in all industrialized countries and among the privileged population of developing countries. Large segments of the population are engaged in jobs such as administration, clerical work and computing in which they are not called upon to carry out physically strenuous effort. Even individuals engaged in occupations traditionally involving manual labor (e.g lumbering, farming and construction), expend much less energy than those workers in generations past, in large measure due to mechanization. While an unprecedented number of Americans engage in exercise, this is far from equivalent to the work-related activity of a previous era, and indeed, such a goal is impractical. Instead, we should be tailoring our diet to correspond to the changing needs engendered by a more sedentary lifestyle.

Paralleling the rise in sedentary lifestyles, obesity and unwanted body weight gain have become correspondingly prevalent in the US. According to the National Center for Health Statistics nearly one-third of U.S. adults are overweight, and 46% of women and 27% of men surveyed in 1985 were trying to lose weight. According to M.R.C. Greenwood, there are 30,000 different methods of weight control. Yet, nearly 95% of individuals who lose weight regain it within the first year. Most attempts to reduce weight have involved indiscriminate cutting of calories. Unfortunately rather than resulting in successful weight reduction, this approach has only resulted in an increase in the incidence of malnutrition, deficiency disease and even psychiatric disorders such as anorexia nervosa.

The only prudent way to reduce body weight without a deterioration in overall health is by application of nutrition science as developed in earlier chapters. Thus, to promote weight reduction, most of the food calories should be optained from unrefined plant products such as whole grains, fresh vegetables and fruits. Few, if any, calories should be derived from animal products apart from milk. That is, meat and poultry should be avoided. Such a diet not only promotes weight reduction, but contributes to maintenance of body weight subsequently.

A 4 oz serving of 81% lean pot-roast beef, for example, will supply twenty times the energy supplied by a similar sized serving of cooked cabbage. Four ounces of steak served as such hardly satiates an individual, whereas, the same meat made into an old-fashioned stew containing onion, carrot, turnip, potatoes, flour and spices, or a casserole with an abundance of unrefined whole grains, vegetables and spices may serve six people sumptuously. Used in this way, vegetable bulk not only dilutes unwanted food calories without curtailing needed nutrients but also brings satiety. Thus, diluting calories with dietary fiber-rich food bestows many benefits to all the three entities of the body.

More than 10% of the western population has been considered overweight and one of the main reasons to this is lack of dietary fiber or bulk. There is an increase in snacking among the population. Snack foods are rich in meat, cheese or items made of refined flour, sugar, salt and fat. They contribute to weight gain. The old-time snacks, such as apples, popcorn, peanuts and roasted chestnuts which were high in fiber provided three physiological barriers against gaining weight: 1. They reduced absorption of calorie rich nutrients such as fat. 2. The act of chewing those foods reduces hunger and craving by creating a sense of satiety and 3. The higher the fiber content, the lower the calorie content of other nutrients.

Looking to the past for the future: traditional high fiber diets

Traditionally, an array of culinary techniques (such as popping, pounding, roasting, frying, soaking, steeping, grinding, fermenting, baking and pickling) were used along with herbs and spices to make unrefined, fiber-rich foods palatable. Many communities used selective techniques to modify unrefined plant ingredients prior to or during cooking. Processing paddy (rice in the husk) to parboiled rice (converted rice), for example, is a complex ancient technique that was used in India, especially in the Udipi area. It is done by steeping paddy in boiling water, so that nutrients and a moderate amount of dietary fiber are retained even after the subsequent removal of the husk. Such preparations extended shelf-life, enriched the grains with nutrients such as vitamin B complex and allowed the grain to retain most of the dietary fiber as well (see Table 10.1). Compared to parboiled rice, brown rice takes much less labor to prepare, has more crude fibers and less nutrients. Its nutrients are subjected to greater loss because they are located superficially and not seeped into the deeper layers of the grain. Polished white rice contains a minimum of both fiber and nutrients.

Culturally, whole grains were selectively prepared to suit the needs of different groups of people such as hard working laborers, the elderly, the convalescent and weaning infants. In the Udipi area, for example, the millet Ragi (*Eleusine coracana*) is used without any modification to make breads or dumplings for hard working laborers while mothers used laborious processes to make "Ragi manni" that retained nutrients and fine coats of the millet, to feed infants. Such special foods kept infants healthy, especially, when breast milk was insufficient. Preparations made out of other whole grains and grits also used to be popular in many communities "Gungi", made of parboiled rice, for example, that we ate with *ghee* or yogurt was a delightful and inexpensive breakfast food for the young, the old and the convalescent in the Udipi area. "Nasha", a Sudanese food made of whole grain sorghum flour to feed infants

TABLE 10.1. Nutrients in 100 g portion of Parboiled, Brown and White Rice. Selected from Nutritive Value of Indian Foods. National Institute of Nutrition, India, 1984.

Food Item	Moisture	Protein	Fat	Fiber	Minerals	B vit.
Rice, Polished	11.7	6.8	0.5	0.6	0,2	2.02
Rice, Brown	13.3	7.5	1.0	0.9	0.6	4.27
Rice, Parboiled	12.6	8.5	0.6	0.9	0.6?	4.39

and the convalescent has been found to retain the original nutrients and bulk of the grains.

Most cultural dishes found throughout the world not only aided in retaining the bulk (dietary fiber) but also enhanced the flavors and tastes of the dishes to suit their population. They also modified or removed excessive amounts of toxic substances such as phytic acid and oxalic acid present in some raw foods. In India, China and Southeast Asia where many greens and tender stems of plants such as spinach, amaranth, kale, turnip, beet and mustard are served as a daily staple, people use special techniques to combine them with ingredients such as cream, yogurt, legumes, nuts, spices, lemon or tamarind juice. By combining cooking with multiple ingredients, the flavor could be enhanced while often neutralizing undesirable or potentially toxic chemicals that are present in natural (unprocessed) plant products.

Various culinary processes practiced by different cultures trained the palate to cherish fibrous texture, flavor and taste. Amaranth, for example, which has a long history of being a staple of the Aztecs, even now is a popular vegetable delicacy all over India. At Annapurna, the vegetarian restaurant we operate in Worcester, Massachusetts, we have experimented by offering culturally based "Ensembles" of Amaranth, Comfry, Cucumber, Girasole and other vegetables to our American patrons with great success. Each Ensemble consists of 8 different dishes, appetizer and soup to bread and entre, made largely from a single vegetable staple, but blended with a variety of other vegetables, grains, lentils, nuts, yogurt and spices so as to make each dish distinctive and enticing as well as nutritious. This is an age-old technique of combining one or two vegetables of the season with different lentils, spices, nuts and yogurt. Such ensembles have become a hallmark of Annapurna Restaurant in the New England area and have helped thousands of Americans to rediscover their taste buds and taste and cherish these vegetables once again!

Most cultures were able to use many vegetables in their entirety including the skin, rind and seeds, because of various pre-treatments and because of the combinations of ingredients with which they were used. Eggplant, an age-old cherished delicacy in Italy, Greece, the Middle-east and most other Asian countries, for example, is used with skin, seeds and all; it is presoaked, treated with lemon or tamarind juice and cooked with spices, lentil, cheese, or yogurt. These reduce the effects of undesirable tannins. Bitter gourd, which is considered inedible in the U.S. is a delicacy in India, China and South East Asia where it is cooked in many special ways. Cassava is a "staple" in many tropical countries. It yields more food per acre (20 tons) than any other crop and requires very little labor to grow. Although, the starch-rich roots are low in protein (1%) and fat, they are rich in minerals and vitamins. The edible leaves, however, are very rich in protein (10%). Some of the varieties of cassava contain a poisonous cyanogenic glycoside. There are traditional methods of preparing cassava roots which eliminate the toxins. Apple cores are discarded along with seeds which are cyanogenetic and poisonous.

In the Udipi cuisine, where ripe gourds and pumpkins are used in their entirety, they are cooked with cereals, lentils, nuts, spices, herbs and yogurt; such preparation brings palatability even to crude fibers and make these foods choice delicacies of the area (see appendix 1). Udipi cuisine has developed its own ingenuity of making bulky fiber-rich vegetables into delightful dishes rather than discarding them as protein poor. Udipi cuisine is known for creating dishes and delicacies from tender as well as ripe vegetables and from fruits of all seasons. Cucumbers, for example, are used for pickles and relishes when tender, for curries and savories when ripe. They make vegetable and fruit savories that could be cooked with spices and herbs while fresh or dried and stored for years to cook when needed. There are preparations that taste best when consumed immediately. Others improve when marinated for a long period.

Many kinds of root and tuber crops such as beet, cassava, carrot, radish and kohlrabi also have been used extensively in their entirety in many cultures. For example, all parts of the radish plant, the fleshy root, leaves, stem tips, flowers and tender pods with seeds are used for making different dishes. In Kauai we enjoyed cooking all kinds of root vegetables sold in farmers markets even though we could not identify them as anything that we had used before. In Mexico City, we ate a delicious soup made out of tender cactus pads with cream and herbs. The techniques of preparing dishes by combining foods that make them dishes nutritious, attractive and tasty is an art of all cultures (see Chapter 19). Dishes such as applesauce made out of unpeeled apples, raw sugar and spices and relishes made of citrus skins with tamarind sauce, raw sugar and spices not only contain dietary fiber such as pectin, pentosans and galactans but also nutrients such as flavonoids and antioxidants. In contrast similar dishes made for mass production contain mainly food calories from white sugar, processed fat and starch along with plenty of artificial colors, flavors and preservatives.

In an experiment, when volunteers were allowed to consume whole apples or apple juice, those who consumed whole apples suffered less temporary hyperglycemia, maintained a more stable blood glucose for a longer period, and experienced a greater sense of satiety than those who consumed apple juice. A scientific survey carried out in Agra, India revealed that people of low socioeconomic groups who consumed fiber-rich chickpeas, had a much lower incidence of elevated plasma glucose and a lower serum cholesterol than those whose diets lacked dietary fiber. Some of these beneficial effects of natural plant ingredients are quite well-known but their mechanisms are still unexplained.

Dietary fiber is not a panacea! Although the diets of Third World populations are often rich in dietary fiber, these people often suffer from malnutrition and consequent susceptibility to infections. The developing world is suffering from malnutrition while the industrialized world suffers from the dietary excess of a sedentary population. What both worlds need is a diet rich in bulk and variety. Bulk in the form of complex carbohydrates provides both dietary fiber and energy while variety, through the consumption of many different foodstuffs, provides the range of nutrients needed including protein, minerals and vitamins for good health and well-being. In many parts of the world, centenarians who have learned to balance their diet and maintain body weight throughout their lives accomplish it by obtaining bulk and variety in their diet. Such healthy people in the world are known to consume nearly 80% of their daily energy from a fiber-rich complex carbohydrate diet. Thus, maintaining health through plant staples has been the basis of good health for all cultures. The time has come for us to understand and accept this!

Selected Sources and Suggested Readings

Milton J. Allison, et al., Oxalate degradetion by gastrointestinal bacteria from humans. *J. Nutrition,* 116: 455-460

James Anderson and Kyleen Ward, 1979. High-carbohydrate, high-fiber diets for insulin-treated men with diabetes mellitus.*American J. Clinical Nutrition,* 32, 2312- 2321

Anonymous, 1990. Dietary fibre. *British Medical J.,* 300, 1479-1480

Anonymous, 1988. Position of the American Dietetic Association: Health implications of dietary fiber. *J. American Dietetic Association,* 88, 216-221

Vivienne C. Aries, et al., 1971. The effect of a strict vegetarian diet on the fecal flora and fecal steroid concentration. *J. Pathology,* 103, 54-56

Sheila Bingham, 1979. Low residue: a reappraisal of their meaning and content. *J. Human Nutrition,* 33,5-16

Sheila A. Bingham, 1990. mechanism and experimental and epidemiological evidence relating dietary fibre (non-starch polysaccharides) and starch to protection against large bowel cancer.*Proc. Nutrition Society,* 49, 153-171

N.A. Blackburn, A.M. Holgate and N.W Read, 1984. Does guar gum improve post-prandial hyperglycaemia in humans by reducing small intestinal contact area? *British J. Nutrition,* 52, 197-204

John H. Bond and Michael D. Levitt, 1978. Effect of dietary fiber on intestinal gas production and small bowel transit time in man.*American J. Clinical Nutrition,* 31,S169-S174

P. Borriello, B. Drasar and A. Tomkins, 1978. Diet and faecal flora: A comparison of rural Northern Nigeria and London. *Proc. Nutrition Society, 37, 40A*

Elizabeth Bright-See, 1988. Dietary fiber and cancer. *Nutrition Today,* July/August, 4-10

B.J. Burke, et al., 1982. Assessment of the metabolic effects of dietary carbohydrate and fibere by measuring urinary excretion of C-peptide. *Human Nutrition: Clinical Nutrition,* 36C 373-380

D.P. Burkitt, A.R.P.Walker and N.S. Painter, 1974. Dietary fiber and diseases. *J. American Medical Association,* 229, 1068-1074

D.P.Burkitt, A.R,P. Walker and N.S. Painter, 1972. Effect of dietary fibere on stools and transit-times, and its role in the causation of disease. *Lancet,* 2. 1408

Peh Yean Cheah and Harris Bernstein, 1990. Colon cancer and dietary fiber: Cellulose inhibits the DNA-damaging ability of bile acids. *Nutrition and Cancer,* 13, 51-57

Wen-Ju Lin Chen and James Anderson, 1981. Soluble and insoluble plant fiber in selected cereals and vegetables. *AmericanJ. Clinical Nutrition,* 34, 1077-1082

Z.T. Cossack, A. Rojhani and A.O. Musaiger, 1992. The effects of sugar-beet fibre supplementation for five weeks on zinc, iron and copper status in human subjects. *European J. Clinical Nutrition,* 46, 221-225

D. Cranston, D. McWhinnie and J. Collin. 1988. Dietary fibre and gastrointestinal diseases. *British J. Surgury,* 75, 508-512

John H. Cummings, 1978. Nutritional implications of dietary fiber. *American J. Clinical Nutrition,* 31, S21-S29

John H. Cummings, 1978. Dietary factors in the aetiology of gastrointestinal cancer. *J. Human Nutrition,* 32, 455-465

J.H. Cummings, et al. 1979. The digestion of pectin in the human gut and its effect on calcium absorption and large bowel function. *British J. Nutrition,* 41, 477-485

John D. Davis and Barbara J Collins, 1978. Distention of the small intestine, satiety, and the control of food intake. *American J. Clinical Nutrition,* 31, S255-S258

Martin A Eastwood and Reginald Passmore, 1984. A new look at dietary fiber. *Nutrition Today,* September/October, 6-11

Martin Eastwood, 1978. Fiber in the gastrointestinal tract. *American J. Clinical Nutrition,* 31, S30-S32

F.R. Ehl, J.B. Robertson and P. J. Van Soest, 1982. Influence of dietary fibers on fermentation in the human large intestine. *J. Nutrition,* 112, 158-166

Sherwood L. Gorbach and Soad Tabaqchali, 1969. Bacteria, bile, and the small bowel. *Gut,* 10, 963-972

K.W. Heaton, 1983. dietary fibre in perspective. *Human Nutrition: Clinical Nutrition,* 37C, 151-170

K.W. Heaton, et al., 1978. How fiber may prevent obesity: promotion of satiety and prevention of rebound hypoglycemia. *American J. Clinical Nutrition,* 31, S281-S284

Lybus Hillman, et al., 1983. Differing effects of pectin, cellulose and lignin on stool pH, transit time and weight. *British J. Nutrition,* 50, 189-195

Charles T.L. Huang, G.S. Gopalakrishna and Buford L. Nichols, 1978. Fiber, intestinal sterolds, and colon cancer. *American J. Clinical Nutrition,* 31, 516-526

David J.A. Jenkins, et al., 1980. Diabetic diets: high carbohydrate combined with high fiber. *American J. Clinical Nutrition,* 33, 1729-1733

David Kritchevsky, 1988. Dietary fiber. *Annual Review nutrition,* 8, 301-328

G. Livesey, 1991. Calculating the energy values of foods: Towards new empirical formulae based on diets with varied intakes of complex carbohydrates. *European J. Clinical Nutrition,* 45, 1-12

T.S. Low-Beer, 1985. Nutrition and cholesterol gallstones. *Proc. J. Nutrition Society,* 44, 127-134

L.M. Morgan, et al., 1979. The effect of unabsorbable carbohydrate on gut hormones. *Diabetologia,* 17, 85-89

L.M. Morgan, et al., 1985. The effect of guar gum on carbohydrate, fat-and protein-stimulation of gut hormone secretion: modification of postprandial gastric inhibitory polypeptide and gastrin responses. *British J. Nutrition,* 53, 467-475

John W. Powels and D.R.R. Williams, 1984. Trends in bowel cancer in selected countries in relation to wartime changes in flour milling. *Nutrition and Cancer,* 6, 40-48

David P. Rose, 1990. Dietary fiber and breast cancer. *Nutrition and Cancer,* 13, 1-8

David P. Rose, et al., 1991. High-fiber diet reduces serum estrogen concentrations in premenopausal women. *American J. Clinical Nutrition,* 54, 520-525

Alasdair H. M. Ross, et al.,1983. A study of the effects of dietary gum arabic in humans. *American J. Clinical Nutrition,* 37, 368-375

Peter J. Van Soest, 1984. Some physical characteristics of dietary fibres and their influence on the microbial ecology of the human colon. *Proc. Nutrition Society,* 43, 25-33

D.A.T. Southgate, 1973. Fibre and the other unavailable carbohydrates and their effects on the energy value of the diet. *Proc. Nutrition Society,* 32, 131-136

David L. Topping, et al.,1988. A viscous fibre (methylcellulose) lowers blood glucose and plasma triglycerols and increases liver glycogen independently of volatile fatty acid production in the rat. *British J. Nutrition,* 59 21-30

David Topping, 1991. Soluble fiber polysaccharides: Effects on plasma cholesterol and colonic fermentation. *Nutrition Reviews,* 49, 195-203

Hugh Trowell, 1976. Definition of dietary fiber and hypotheses that it is a protective factor in certain diseases. *American J. Clinical Nutrition,* 29, 417-427

Alan C. Tsai, et al., 1983. Effect of soy polysaccharide on gastrointestinal functions, nutrient balance, serum lipids, and other parameters in humans. *American J. Clinical Nutrition,* 38, 504-511

Karen J. Wedekind, Howard R. Mansfield and Larry Montgomery, 1988. Enumeration and isolation of cellulolytic and hemicellulolytic bacteria from human feces. *Applied and Environmental Microbiology,* 54, 1530-1535

Walter C. Willett, 1991. Diet and Human cancer of the breast, colon and prostate. *European J. Clinical Nutrition,* 45, 19-21

Marianne Stasse Woltuis, et al., 1980. Influence of dietary fiber from vegetables and fruits, bran or citrus pectin on serum lipids, fecal lipids, and colonic function. *American J. Clinical Nutrition,* 33, 1745-1756

As has been stated in several connections, a diet which conforms to the true nutritive requirements of the body must necessarily lead toward vegetable foods. In no other satisfactory way can excess proteid be avoided, and at the same time the proper caloric value be obtained. This does not mean vegetarianism with a corresponding diminution in the typical animal foods. This raises the question of the possible relation of diet to the bacterial processes of the intestine, knowing, as we do, that the latter are of primary importance in the causation of certain forms of auto-intoxication etc. . . .

– Russell H. Chittenden, *The Nutrition of Man,* 1906

PART C
Our Internal Environment

11

Digestion, Absorption and Beyond

Abstract: Nutrients become available to the body's cells only when food ingredients are converted into small molecules in the G.I. tract by processes collectively known as digestion. Digested nutrients are specifically recognized and transported across epithelial cells of the G.I. tract, especially in the small intestine. These processes are collectively known as absorption. The composition of food affects the amount of acid secretion (increased by dietary protein), transit time out of the stomach (slowed by dietary protein and fat) and transit time out of the small intestine (slowed by dietary fiber). The rate of absorption of specific nutrients depends on the overall composition of ingested food. For example, excess phosphate interferes with absorption of other minerals; iron absorption is influenced by the acidity in the stomach; fiber delays absorption of simple sugars. The circulatory system distributes absorbed nutrients to cells throughout the body for immediate use or for storage. The residue from our food that is unabsorbed passes into the colon and is partly digested by the normal microflora. The remaining residue along with the microbes themselves, make up the feces which is regularly eliminated. Satiety is a subjective feeling of suficient food consumption which can be achieved by several different mechanisms including high protein, high glucose or high bulk diets.

Satiety achieved by a high protein diet carries the risks associated with excess protein consumption (see chapter 5). Satiety achieved by a diet of simple sugars alone is transient and counter-homeostatic in that blood glucose rises rapidly only to fall rapidly in a short time. Bulk in the form of fiber contributes to satiety by distension of the G.I. tract which, via signals to the brain, removes the desire to eat and by slowing the absorption of glucose (see chapters 9 and 10). Thus a diet of complex carbohydrates provides the advantages of glucose-mediated satiety over protein-mediated satiety. Moreover its fiber content removes the disadvantages that would be associated with a simple sugar diet alone. Thus the composition of food in terms of protein and fat (enriched in meat) versus complex carbohydrates and dietary fiber (enriched in plant products) is crucial for proper G.I. tract functions. Bulk and variety of complex carbohydrates, as achieved through a diverse plant staple-based diet, is the surest way to maintain G.I. tract homeostasis.

The human gastrointestinal (G.I.) tract stretches to nearly 30 feet from the mouth to the anus. The intestines make up most of its length. According to Fritz Kahn, a German biologist, the intestinal length in animals correlates with, and presumably reflects evolutionary adaptation to, their diet. Thus the intestine of a carnivore is relatively short, measuring approximately five times the length of the animal's body. In contrast, the intestines of a herbivore may be as much as sixteen times as long as its body. On this scale the human intestine is approximately eight times the length of the body. The human G.I. tract is a structure adapted to digest an omnivorous diet containing a variety of bulky plant staples.

The walls of the G.I. tract are composed of four layers: a mucosa consisting of epithelial cells on the inner surface, connective tissues associated with which are found cells of the immune system as well as secretory glands, and muscle fibers involved in movement of the G.I. tract (termed peristalsis). All of these layers are connected by blood vessels and networks of nerves. One set of nerves controls the muscle fibers while another set controls fluid transport across the epithelial cells. The G.I. tract secretes as well as absorbs large volumes of fluids. Among the most important G.I. secretions are hydrochloric acid, bicarbonate (an acid-neutralizing solution), digestive juices (all of which are released into the G.I. lumen) and hormones released into the bloodstream. The G.I. tract is sensitive to the chemical environment of the food with which it is in contact. The blood vessels and nerve endings in the mucosa help to maintain communication between the G.I. tract and the rest of the body. The effect of the specific nutrient composition of food on G.I. tract functions, such as movement and secretion, are different in different regions of the G.I. tract. Let us consider some of the different effects of food composition on function of the different regions of the G.I. tract

Mouth, oropharynx and esophagus

The flow of saliva starts in the mouth when stimulated by the sight and aroma of familiar foods and the feelings of appetite and hunger. Salivation is a signal to begin other digestive processes such as chewing. All these functions are regulated by complex homeostatic mechanisms. The sense of taste, for example, enables 10,000 taste buds on the tongue to identify to select foods belonging to four basic tastes: sweet, sour, salt and bitter. The secretion of saliva increases as chewing and mixing progresses and their coordination enhances taste.

Nuts, seeds, and bulky fibrous structures of vegetables and fruits have to be crushed, chewed and broken down to release nutrients such as starch, protein and sugars from them. This is not true for meats which are readily digested without such activity. The human mouth is well equipped for chewing. Human adult teeth, for example, can exert as much as 25-50 lb/in ^{2} pressure and the molars as much as 200 lb pressure to process the food. Even though the saliva is 99.5% water it contains important enzymes that digest starch and soften the ingredients of the food. Depending upon the composition of the food being chewed, a healthy adult can produce up to 2 liters of saliva daily. Continued activities of the mouth also initiate the flow of neurohormones that stimulate digestive secretions such as gastric juice in the stomach, bile from the liver and enzymes and bicarbonate from the pancreas and other glands even before the food reaches these parts of the G.I. tract. The chewed and mixed mushy food is transported into the esophagus by the act of swallowing and from there into the stomach.

Stomach

Nearly a quart of chewed and partially digested material (termed chyme) is retained in the stomach for approximately 2-4 hours. The exact retention time depends largely on the ratio of animal protein and fat (e.g. meat) to plant staples (e.g. complex carbohydrate) in the diet.

Increasing the ratio of meat to plant products in the diet prolongs the retention time of food and increases the strength and the amount of hydrochloric acid (HCl) secreted in the stomach. In contrast, a high ratio of complex carbohydrates (e.g. plant products) to protein and fat (e.g. meat) reduces both retention time and production of acid. Secretion of hormones and enzymes, and the squeezing and mixing actions (peristaltic movements) that propel the chyme, are also influenced by the composition of food. All digestive processes including acid production are precisely controlled functions. A certain minimum concentration of stomach acid secretion is required to digest chyme. Production of an excessively dilute acid may leave foods undigested or encourage the growth of incoming pathogenic microbes. However, excessive acid secretion can damage the mucosa, potentially resulting in an ulcer.

Small intestine

The chyme leaves the stomach in small spurts and enters the small intestine, a 20-25 feet long continuous narrow tube of about 1" diameter. The circular smooth muscles along its entire length undergo oscillating and contracting peristaltic movements which forces the chyme to and fro, ultimately towards the large intestine. The inner surface layers of the small intestine are highly folded and project into the lumen as finger-like villi and hair-like microvilli. Such foldings increase the small intestine surface area nearly 600-fold for digestion of the chyme and absorption of its nutrients. Just how long the small intestine retains the chyme depends upon many variables including the composition of the food and digestive secretions, and the pH of the environment. Rates of nutrient absorption can also affect satiety. For example, tryptophane, which is normally in short supply in the body gains entry into brain tissue after a complex carbohydrate meal. As a result seratonin synthesis is enhanced, brain signals are amplified and the mood of the individual is affected. The complex homeostatic mechanisms of the autonomic and enteric nerve networks regulate these functions to achieve efficient digestion and absorption of nutrients from the chyme.

Normally, in the small intestine, chyme derived from plant staples moves more slowly than does that derived from meat staples. Even among plant staples, factors such as nutrient composition and the kind of dietary fiber present make a significant difference in the extent of chyme retention, digestion and absorption of nutrients. Complex carbohydrates such as guar gum, present in cooked leguminous seeds (beans and lentils), for example, resist digestion. As a result, nutrients (e.g. glucose) are released more slowly and their absorption into the the bloodstream is slowed. The rate of release of glucose also influences the secretion of hormones like insulin into the blood, perhaps accounting for epidemiologic studies indicating that a diet rich in legumes may prevent or ameliorate some cases of diabetes mellitus. Therefore a generous intake of high fiber complex carbohydrate has been recommended for patients with diabetes.

The nutrient pool in the intestine includes protein not only from the food consumed but also from the protein contained in secretions and sloughed cells of the G.I. tract itself. As many as 100 million cells per minute, for example, are sloughed off from the intestinal wall alone. In less than three days the entire lining of the intestinal wall is replaced. Its contribution may amount to as much as 250 g of cells and 40 g of protein per day. How much of this will be digested and absorbed depends on many factors including the amount of protein present in the diet, the age and health of an individual and the pH of the chyme. The acidic chyme of the stomach is neutralized in the small intestine by bicarbonate secretion from the pancreas and the bile from the liver. Acidity of chyme in the duodenum is one of the factors that controls the rate of gastric emptying. The general chemical environment is modified by the type and amount of dietary fiber.

Pancreas

The pancreas is a lobed organ made up of clusters of two kinds of glands, one termed exocrine (that secrete digestive enzymes into the intestine) and one termed endocrine (that secrete the hormones insulin and glucagon, which regulate carbohydrate metabolism, into the bloodstream). The exocrine secretions pour into the small intestine as chyme arrives from the stomach. These pancreatic secretions contain a variety of enzymes that digest polysaccharides, proteins and fats. These enzymes are suspended in an alkaline bicarbonate-rich fluid which serves to neutralize the acidity of chyme as it enters the small intestine. The pancreatic enzymes work efficiently only in neutral and alkaline pH, and are inactivated by acid pH.

Depending upon the composition of the meal, the volume of chyme is expanded from approximately 2 liters to 9 liters with almost all of the nutrients and 90% of the fluids and salts absorbed into the bloodstream from the intestine. Ultimately, only half a liter of residue consisting of dietary fiber and internal secretions may enter the colon.

Liver

The liver plays a dominant role in metabolism. The liver is also one of the most active recycling organs of the body. Normally, it produces 3-8 g of bile salts into the small intestine per day. Only 5% of this is eliminated via the colon while the rest is recycled. Depending upon the amount of fat digested, as much as 15 g of bile may be recycled per meal. The liver also recycles amino acids derived from the digestion of proteins. It stores sugars as glycogen and fat. Among its many important functions, the liver also specializes in degrading and detoxifying drugs and foreign substances (xenobiotics) and the body's own metabolic products (see Chapter 12).

Bile, a detergent-like solution secreted by the liver and stored in the gallbladder also contributes to pH adjustment of chyme in the small intestine. Bile consists of bile salts, cholesterol, lecithin and other chemicals and is essential for the digestion and absorption of fat and cholesterol. The presence of fat and cholesterol in the diet also influence the overall synthesis, storage and secretion of bile. Excess cholesterol in the diet may lead to higher concentrations of cholesterol in stored bile and cause the formation of gallstones. Small gallstones may pass through the G.I. system but large ones may cause obstruction, pain and infection.

A damaged liver affects not only the digestion and absorption of fat in the small intestine but also the homeostasis of the entire body. A full description of the effects of the liver is beyond the scope of this book. However it should be noted that the liver has effects on function of a wide range of other systems including the brain, immune system and reproductive system.

Colon

The colon is an 8 feet long extension of the small intestine. It is wider than the small intestine and ends in a muscular opening, the anus. The inner wall of the colon is not convoluted and there are no villi or micro villi. As a result, its surface area is only 1/30th that of the small intestine. It does not produce its own enzymes to digest its contents but utilizes the enzymes of its microbial residents. The main functions of the colon include absorbing liquids, concentrating its contents into a semi-solid form, fostering the proliferation of resident microbes and propelling solid waste of their body, along with microbial cells, towards elimination. Primarily, it is a reservoir to accumulate and concentrate food waste until it is eliminated as feces. Microbial cells normally constitute one-third of the wet weight of the feces.

Unlike the stomach and the small intestine that discourage settlement of microorganisms, the environment of the colon fosters microbial colonization. It is the only organ of the G.I. tract that is ideally suited for, and benefits from, supporting the growth of an enormous population of microbes. At any one time, the colon may contain one hundred trillion (10^{14}) microorganisms belonging to many different genera and species. The microorganisms generate enzymes that are different from those produced by the human body. The microbial enzymes can break down materials that would be otherwise indigestible. They also carry out chemical transformations of a variety of substances including bile acids, hemicelluloses and drugs. The kind of activities and the transformation of chemicals brought about varies with changes in the microbial population (see Chapter 13) and the diet.

Normally, the colonic microbes are fermentative organisms and they prefer metabolizing carbohydrate over protein and fat. The majority of the colonic microbes do not need any oxygen (they are termed strict anaerobes or facultative organisms) or needs very little oxygen (microaerophilic). They are capable of fermenting nearly 70% of the available dietary fiber and produce various organic acids, short chain fatty acids and gases. Such acidic by-products have a laxative effect to propel bulky feces and protect the colon's environment against pathogens. Insufficient dietary fiber and carbohydrate residue in the colonic contents encourages the growth of species of colonic microorganisms that prefer to metabolize protein and fat over carbohydrate (proteolytic organisms). Such organisms produce urea, ammonia, amines and phenolic compounds as byproducts. These byproducts have neither the laxative effect nor maintain an acidic environment in the colon. Instead they promote an alkaline environment and fecal stagnation. Lack of dietary fiber also has a direct effect of promoting the formation of hard feces and delayed defecation (constipation).

Chronic constipation, "irregularity," changes microbial activity in the colon. The accumulation of byproducts that accompanies constipation may result in headaches, loss of appetite, nausea and mental depression. It may also be responsible for abdominal pain, irritation and disfunction of the bowel as manifest in other disorders such as hemorrhoids and diverticular disease (see Chapter 6). Retention of feces for longer than 24 hrs creastes an environment in which otherwise harmless microbial products may be transformed by microbes into tumorigenic, carcinogenic and biologically active compounds. High residue diets contribute on the average as much as 40 g of dietary fiber, and produce up to 300 g of feces which is bulky and soft. In contrast, low residue diets supply as little as 7 g of fiber and produces constipated stools which are small, hard and faceted. They slow and extend the transit time out of the colon and decrease the frequency of evacuation. A low residue diet is known to increase the transit time from 25 hours to greater than 57 hours and the frequency of bowel movements from one per day to one in several days.

Irregular bowel behavior affect not only the colon's environment but also the well-being of the entire body. According to R.P. Walker, Head of the Human Biochemical Research Unit in South Africa, cancer causes about 10-20% of total deaths, and colon cancer alone 2-4% of all deaths. The incidence of colon cancer is higher in economically advanced countries where the diet is rich in food of animal origin and poor in plant staples, hence poor in dietary fiber and residue. Surveys done in various parts of the world also demonstrate that pattern: a lack of fiber in the diet correlates with coincidences of increased problems of the bowl and cancer of the colon. According to the British scientist K.W. Heaten, an average Englishmen produces about 100g of stool per day while vegetarians produce 225 g and Asians and Africans 300-500g. According to D.P. Burkitt, H.C. Trowell and others, many African groups who eat fiber-rich complex carbohydrate diets, rarely suffer from non-infectious colonic diseases. This is also evident in the U.S where Seventh-Day Adventists who consume little meat have a lower incidence of colonic diseases than those who eat meat as a staple.

Dietary fiber is able to influence the environment of the colon because it is the major dietary constituent to reach the colon relatively unaffected by digestive processes and because it promotes fermentative microbial growth. Dietary fiber reduces the availability of rich nutrients by dilution, by reducing absorption, and by promoting rapid elimination. Thus fiber-rich foods lower serum cholesterol concentrations by approximately 15- 20%, while refined sugar and white flour actually increase blood cholesterol levels. Thus also, dietary fiber may prevent saturated fat, bile, phosphate, sulfur and the residue of drugs and xenobiotics from being available for absorption by the body or metabolism by its colonic microbes.

According to reports, reduced acidity of the colonic environment may promote cell proliferation and tumorigenesis in the colon. Thus, individuals with a lower incidence of colonic cancer had a fecal pH range of 5.5-7 while those with higher cancer rates had a fecal pH above 7.0 (alkaline). The mean stool pH of a Seventh-Day Adventist population was 6.5. Similarly, prostate cancer in men and breast cancer in women also have been linked to high meat and low dietary fiber consumption. The basis for these epidemiologic correlations has been suggested by studies demonstrating that microbes can transform bile acids such as cholic acid and deoxycholic acid into carcinogenic compounds. These transformations takes place at pH 7.0. and above. At stool pH of 6.0 such transformation was reduced and lower stool pH is largely did not occur.

Over three billion people around the world get over 75% of their food energy from plant staples. They suffer the least from "affluent diseases" largely because of their diet. Meanwhile, the 500 million people of the western world, may get only 50% or less of their daily food energy from plant staples. It is in these industrialized countries that the affluent diseases have reached epidemic proportions (see Chapter 4). Thus, according to many investigators, the diabetes and obesity that are common among the populations of industrialized countries may be related to the lack of plant staple in the diet. Increased consumption of refined sugar, flour and other products that are poor in dietary fiber may also interfere with the homeostatic energy distribution. It is a well established, for example, that the energy obtained from fiber-rich legumes and vegetables is able to maintain a more stable blood glucose and body weight than an equal amount of energy obtained from a diet rich in meat, white flour and refined sugar, which are poor in fiber.

Equal numbers of food calories obtained by eating a whole apple or drinking apple juice have entirely different consequences on the digestive system and on the distribution of energy to the three entities of the body. The processes of chewing, mixing and bulking of fiber-rich apple exercises the G.I. tract and its muscles, and regulates production of hormones, enzymes and digestive secretions. The resultant release and absorption of glucose in small quantities brings about satiety. The glucose from apple juice, on the other hand, is rapidly absorbed, flooding the blood stream with sugar and compromising the regulation of the G.I. tract. The lack of bulk in juice fails to support healthy colonic functions such as maintenance of an acidic colonic environment.

According to some scientists, prolonged consumption of fiber-poor diets may alter the central nervous system to bring about or exacerbate disorders such as obesity in some individuals. Optimal human nutrition involves more than the supply of adequate energy and nutrients. It involves slow-paced digestion and absorption and rapid eliminating of certain materials and their byproducts. By evolution, all the digestive processes of the human body have been built around bulk and variety of complex carbohydrates. When the diets of traditional cultures supplied plant staples to meet roughly 80% of energy needs, the homeostatic mechanisms maintained the physiological energy economy of the body through appetite and satiety.

Over the past 100 years we have seen that "a little knowledge is a dangerous thing." "Scientific" human nutrition has erroneously applied modern knowledge about specific nutrients to make recommendations regarding the optimal human diet. In doing so it has shifted priority from the bulk and variety of the traditional diet to a focus on the abstract biological values of nutrients (richness of nutrients). Consequently, as nations became more affluent, the diets of their populations switched from plant staple to meat staples (see Chapter 4). Low-fiber foods have increased from approximately 8% in developing countries to over 58% in western countries. Such changes in the diet have altered the regulation of mind, body and colonic microflora. The rising incidence and prevalence of the affluent diseases is in part a consequence of such dietary changes and the fiber-poor modern diet (Figure 11.1).

Selected Sources and Suggested Readings

Philip H. Abelson, 1973. Prevention of cancer.*Science,* 182, 1

Bal K. Anand, 1961. Nervous regulation of food intake. *Physiological Reviews,* 41, 677-705

Claude Andrieux, et al., 1989. Effects of some poorly digestible carbohydrates on bile acid bacterial transformations in the rat. *British J. Nutrition,* 62, 103-119

Anonymous, 1990. Dietary fiber, food intolercance, and irritable bowel syndrome. *Nutrition Reviews,* 48, 343-347

Anonymous, 1990. The liver provides glutamine to nourish other organs. *Nutrition Reviews,* 48, 197-199

Anonymous, 1963. Coma and the colon. *Lancet,* 1, 310-311

Kay M. Behall, et al., 1973. Amylase and protein in parotid saliva after load doses of different dietary carbohydrates. *J. American Clinical Nutrition,* 26, 17-22

S.R. Bloom and J.M. Polak, 1978. Gut hormones. *Proc. Nutrition Society,* 37, 259-271

Bengt Borgstrom, 1967. Absorption of fats. *Proc. Nutrition Society,* 26, 34-46

Robert S. Bresalier and Young S.Kim, 1985. Diet and colon cancer. *New England J. Medicine,* 313, 1413-1414

Doris H. Calloway, Dominic J. Colasito and Richard D. Mathews, 1966. Gases produced by human intestinal microflora. *Nature,* 212, 1238-1239

William B. Castle, et al.,1989. The relationship of disorders of the digestive tract to anemia. *Nutrition Reviews,* 47, 262-266

James Christensen, 1985. The response of the colon to eating. *American J. Clinical Nutrition,* 42, 1025-1032

John H. Cummings, 1983. Fermentation in the human large intestine: Evidence and implications for health. *Lancet,* 1, 1206-1208

Bess Dawson-Hughes, 1986. Osteoporosis and aging: gastrointestinal aspects. *J. American College of Nutrition,* 5, 393-398

Health problems in Europe with possible nutritional links

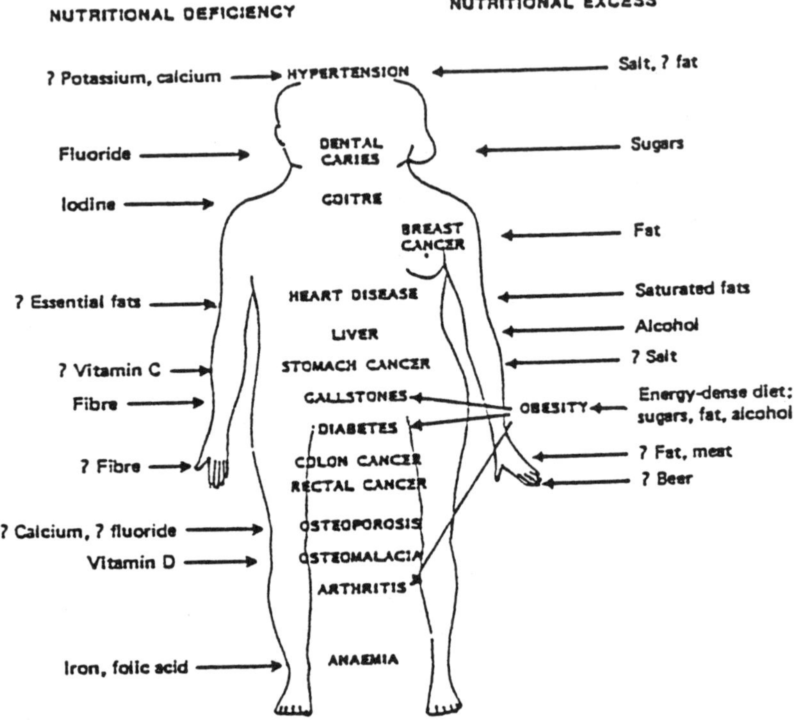

Figure 11.1. Nutritional causes of diseases are indicated as due to excess or deficiency of nutrients. Question marks refer to speculative or theoretical causes not yet supported by specific evidence,

(W.P.T. Jones, 1988. By permission of World Health Organization)

Note. Individual susceptibility to the prevailing diet is important in both nutritional deficiency and excess. The nutritional components have only been tentatively linked to many of the conditions shown.

Ghislain Devroede, 1978. Dietary fiber, bowel habits, and colonic function. *American J. Clinical Nutrition,* 31, S157-S160

René Dubos et al., 1965. Indigenous normal, and autochthonous flora of the gastrointestinal tract. *J. Experimental Medicine,* 122, 67-76

Hans Englyst and John Cummings, 1987. Digestion of polysaccharides of potato in the small intestine of man. *American J. Clinical Nutrition,* 45, 423-431

O. Gregor, R. Toman, and F. Prusova, 1969. Gastrointestinal cancer and nutrition. *Gut,* 10, 1031-1034

Susan J. Henning, 1986. Development of the gastrointestinal tract. *Proc. Nutrition Society,* 45, 39-44

Michael J. Hill, 1975. Metabolic epidemiology of dietary factors in large bowel cancer. *Cancer Research,* 35, 3398-3402

Roger Jones, Susan Lydeard, 1992. Irritable bowel syndrome in the general population. *British Medical J.* 304, 87-90

Fritz Kahn. *Man in Structure and Function.*vol.1, Alfred A Knopf, New York, 1943

R. Kenworthy, 1967. Influence of bacteria on absorption from the small intestine. *Proc. Nutrition Society,* 26, 18-23

Roger Lewis and Sherwood Gorbach, 1972. Modiffication of bile acids by intestinal bacteria. *Archives Internal Medicine,* 130, 545-548

Richard D. Mattes, 1987. Sensory influences on food intake and utilization in humans. *Human Nutrition: Applied Nutrition,* 41A, 77-95

David J. Mela and Richard D. Mattes, 1988. The chemical senses and nutrition: Part 1. *Nutrition Today,* March/April, 4-9

John E. Morley, et al., 1982. The role of the endogenous opiates as regulators of appetite. *American J. Clinical Nutrition,* 35, 757-761

Harold L. Newmark and Joanne R. Lupton, 1990. Determinants and consequences of colonic luminal pH: Implications for colon cancer. *Nutrition and Cancer,* 14, 161-173

Donald Novin et al., 1985. Is there a role for the liver in the control of food intake? *Americn J. Clinical Nutrition,* 42, 1050-1062

Sidney F. Phillips and Alison M. Stephen, 1981. The structure and function of the large intestine. *Nutrition Today,* November/December, 4-12

Bandaru S. Reddy, Anthony Mastromarino and Ernst L. Wynder, 1975. Further leads on metabolic epidemiology of large bowel cancer. *Cancer Research,* 35, 3403-3406

J.A. Robertson, 1988. Physiochemical charactristics of food and the digestion of starch and dietary fibere during gut transit. *Proc. Nutrition Society,* 47, 143-152

Chester B. Rosoff and Harvey Goldman, 1968. Effect of the intestinal bacterial flora on acute gastric stress ulceration. *Gastroenterology,* 55, 212-222

Ann-Sofie Sandberg, et al., 1982. The effect of citrus pectin on the absorption of nutrients in the small intestine. *Human Nutrition: Clinical Nutrition,* 37c, 171-183

Brittmarie Sandstrom, 1988. Fators influencing the uptake of trace elements from the digestive tract. *Proc. Nutrition Society,* 47, 161-167

Barbara O. Schneeman, 1987. Dietary fiber and gastrointestinal function. *Nutrition Reviews,* 45, 129-132

D. B. A. Silk, G.K. Grimble and R.G. Rees, 1985. Protein digestion and amino acid and peptide absorption. *Proc. Nutrition Society,* 44, 63-72

Eliot Stellar and Eileen Shrager, 1985. Chews and swallows and the microstructure of eating. *American J. Clinical Nutrition,* 42, 973-982

Stephen Strobel, 1986. Allergenicity of feeds and gastrointestinal immunoregulation in man and experimental animals. *Human Nutrition: Applied Nutrition,* 40A (Suppl.1.) 45-54

A Tamm and K. Villako, 1971. Urinary volatile phenols in patients with intestinal obstruction. *Scand. J. Gastroenterology,* 6, 5-8

A.B.R. Thomson, 1989. Intestinal aspects of lipid absorption. *Nutrition Today,* July/August, 16-20

Kerstin Uvnas-Moberg, 1989. The gastrointestinal tract in growth and reproduction. *Scientific American,* July, 78-83

J.H. Weisburger, 1985. Nutrition and carcinoma of the large intestine. *Proc Nutrition Society,* 44, 115-120

Tadataka Yamada,1985. Gut hormone release induced by food ingestion. *American J. Clinical Nutrition,* 42, 1033-1039

12

Elimination Decreases Internal Pollution

Abstract: Organisms, and the cells and tissues of which they are composed, have evolved mechanisms for both acquiring nutrients and for eliminating wastes. The renal, gastro-intestinal (including liver), circulatory and respiratory systems are all involved in waste elimination in humans and all vertebrate animals. Urine produced by the kidney is the route of elimination of water soluble substances including excess nutrients in the bloodstream. Feces generated in the GI tract is the route of elimination of undigested food materials. The major excretory role of the lungs is elimination of carbon dioxide. The human body is a limited ecosystem with respect to capacity for waste elimination. Moreover, that capacity for elimination of wastes normally decreases due to cell loss and dysfunction with age. Excess nutrients, toxic by-products and xenobiotics (e.g. ingested drugs and environmental polutants) all can be causes of disease and degeneration through mechanisms including direct toxicity, carcinogenic effects and inappropriate deposition of substances (e.g. cholesterol in arteries causing athrosclerosis). Rapid transit of fecal waste through the colon is important because prolonged exposure to fecal materials that contain biologically active products of microbial metabolism, results in local irritation and other damaging effects on the epithelial cells of the colonic lumen that can cause cancer. Absorption of fecal substances can also be harmful. Therefore it is prudent to maintain homeostasis by minimizing generation of wastes with high toxic potential (e.g. of protein and fat metabolism) rather than by making the excretory organs work harder to eliminate a larger amount of toxic or potentially toxic wastes. The affluent diet, characterized by high fat, high protein and low complex carbohydrates fails to do this. Perhaps as a result, degenarative diseases, including those of the excretory organs, are on the increase.

In Chapter 3 we compared the energy economy of the human body to that of a city. In a city, people bring in materials, build and demolish structures and generate both valuable products and wastes. Products are transported, utilized, or stored and wastes are disposed of or recycled. Unless all of these activities are coordinated, the environment will deteriorate. Maintaining a healthy internal environment in the human body, a large community of trillions of living cells, has similarities to the maintenance of a city. The wastes are generated from the nutrients, non-nutrients and xenobiotics (ingested drugs or environmental pollutants) that enter the body, and from the activities of the body's cells and microbes. An adult human, for example, replaces 1% of it's 30 trillion red blood cells daily. The number of microbes in the colon exceeds the total number of body cells and their metabolic activity is much higher than that of the body's cells (see Chapter 13).

The homeostatic mechanisms that maintain the internal environment of cells evolved over 3 billion years ago with the primitive cellular organisms that originated in primeval seas. The cell membranes of the primitive organisms regulated incoming nutrients and outgoing wastes and protected the internal environment of the cells. Such regulation of materials has become tremendously complex in multicellular organisms. In the higher animals, various systems of the body have also evolved to carry out the processes of transport, regulation, recycling and elimination of wastes. Primary among these are the circultory, respiratory, gastro-intestinal (including liver) and renal systems, each performing multiple functions.

Waste processing is regulated by the homeostasis of the body. The only nutrient that the body can store in large amounts is fat and the only dietary ingredient that can be disposed of in large amounts is dietary fiber. Any other means of storage and elimination in large amounts compromises homeostasis, risking the health and longevity of the body.

Any excess of ingested substances that are difficult to eliminate, and their byproducts, can be viewed as pollutants with the potential to contribute to degenerative diseases (see Chapter 4). The richer the food we consume, the more by-products are produced which are hard to store or eliminate (see Chapter 7). Cholesterol, for example, is a normal metabolite of the body. It is essential for all cells and it is present in large quantities in some tissues such as the brain and in some body fluids such as bile. A healthy body produces enough cholesterol to meet its needs (see Chapter 11). However, when increased meat and eggs in the diet overwhelms the homeostatic mechanism of the body, cholesterol can accumulate in the walls of arteries causing atherosclerosis (a form of internal pollution). As important, excess cholesterol intake results in large amounts of cholesterol available in the colon for transformation into toxic and carcinogenic compounds by microbes.

The circulatory system, continuously transports both nutrients and hormones and collects wastes. The human circulatory system is very sophisticated as the following will illustrate. Capillaries are the most narrow (thinner than a hair) vessels that carry blood to all tissues. The total length of the capillaries measure over 60,000 miles long. No cell surface is more than 0.15 mm away from a capillary, which helps rapid exchange of materials between cell and the circulatory system. The arteries, the vessels that deliver nutrients and oxygen (O_2) and the veins that collect wastes of the cells such as carbon dioxide (CO_2) travel separately. While the arterial capillaries distribute blood with nutrients, another network of venous capillaries collects blood with wastes which returns to the circulation through the veins (Figure 12.1). The veins carry their load to cleansing stations (excretory organs) such as the lungs, the kidneys and the liver. Any nutrients, non-nutrients and xenobiotics that are absorbed by the body as food or as contaminants pass through the circulatory system. The circulatory system aids the body to sort gaseous and soluble materials that enter the body. Most of the gaseous materials get recycled or eliminated via the lungs. The water-soluble materials are eliminated through the kidneys. Finally, solid or water insoluble wastes are eliminated, for some substances with the help of bile, via the GI tract as feces.

Varying by the age of the person and the environment, the blood carries both nutrients absorbed from the G.I. tract and certain metabolic by-products such as carbon dioxide, ammonia, urea and uric acid. These by-products are either materials that can be stored as fats of various kinds or compounds that can be eliminated as waste. Ordinarily, very little that cannot be stored as fat or that cannot be eliminated as waste remains in the bloodstream. In healthy conditions, for example, neither glucose nor uric acid in the blood can increase beyond a certain level. Even water cannot accumulate in excess in the blood, as the same amounts are taken in and eliminated daily, precisly maintaining the fluid balance of the body (see Chapter 10). Normally, young growing organisms utilize, recycle and eliminate metabolites more efficiently than older organisms.

The lungs work interdependantly with the kidneys, liver and colon to eliminate the gaseous wastes such as carbon dioxide (CO_2), hydrogen sulphide (H_2S), methane (CH_3), and ammonia. Many gases, especially CO_2, are largely eliminated through the lungs. This highly efficient exchange of gasses takes place within the extremely permeable epithelial pockets of the lungs, the alveoli, and the blood flowing through the capillaries. A sticky mucus fluid film traps particles and ciliated cells that line the respiratory passages sweep the particulates up towards the throat to keep more than 300 million alveoli of the lungs clean. A part of the CO_2 generated by cellular metabolism is eliminated by the lungs and the rest is recycled as bicarbonate ions to maintain the acid-base balance of blood. However, contaminants in polluted air increase the workload of lung tissue and reduce their efficiency. The dirty air we breath may bring into the lungs 30-50 lb. of dust in a lifetime. Toxic molecules that are present in polluted air or cigarette smoke poison the cells, inhibit ciliary

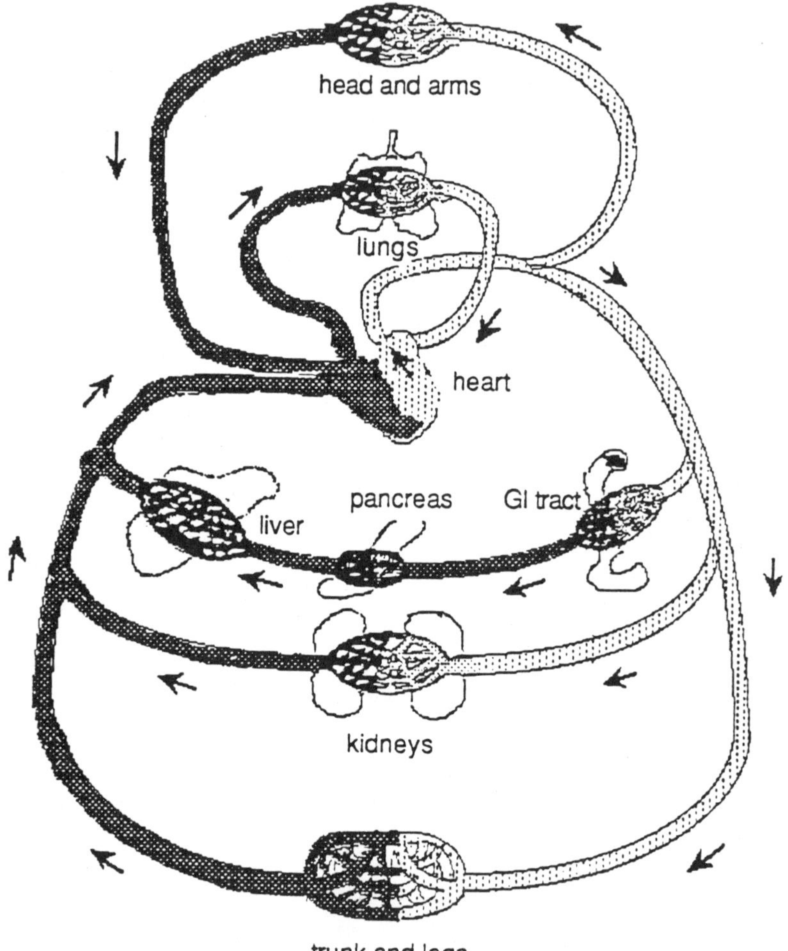

Figure 12.1. Blood flow in the human body. Dark shading refers to venous (deoxygenated) blood; light shading refers to arterial (oxygen-rich) blood. Arrows indicate direction of blood flow. Arterial and venous systems connect at capillary beds.

movement and drastically reduce the cleansing function of the lungs, resulting in respiratory tract infections, asthma and cancer.

Most soluble wastes are carried by the veins to the urinary system. The urinary system consists of the kidneys,the ureters, the bladder, and the urethra. The kidneys contain millions of blood capillaries twisted into little coils and sacs, wastes are strained through these sacs and collected in tubules which drain through the ureters into the urinary bladder. The kidneys have special access to the arteries and the veins and they process most of the liquid wastes of the body through their filtering system. Out of 6 quarts of blood that an heart pumps every minute, nearly 20% of it flows through the urinary system. The urinary system is specialized to efficiently filter, cleanse and recycle the liquld components of blood, generating urine as waste. Approximately 60 liters of blood filters daily through kidneys and roughly 1.5 liters of urine is generated and eliminated from the body. In a sense, urine is highly modified blood, from which most substances including water, glucose and salts first removed are reabsorbed and nearly 99% returned to the blood stream for recycling. The ammount of fluid discarded in urine is related to the fluid intake and metabolic fluid generated in the body. While regulating intravascular fluid volume, the kidneys also coordinate other important functions of the body such as ionic balance and acid-base balance. The urine of a healthy adult is approximately 95% water and the rest is by-products of the body such as urea, uric acid, ammonia, sulfate, phosphate and other minerals. Urea is the principal constituent. Excretion of urea decreases when the diet is low in protein and increases with a high protein diet.

In western countries increased meat, sea food and other animal protein in the diet contributes to many degenerative diseases associated with uric acid. The uric acid content of urine also corresponds to dietary protein intake, increasing most with the consumption of organ meats which have a high purine content. Purines are nitrogenous compounds that are derived from nucleic acids. Sloughed off body cells, which may increase with old age and during chronic ailments, also generate uric acid. Plant staples have 12-40 times less purine content than seafood and organ meats. In 24 hours as much as 0.7 g of uric acid may be eliminated in urine. Increased uric acid production causes increased uric acid content in the blood because only a limited amount of it can be eliminated in the urine. When production exceeds elimination, the uric acid may deposit as crystals in the joints, causing gout, or as stones in the kidneys.

Other by-products of nutrients and non-nutrients may also accumulate in the blood when the efficiency of the kidneys is reduced. Non-nutrients such as food additives and drugs also can accumulate in the blood if the kidneys' capacity to eliminate them is reduced. Anything that weakens the capacity of kidneys increases the internal pollution of the body and causes deterioration of the body. Vigorous exercise, for example, can generate more lactic acid than can be cleared by liver and kidney at one time. Professional athletes, especially those who consume high protein diets, have more kidney and urinary tract problems than others. A decreased clearing capacity of the urinary system encourages the accumulation of many metabolic by-products in the blood. The blood and urine rich in these substances become an attractive medium for various disease and cancer causing cells.

Breakdown products of various amino acids such as tyrosine and tryptophan, food additives such as cyclamate, and xenobiotics such as red dye can become bladder carcinogens. Tyrosine, an amino acid, for example, can be metabolized by bacteria to yield compounds such as phenols and p-cresol which promote benign and malignant tumors. Various by-products of food additives such as cyclamate and nutrasweet found in the urine have been implicated in certain types of bladder and brain tumors.

Any nutrients, non-nutrients and xenobiotics that are not absorbed into the blood from the G.I. tract collect in the colon as solid wastes to be eliminated as feces (see Chapter 10). Unless feces are eliminated frequently, many substances in the colon are reabsorbed into the blood as such or after undergoing biotransformation by the colonic bacteria. The infrequent emptying of the bowl is constipation. It causes stagnation of nutrients and by-products. This condition is a good example of internal pollution. Carnivores produce firmer, less bulky feces than omnivores and herbivores. While bulky feces promotes frequent elimination that carries toxic wastes and carcinogenic substances along with it, a harder feces results in infrequent bowel action and incomplete evacuation. The amount of feces produced daily may vary from 100 g in high meat consumers to 350 g or more in vegetarians. In general, affluent people of industrialized societies who consume more meat in their diet have more constipation than those in developing countries who consume less meat and more bulk. According to published reports, high meat eaters have two or less bowel movements per week compared to bowel movement once or twice a day among people in developing countries who consume the traditional high roughage diets. Depending upon the diet, more than 1% of the adult population suffers from constipation. It may afflict as many as 3% of the young and 20% of the elderly of the western countries. According to a report, 42% of the patients admitted to a geriatrics ward had fecal impaction (severe constipation). It is more common in women than in men.

Under constipated conditions, various residues, such as those from beans, can produce flatulence and abdominal discomfort. Intestinal gas, flatus, is the product of two different processes carried out by specific groups of microbes; fermentative and methanogenic. Together they produce carbon dioxide (CO_2), hydrogen,(H_2), methane (CH_4) and hydrogen sulphide (H_2S) in the colon. How much of each of these gases are generated depends upon fermentative nature of the colon and food residue present. Methanogenic transformations are favored under neutral or alkaline conditions and suppressed in an acidic environment. Intake of yogurt and complex carbohydrate-based meals (whole grains) create an acidic colonic environment and thereby diminish flatulence.

The lack of a fermentative colonic environment (see chapter 13) encourages the growth and proliferation of proteolytic bacteria (those that break down protein). They in turn biotransform many wastes such as urea to ammonia and amino acids to bioamines. This occurs more when the colon is rich in proteinaceous residues, the result of a high meat diet. The proteolytic bacteria can convert the residues of proteins and xenobiotics to procarcinogens and carcinogens (see Chapter 11). A high protein diet causes increased production of urea in the colon. When more urea is available to the colonic bacteria, the urea is transformed to ammonia. Increased ammonia in the colon also alters the colonic environment towards neutral or alkaline pH. Likewise changes in the bacterial population occur. At the beginning of the 20th century it was observed that the ingestion of excess meat aggravated the clinical symptoms of kidney patients. When their dietary protein was reduced to roughly 20-30 g daily, the level of blood urea went down and so did the content of ammonia in the colon. A high levels of ammonia in the bowel also inhibits cell functions and may predispose to viral infections. Its excess may also contribute to neoplastic transformation in the colon.

When the diet is rich in dietary fiber even many xenobiotics such as lead, pesticides and other toxic substances are largely eliminated. Poisoning caused by an accumulation of lead in the body is an age old problem of human civilization. Now, virtually all countries have polluted their soil, air and water with lead and other toxic substances. Even a minute quantity of lead causes poisoning in children when it enters the blood and soft tissues. The body has homeostatic mechanisms to decrease blood lead levels either by storing a moderate amounts of lead in the hair, bones and teeth and by eliminating it in small amounts in the urine. However, these basic homeostatic mechanisms become ineffective in people whose diet lacks universally protective foods such as milk and plant products rich in fiber (see Chapter 15). Experimental studies of animals and epidemiological studies of children have shown that lead poisoning can be avoided or reduced by increasing consumption of protective foods.

Since the turn of the century, diets in all industrialized countries have inflicted a heavy burden on the colon and other organs of elimination by increasing dietary protein, fats and xenobiotics, and decreasing foods rich in dietary fibers. As a result, the ailments of internal pollution, including cardiovascular disease and cancer, have become the predominant diseases in industrialized countries in the twentieth century. This has been worsened in both developed and developing countries by food additives, hormones and antibiotics fed to meat animals, and pesticides and herbicides used in agricultural crops (external pollution). As long as our internal and external environments remain polluted we will lose in health and longevity. Consumption of high fiber diets will help to reduce these ill effects.

Selected Sources and Suggested Readings

Anonymous, 1990. Pesticides in the third world. *Lancet, 336, 1437*

Anonymous, 1982. Mutagen implicated in human colon cancer. *Chemical Engineering News,* September 27, 22-23

Anonymous, 1973. Internal pollution. *Lancet,* 1, 1071

Anonymous, 1971. Effects of dietary changes on kidney metabolism. *Nutrition Reviews,* 29, 95-97

Anonymous, 1968. Dietary protein and acute renal failure. *Nutrition Reviews,* 26, 44-47

H. Babich and D.L. Davis, 1981. Food tolerance and action levels: Do they adequately protect children? *BioScience,* 31, 429-438

Harvey Borden, 1906-7. The elimination of Indoxyl sulphate in the urine of the insane. *J. Biological Chemistry,* 2, 575-601

Barry Brenner, Timothy W. Meyer, and Thomas H. Hostetter, 1982. Dietary protein intake and the progressive nature of kidney diseases: *New England J. Medicine,* 307, 652-659

C.L. Brown, M. J. Hill and Peter Richards, 1971. Bacterial urease in uremic men. *Lancet,* 2, 406-408

George T. Bryan, 1971. The role of urinary tryptophan metabolites in the etiology of bladder cancer. *American J. Clinical Nutrition,*24, 841-847

William H. Chambers, 1923. The hydrogen ion concentration of the blood in carcinoma. *J. Biological Chemistry,* 60, 229-254

Peh Yean Cheah, 1990. Hypotheses for the etiology of colorectal cancer – An overview. *Nutrition and Cancer,* 14, 5-13

David B. Clayson, 1975. Nutrition and experimental carcinogenesis: A Review. *Cancer Research,* 35, 3292-3300

A. M. Connell, et al., 1965. Variation of bowel habit in two population samples. *British Medical J.* 2, 1095-1099

G.J. Davies, et al., 1986. Bowel function measurements of individuals with different eating patterns. *Gut,* 27, 164-169

W. Denis, 1917. The influence of the protein intake on the excretion of creatine in man. *J. Biological Chemistry,* 30, 47-51

J.W.T. Dickerson and R. Walker, 1974. Nitrogen, age and drug metabolism. *Proc. Nutrition Society,* 33, 191-196

Martin Eastwood and Laureen Mowbray, 1976. The binding of the components of mixed micelle to dietary fiber. *American J. Clinical Nutrition,* 291461-1467

Louis R. Ember, 1980. Nitrosamines: assessing the relative risk. *Chemical Engineering News,* March 31, 20-26

Benjamin H. Ershoff, 1974. Antitoxic effects of plant fiber. *American J. Clinical Nutrition,* 27, 1395-1398

Martin H. Floch, 1976. Diet, Bacteria, and the Colon. *American J. Clinical Nutrition,* 29, 1409-1484

Otto Folin and W. Denis, 1912. Protein metabolism from the standpoint of blood and tissue analysis. *J. Biological Chemistry,* 11, 87-95

Frank H. Gardner, 1962. Nutritional management of chronic diarrhea in adults. *J. American Medical Association,* 180, 147-152

J.S.S. Gear, et al., 1981. Fibre and bowel transit times. *British J. Nutrition,* 45, 77-82

Sherwood L.Gorbach and Soad Tabaqchali, 1969. Bacteria, bile, and the small bowel. *Gut,* 10, 963-972

Norton J. Greenberger, Samad Saegh and Richard D. Ruppert, 1968. Urine indican in malabsorptive diorders. *Gastroenterology,* 55, 204-211

M.I. Gurr, 1990. The nutrition of microbes and man. *British J. Nutrition,* 63, 5-6

N.Y. Haboubi, R.D. Montgomery, 1992. Small-bowel bacterial overgrowth in elderly people: Clinical significance and response to treatment. *Age and Ageing,* 21, 13-19

Juliana T. Hauser, 1986. The human hotel. *Carolina Tips,* Carolina Biological supply Co., 49, 21-23

C. Ioannides and D.V. Parke, 1979. Effect of diet on the metabolism and toxicology of drugs. *J. Human Nutrition,* 33, 357-366

Attallah Kappas and Alvito P. Alvares, 1975. How the liver metabolizes foreign substances. *Scientific American,* 232, 22-31

Jan Koch-Weser and Edward M. Sellers, 1976. Drug Therapy. *New England J. Medicine,* 294, 311-315

J.P. Lambert, et al., 1991. The value of prescribed "high-fibere" diet for the treatment of the irritable bowel syndrome. *European J. Clinical Nutrition,* 45, 601-609

K.O. Lewis, 1991. What are the causes of a raised plasma urea concentration with unchanged creatinine concentration ? *British Medical J.* 302, 651

Joachim G. Liehr, 1991. Vitamin C reduces the incidence and severity of renal tumors induced byestradiol of diethylstilbestrol. *American J. Clinical Nutrition,* 54, 1256S-12660

C.L. Long, M.J. Jeevanandam and J.M. Kinney, 1978. Metabolism and recycling of urea in man. *American J. Clinical Nutrition,* 31, 1367-1382

Albert B. Lowenfels, 1983. Is increased cholesterol excretion the link between low serum cholesterol and colon cancer? *Nutrition and Cancer,* 4, 280-284

Edward Majchrowicz and Jack H. Mendelson, 1970. Blood concentrations of acetaldehyde and ethonal in chronic alcoholics. *Science,* 168, 1100-1102

Charlotte Mangum David Towle, 1977. Physiological adaptation to unstable environments. *American Scientist,* 65, 67-75

Elizabeth A. Melcher, Michael D. Levitt and Joanne L. Slavin, 1991. Methane production and bowel function parameters in healthy subjects on low- and high-fiber diets. *Nutrition and Cancer,* 16, 85-92

Helene Martelli, et al., 1978. Some parameters of large bowel motility in normal man. *Gastroenterology,* 75, 612-618

Jon J. Michovicz and H. Leon Bradlow, 1991. Altered estrogen metabolism and excretion in humans following consumption of indole-3-carbinol. *Nutrition and Cancer,* 16, 59-66

Randy Moore, 1992. Changing our attitude about the environment. *American Biology Teacher,* 54, 132-133

Irvine H. Page, 1972. Blood- the circulatory computer tape. *Perspectives in Biology and Medicine,* 15, 219-220

E.J. Pantuck, et al., 1976. Stimulatory effect of vegetables on intestinal drug metabolism in the rat. *J. Pharmacology and Experimental Therapeutics,* 198, 278-283

Charles W. Parker, 1991. Environmental stress and immunity: Possible implications for IgE-mediated allergy. *Perspective in Biology and Medicine,* 34, 197-211

Bandaru S. Reddy, et al., 1978. Metabolic epidemiology of large bowel cancer.*Cancer,* 42, 2832-2838

Arnold E. Reif, 1981. The causes of cancer. *American Scientist,* 69, 437-447

Christian Remesy and Christian Demigne, 1988. Specific effects of fermentable carbohydrates on blood urea flux and ammonia absorption in the rat cecum. *J. Nutrition,* 119, 560-565

Peter Richards, 1972. Nutritional potential of nitrogen recycling in man. *American J. Clinical Nutrition,* 25, 615-625

E. Ritz, et al., 1978. Protein restriction in the conservative management of uremia. *American J. clinical Nutrition,* 31, 1703-1711

J.A. Robertson and M.A. Eastwood, 1981. An examination of factors which may affect the water holding capacity of dietary fibre. *British J. Nutrition,* 45, 83-88

Carl P. Sherwin, 1917. Comparative metabolism of certain aromatic acids. *J. Biological Chemistry,* 31, 307-310

Laura Tangley, 1987. Regulating pesticides in food. *BioScience,* 37, 452-456

Rodney Taylor, 1990. Management of constipation. *British Medical J.* 300, 1063-1064

Ruth C. Theis and Stanley R. Benedict, 1918. Phenols and phenol derivatives in human blood in some pathological conditions. *J. Biological Chemistry,* 36, 99-103

A.J. Vince, et al., 1990. The effect of lactulose, pectin, arabinogalactan and cellulose on the production of organic acids and metabolism of ammonia by intestinal bacteria in a fecal incubation system. *British J. Nutrition,* 63, 17-26

Willard J. Visek, 1979. Ammonia metabolism, urea cycle capacity and their biochemical assesment. *Nutrition Reviews,* 37, 273-282

Willard J Visek, 1978. Diet and cell growth modulation by ammonia. *American J. Clinical Nutrition,* 31, S216-S220

T. Wang, et al., 1978. Volatile nitroamines in normal human faeces. *Nature,* 276, 280-281

Enrique Wolpert, Sidney F. Phillips and W.H.L. Summerskill, 1971. Transport of urea and ammonia production in the human colon. *Lancet,* 2, 1387-1390

Keith Wrenn, 1989. Fecal implication. *New England J. Medicine.* 658-662

Oliver M. Wrong and Angela Vince, 1984. Urea and ammonia metabolism in the human large intestine. *Proc. Nutrition Society,* 43, 77-86

Vernon R. Young, 1981. Protein metabolism and nutritional state in man. *Proc. Nutrition Society,* 40, 343-359

The artificial condition of civilized life, sedentary habits, concentrated foodstuffs, false modesty, ignorance and neglect of bodily needs, have produced a crippled state of the colon as an almost universal condition among civilized men and women.

Intestinal toxemia or autointoxication is the most universal of all maladies, and the source of autointoxication in the colon with its seething mass of putrefying food residues.

– John Harvey Kellogg, *The Itinerary of a Breakfast,* 1926.

13

Our Microbes in Nutrition and Health

If the condition of a free and happy life is to meet the Claude Bernardian demand for maintenance of the fixity of the internal milieu, we cannot afford to remain in ignorance of what friends and enemies our intestines harbor.
– Carl Lamanna, 1972

Abstract: The normal microbial population of the G.I. tract, largely limited to the colon, comprises species that are permanent residents as well as transients which enter from the outside world. This third entity within human beings is unlike the other two (the brain and the other organs of the body) in that it is not inherited, but rather, develops after birth under the influence of the diet. When well established it is a powerful player in maintaining homeostasis. When developed inappropriately, the result is susceptibility to a wide range of disease. The beneficial role of normal microbial flora includes the establishment of a G.I. tract environment inhospitable to most pathogens and the production of beneficial substances including certain vitamins and short chain fatty acids. The diet is a powerful influence on the composition and stability of the colonic microbial flora. Fermentative bacteria are the natural inhabitants of the colon on a diet of plant products and complex carbohydrates while a range of proteolytic species are favored in high-protein and high fat meat-staple diets. Fermentative bacterial populations are associated with improved longevity and quality of life, and a range of disorders can be ameliorated or, in some instances possibly, even prevented, by maintenance of a fermentative colonic bacterial population.

In Chapter 1 we divided the human body into three entities: the brain, the body and the intestinal microflora. The first two entities begin to interact even before birth and their roles in adult health has been well recognized by scientists. However, the intestinal microflora acquired at birth and established during the nursing period, which also contributes tremendously to adult nutrition and health, has been largely ignored by contemporary nutritional science. Yet, fermentative intestinal microflora and the colonic ecology they establish is a major contributor to the influence of diet on health, in all higher animals including humans. Evidence suggests that humans benefit immensly from the maintenance of a stable fermentative microbial environment in the colon (see Chapter 11).

In Greek the term micros means small and bios means life. Thus microbes are the diverse organisms that cannot be seen with unaided human eyes. The microbes were not known until Antony Leeuwenhoek, a Dutchman, invented the microscope. Leeuwenhoek, for the first time in 1673, saw millions of tiny organisms when he picked his teeth and examined the material under his microscope. He called them "animalcules." He calculated that it took approximately a million bacteria to make a particle of the size of a sand grain. Since then, the microbial world has been explored extensively. It consists of organisms such as viruses, bacteria, fungi, yeasts, protozoa and algae. Such single-celled organisms evolved a billion years before higher living forms including human beings.

Microbes are everywhere. They have been found in hot springs, in freezing water, in the mountain air, on the deep ocean floor, inside plants and animals and on rotting woods and soils. Some of them are intimately associated with all animals including human beings. Plants, animals and humans also have evolved to interact with microbes. Microbes are capable of adapting to a wide range of nutrients and environmental conditions extremely rapidly. Most intestinal bacteria are capable of reproduction by doubling every 20 minutes. No pant or animal can match that rate of reproduction. It has been calculated that a single bacterium with a generation time of 15 minutes would produce enough cells that would cover the entire Earth one foot deep within less than 2 days if optimum growth conditions could be maintained. However, this does not happen because the growth rate slows down rapidly as the number of cells increase and available nutrients diminish.

Each of the diverse species of microbes have evolved to thrive in a specific environmental niche for themselves. The most abundant microorganisms, the bacteria, may measure as small as 0.1 cubic micrometers. Bacteria are 10 to 100 times smaller than most cells of higher organisms. They exist in three basic forms; spherical, rods and helical, and as singles, doubles, groups or chains. Some have appendages for swimming and others have perfected mechanism for adhering to their hosts (Figure 13.1). The microorganisms need to absorb their foods in liquid form through their cell surfaces. To achieve this condition they sometimes secrete powerful enzymes which digest solids and thereby release nutrients. Perhaps most amazing about bacteria is the enormous diversity of metabolic types that occur. Moreover they grow 3 to 10 times as fast as the fastest growing cells of most higher organisms.

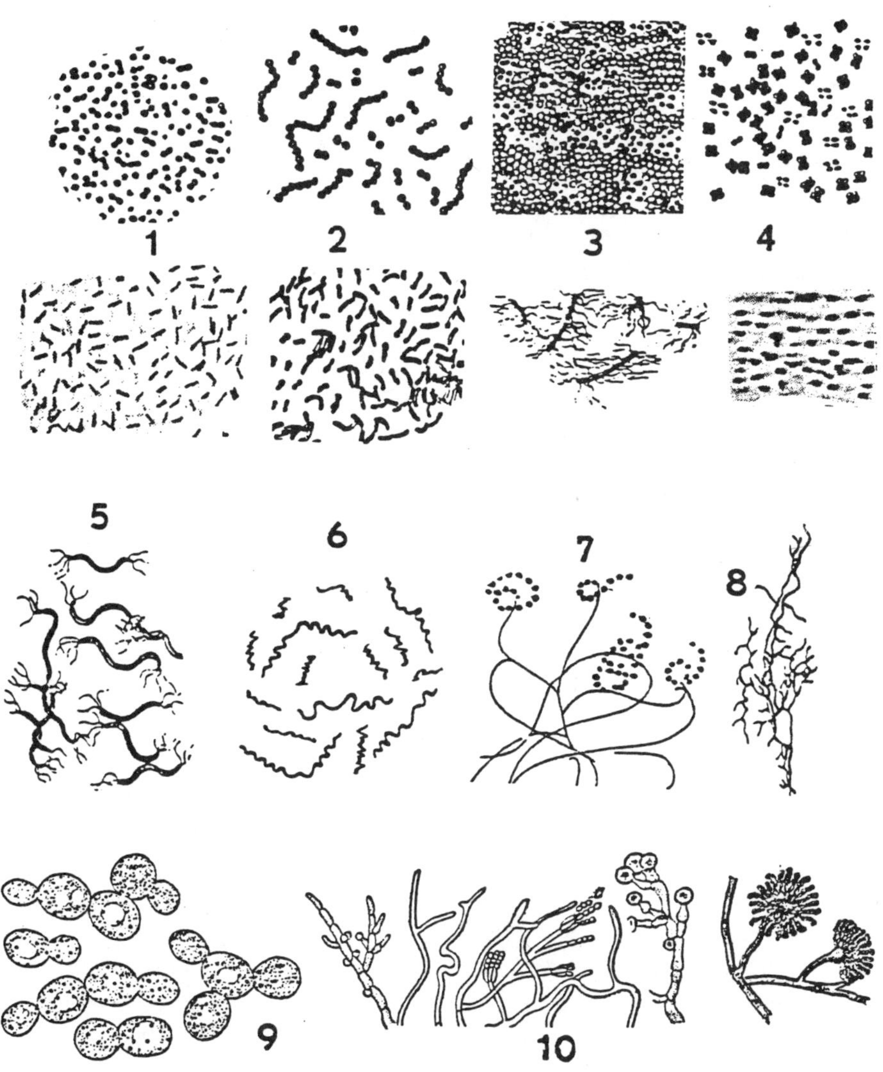

Figure 13.1. Some common bacteria. Top row: 1. a *Micrococcus,* 2. a *Streptococcus,* 3. a *Staphylococcus,* 4. a *Sarcina*. Second row. 1. *Escherichia coli,* 2. a non-motile *Bacillus*, 3. a motile *Bacillus*, 4. endospores, Third row. 5. a *Spirullum*, 6. a *Spirochaete*, 7. a *Streptomycete*, 8. an *Actinomycete*, Fourth row. 9. a yeast, and 10. several common fungi (molds).

Much information about interactions between the normal microbes that reside in the colon and their animal (including human) hosts has been collected by using germ-free animals as experimental models. These animals are obtained by caesarean sections to prevent the normal aquisition of microbes from their mothers during delivery. These animals are then maintained under sterile conditions that prevent their subsequent establishment of a normal microbial population. Compared to conventional animals the germ-free animals are much more susceptible to infection, stress and deficiency diseases. They frequently develop anatomical abnormalities such as incomplete mucosa and an enlargement of the cecum (Figure 13.2). They develop deficiencies of various nutrients such as vitamins and amino acids. Their anatomic morphology, nutritional needs and functions return to normal after the natural bacteria are introduced. The adaptation of microbes to their hosts, dates back hundreds of millions of years. Even termites have as many as one hundred billion friendly microbes per gram content of their G.I. tract. As with other animal species, germ-free termites are unable to survive in a healthy condition.

Fermentative microbes such as lactic acid bacteria (e.g. those found in yogurt) generally play beneficial roles for their healthy animal hosts. It is only a small minority of gut microbes which actually cause disease in their hosts. They build communities and an ecosystem pertinent to that environment (i.e., to the particular host and substrates to which they have adapted). The particular colonic microbial flora that is established depends on the diet and other features of host homeostasis. All animals and humans interact with their normal microbes to obtain many nutrients and other benefits. Many omnivores, for example, get vitamin B12 and vitamin K from their colon microflora. Moreover, the colon microbes defend their hosts against microbial pathogens by preventing establishment of such pathogens in the G.I. tract.

A healthy human colon harbors as many as one hundred trillion (10^{14}) microbes representing many different species. Most of these microbes are members of so-called indigenous species, i.e. those that are permanent residents. Some however are transients which enter the body as contaminants of food, water and soil. Besides existing in the colon, large numbers of microbes of specific types reside on other body surfaces such as the skin, mouth and vagina. However, under healthy conditions most internal organs of the body such as the brain, heart and liver are completely sterile. Thus the term intestinal microflora refers to specific types of microorganisms that flourish primarily in the colon

The transient microbes that enter the colon may be friendly, or unfriendly pathogens. Some transients may remain harmless until a favorable opportunity arises and then they become mild or serious pathogens. Thus it is not always easy to distinguish harmful from harmless transients. *Candida albicans*, for example, is a transient yeast often found as a part of the microflora of the healthy human body. However, it may become a mild or serious pathogen for people whose immune defences have been weakened by malnutrition, over-

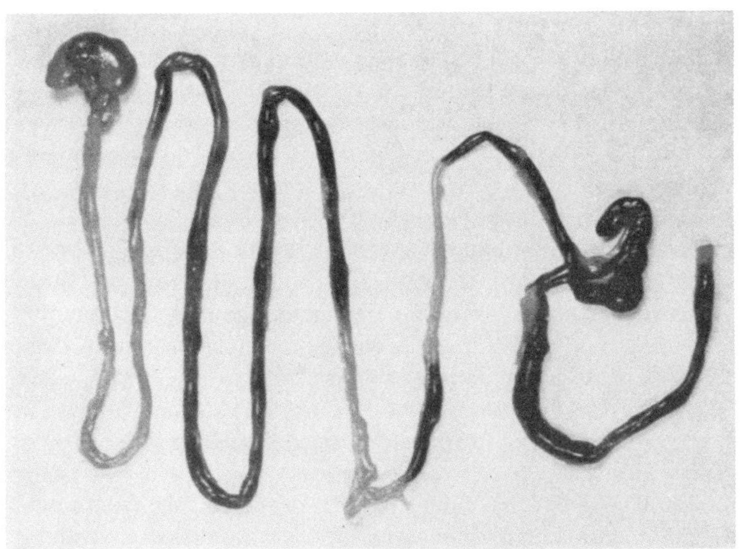

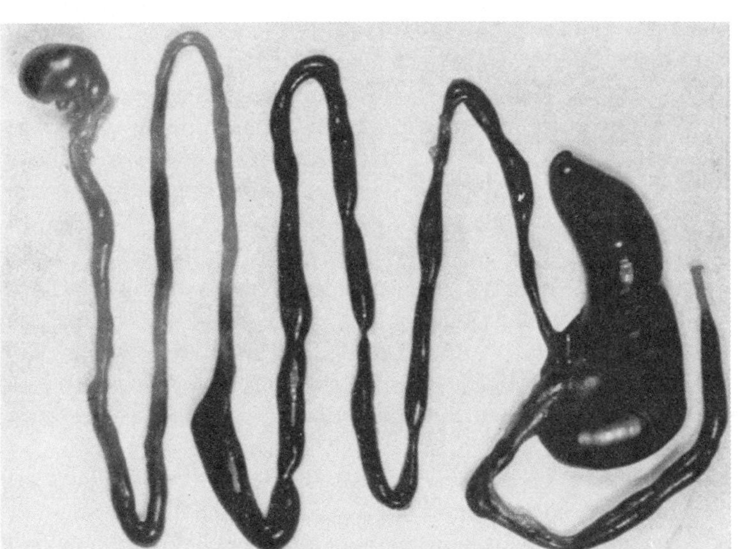

Figure 13.2. G.I. tract of a germ-free mouse (left) is compared to that of a normal mouse (right). Notice the enormous size of caecum of the germ-free caecum. Structural and metabolic abnormalities occur in germ-free animals. (Contributed by Dr. H.A. Gordon)

nutrition, chronic disorders such as diabetes, infectious diseases such as AIDS, and destructive habits such as alcohol and drug abuse.

All animals acquire a distinctive population of permanent microbial residents very early in life. These microbes are maintained by the specific diet and environment of the organism. Both mice and humans, have lactic acid producing indigenous bacteria, but the particular species, and hence the biochemical activities they perform in their hosts, are not same. In humans, under the conditions of a high roughage diet, fermentative species dominate the indigenous flora while proteolytic (protein-digesting) species are suppressed. However, changing the diet and lifestyle of a person can quickly alter their relative prevalence their specific microbes very early in life.

Approximately 30% of the volume of the contents of the human colon are microbes. Most of them prefer to metabolize carbohydrates fermentatively. The metabolic activities of these organisms determine the chemical environment and the ecology of the colon. As a consequence of evolution, these microbes display a tremendous versatility in their ability to proliferate, transform chemicals and scavenge nutrients from the ingested foods of the host. In a healthy adult the bifidobacteria, lactobacilli, the coliforms, and bacteroides exist as a mutually interacting ecosystem. The relative numbers in each group may vary from time to time but the overall stability of the gut microflora does not alter readily unless individuals change their diet or lifestyle drastically.

Bifidobacteria and other acidogenic (fermentative) bacteria which cannot tolerate oxygen (strict anaerobes) are associated in the colon with those that love oxygen (aerobes) or tolerate it (facultative anaerobes). By utilizing products each other cannot tolerate, or by generating secondary products that are valuable metabolites, different microbes establish a mutually supportive environment. Thus their relationship to each other resembles in some ways their symbiosis with their human host, and makes a well adapted microbial population a particularly resilient barrier to the permanent establishment of normally transient species. The beneficial role played by microbes in the human colon includes subtle features such as diminution of lactose intolerance (inability of the host to digest milk sugar), which can be offset by the presence of a large population of lactase-producing microbes. Likewise, patients with liver failure are particularly sensitive to the presence of proteolytic microflora which can generate more ammonia than their diminished hepatic clearance mechanisms can handle, resulting in coma. (see Chapter 11).

Around 1900, Tissier, a French scientist reported that the bifidobacteria were the dominant microbes in the feces of all healthy breast fed infants. This was confirmed to be true for infants in many parts of the world. Bifidobacterial domination was responsible for the acidity (pH 5.0), liquid consistency and cheesy odor of the feces of the nursing infants. The feces (meconium) of many rural Guatemalan infants examined within four hours after natural birth showed a mixed bacterial population, but after four days of nursing the bifidobacteria rapidly increased to a population of 100 billion cells comprising almost 100% of the colon flora. Paul György, a physician researcher attributed bifidobacterial growth to the unique composition of breast milk, a food rich in diverse sugars and low in protein concentration (see Chapter 16).

Why is establishment of bifidobacterial predominance of the infants colonic microflora so important? These microbes adhere firmly to the mucosa, allowing it to be thickly populated, thereby suppressing establishment of potential pathogens. Furthermore acids and other chemicals produced by the bifidobacteria inhibit the growth of many undesirable organisms in the colon environment. When breast-fed infants encounter pathogens such as Escherichia, Shigella and Salmonella that can cause diarrheal diseases, they fare far better than formula-fed infants not only because of immunoglobulins ingested in the milk, but also because of their microbial environment. The colon microflora of formula-fed infants and children after weaning resemble more closely the mixed microflora of the adults (see Chapter 16). Their stool characteristics, consistency, pH and odor all resemble those of adults. The pH of the feces varies between 6.0 and 7.0. However, as long as the diet remains rich in bulk and diverse carbohydrates, the colon microbial population will remain stable, fermentative and beneficial.

As early as 1907, Eli Metchnikoff, a Russian microbiologist working at the Pasteur Institute in Paris, noticed that Bulgarian peasants, maintained striking health and longevity. He suspected that their excellent health was related to their diet and noted that they habitually consumed large quantities of fermented milk (yogurt and buttermilk). He postulated that fermented milk, rich in lactic acid bacteria, flood the intestine and reduced the activity of undesirable microbes, with marked effects on health and longevity. These and other observations led Metchnikoff to propose a theory of "autointoxication." In spite of many controversial aspects, his work remains a classic in the microbiologic literature, even to this day.

Around the 1920's, investigators such as Leo Rettger of Yale University tried to derive beneficial results by populating the G.I. track with lactic bacteria. It became quite evident that a stable population of acidogenic bacteria cannot be maintained in the colon without a diet rich in complex carbohydrates (see Chapters 5 and 6). Muting and associates in the 1960's reported that they were able to prevent hepatic encephalopathy in many of their liver cirrhosis patients by incorporating fermentative bacteria that reduced the production and accumulation of ammonia in the colon by suppressing ammonia producing proteolytic bacteria.

In the 1900's, Christian Herter and Arthur Kendall, two American microbiologists found that the intestinal microflora of monkeys fed with eggs (a high protein diet) became proteolytic. The monkeys became drowsy and their urine and feces showed toxic products of putrefaction such as indican, indole and aromatic acids. In the 1940's Frederick Gale and others microbiologists reported that intestinal microbes can metabolize amino acids into ammonia and bioamines such as indican, indole and histamine and aromatic and phenolic compounds. All of the byproducts can cause deleterious effects to their hosts. From experimental animals they also isolated many bacteria that metabolize various amino acids. A microbiological process of protein decomposition under anaerobic conditions (putrefacation) is carried out by colonic microbes. This process generates foul-smelling compounds that are quite toxic.

According to some reports microbial metabolites of the amino acid tryptophan, such as skatole and indole, may have a role in diverse ailments including schizophrenia, rhumatoid arthritis, hepatic coma, pulmonary edema, exacerbation of emphysema, allergic reactions, induction of certain cancers, and development of stomach ulcers. The primary factors that influence the microbes to produce bioamines from various amino acids are the availability of amino acids, the pH and the kinds of bacteria populating the colon. Depending upon the amount of, and conditions in which, the amino acid tryptophan is available to certain colon bacteria, hazardous metabolites such as tryptamine, indole and skatole may be produced. According to W.T. Irwine and associates of the University of London, when meat in the diet supplies a considerable amount of the amino acid L-histidine, the bacteria transform histidine to histamine by decarboxylation. Even small amounts of bioamines such as histamine, tryptamine and tyramine absorbed at physiological doses, especially when the liver fails to inactivate them, can have grave consequences as indicated above.

Many scientists have come to the conclusion that people constantly exposed to the lactic acid bacteria that are abundantly found on green plants, in milk and in fermenting foods, maintain a stable fermentative microflora. This colonic bacterial population prevents proliferation of pathogenic and undesirable microbes, thereby protecting human health.

In 1961 a German scientist, H. Haenel, examined many Bulgarians over the age of 80 years and found that there was little change in the indigenous intestinal microflora with age. He attributed the stability of their intestinal microflora to lifelong maintenance by their diet rich in carbohydrates, and especially, their high consumption of milk and yogurt.

In 1972 the British scientists, B.S. Draser and M.J. Hill compared the fecal flora of people living in Uganda, India and Japan whose diet consisted of carbohydrate rich staples (banana and rice) with those of people living in England, Scotland and the U.S. whose dietary staple was meat. They found that increased animal protein and fat increased the number of bacteroides in the fecal flora. Long term animal experiments also showed that bulky carbohydrate diets increase acid producing fecal flora whereas meat staple diets favor clostridia.

In 1989 Yoshimo Benno, a Japanese scientist, and his colleagues, compared the colon microflora of a group of healthy elderly persons in rural areas whose median age was 84 and who consumed a high residue diet to that of individuals living in Tokyo City whose median age was 68 and consumed a low residue diet. He reported that the people of the rural areas had a larger bifidobacterial population and a much smaller number of clostridia and enteric bacteria than the urban group. He also found that such disparities can be remedied to a large extent by changing from a low residue diet to one of high residue. American scientists who examined the fecal flora of group on various diets found that Seventh-Day Adventists and other healthy vegetarians had higher counts of fermentative bacteria and smaller numbers of coliforms and clostridia than others.

In addition to their role in preventing colonization of the colon with undesirable microbes, the fermentative microflora of the colon contribute to the welfare of the human body by producing a variety of beneficial chemicals such as acetic, butyric and propionic acids from carbohydrate residue scavenged from dietary waste. These compounds are taken up and used as energy sources by both microbes and their human hosts. Such organic acids may provide over 500 food calories daily for humans. These compounds may also be inhibitory to the establishment of many transient microbes and even to the development of neoplastic cells.

Likewise, fermentative microflora are an important source of vitamins. Generally germ-free animals are noted to be deficient in vitamin B1, B2, B6, B12, pantothenic acid, biotin and vitamin K. These deficiencies gets corrected when indigenous bacteria are introduced into their G.I. tracts. Healthy omnivores, including humans, obtain significant amounts of vitamin K and B12, among others, from their gut microflora. Presumably for this reason, healthy vegans (those who do not consume any animal products at all), do not suffer from deficiencies of these vitamins.

Germ-free animals are observed to instinctively eat the feces of conventional animals (coprophagy) and thereby establish a normal microbial flora, which usually corrects their vitamin and other nutritional deficiencies. Compared to conventional animals, germ-free animals also have a very slow rate of cholesterol metabolism. Their cholesterol metabolism can be improved with the introduction of certain indigenous bacteria.

A delicate equilibrium exists among various groups of colon microbes. Factors such as changes in lifestyle, stress, old age, undernutrition, overnutrition, G.I. motility (e.g. as a complication of diabetes and other chronic diseases) can all alter the microbial population. The alterations that take place in the change from nursing to weaning or from youth to old age will not, by themselves, alter the stability of fermentative bacteria as predominant in the colon. The fermentative character of the bacterial population can be changed, however by the diet. When volunteers were fed with a chemically balanced liquid diet devoid of bulk, the total population of microbes and the quantity of feces voided decreased drastically and bifidobacteria and lactobacilli largely disappeared. Microbial changes also occur in the G.I. tract of people who are chronically depressed, in people subjected to longtime chemotherapy, after surgery and other forms of stress.

Since the 1940's, dietary changes such as consuming a low residue and high meat diet, the use of food additives such as cyclamates and aspartame, the use of hormones and antibiotics in raising meat animals and the increased use of pesticides in raising food crops all have contributed to altering the indigenous beneficial colon microflora, especially in the industrialized countries (see Chapter 4 and 11). Some scientists believe that such changes have altered the indigenous microflora so much that many individuals have become compromised hosts for pathogens with a weakened first line of defence. This may make them easy targets for invasion by transient bacteria such as Legionella (which causes Legionnaire's disease). Physiological factors such as chronic malabsorption, constipation and degenerative diseases also make individuals vulnerable to disseminating pathogenic transients from the colon to other parts of the body. In such cases, the issues of the cause and the consequence of disease become confused. The current AIDS epidemic is an example of this kind of situation where common pathogens unable to infect individuals with an intact immune system but can cause overwhelming disease in the immunocompromised AIDS patient.

Around 1950's many scientists noticed a correlation between the frequency of bowel cancer and the quantity of meat consumed. M.J. Hill and co-workers in England documented the increased number of carcinogen producing bacteria in the bowel of animals fed with a high meat diet. During the 1970's they experimented by placing five volunteers on high-beef diet and a control group on a meatless diet for about four weeks. The fecal flora of those consuming a high meat diet showed dominating bacteroides whereas the other group had more coliforms. This trend was evident in several studies. Other scientists in many parts of the world who compared fecal samples of people at low risk of cancer to those at high risk found a remarkable similarity to people who consumed a diet rich in plant staples and those who consumed diet rich in animal protein and fat, respectively.

Scientists also found that the fecal samples obtained from people at high risk of cancer contained more bile acid and the microbes that metabolize them to carcinogens than did a low risk group. They also found a large number of clostridia in the gut microbial populations of high risk people and in cancer patients. The American scientists Ernst Winder, B.S. Reddy and others engaged in cancer research found that cancer patients with cancers of the large intestine excreted increased bile acids. Whether from Japan or Scotland, those who consumed a western type diet had more clostridia and bacteroides whereas those who consumed a diverse carbohydrate-rich bulky diet had more fermentative microflora. Many of these investigators came to the conclusion that the intestinal bacteria modify a very wide range of chemicals that reach the colon, such as protein, fat and cholesterol of dietary origin, bodily secretions, food additives, pesticides and heavy metal contaminants and generate carcinogens, precarcinogens or cocarcinogens.

Studies suggest that high meat and low residue diets aid the microbial transformation of chemicals and predispose individuals to many cancers including colon, breast and of prostate. Epidemiologic investigations have also shown that the mortality rate from those cancers is high in industrialized countries where meat consumption is also high and that mortality from those cancers is low among people of developing countries who consume a higher proportion of complex carbohydrates in their diet. Breast tumors have been induced in experimental animals by feeding them with beef diet or a diet rich in animal fat. The fecal flora of such animals also showed a larger number of microbes that were selected for metabolizing steroids, bile acids, aromatic and phenolic compounds compared to control animals fed a regular chow diet.

Healthy animals herded for slaughtering are also known to shed Salmonella suddenly. Administering broad spectrum antibiotics also increases the number of Candida albicans and other fungi in the human gut microflora.

According to microbial ecologists, many pathogens become established when the indigenous microflora is diminsihed. Shigella infection, for example, is known to take place when the normal coliform population that keeps them in check is weakened or disrupted.

Carl Lamanna, a distinguished American microbiologist addressing the 2nd International Symposium on intestinal mcirobiology pointed out that we have dynamic microbiological systems that are disturbed by changes in our diet and habits, and as a result, the microbes are capable in turn, of changing from friend to foe.

Scientific studies done around the world show that diet rather than nationality (genetics) is primarily responsible for many cancers. Many scientists are of the opinion that the intestinal microflora, which is intimately connected with the diet, and which constitute an integral part of the human environment, may be involved in causing or preventing 80% of certain types of human cancer. As René Dubos, a well known microbiologist pointed out, the microorganisms are so versatile that many characteristics that we take for granted as genetic changes in reality may be caused by colonic microbial action.

Selected Sources and Suggested Readings

Gerald D. Abrams, 1969. Effects of the normal flora on host defences against microbial invasion. *Germ-Free Biology,* 197-206

Atif B. Award, Peter J Horvath, and Martha S. Andersen, 1991. Influence of butyrarte on lipid metabolism, survival, and differentiation of colon cancer cells. *Nutrition and Cancer,* 16, 125-133

Helen Baldwin, 1909-1910. Observations on the influence of lactic acid ferments upon intestinal putrefaction in a healthy individual. *J. Biological Chemistry,* 7, 37-48

John C. Banwell and Sherwood L. Gorbach, 1969. Tropical sprue. *Gut,* 10, 328-333

Henri Beerens, C. Romond, and C. Neut, 1980. Influence of breast-feeding on the bifido flora of the newborn intestine. *Americn J. Clinical Nutrition,* 33, 2434- 2439

Rodney D. Berg, 1980. Mechanisms confining indigenous bacteria to the gastrointestinal tract. *American J. Clinical Nutrition,* 33, 2472-2484

Olaf Bergeim, et al., 1941. Relation of volatile fatty acids and hydrogen sulphide to the intestinal flora. *J. Infectious Disease,* 69, 155-166

H. Bernhardt and Philip S. Hench, 1931. Bacteriology of the blood in chronic infectious arthitis. *J Infectious Disease,* 49, 489-496

Debra Jan Bibel, 1988. Elie Metchnikoff's bacillus of long life. *ASM News,* 54, 661-665

Victor D. Bokkenheuser, Jeanette Winter and William G. Kelly, 1978. Metabolism of biliary steroids by human fecal flora. *American J. Clinical Nutrition,* 31, S221-S226

T.D. Bolin, et al., 1970. Lactose intolerance in Singapore. *Gastroenterology,* 59, 76-84

J. Harvey Borden, 1906-1907. The elimination of indoxyl sulphate in the urine of the insane. *J. Biological Chemistry,* 2, 575-601

George H. Bornside, 1978. Stability of human fecal flora. *American J. Clinical Nutrition,* 31, S141-S144

George T. Bryan, 1971. The role of urinary tryptophan metabolites in the etiology of bladder cancer. *American J. Clinical Nutrition,* 24, 841-847

George T. Bryan, 1966. Quantitative studies on the urinary excretion of indoxyl sulfate (indican) in man following administration of L-tryptophan and acetyl-L- tryptophan. *American J. Clinical Nutrition,* 19, 105-112

M.P. Bryant, 1978. Cellulose digesting bacteria from human feces. *American J. Clinical Nutrition,* 31, S113-S115

D.H. Calloway and S.E. Burroughs, 1969 Effect of dried beans and silicone on intestinal hydrogen and methane production in man. *Gut,* 10, 180-184

I.T. Cavalli-Sforza and A. Strata, 1986. Double-blind study on the tolerance of four types of milk in lactose malabsorbers and absorbers. *Human Nutrition: Clinical Nutrition,* 40C, 19-30

Steven K. Clinton, PI-Hsueh Shirley and Willard J. Visek, 1985. The combined effects of dietary protein and fat on prolactin in female rats. *J. Nutrition,* 115, 311-318

Marie E. Coates, 1973. Gnotobiotic animals in nutrition research. *Proc. Nutrition Society,* 32, 53-58

John H. Cummings, Fermentation in the human large intestine: Evidence and implications for health. *Lancet,* 1, 1206-1208

Michael DeVrese, Birgit Keller and Christian A Barth, 1992. Enhancement of intestinal hydrolysis of lactose by microbial B-galactosidase (EC 3.2.1.23) of Kefir. *British J. Nutrition,* 55, 67-75

Lennart Domellof, et al., 1982. Fecal sterols and bacterial B-glucuronidase activity: A preliminary metabolic epidemiology study of healthy volunteers from Umea, Sweedn, and Metropolitan New York. *Nutrition and Cancer,* 4, 120-127

René Dubos, Russell W. Schaedler and Richard Costello, 1963. Composition, alteration, and effects of the intestinal flora. Federation Proceedings, 22, 1322-1329

B.S. Draser and M.J. Hill, *Human Intestinal Flora.* Academic Press, London New Yok, 1974.

B.S. Draser, et al., 1973. The relation between diet and the gut microflora in man. *Proc. Nutrition Society,* 32, 49-52

B.S. Draser and M.J.Hill, 1972. Intestinal bacteria and cancer. *American J. Clinical Nutrition,* 25, 1399-1404

H. Eyssen, 1973. Role of gut microflora in metabolism of lipids and sterols. *Proc. Nutrition Society,* 32, 59-63

Custy F. Fernandes and Khem M. Shahani, 1989. Lactose inteolerance and its modulation with lactobacilli and other microbial supplements. *J. Applied Nutrition,* 41, 51-64

Martin H. Floch, Sherwood L. Gorbach and Thomas D. Luckey, 1970. Introduction. Symposium on Intestinal Microflora. *American J. Clinical Nutrition,* 23, 1425-1426

Rolf Fretter, 1974. Interactions between mechanisms controlling the intestinal microflora. American J. clinical Nutrition, 27, 1409-1416

Ernest F. Gale, 1940. 102. The production of amines by bacteria. *Biochemical J.* 34, 846-852

L.S. Gall, 1970. Normal fecal flora of man. *American J. Clinical Nutrition,* 23, 1457-1465

Stewart A.W. Gibson, et al., 1989. Significance of microflora in proteolysis in the colon. *Applied and Environmental Microbiology,* 55, 679-683

Sherwood L. Gorbach, 1967. Population control in the small bowel. *Gut,* 8, 530-532

N.Y. Haboubi, R.D. Montgomery, 1992. Small-bowel bacterial overgrowth in elderly people: Clinical significance and response to treatment. *Age and Ageing,* 21, 13-19

Helmut Haenel, 1970. Human normal and abnormal gastrointestinal flora. *American J. Clinical Nutrition,* 23, 1433-1439

H. Haenel, 1951. Some rules in the ecology of the intestinal microflora of man. *J. Applied Bacteriology,* 24, 242-251

Bernard J. Haverback, Barbara Dyce and Heriberto V. Thomas, 1960. Indole metabolism in the malabsorption syndrome.*New England J. Medicine,* 262, 754-757

C.A. Herter and A.I. Kendall, 1909-1910. The influence of dietary alternations on the type of intestinal flora. *J. Biological Chemistry,* 7, 203-217

M.J. Hill et al., 1975. Faecal bile-acids and clostridia in patients with cancer of the large bowel. *Lancet,* 1, 535-539

M.J. Hill, P Goddard, and R.E.O. Williams, 1971. Gut bacteria and aetiology of cancer of the breast. *Lancet,* 2, 472-473

Elsie Hill and W. R. Bloor,1922. Fat excretion, *J. Biological Chemistry,* 53, 171-177

Eileen Hilton, et al., 1992. Ingestion of yogurt containing *Lactobacillus acidophilus* as prophylaxis for candidal vaginitis. *Annals of Internal Medicine,* 116, 353-357

Jos H.J. Huls in t Veld and Robert Havenaar, 1991. Orobiotics and health in man and animal. *European J. Clinical nutrition,* 45, 29-31

E.F. Hungate, 1978. Bacterial ecology in the small intestine. *American J. Clinical Nutrition,* 31, S125-S127

Henry Isenberg and James Berkman, 1970 ?. The role of drug-resistant and drug-selected bacteria in nosocomial disease. *Annals New York Academy of Sciences,* 52-58

Henry D. Isenberg, et al., 1960. Factors leading to overt monilial disease. *Antibiotics and Chemotherapy,* 10, 353-363

Yasuo Kawai, et al., 1980. Distribution and colonization of human fecal streptococci. *American J. Clinical Nutrition,* 33, 2458-2461

Arthur Kendall and Chester J. Farmer, 1912-1913. Studies in bacterial metabolism. VII. *J. Biological Chemistry,* 13, 63-70

Joseph C. Kolar, et al., 1984. Yogurt- An autodigesting source of lactose. *New England J. Medicine,* 310, 1-3

Malcolm Koo and A. Venkateshwer Rao, 1991. Long-term effect of bifidobacteria and neosugar on precursor lesions of colonic cancer in CF1 mice. *Nutrition and Cancer,* 16, 249-257

B.T. Lingappa and Yamuna Lingappa, 1969. Autoantibiotics. Worcester, *Medical News,* May, 5-6

Thomas D. II. Luckey and Martin H. Flock, 1972. Intestinal Microbiology. II. International Symposium. *American J. Clinical Nutrition,* 25, 1291-1490

T.D. Luckey, 1970. Introduction to the ecology of the intestinal flora. *American J. Clinical Nutrition,* 23, 1430-1432

Thomas D. Luckey. *Germfree Life and Gnotobiology.* Academic Press, New York. London. 1963

William A. A. G. Macbeth, Edward H. Kass and William V. McDermott, 1965. Treatment of hepatic encephalopathy by alteration of intestinal flora with *Lactobacillus acidophilus. Lancet,* 1, 399-403

Bruce R. Maier, et al., 1974. Effects of a high-beef diet on bowel flora: a preliminary report. *American J. Clinical Nutrition,* 27, 1470-1474

A.K. Mallett, I.R. Rowland, 1990. Bacterial enzymes: Their role in the formation of mutagens and carcinogens in the intestine. *Digestive Disease,* 8, 71-79

Lynn Margulis, David Chase, and Ricardo Guerrero, 1986. Microbial communities. *BioScience,* 36, 160-170

Ph. Marteau, Ph Pochart, 1991. Effect of probiotics on intestinal metabolism. *European J. Clinical Nutrition,* 45, (Suppl.2) 35-37

Philippe Marteau, et al., 1990. Effect of the microbial lactate (EC 3.2.1.23) activity in yogurt on the intestinal absorption of lactose: an in vivo study in lactase-deficient humans. *British J. Nutrition,* 64, 71-79

Margaret C. Martini, et al., 1987. Lactose digestion by yogurt B-galactosidase: influence of pH and microbial cell integrity. *American J. Clinical Nutrition,* 45, 432-436

Michael I. Mcburney Peter J. Van Soest and Joseph l Jeraci, 1987. Colonic carcinogenesis: the microbial feast or famine mechanism. *Nutrition and Cancer,* 10, 23-28

I. Nakoneczna, J.C. Forbes and K.S. Rogers, 1969. The arthitogenic effect of indole, skatole and other tryptophan metabolites in rabbits. *American J. Pathology,* 57, 523-532

D.P. Nelson and L.J. Mata, 1970. Bacterial flora associated with the human gastrointestinal mucosa. *Gastroenterology,* 56, 56-61

Albert D. Newcomer, and Douglas B. McGill, 1984. Clinical importance of lactase deficiency. *New England J. Medicine,* 310, 42-43

D. Parratt, 1980. Nutrition and immunity. *Proc. Nutrition Society,* 39, 133-140

James A. Poupard, Intisar Husain, and Robert F. Norris, 1973. Biology of bifidobacteria. *Bacteriological Reviews,* 37, 136-165

L.F. Rettger and H.A. Chaplin. *A Treatise on the Transformation of the Acidophillus and its Therapeutic Applications.* Yale University Press, 1921

Leo Rettger and Clyde R. Newell, 1912-1913. Putrefaction with special reference to the proteus group. *J. Biological Chemistry,* 13, 341-346

Edmund A. Richards, F.R. Steggerda and A. Murata, 1968. Relationship of bean substrates and certain intestinal bacteria to gas production in the dog. *Gastroenterology,* 55, 503-509

Ian Rowland, 1981. The influence of the gut microflora on food toxicity. *Proc. Nutrition Society,* 40, 67-74

W.E. Sandine, et al., 1972. Lactic acid bacteria in food and health: A review with special reference to enteropathogenic *Escherichia coli* as well as certain enteric diseases and their treatment with antibiotics and lactobacilli. *J. Milk Food Technology,* 35, 691-702

Dwyne C. Savage, 1979. Introduction to mechanisms of association of indigenous microbes. *American J. Clinical Nutrition,* 32, 113-118

R.W. Schaedler, 1973. The relationship between the host and its intestinal microflora. *Proc. nutrition Society,* 32, 41-47

Khem M. Shahani, and Amada D. Ayebo, 1980. Role of dietary lactobacilli in gastrointestinal microecology. *American J. Clinical Nutrition,* 33, 2448-2457

Charles J. Smith and Marvin P. Bryant, 1979. Introduction to metabolic activities of intestinal bacteria. *American J. Clinical Nutrition,* 32, 149-157

H. William Smith, 1965. Observations on the flora of the alimentary tract of animals and factors affecting its composition. *J. Path. Bact.* 89, 95-122

M.L. Speck, 1975. Interactions among lactobacilli and man. J. *Dairy Science,* 59, 338-343

H. Spiera, 1966. Rheumatoid arthritis. *Arthritis and Rheumatism,* 9, 318-324

Katherine Sprunt, 1980. Normal throat bacteria protect against infection. NIH Division of Research Resources, The general Clinical Research Center at Babies Hospital, *Resource Reporter,* September, 1-4

R. Walker, 1973. The influence of gut micro-organisms on the metabolism of drugs and food additives. *Proc Nutrition Society*, 32, 73-78

Karen J. Wedekind, Howard R. Mansfield and Larry Montgomery, 1988. Enumeration and isolation of cellulolytic and hemicellulolytic bacteria from human feces. *Applied and Environmental Microbiology,* 54, 1530-1535

H.S.Wiggins,et al., 1969. The origin of fecal fat. *Gut,* 10, 400-403

Tracy D. Wilkins, et al., 1980. Characterization of a mutagenic bacterial product in human feces. *American J. Clinical Nutrition,* 33, 2513-2520

James P. Witter, S. John Gatley and Edward Balish, 1981. Evaluation of nitrate synthesis by intestinal microorganisms in vivo. *Science,* 213, 449-450

PART D

A Diet Tailored by Evolution

14

Human Evolution, Traditional Culture and Diet

Abstract: Omnivores (including primates) have evolved to be nourished by complex carbohydrates. Ancient populations had firm ideas as to what constituted wholesome food based on the experience of earlier generations and by their environment, technology and economy. These diets were, in general, characterized by the presence of a variety of complex carbohydrate food types, especially prior to the full scale development of commercial agriculture. These diets were also characterized by low nutrient density due to the presence of bulk (undigestible fiber), simply because the technology for extensive food processing (by which modern preparation removes indigestible fiber), was not in existence. Since our ancestors and other primates evolved consuming such diets, it is not surprising that our physiological economy is optimized when nourished by complex carbohydrates. Likewise, it is only natural that the subsequently such diets would be incorporated into culture as it developed. Traditional philosophical and medical systems incorporated these diets. The Indian systems of Yoga and Ayurvedic medicine are discussed as examples. The scientific and industrial revolutions of the last century have changed the way people live and the diets they eat, by emphasizing protein, refined food products and concentrated nutrients. Unfortunately, this approach is largely disconnected from the evolutionary and cultural history that determine what constitutes the optimal diet for humans as reflected in cultural dietary traditions characterized by bulk and variety of complex carbohydrates.

Pre-Historic and Traditional Cultures and their Diets

The adaptation of humans to a sub-saturated diet of bulk and variety has a long history. Adaption to variety and bulk can be traced from herbivores to the omnivorous primates, our closest ancestors. Primates are known to consume a wide variety of plants and plant parts for their flavors, unlike carnivores who have adapted to concentrated nutrients with less variety. Wild populations of monkeys have been known to select and consume over a hundred varieties of plants and their parts. Pre-historic people also had a diet rich in bulk and variety because the large number of food plants available to them then contributed more dietary fiber than is obtained from a diet of selected cultivated plants. Plants of great variety complemented the nutrients of their diet and regulated their bowel.

Humans evolved with this diet, which became part of the legacy of the peoples to ancient cultures. The four thousand year old word "Annapurna" means wholesome food in Sanskrit. It conveys the meaning that wholesome food is one which maintains the well-being of all parts of the body. Wholesome food contained preparations made out of various grains, pulses, nuts, vegetables and fruits, herbs and spices in addition to milk, yogurt and butter. The early Hindus were obsessed with their dietary regimen. During the Vedic period they spent an enormous time thinking about, deliberating on and developing various dietary disciplines. They developed a dietary philosophy (vegetarianism), a discipline of life itself (yoga) and a system of medicine (Ayurveda) with diet central to each. The lifestyle which evolved then integrated not only the external environment but also the cosmos (see Chapter 20).

The discipline of yoga emphasized diet as the most influential factor in the promotion of positive health for the mind and the body. Positive health was defined as the condition of being free from sickness, feeling jubilant and taking an active part in all aspects of natural life. The composition of the diet was thought to influence growth, health, behavior, intellectual development and longevity of the body. Even as early as the 7th century, the Hindu physician Susruta diagnosed diabetes as a sickness and tried to remedy it through a dietary regimen. The belief that through diet one can influence the health, behavior and intellectual capacity of people lead the Hindus to develop dietary guidelines to achieve social goals. A lacto-vegetarian diet was prescribed to develop the mind over the body and bring about intellectual achievement, gentleness and a philosophical attitude. Rich food such as meat and other animal products were used to promote physical strength, robustness and a warrior like attitude.

Occasional fasting and sub-saturated or meager diets were suggested for prolonging healthy life after middle-age. Special diets were prescribed for pre-puberty, post-puberty, during pregnancy, after childbirth and even for life after retirement. The ancient Hindus divided the society (cast system) according to people's professions and prescribed various dietary regimens to improve their adaptation to their work. Over the course of time the system was corrupted into a mechanism of repression. All sedentary intellectuals (Brahmins and Vyshyas) were restricted to a lacto-vegetarian diet, professional military (Kshatriyas) and hard working farmers and laborers (Shudras) were allowed to eat meat, fish and other animal products. Irrespective of their professions, middle-aged people were encouraged to decrease the rich foods in their diet and to observe more fasts than feasts. The young and pregnant women were encouraged to eat plentifully and avoid fasting. Both authors were raised in families which followed these dietary traditions for centuries.

Even though no scientific evaluation of such a dietary regimen had been made, many generations of Hindus have grown up being nourished in this way. These dietary regimens were not restricted to one area of the country even though the varieties of foods consumed varied slightly from region to region. People in the north and northwest for example, used wheat as the primary staple whereas people in southern and eastern India used rice and millet. Variations in eating existed even from family to family. However, the dietary philosophy and principles integrated the people of all regions. Currently, less than 10% of the population of India profess to be lacto-vegetarians. They reside in all regions of the country.

Ayurveda, the ancient Hindu medicinal system still popular in India, is deeply rooted in the belief that diet is responsible for positive health because it strengthens the self-healing innate power of the body, the Atma (what we might call homeostasis). The factors that strengthen and stabilize Atma can also influence the faculties of mind and change the individual's behavior towards positive thinking. When the diet fails to support the self-healing power, then discomfort or illness of the mind and the body (alasya) follows. Alasya may be due to improper or inadequate diet, sleep, elimination or conflicting rhythms of the body; or it may be due to changing factors in the external environment and the cosmos. All these factors were taken into consideration in preventing and curing diseases. All cures were intended to strengthen and stabilize the self-healing powers of the body more than to eliminate the "disease" or the diseased part.

Belief in strengthening the self-healing power through dietary disciplines also existed in other ancient cultures, such as the Chinese, Arabic and Greek. The Hippocratic system, which is the basis for modern medicine, also emphasized diet and self-healing. The native Americans and people of Africa believed in the healing power of diet. All of them utilized various plant ingredients. They utilized juices, extracts, decoctions, pastes and even ashes of leaves, bark, roots, fruits and seeds. These supplied missing ingredients to the diet and stimulated self-healing. Plant components such as antioxidants, flavinoids, carotenes, alkaloids, lecithins and various trace components can also bring about physiological effects such as sedating or stimulating certain organs, repairing muscles or regulating elimination. In Indian folklore, coffee, tea and various herb and spice decoctions (Kashaya) for example, were used as remedies for fever and mild forms of illness. Drinks made of poppy seeds and of ripe cashew fruits were used as mild sedatives. Other ancient cultures also utilized botanicals such as coca leaves, peyote and hallucinogenic mushrooms for relaxation. Some of these dietary ingredients (e.g. areca nuts and betel leaves) in variety and diluted forms served as stimulants but not necessarily as addictives (e.g. when used without tobacco). However, some natural products that are not addictive in their unprocessed form can become addictive when active ingredients are purified and concentrated. Use of such products was prohibitted by the yogic school of thought because they were felt to be "tamasic" (degrading and corrupting).

It was believed that excessive consumption of rich foods in middle age would cause ailments such as arthritis and other crippling diseases. Thus, even during festivities, people of middle and old age avoided rich foods. Traditionally, all over India, especially in the Udipi area, fried foods, sweets and nuts were eaten only occasionally. For those who did indulge in such dietary excesses, feasts were typically followed by fasts, which regulated the appetite and compensated for overeating. Many cultural practices promoted taste for varying seasonal foods and coordinated rhythmic cycles of the body. A rice staple diet was supplemented with lentils, milk, buttermilk in variety and bulk. While fish or meat were eaten by many, its consumption was small in amount and was suited to their life-style and environment.

Advantages Inherent in Traditional Diets

Traditional cultural diets are wholesome because they supply nutrients considerably diluted with bulk and in variety. A traditional Udipi dinner, for example, contains 10-15 different items each of which is made of 6 or more of unprocessed ingredients (leafy greens, lentils and whole grains). Even in unsophisticated traditional families of modest means, 2 to 3 different vegetables were served daily. Combining a variety of available food ingredients into dishes such as Indian curries, American stews, Italian pastas with sauce and Mexican tortillas with beans, rice and salsa are examples of traditional foods of various cultures that provided dilute nutrients with bulk and variety. Such diets did not burden the homeostatic regulation of the body with any one nutrient in high concentration. Adaptation of the body to variety and bulk played a major role in simplifying the appetite, controlling food calories and in achieving satiety, in many cultures. Sadly, recent surveys suggest that less than 1 in 4 Americans consumes such a diet today.

Many food ingredients such as sugars, fats and oils, vitamins, and minerals affect the entities of the body differently depending on whether they are provided as concentrated substances or in a sub-saturating form. For example, sugar consumed naturally in the form of oranges, grapes and apples has a very different effect on glucose absorption into the bloodstream and insulin secretion than does concentrated sweets. Thus, patients with diabetes mellitus are strongly urged to avoid concentrated sweets but are encouraged to consume moderate amounts of fresh fruit.

Vegetable oils consumed as part of natural products rarely cause hyperlipidemia or obesity, but often do so when stripped of all associated ingredients (see Chapter 8). Fat soluble vitamins and trace minerals consumed as high-roughage plant products which contain them are generally beneficial, even in large amounts. However toxicity can rapidly occur when they are ingested in purified and concentrated form (see Chapter 9 and 10).

Even relatively toxic chemicals such as indoles and isothiocynates exist naturally in dilute form in most cruciferous vegetables such as broccoli, cabbage and cauliflower. Not only are they NOT toxic in this form, but consumption of such vegetables have been found to reduce tumors that develop in carcinogen treated mice. Phytic acid, considered to be toxic, may make up as much as 3% of the dry weight of most legumes. Yet, legumes have been part of the healthy diets in almost all ancient cultures. Recent investigations have shed light on this seeming paradox: it has been shown that sub-saturating amounts of phytic acid increase the oxygen holding capacity of red blood cells and, thereby, may reduce the incidence of heart attacks and strokes.

Unprocessed plant materials contain many substances which are produced by the plants to serve as natural antibiotics or pesticides. These chemicals protect the plants from attack by insects and microbes. While they can also be toxic to humans if consumed in a concentrated form devoid of bulk, in their natural dilute state they may serve as a valuable form of dietary therapeutics. Even dietary fiber, a component of plant material, for example, consumed as dietary bulk stimulates the bowel and prevents constipation. However, an excess of fiber as an additive without associated nutrients, can cause diarrhea. Ayurvedic medicine considers bowel regularity basic to preventive medicine, and utilizes many plant materials to regulate the bowels.

Many plant species, which formerly were used in multiple varieties are now used in much more limited ways. The potato, a prominent food crop of industrialized countries, was introduced to Europe around 1500s by the Conquistadors. Many varieties of potato can serve as a food staple yet now there is only one high yielding white variety widely available. Yet the potato still serves as a staple to many millions of people of developing countries. Bananas and rice, staples to millions of people in the world, used to exist in hundreds of varieties where now but a few high yielding varieties are common. Likewise, the early native Americans living in North America used several hundred species of plants for food and medicine. According to anthropologists, hunter-gatherers derived abundant variety and bulk by consuming a wide variety of fruits and nuts in their broadest botanical sense.

When scientific nutrition shifted the emphasis from a wholesome diet with variety and bulk to valuing primarily the protein component of foods (the concept of biological value) they elevated the importance for the recommended diet of foods such as meats and eggs, rich in protein, over beans and whole grains rich in bulk (see Chapter 4). Efforts to increase consumption of such favored nutrients, especially protein, lead to the breeding of plants that yielded more protein or which had an abundant yield that could be fed to livestock for meat production. Gradually, the focus of agriculture in many industrialized countries including the U.S., became the production of crops related to meat production. Consequently, the numerous local plant varieties that fed people according to their environment and philosophy dwindled around the globe. Production of many varieties of whole grains, legumes, bananas and peanuts that served as staples, was also reduced. Vegetables such as amaranth, girasol, kohlrabi and fruits such as guava, jackfruit and pomegranate are becoming rare species even in the developing countries. In addition, fiber considered bulky was removed to concentrate nutrients. Even the "Green revolution" encouraged farmers to cultivate only those food crops that either had a high yield or a high protein content. Such efforts increased the yield of grain production as much as 100%. However, i t also reduced the variety of food plants from approximately 3,000 species to as few as 20 that serve key investment and marketing criteria.

Humans have survived with, and evolved for three million years on, a diet of bulk and variety. More cultures have fared better with a wholesome diet of bulk and variety than any other kind of diet. Over the past century, dietary recommendations emphasizing nutrient density over bulk and variety, hence favoring protein (especially animal) over unprocessed plant products, have resulted in decreased cultivation and availability of a wide variety of plant products and detrimental effects on health. A diet high in bulk and variety supplied by complex carbohydrates is the best diet for the people of affluent countries whose lives have become extremely sedentary. It is also the best diet for people of developing countries where supplying inexpensive healthy food is the priority. It is the kind of diet which has tailored the body's organ systems over the course of primate evolution.

Selected Sources and Suggested Readings

Roy M. Acheson and D.R.R. Williams, 1983. Does consumption of fruit and vegetables protect against stroke? *Lancet,* 1, 1191-1193

Anonymous, 1992. Improving America's diet and health: From Recommendations to action. *Nutrition Today,* January/February

Anonymous, 1991. Diet, nutrition and the prevention of chronic diseases. A report of the WHO Study Group on diet, nutrition and prevention of noncommunicable diseases. *Nutrition Reviews,* 40, 291-301

Anonymous, 1982. *Diet, Nutrition, and Cancer. Committee on Diet, Nutrition, and Cancer.*. National Academy Press, Washington DC, 1982

Este Armstrong, 1983. Relative brain size and metabolism in mammals. *Science,* 220, 1302-1304

James R. Bindon, 1982. Breadfruit, banana, beef, and beer: Modernization of the Samoan diet. *Ecology of Food and Nutrition,* 12, 49-60

Gladys Block, Blossom Patterson, and Amy Subar, 1992. Fruit, vegetables, and cancer prevention: A review of the epidemiological evidence. *Nutrition and Cancer,* 18, 1-29

D.A. Booth, 1978. Neurochemistry of appetite mechanisms. *Proc. Nutrition Society,* 37, 181-191

Marian Burros, 1988. What Americans really Eat: Nutrition can wait, survey finds. *New York Times,* January 6, 15-17

D.H. Buss, 1977. Food habits in Britain. *Proc. Nutrition Society,* 36, 247-253

William E. Conner, et al., 1978. The plasma lipids, lipoproteins, and diet of the Tarahumara Indians of Mexico. *American J. Clinical Nutrition,* 31, 1131-1142

M.A. Crawford, 1968. Food selection under natural conditions and the possible relationship to heart disease in man. *Proc. Nutrition Society,* 27, 163-172

David Cuthbertson, 1967. The influence of feeding patterns on nutrient utilization. *Proc. Nutrition Society,* 26, 143-144

Theodosius Dobzhansky, *Mankind Evolving.* Yale University Press, New Haven, 1962

J.V.G.A. Durnin, et al., 1972. How much food does man require? *Nature,* 242, 418

S. Boyd Eaton, 1990. What did our late paleolithic (Preagricultural) ancestors eat? *Nutrition Reviews,* 48, 227-229

Jonathan Fielding, et al., 1978. A program to prevention in Massachusets. *Preventive Medicine,* 7, 564-640

Stephen Jay Gould. *Ever Since Darwin.* W. W. Norton, New York, 1977

Stephen Jay Gould. *The Mismeasure of Man.* W.W. Norton, Ney York, 1981

Jane Goodall. *In the Shadow of Man.* Houghton Miffin, Boston, 1971

Morris Goodman, 1982. Biomolecular evidence on human origins from the standpoint of Darwinian theory. *Human Biology,* 54, 247-264

William Gooddy and M.D. Lond, 1958. Man and the nervous system. The brain as a clock. *Lancet,* 1. 1139-1144 ?

Louis E. Grivetti, 1981. Cultural nutrition: Anthropological and geographical themes. *Annual Review of Nutrition,* 1, 47-68

Bernard Guenault, 1985. New plants and plant products as food. *Proc. Nutrition Society,* 44, 31-35

Steve Harakeh and Raxit J.Jariwalla, 1991. Comparative study of the anti-HIV activities of ascorbate and the thiol-containing reducing agents in chronically HIV-infected cells. *American J. Clinical Nutrition,* 54, 1231S-1235S

Robert A. Jacob, et al., 1991. Immunocommpetence and oxidant defense during ascorbate depletion of healthy men. *American J. Clinical Nutrition,* 54, 1302-1309

Sissel Johannessen and Christine A. Hastorf, 1989. Corn and culture in Central Andean Prehistory. *Science,* 244, 690-692

Thomas H. Jukes, 1992. Historical perspective: Antioxidants, nutrition, and evolution. *Preventive Medicine,* 21, 270-276

K.E.Bach Knudsen and L. Munck, 1988. Effect of cooking, pH and polyphenol level on carbohydrate composition and nutritional quality of a sorghum (Sorghum bicolor L. Moench) food, ugali. *British J. Nutrition,* 59, 31-47

Gina Bari Kolata, 1975. Human evolution: Life-styles and lineages of early hominids. *Science,* 187, 940-942

Henry S. Koopmans, 1985. Satiety signals from the gastrointestinal tract. *J. Clinical Nutrition,* 42, 1044-1049

Roger Lewin, 1984. Man the scavenger. *Science,* 224, 861-862

L. Michael Lerner, 1954. *Genetic Homeostasis.* Dover Publications, New York, 1954

Roger Lewin, 1988. New views emerge on hunters and gatherers. *Science,* 240, 1146-1148

Martha P. McMurry, et al., 1991. Changes in lipid and lipoprotein levels and body weight in Tarahumara Indians after consumption of an affluent diet. *New England J. Medicine,* 325, 1704-1708

Anne S. Moffat, 1990. China: A living lab for epidemiology. *Science,* 245, 553-555

Anne Murcott, 1982. Food habits and culture in the UK. *Proc. Nutrition Society,* 41, 203-?

S.J. D. O'Keefe, N. Ndaba and A. Woodward, 1985. Relationship between nutritional status, dietary intake patterns and plasma lipoprotien concentrations in rural black south Africans. *Human Nutrition: Clinical Nutrition,* 39C, 335-341

Steve Olson, 1982. Why is the Sea constant? *Science 82,* 3, 112

Aviva Palgi, 1980. Evaluation of the dietary intake of the Israeli population, 1949-1977. *Ecology of Food and Nutrition,* 9, 157-165

John D. Palmer, 1977. Human rhythms. *BioScience,* 27, 93-99

Linus Pauling, 1991. Effect of ascorbic acid on incidence of spontaneous mammary tumors and UV-light-induced skin tumors in mice. *American J. Clinical Nutrition,* 54, 1252S-1255S

G.L.S. Pawan, 1974. Drugs and appetite. *Proc. Nutrition Society,* 33, 239-243

Roland L. Phillips, et al., 1978. Coronary heart diseases mortality among Seventh-Day Adventists with differning dietary habits: A preliminary report. *American J. Clinical Nutrition,* 3, S191-S198

Leslie Roberts, 1988. Diet and health in China.*Science,* 240, 27

John R.K. Robson, 1978. Fruit in the diet of prehistoric man and of the hunter-gatherer. *J. Human Nutrition,* 32, 19-26

Guillermo L. De Romana, et al., 1980. Utilization of the protein and energy of the white potato by human infants. *J. Nutrition,* 110, 1849-1857

Julia M. Rux, 1981. Thoughts on culture, nutrition and the aged. *J. of Nutrition for the Elderly,* 1, 15-19

Jose E. Dos Santos, et al., 1979. Relationship between the nutritional efficacy of rice and bean diet and energy intake in preschool children. *American J. Clinical Nutrition,* 32, 1541-1544

R.B. Singh, et al., 1989. Dietary modulators of blood pressure in hypertension. *European J. Clinical Nutrition,* 44, 319-327

H.C. Sherman and A.O. Gettler, 1912. The balance of acid-forming and base-forming elements in foods, and its relation to ammonia metabolism. *J. Biological Chemistry,* 2, 323-338

Timo E. Strandberg, et al., 1991. Long-term mortality after 5-year multifactorial primary prevention of cardiovascular diseases in middle-aged men. *J. American Medical Association,* 266, 1225-1229

Jenny Storer, 1977. 'Hot' and 'Cold' food beliefs in an Indian community and their significance. *J. Human Nutrition,* 31,33-40

E. Neige Todhunter, 1965. The evolution of nutrition concepts- Perspectives and new horizons. *J. American Dietetic Association,* 46, 120-128

Lilian U. Thompson et al., 1991. Mammalian lignan production from various foods. *Nutrition and Canmcer,* 16, 43-52

Malulee Tuntawiroon, et al., 1990. Rice and iron absorption in man. *European J. Clinical Nutrition,* 44, 489-497

Joseph T. Vanderslice and DarlaJ. Higgs, 1991. Vitamin C content of foods: sample variability. *American J. Clinical Nutrition,* 54, 1323S-1327S

Noel D. Vietmeyer, 1986. Lesser-known plants of potential use in agriculture and forestry. *Science,* 232, 1379-1384

G.R. Wadsworth, 1978. The use, dietary significance and production of fruit. *J. Human Nutrition,* 32, 27-40

Sherwood L. Washburn, 1978. Evolution of man. *Scientific American,* 239, 194-212

David Wilson, 1976. On the nature of consciousness and of physical reality. *Perspectives in Biology and Medicine,* 19, 568-580

Ernst L. Wynder, 1976. Nutrition and cancer. *Federation Proceedings* 35, 1309-1315

Hisato Yoshimura, 1961. Adult protein requirements. *Federation Proceedings.* 20. 103-110

John Yudkins, 1964. Patterns and trends in carbohydrate consumption and their relation to disease. *Proc. Nutrition Society,* 23, 149-162

15

Protective Foods Prevent Disease

Abstract: A number of observations suggest that the value of a diet is determined not only by its caloric and specific nutrient content, but also, by the ability of some foods to offset deleterious features of others. This aspect of holism in nutrition (see Chapter 2) was recognized by E. Vernon McCollum, a pioneering nutritionist of the early 1900's. He termed them "protective foods". What features make certain foods "protective"? We have seen that high dietary fat and protein, low dietary fiber and saturation of nutrients as occurs in a meat-staple diet, contribute to the widespread problems of obesity and constipation and are causally associated with degenerative diseases and cancer. We have discussed the value of glucose rather than amino acids as an energy source (see Chapters 3 and 5), the beneficial roles of dietary fiber (see Chapter 10), the importance of fostering a stable beneficial microbial population, (see Chapter 13), and the nutritional implications of a diet subsaturating in various minerals (e.g. iron) and nutrients (e.g. amino acids) as a means of promoting resistance to disease. Yet we have also seen that a diet of simple sugars is not the best way to get glucose, that mineral supplmentation is a tricky business (see Chapter 8), and that natural sources of fiber serve automatically to provide not only bulk but also nutrient variety and, by dilution and binding, nutrient subsaturation (see Chapter 9 and 10). Protective foods are those such as milk, green, leafy vegetables, and fruit, rich in complex carbohydrates which display all of these beneficial features (e.g. of glucose for energy metabolism of mineral, vitamin and antioxidant variety, or nutrient dilution and binding) while either mitigating the negative aspects of each of these components in isolation or providing additional benefits (e.g. the possibilities of substitution through variety, see Chapter 7). Such "protective foods" were plentiful in traditional diets, but have been neglected in recent decades by a nutrition science obsessed with reductionist views of food value and food industries geared to refined products(see Chapter 14). Studies suggest that an increase in consumption of protective foods would result in improved health of the population: decreased constipation and obesity, decreased nutritional deficiencies and diminished incidence of degenerative diseases would be a likely outcome of dietary modification.

E. Vernon McCollum, of the Johns Hopkins University, and his associates found that ancient Asian cultures which had long stable records of maintaining health, always promoted whole grains and leafy vegetables in their diet. Their regular diet included legume seeds, tubers, roots and green leaves of all kinds that made up for the micronutrients lacking in cereal grains and meat. McCollum also noticed that traditions that lacked milk in their diet substituted for it with various vegetable products such as soybeans and chickpeas for adults, while emphasizing milk in the children's and women's diet. Eskimos, for example, consumed ingredients such as willow greens and berries as valuable foods for maintaining health. Where milk was unavailable, the population consumed more green leaves which are rich in minerals (including calcium) and vitamins thereby compensating for the lack of milk.

McCollum concluded that unless milk, leafy vegetables and fruits are emphasized in the human diet, obtaining excessive calories from meat, poultry, cheese and refined sugar and flour may endanger people's health. He reasoned that milk, fruits and leafy vegetables that add more micronutrients into the diet compensate for the ill-effect of non-protective foods such as white flour, sugar and meat which supply protein and energy but lack other essentials. Milk and the leafy vegetables are the only foods that could make up for the deficiencies of cereal grains, tubers, roots and meats. In 1918 McCollum proposed the phrase "Protective Foods" to emphasize the importance of milk and plant products in human diet. Many scientists became aware that decreasing meat and refined products in the diet was necessary to compensate for the increasingly sedentary life brought about by technology.

A gradual transition from traditional diets to diets influenced by nutritional science took place from the eighteenth century to the beginning of the twentieth century. Unfortunately, it involved analysis of foods based on a flawed understanding of the relationship of food ingredients to energy, and an incomplete understanding of the fundamentals of carbohydrates, proteins and lipid metabolism in relation to the human body and its physiology. During these elaborate investigations, maintaining the variety and bulk in the diet (features that were found in traditional cultural diets) was thought to be less important than providing concentrated nutrients as a means of "improving" the quality of the diet (see Chapter 6). As a result, refining and improving food by processing inadvertently removed many associated minerals, vitamins and antioxidants (see Chapter 14). As it became popular to consume processed foods, fresh produce and whole grain consumption declined. These lead to large scale deficiency diseases such as beriberi, pellagra, rickets and scurvy in many parts of the world including Europe (see Chapter 9).

In Asia, for example, for many years the natives consumed hand-pounded brown rice as their dietary staple. However, when promotion of the milling industry popularized refined and polished white rice, the consumption of brown rice declined. The natives who consumed polished white rice as staple, without supplementing it with fresh produce and milk, began suffering from beriberi, a complex deficiency disease involving the swelling of peripheral nerves and leading to paralysis. Beriberi spread in the majority of countries where white rice replaced brown rice as a staple. Around that period, Robert McCarrison, an officer in the Indian Medical Service, noticed that natives in places such as near the Himalayas, upper Egypt and northern Nigeria, lead long lives with continued vigor, fertility and physical health. He ascribed this strikingly superior health to the fact that their infants were breast fed and the adults consumed natural foods of whole grains, fruits and leafy vegetables with some milk and dairy products.

According to his report, those natives suffered from a much lower incidence of deficiency diseases, compared to other parts of Asia. Moreover they avoided the high incidence of gastrointestinal problems and cancer that were common in the Western population that he was familiar with. According to him, while Asian populations were inflicted with deficiency diseases, as much as 25% of the Western population were suffering from noninfectious ailments such as dyspeptic or colonic diseases. He felt that the colonic problems were caused either by the state of colonic bacteria flora or the conditions that brought changes in their colonic environment. In general, he felt that deficiency ailments and the colonic diseases were due to the lack of some essentials in the diet or were due to certain excesses that indirectly caused the lack of essentials in the diet. The emergency caused by the spread of deficiency diseases and the shortage of food caused by World War I brought a great need to improve and conserve food, especially in European countries.

The Danish government, for example, established a Nutrition Research Laboratory under the supervision of a physician, Mikkel Hindhede, to conduct elaborate animal experiments and study the mass feeding of people (see Chapter 7). Other European countries also undertook various means of improving the diet, such as supplementing the children's diet with milk and campaigning to increase production and consumption of domestically grown food crops. Many scientists including McCarrison supported the scientific view held by Hindhede that almost all prevailing health problems were related to the food and drink that people consume. However, neither the epidemic of deficiency diseases nor the awareness of food shortages reached North America until 1917. This was because, unlike other parts of the world, North America did not lack food resources. According to European commentators, if there was ill health in America due to diet, it was not due to shortage of food but because of liberalized consumption of meat.

Pellagra, a deficiency disease which starts with skin lesions and gum bleeding and becomes more complex as time passes, for example, was not noticed in the U.S. until after 1900 even though it had prevailed in many parts of Europe and Asia since 1735 (see Chapter 9). It then became epidemic in the U.S. when consumption of fresh produce and milk declined drastically and the use of meat and refined products increased. This was partly due to people's ignorance of their dietary needs and partly because of a lack of refrigeration to keep fresh produce and milk. Although many rural families had lived for generations on a very limited diet without deficiency diseases they appeared in epidemic proportion when people began consuming highly refined foods in large quantities. The main reason for this was that fresh produce and milk were expensive and not easily available. Refined products such as white flour, white sugar, white bread, canned, packaged and chemically treated foods were popularized as "clean and pure" healthy foods and they were easily available.

The cases of pellagra in the U.S., began to increase when old local grist mills were replaced by more "efficient" mills which produced more refined cereals. It was noted to be more common in southern states than in eastern or western states. A group of scientists lead by Joseph Goldburger of the U.S. Health Service was able to trace the disease to a deficient diet. By 1915, the scientists knew that pellagra could be prevented or cured by greater use of milk, fruits and leafy vegetables. However, scientists did not identify the exact factor, called "PP," a part of the vitamin B complex, until 1937. By 1915 many scientists in the U.S. felt that not only pellagra but also many other deficiency diseases might be related to a lack of milk, fruits and leafy vegetables in the diet. Deficiency symptoms were found even in some prosperous communities where people lacked fresh produce and milk in their diet. Children became frequent victims of deficiency diseases (see Chapter 9).

All these developments brought a new awareness among U.S. scientists of the need to explore and find an adequate diet that contains the needed essentials in addition to the major nutrients, carbohydrate, protein and fat. The consensus was that health and longevity could be improved by making appropriate choices in daily food. An average individual accumulates knowledge until around the age of 50, and unless healthy adulthood is extended far beyond that age people cannot utilize their knowledge to maximal advantage. Therefore, concerned scientists wanted to use the science of nutrition to find a prudent diet that extends the healthy life span of the population and enhances the vitality and efficiency of the people.

As early as 1906 Gowland Hopkins, a British scientist reported that the addition of milk even in small quantities supplied unknown nourishing substances to experimental animals and improved their health. He ascribed these benefits to an "accessary food factors" (see Chapter 9). Henry Sherman of Columbia University found that enriching a diet already adequate in food calories with milk improved the vitality and longevity of laboratory animals, in addition to increasing their growth. He showed that milk might supply substances that would stimulate the body's self- regulatory processes and bring buoyant health rather than merely passable health. Sherman and other scientists found that animals fed with 5 parts by weight of ground whole-wheat could have their diet adequately balanced by one part by weight of dried whole milk; however, increasing amounts of milk made the diet better for all ages and improved the reproductivity and longevity of animals. He found that the diet built around whole grains and milk improved vitality of not only the young but also of the adults and the elderly.

Many scientists engaged in research involving protective foods found that many deficiency diseases could be prevented if people consumed large amounts of protective foods. In addition, World War 1 brought more urgency to improving health through protective foods because both meat and refined foods were scarce. For the first time, human nutrition became part of the public domain in the U.S. According to reports, more than 20 federal government agencies directly or indirectly became involved in human nutrition during the 1930's. Their efforts and results were translated into policy interventions at the state and municipal levels. In addition, many higher educational institutions and welfare agencies were also involved in educating people in hygiene, food and healthy living. Promotion of protective foods was received with great enthusiasm. All Americans were encouraged to substitute fresh vegetables and fruits for refined flour, meat and sugar in their diets. According to one report, the enthusiastic people of New York City alone converted over a million acreage of city junk lots into vegetable gardens that produced $350,000,000 worth of fresh produce. All over the U.S. "Every Garden a Peace plant" became a popular slogan. Scientists, who were responsible for discovering many vitamins, went out of their way to emphasize the value of protective foods rather than to encourage the use of vitamins as their substitutes. Many philanthropic individuals and consumer groups joined to teach prudent nutrition that emphasized consuming adequate amounts of protective foods. Organizations such as the New England Kitchen in Boston, were set up to teach people how to eat better, because it was found that people were consuming 2/3 or more of their food calories as baker's bread, pies, cake and doughnuts, with tea or beer as a drink. McCollum argued that no other food combinations provided for the supply and assimilation of calcium in the human diet as did protective foods. Scientists found that the body's ability to assimilate calcium is impaired by the consumption of a diet low in calcium, low in fiber and high in protein (see Chapter 7). The consensus among scientists was that the nation as a whole should shift the priority in the human diet from meat to protective foods which are poorer in calories but richer in variety of micronutrients. Some even felt that a political slogan of 1896 "Full dinner pail," which evoked abundance of variety and bulk was more prudent than the one of 1928 "a chicken in every pot", which advocated excessive consumption of meat. Professors Henry Armsby, Director of Pennsylvania State College, produced economics of investment in favor of protective foods. According to him, in energy values, a dairy cattle as milk yielded 18% of what it consumed, whereas a beef cattle, as meat yielded only 4% of what it consumed. Similarly, a soil conservation program was found to be more attractive to dairy farmers and vegetable and fruit growers than to cotton growers, who then received reduced federal money. By 1928 meat consumption was the lowest it had been in 6 years. In spite of this, many scientists argued that Europeans had a better diet than Americans because their cereals were less refined and they consumed less meat and more whole grain bread. Statistics showed that improving the diet with protective foods made many deficiency diseases decrease in incidence. It was found that economically privileged groups of people who had better knowledge of nutrition and consumed more protective foods derived better health benefits from them than those who lacked this knowledge.

A survey of Ivy League college students from well-to-do families showed that not only did they increase their stature and improved their health, they also performed far better intellectually than their parents and than students from other socioeconomic groups. In contrast, approximately 53% of school children belonging to low socioeconomic groups consumed less protective foods in their diet and suffered more from deficiency diseases such as pellagra and night blindness. In addition, their performance in school also suffered. Scientists and politicians alike discovered that benefits gained by supplying protective foods to all people may outweigh the expense involved in supplying them. For the first time they felt that a prudent diet was not expensive because it saved the expenses involved in sickness and gave a bonus of improved health. They felt that city workers suffering from ill-health due to a lack of protective foods were a greater economic drain than the expenses involved in making protective foods easily available to them.

According to many published reports, consumer education not only popularized protective foods but also decreased the purchase of luxury foods such as meat, eggs, white sugar and white flour. A Government survey of 373 cities indicated that milk consumption increased from 43 gallons per capita in 1920 to 55 gallons in 1926. Similarly, per capita consumption of fruits and vegetables also increased. Consumption of oranges alone for example, increased from 14 pounds in 1919 to 25 pounds in 1931, in spite of reduced facilities to store and distribute them. A survey of families eating habits showed that the number of food items consumed from the 19th century to the 20th century jumped from 55 to 81. Increased emphasis on protective foods showed that both boys and girls entered college better developed at a slightly earlier age than their parents.

In the 1930's professor C. M. McCay at Cornell, working with experimental animals, found that unlimited food calories supplied in an appetizing combination of foods increased the animal's growth rapidly, but shortened its longevity. Other scientific investigations also revealed that beyond a certain extent, increased body size even in humans may unduly tax organs such as the heart and kidneys and promote degenerative diseases at an early age. Consequently, people received more intensive nutrition and health education in the 30's than they did ever before. Consumers were reached through various channels such as schools, factories and families and they were persuaded to spend less on meat, eggs, sweets and flavorings and more on protective foods. Model meals containing more protective foods were served by the Bureau of Home Economics to encourage people to consume whole-wheat bread (mottled loaf) instead of white bread; and to cultivate their taste from meat to whole grains.

Many physicians encouraged their patients to include plenty of protective foods in the diet of their families. The efforts began showing results. For example, Dr. Lowell Langstroth published the result of his study in the Journal of American Medical Association (JAMA) in 1929, after examining 501 patients who were over 35 years. According to him, a good correlation existed between the amount of protective foods consumed and the prevalence of degenerative diseases. Among those who included 5% or less of protective foods in their diet, 70% suffered disorders such as arthritis, diabetes and gastrointestinal diseases, whereas of those whose diets included 40% protective foods, only 45% had degenerative diseases. When he placed 174 patients on 70% protective foods, 73% were found to be either cured or much relieved of their distresses. The incidence of degenerative disease was also higher among the poor who used smaller quantities of protective foods.

Increase in consumption of protective foods not only curtailed degenerative diseases of the elderly but also decreased children's visit to the doctor's office. Many scientists felt that supplying liberal amounts of protective foods was more economical for the country because they were potentially the most inexpensive foods and they reduced most medical bills. In spite of this, protective foods remained relatively more expensive at retail than refined products and other processed staples. The well to do ate more protective foods than the less prosperous. In the southern states, many families went without protective foods, especially milk, because the landlords preferred them to grow cotton or other cash crops and not fruits and vegetables. Moreover storage of fresh produce was difficult. As a result of lack of protective foods, deficiency diseases such as pellagra became common.

Poor families had problems for not only obtaining protective foods but also in utilizing whatever was available to them because of a lack of storage facilities. People in Mississippi, for example, produced more, but consumed less fresh milk in the summer months because milk spoiled faster during the summer. In South Carolina only 63% of the farmers reported milking of cows; in Arizona, 43%, while 82% of the farmers in New York and 92% in Wisconsin milked cows. Wherever the diet lacked milk, poor health increased. Themes such as "milk week" and "eat more wheat" slogans encouraged people to reduce meat and refined food consumption and increase consumption of protective foods. The food stamp program encouraged poor families to increase protective foods in their diet and also helped to reduce agricultural surpluses. But according to one report, even though 31% of food stamps were used to purchase fresh fruits and vegetables, the per capita amount of these products remained inadequate.

A survey taken in Boston in 1937 showed that 49% of the 18,000 families on relief in the City were purchasing no milk and on the average they were drinking less than 3 pints a week. When milk was supplied free to families on relief and with minimal expense to wage earners, milk consumption jumped from 14,000 quarts to 120,000 quarts per day. This angered and aggravated many industries. So much so, that even the advice given by the U.S. Health Service to eat less meat during warm weather was protested by the meat industries. A counter current which existed to support the views of the meat and processed food industries gained strength as the depression years came to an end. Many scientists also joined the campaign to deemphasize protective foods or to include eggs in the diet. These workers overlooked or were ignorant of the fact that unlike milk, any residue of which ferments in the colon, high protein egg residue promotes putrefaction resulting in an unhealthy colonic environment optimal for microorganisms that are not beneficial to maintaining a health (see Chapter 13). According to a recent report, a higher colon cancer incidence has been detected among those who consume more eggs. As the 40's passed, the promotion and popularity of protective foods declined, and non-protective foods dominated by fast foods and soft drinks became popular. Members of the generation of the 1950's even lost their taste for protective foods. They cultivated tastes for snacks made of meat, eggs, refined flour and sugar and soft drinks which were made conveniently available to them.

Decreased consumption of protective foods and increased consumption of fast foods began to contribute to health problems attributed to a lack of calcium, dietary fiber and complex carbohydrates. (see Chapter 5). More than 6 million Americans, especially postmenopausal women, suffer from bone fractures as a result of osteoporosis. Hip fractures alone cost the nation more than one billion dollars per year. More than 10-15% develop reduced bone density as early as age 25. Imbalanced calcium in the diet also has a correlation with other ailments such as hypertension, colorectal cancer and lead poisoning of young children (see Chapter 10).

According to Denis P. Burkitt, a British medical scientist, Earnst Wynder, an American medical scientist, and others, almost all degenerative diseases of Western Society have increased with the increased consumption of meat and refined foods. This was verified by epidemiological studies carried out in various parts of the world. The one reported from Japan illustrates the issue. The food calories in the traditional Japanese diet, for example, came from plant products such as rice, wheat, soybean and various vegetables and fruits, even though fish remained an important item. People had smaller stature but maintained better health and longevity. They suffered less from degenerative diseases and there were more centenarians among them. Between 1950-1963 the average total calories consumed by Japanese remained constant around 2,097 Kcal/day. Rice alone provided 57% of the total calories.

However, in the 1970's the Japanese Council of Nutrition, which followed the U.S. model, recommended increasing food intake to 2,300 Calories, including 75g of protein out of which 30g was from animal products. The diet drastically reduced the quantity of complex carbohydrates and changed the ratio of animal to plant products. The changed diet that brought larger physique and stature also increased cholesterolemia causing vascular and degenerative diseases. Malignant cancers also increased among this population. Obesity emerged as a potential health problem among affluent school children. According to Takashi Hirayama of the National Cancer Research Institute, Tokyo, both mortality and morbidity increased sharply in the age group of 45-59. The risk was 8.5 times higher in women of high socioeconomic groups who ate meat daily than in women who did not. Recently, these findings have been underscored by data presented by Gladys Block and associate at the U.C., Berkeley that links increased dietary intakes of fruits and vegetables to lower incidences of a variety of types of cancer (including colon, breast cerevix and G.I. tract cancers).

Increased health problems led to increased use of both prescribed and over the counter medicines in all parts of the world. In the U.S., pharmaceutical companies provided many fewer drugs in the 1930s, many of them of herbal origin, compared to today. When petroleum and coal tar products began replacing herbal medicines, the priority shifted from prevention to treatment. Constipation, is a good example of a disorder which traditionally was prevented by mere dietary adjustments. With the rise in pharmaceuticals, it is now commonly treated with a range of medicines. A direct consequence of this change has been a marked rise in disorders such as diverticular disease. Now the Physician's Desk References alone lists over 5,000 medicines. This pharmaceutical approach to disorders that should be dealt with through physiological dietary manipulation is a major contributor to the current explosion in the cost of health care.

In the 1970's the U.S. Senate Select Committee on Nutrition and Human Needs proposed dietary goals for the United States. The first of the 6 dietary goals, called for increasing consumption of complex carbohydrates. The goal suggested almost doubling of consumption of whole grains, fruits and vegetables and decreasing consumption of meat, poultry, fish and sugar. These recommendations were not acted upon. Instead of increasing the provision of protective foods, in the 1980's there were proposals to replace vegetables with catsup and fruit with candy bars in children's lunches. People eat what is popular and conveniently available. Unless a healthy human diet as a form of preventive therapy is accorded a position of priority, health care costs will continue to escalate. Making protective foods widely available and educating people to consume them cost very little compared to treatment of diseases.

Selected Sources and Suggested Readings

Anonymous, 1986. Diet and coronary disease. *Nutrition Today,* March/April, 26-33

John C. Bailar III and Elaine M. Smith, 1986. Progress against cancer? *New England J. Medicine,* 314, 1226-1232

Gladys Block, Blossom Patterson and Amy Suber, 1992. Fruit, vegetables, and Cancer Prevention: A review of the epidemiological evidence. *Nutrition and Cancer,* 18, 1-29

Gladys Block, 1991. Dietary guidelines and the results of food consumption surveys. *American J. Clinical Nutrition,* 53, 356S- 357S

Jane Broady, 1982. How diet can affect mood and behavior. *New York Times,* November, 17

S. Boyd Eaten, 1990. What did our late paleolithic (preagricultural) ancestors eat? *Nutrition Reviews,* 48, 227-228

C.L. Brown and M.J. Hill, 1971. Bacterial urease in uremic. *Lancet,* 2, 406-408

Alastair M. Connell, 1976. Natural fiber and bowel dysfunction. *American J. Clinical Nutrition,* 29, 1427-1431

Richard O. Cummings. *The American and His Food.* University Chicago Press, chicago, 1940

L.G. Darlington and N.W. Ramsey, 1991. Diets for rheumatoid arthritis. *Lancet,* 338, 1209

Harry G. Day, 1981. The nutrition legacies of E.V. McCollum. *Nutrition Today,* January/February, 26-29

Cortez F. Enole,Jr., 1979. The twenty-five-year century. *Nutrition Today,* March/April, 29-35

George H. Fathauer, 1960. Food habits- an anthropologist's view. *J. American Dietetic Association,* 37, 335-338

Jane V. Goodall. *In the Shadow of Man.* Houghton Miffin, 1971

J. A. E. Goy, et al., 1976. Fecal characteristics contrasted in the irritable bowel syndrome and diverticular disease. *American J. Nutrition,* 29, 1480-1484

Louis E. Grivetti, 1978. Culture, diet, and nutrition: Selected themes and topics. *BioScience,* 28, 171-177

William Insull Jr., Toshio Olso, and Kenzaburo Tsuchiya, 1968. Diet and nutritional status of Japanese. *American J. Clinical Nutrition,* 22, 753-777

W.P.J. James, 1991. Future of nutritional science: Challenges for the year 2000. *European J. Clinical Nutrition,* 45, (Suppl. 2), 2-7

Mishrilal Jain and Kamal M. Jain, 1973. The science of Yoga: A study in perspective. *Perspective in Biology and Medicine,* 17, 93-101

Najia Karim, et al., 1986. Modifications in food consumption patterns reported by people from India, living in Cincinnati, Ohio. *Ecology of Food and Nutrition,* 19, 11-18

Charles Glen King, 1970. Notes on the history of nutrition in *America. J. American Dietetic Association,* 56, 188-190

H.V. Kuhnlein, N.J. Turner and P.D. Kluckner, 1982. Nutritional significance of two important root foods (springbank clover and pacific silverweed) used by native people on the coast of British Columbia. *Ecology of Food and Nutrition,* 12, 89-95

Lowell Langtroth, 1929. Relation of the American dietary to degenerative diseases. *J. American Medical Association,* 93, 1607-1613

E.M. Leeper, 1978. Senator McGovern on dietary goals: Without nutrition education 'everything else is lost'. *BioScience,* 28, 161-164

Robert McCarrison, 1922. Faulty food in relation to gastrointestinal disorder. *J. American Medical Association,* 78, 1-8

E. V. McCollum. *A History of Nutrition.* Houghton Miffin, 1957

E. V. McCollum, N Simmonds and W. Pitz, 1917. The supplementary dietary relationship between leaf and seed as contrasted with combinations of seed with seed. *J. Biological Chemistry,* 30, 13-19

Michael I. McBurney and Lilian U. Thompson, 1990. Fermentative characteristics of cereal brans and vegetable fibers. *Nutrition and Cancer,* 13, 271-280

Edward J. Mosoro, 1992. Retardation of aging processes by food restriction an experimental tool. *American J. Clinical Nutrition,* 55, 1250S-1252S

John Boyd Orr, William Thompson and R.C. Garry, 1935. A long term experiment with rats on ahuman dietary. *J. Hygiene,* 35, 476-497

Lot B. Page, et al., 1981. Blood pressure of Qash'qui pastoral nomads in Iron in relation to culture, diet, and body form. *American J. Clinical Nutrition,* 34, 527-538

Sushma Palmer and Susan Berkow, 1986. Nutrition education in American Medical Schools. *Nutrition Today,* January/Februery, 5-15

Leslie Roberts, 1988. Diet and health in China. *Science,* 240, 27

John R. K. Robson, 1978. Fruit in the diet of prehistoric man and of the hunter-gatherer. *J. Human Nutrition,* 32, 19-26

G.P. Savage, 1990. Nutritional value of sprouted mung beans. *Nutrition Today,* May/June, 21-24

Albert Szent-Gyorgyi, 1976. The electronic theory of cancer. *International J. Quantum Chemistry.* Quantum Biology Symposium, 3, 45-50

Jonathan B. Tucker,1986. Amaranth: the once and future crop. *BioScience,* 36, 9-13

Regina G. Ziegler, 1991. Vegetables, fruits, and carotenoids and the risk of cancer. *American J. Clinical Nutrition,* 53, 2515-2595

Margareta Wandel, et al., 1984. Heaty and cooling foods in relation to food habits in a southern Sri Lanka community. *Ecology of Food and Nutrition,* 14, 93-104

Gordon Young, 1975. Salt the essence of life. *National Geographic,* September 19,

Regina G. Ziegler, 1991. Vegetables, fruits, and carotinoids and the risk of cancer. *American J. Clinical Nutrition,* 53, 251S-9S

Alan Zukerman, et al., 1989. Cardiovascular risk factors among black school-children: comparison among four know your body studies. *Preventive Medicine,* 18, 113-132

16

Milk:
Food Tailored by Evolution

Abstract: Milk is a quintessential "protective" food unique to mammals. Here we discuss the physiology of milk as a nutrient, explain how it is tailored to the needs of the species and discuss its role in a wholesome diet. The special role of milk in nutrition isthat i) it contains an enormous diversity of nutrients, ii) these nutrients are present as a very dilute solution at subsaturating concentrations, and iii) it is rich in lactose, a sugar absorbed extremely slowly which assists in calcium absorption. The diversity of nutrients in milk prevents deficiencies that might otherwise interfere with development. At the same time, the subsaturating concentration of nutrients permit optimal establishment of homeostatic mechanisms and forms a barrier to pathogens by forcing them into unfavorable competition for nutrients. Examples of the role of breast milk in carbohydrate, protein, lipid and iron metabolism of the developing infant are discussed. In addition, the nutrients of breast milk initiate the selection of an optimal intestinal microbial flora. Finally, milk provides a universal standard for human infant nutrition. While human milk is optimal for human babies, cow's milk provides a reasonable nutritional standard attainable for adults. No other single food can provide the dietary needs for all ages as well as milk.

All living beings start their lives with specific evolutionary foods. Plant embryos are fed by their own endosperm, fish and bird embryos are fed by their own yolk and mammals such as mice, monkeys and human infants are fed by their mother's breast milk. These evolutionary foods are tailored to the needs of each individual species and adapt the newborn to their new environment. Supporting this conclusion are studies which show that breast-fed infants are healthier and more resistant to infection than formula-fed infants. Milk as a generic food of mammalian offsprings, provides a variety of nutrients in ratios tailored to the needs of different species. Milk of mice, for example, contains over 11% protein, consistent with their very short lifecycle and hence, need for rapid growth and maturation. Human breast milk on the other hand, contains less than 1.0% protein, consistent with the longer lifespan and more prolonged period of development in humans.

The composition of milk produced by various species correlates with their adult diets. Thus, the milk of herbivores and omnivores are rich in lactose (carbohydrate) and low in protein whereas milk of carnivores are rich in protein. Even though milk is a complete food in terms of its distribution of nutrients, it is too dilute to be the exclusive food past infancy. Human milk, for example, contains nearly 88% water and 12% solids. However, animal milk (e.g. of cows or goats) is an excellent supplemental food for adults (Table 16.1).

While the milk of various species have similar nutrients, the amounts and ratios of those nutrients are species specific. Lactose, the milk sugar, for example, is a common constituent of both cow and human milk; however, it is present at a distinctly higher concentration in human milk compared to that of the cow. Human milk has over 100 different constituents in various ratios compared to the milk of other species. Human milk is a unique secretion evolved to serve the complex nutritional needs of human infants. It is a universally standardized model food of evolution that provides the optimal dietary needs to all human infants irrespective of their socioeconomic and environmental differences.

Even though animal experiments show that the composition of milk varies with maternal diet, crucial ingredients such as protein, carbohydrate and trace minerals of the human milks have been found to be unaffected by variations in the dietary intake of mothers, except in extreme malnutrition. Analysis of breast milk samples obtained from well nourished Swedish, Australian and from two different socioeconomic groups of Ethiopian mothers have been found to have few differences in their constituents. A study of 20,000 children for 5 years showed that infants fed with cow's milk-based formula may have 7 times more risk in developing eczema than breast-fed infants. Conversely, another study showed that nearly 20% of children who suffered from allergic diseases such as eczema, asthma, hay fever and specific reactions to food were those who did not get the protective benefits of breast milk in their infancy.

What makes milk truly special is that it contains an enormous diversity of nutrients – all at subsaturating concentrations. Not only nutrient diversity but also nutrient dilution is a protective feature of milk in human infant nutrition. Both of these features are conducive to maintenance of homeostasis.

In a healthy mother the output of colostrum (the first thick secretion from the breast after birth), starts at a rate of less than 100 ml/day. Later, as early milk, output increases rapidly to reach up to 700 ml/day during the first month of full breast-feeding and levels off at 800 ml/day at 6 months. The volume output after the first month has been found to vary significantly in relation with weight of infants. Its composition also may vary from day to day and even

TABLE 16.1. Comparison of Milk of Different Animals (100 g portion). Notice with special attention carbohydrate, protein and mineral content of human milk and their enery equivalents.Selected from Journal of Biological Chemistry, 1916, 1919, 1937, 1940, and *Nutritive Value of American Foods.* Handbook No. 456. U.S.Department of Agriculture, 1975.

Milk source	%Water	Carbohy.	Prot.	Fat	Minerals
Human	87.6	7.0	1.2	3.8	0.21
% Energy	0.0	42	7.0	51	0.0
Goat	86.9	4.4	3.8	4.1	0.85
% Energy	0.0	26	21	53	0.0
Cow	87.3	4.8	3.0	3.7	0.72
% Energy	0.0	30	19	52	0.0
Cat	81.6	5.0	10	3.3	0.5
% Energy	0.0	22.0	44.0	34	0.0

during one single nursing period. It has been found that at the end of nursing it may contain 4-5 times more lipids and 1.5 times more proteins than at the beginning.

Composition of colostrum is different from early milk of the first 6 weeks after childbirth. Copper (Cu) concentration for example, goes down from 1.34 ug/ml of colostrum to 0.2 ug/ml of mature milk; cholesterol content also goes down drastically. Early milk likewise is high in many constituents compared to mature milk. The concentration of protein, for example, drastically reduces from 12-13% on day one to 2% on day five and less than 1% in mature milk. Concentration of nutrients such as protein, lipid, iron (Fe), calcium (Ca), sodium (Na) and potassium (K) also vary in the breast milk of a preterm and that of a full-term infant. The mean Ca content increases from 20mg/100ml for early milk to 30mg/100ml for mature milk. However, in all cases lactose content of milk remains stable. While the concentration and ratios of nutrients change, their diversity remains throughout the lactating period. Human colostrum, for example, has roughly 30 more components than cow's milk.

Nutrients of breast milk are tailored to meet growth and developmental needs of the infant's brain and the body and to initiate the ecological succession of intestinal microbial flora. The amount of milk that an infant gets, correlates with the baby's suckling which in turn depends upon its appetite and velocity of growth. Production of the enzyme lactase needed to digest lactose, the milk sugar, increases in the intestine as infant increases its suckling habit and consumes more milk; while digested lactose supplies energy to the brain and other parts of the body, the undigested lactose supplies the major nutrient to initiate the development of fermentative bacterial flora in the colon (see Chapter 13). During the intervening period from breast-feeding to weaning, breast-milk plays a significant role in coordinating the utilization of nutrients by brain, body and microflora. breast feeding is adapted to control the supply of nutrients among the entities, brain, body and the microflora, in an optimal manner. Let us consider the homeostasis of a few key nutrients in milk.

Iron

Iron is a crucial nutrient not only for the developing infant but also for the growth of transient microbes such as pathogenic bacteria. Breast milk is naturally quite low in iron and what iron it contains is tightly bound to the protein lactoferrin and dispersed into the milk fat globules. Such tight binding and dispersion improves iron bioavailability. It also serves to withhold iron from pathogens, thereby providing the infant with another line of defense against infection. These features of low concentration and tight protein binding of essential nutrients such as iron are believed to be an important contribution to the phenomenon that breast-fed infants are more resistant to childhood infections by transient pathogens.

Lipids

The exclusively breast-fed infant receives roughly 52% of its energy from lipids, 41% from carbohydrates and 7% from proteins. Breast milk lipids are of various sorts, some in very minute quantities. They generally exist as globules. The total lipid content of breast milk increases gradually from approximately 2.8% of colostrum to more than 4% in mature milk. In addition to providing energy, the lipids also supply essential substances such as phospholipids, cholesterol, saturated (SFA) and unsaturated fatty acids (USFA), medium chain fatty acids (MCFA) and polyunsaturated fatty acids (PUFA). These nutrients participate in functions of all three entities, and they are especially important in the development of the brain. Out of 30 different fatty acids (FAs) identified in the breast milk, the ones that are rich in colostrum are those that have been found to be rich in brain tissues.In addition, cholesterol has been proposed to play a unique role in regulating appetite and satiety of infants. While total lipid content increases from colostrum to mature milk, the cholesterol and phospholipid content goes down gradually and level off in mature milk. Nevertheless mature human breast milk contains twice as much cholesterol and six times as much lecithin as does mature cow's milk.

The USFA accounts for 56% of the FA in human colostrum and 54% of the FA in mature human milk. Such a ratio stimulates use of USFA more than SFA. According to reports analysis of colostrum and mature milk samples revealed that colostrum is richer in PUFAs such as arachidonic and linolenic acids than mature milk. Human milk contains twice the amount of octadecadienoic acid than does cow's milk; this compound is a precursor to several important regulatory substances. Most FAs are synthesized in the breast (mammary glands) and their content have been found to vary with maternal diet. Breast milk contains 7% linoleic acid compared to 1% of cow's milk. Infant formulas (breast milk substitutes) contain vegetable oils in place of the naturally occurring mix of specialized lipids.

The milk of Egyptian women whose diet is richer in plant staples compared to American women has been found to have significantly greater amounts of USFAs such as oleic, linolenic and arachidonic acids. They have been found to have a role in increasing infants resistance to disease. Linolenic acid which normally varies between 8-10% of breast milk fat of Western women, has been found to occur up to 18% in Egyptian women. The MCFAs are also known to vary with the maternal diet. They enhance absorption of essential nutrients such as minerals and amino acids in the gastrointestinal (G.I.) tract. When dietary habits of mothers in three countries Tanzania, Curacao and Surinam were correlated with MCFA production of milk it was found that breast milk of Tanzanian and Surinam mothers whose diet was rich in carbohydrate had highest percentage of MCFA compared to Curacao mothers who had more protein and fat in their diet.

Lactose

Human milk is particularly rich in lactose, a special sugar that is synthesized from blood glucose, exclusively in the mammary glands. Lactose is a disaccharide made of two monosaccharides glucose and galactose (see Chapter 9). The disaccharide sucrose, but not lactose, is found abundantly in plants. The milk of sea mammals is devoid of lactose, while cow's milk has 4.8% compared to human milk which has nearly 7.0% lactose (see table 16.1). Lactose is one component which does not vary with changes in mother's diet or at different times during the nursing period. Lactose has least sweetness compared to other sugars that exist in the body, and it is the only sugar that, apart from serving as an energy source, is a major protective nutrient. It plays a unique role in the growth and development of brain and body and in establishment of the protective gut bacteria of the human infant:

- Lactose is used in the synthesis of galactosamine, glycoproteins and glycolipids found in particular abundance in the brain and nerve tissues.
- There are indications that lactose may play a role in the infant's body development. Obesity is much more prevalent among children who were formula-fed compared to exclusively breast-fed as babies.
- Unlike glucose or sucrose, lactose is selectively used by only specific kinds of microbes. As a result of this selective utilization of lactose, proper succession of gut bacteria is promoted, resulting in establishment of normal microflora and a barrier to pathogens.

Lactose also influences bioavailability of many major nutrients such as protein and calcium and minor nutrients such as iron, zinc and copper. Chemically lactose and sucrose (white sugar) are disaccharides that contain glucose molecules; their effects on the body are very different. Dietary lactose increases the bioavailability of many nutrients and yet does not interfere in the homeostatic regulation of appetite and satiety of infants. Sucrose however, has been linked to the development of obesity and manifestation of diabetes mellitus. Breast-fed infants are rarely obese. However, formula-fed infants are known to have higher energy intake and expenditure and grow more rapidly than those of breast-fed infants. A group of infants born in 1980 checked over the first year was found to have similar status of weight gain as those in 1933, both infants were predominantly breast-fed; however, the control group of 1964 who were largely formula-fed appeared heavier at all ages four weeks after birth.

Around the 1950s when milk supplemental programs for school children were popularized, the phenomenon of lactose intolerance became evident. Since then, it has been found that as many as 75% of school children who complained of symptoms of lactose intolerance at the beginning of the program had begun to experience gradual decrease in their symptoms, often resulting in complete recovery. This phenomenon has been observed even among adults in both developing and industrialized countries. Many scientists are of the opinion that milk allergies, including lactose intolerance, may be a consequence of milk and milk product (e.g. yogurt) deprivation from infancy. Lactose digestion which depends on increased activity of the enzyme lactase and the lactose digesting bacteria in the gut may need to be cultivated by providing lactose for a period of time. In addition to lactose, breast milk has as many as a dozen different sugars and sugar-derived compounds such as oligosaccharides, amino sugars and sialic acid; each one of them is likely to have a specific physiological role in the body. Oligosaccharides occur at ten-fold higher concentration in breast milk than in cow's milk. Moreover they are found in a dozen different forms. They are believed to have a significant role in the establishment of beneficial gut bacteria.

Amino acids and protein

The ratio of overall protein to energy content in milk is greatest in fast growing species compared to slow growing ones. The human infant, for example, takes 180 days to double its body weight compared to 6 days for a mouse. Human breast milk may have as low as 0.8% protein in contrast to the 11-12% protein composition of mouse milk. Even the milk of large mammals is quite low in protein. That of a rhinoceros is 1.4%; that of a camel or elephant is 3.0%; cow's milk has 3.3% protein and baby formulas typically have 1.5%.

The percentage of protein used to make formula was based upon early studies suggesting 1.2% protein value of breast milk. However this was calculated assuming a total protein nitrogen (PN) to non protein nitrogen (NPN) ratio similar to other animal tissues. Unlike the breast milk of other animals, the milk of primates, especially humans, is very rich in NPN. Human milk contains 25% NPN compared to 5% of cow's milk. When corrected for this difference, the calculated human breast milk protein composition must be reduced to 0.8%. Cow's milk is a good substitute for human breast milk because, like human milk it is relatively low in protein. Moreover, although cow's milk contains a lower ratio of NPN to PN than does human milk, its NPN content is nevertheless higher than that of other domesticated animals.

A low protein content leads a food to be considered poor in essential amino acids (EAA), and hence, of low biological value. Compared to cow's milk breast milk is poorer in its biological value of protein. It is also poorer in the EAA methionine, cystine and tyrosine. However, breast milk is richer in the EAA tryptophan which plays a greater role in neurotransmitter function of the brain. Excess tyrosine has been found to interfere with tryptophan function. In healthy mothers the protein content of milk, especially NPN, is known to remain without fluctuation. This is reflected in similar content of NPN in breast milk of well nourished mothers of both industrialized and developing countries. Thus it may be the case that human milk has evolved its unique composition in order to serve as a specialized food for brain development. By implication, body growth during infancy, and hence the biological value of protein nutrition, is of secondary importance.

When warm milk is acidified, a coagulated precipitate, termed curds, is formed. Milk protein can be distinguished into the proteins that occur in whey (a watery fluid that separates from curdled milk) and casein, the major protein that forms curds. In early milk, as much as 60% of milk protein is whey protein; this may gradually decrease to 40% in mature milk. Milk of other animals, especially cow's milk also contains similar proteins but in different ratios. Cow's milk contains 20% of milk protein as whey protein and is richer in beta lactoglobulin whereas alpha lactalbumin is the major whey protein of human breast milk. In spite of these relative differences, whey is generally rich in several kinds of proteins such as alpha lactalbumin, lactoferrin, lysozyme and immunoglobulins which have physiologically important roles in the infant's health and resistance to disease. Human colostrum and early milk are richer in immunoglobulins (such as IgA and IgG), lactoferrin, lysozyme and macrophages than is mature milk. They all have specific roles in regulating nutrients such as iron and maintaining infants resistance to infections. The IgA content of colostrum, for example, is many-fold higher on day one compared to day five. The casein in human milk forms much softer curds compared to that of cow's and hence is easier for human infants to digest. Moreover the ratio of calcium (Ca) to phosphorus (P) of human milk casein differs from that of cow's milk.

Human milk which is poor in EAAs is quite rich in non-essential amino acids (NEAs). Human milk contains roughly four fold more taurine, a NEA, than cow's milk. Taurine is considered an animal product because it does not exist in plants. Taurine occurs in high concentration in human skeletal muscle, heart, brain and other tissues. Fetal brain contains nearly twice the amount of taurine than does the adult brain. Taurine synthesis in the brain reaches a peak during the neonatal period and gradually decreases during postnatal life. In human milk taurine accounts for 13% of the total free AA pool. It increases from 5 mg/100 ml to about 15 mg/100 ml during the first five weeks of lactation and remains as a significant fraction in mature milk. Taurine may play a major role in central nervous system and cardiovascular regulation and even in the detoxification functions of the liver. It has been suggested to influence cholesterol regulation. The total taurine content of the body is homeostatically regulated by the kidneys. When taurine intake in the diet is eliminated, renal excretion is diminished. Healthy mothers who are vegans (vegetarians who do not consume any animal products) have as much taurine in their milk as do omnivorous mothers. Compared to breast- fed infants formula-fed infants have lower concentrations of taurine in both their plasma and urine. Clearly taurine is likely to play a range of important physiological roles that remain to be fully understood. The observations noted here merely hint at its importance, as do reports that taurine supplementation in children have a favorable effect in disorders as diverse as cystic fibrosis and epilepsy. Given this likely importance, the distinctive content of taurine in human milk should not be ignored.

The overall nutritional constituents of milks in general, and human milk in particular, resemble more a plant rather than animal staple diet. Like plant products the milks are the only animal products that are rich in carbohydrates and in unsaturated fatty acids, especially the PUFAS. Their PN:NPN ratio resembles more of plant than animal products. They are also rich in nutrients such as calcium, potassium and low in sodium, phosphorus and cholesterol. Milk is one of the animal products that is low in protein in general, and methionine an essential amino acid, in specific. As such, milk is a generic food that builds a bridge between diets based on plant and animal products.

Milk and the development of normal microbial flora

The fetus is completely protected by the mother's defence mechanisms until birth. Subsequently, it faces a hostile microbial environment. The composition of breast milk makes the environment of the GI tract more congenial to the normal microbial flora. Fermentation of the high levels of lactose present in milk brings about an acidic pH. Many acid metabolites of lactose such as acetic, lactic, succinic and formic acids are produced in the gut and prevent the establishment of transient pathogens. Together these features selectively foster beneficial microbes and gradually replace the mixed bacterial population initially acquired by the infant's colon with one composed overwhelmingly of certain species of acid-generating and acid-loving bacteria known collectively as bifidobacteria (a kind of fermentative rod-shaped bacteria) . If not for these features of breast milk composition that favor the rapid establishment of beneficial bacteria, the infant might not successfully adapt to its new extra-uterine environment.

In healthy pregnant women, adaptations to protect the infant, such as accumulation of glycogen and change of pH in the vagina, accelerate during the third trimester of the pregnancy. In addition, many beneficial substances such as lactoferrin, lysozyme and oligosaccharides are maintained in higher concentration in colostrum than in mature milk. So called "bifidus factor" (an amino sugar) was isolated from breast milk and found to promote dominance of bifidobacteria. Human milk is about forty times richer in "bifidus factor" than cow's milk.

Milk and brain development

Like other newborn animals, human infants initially have many physical and physiological inadequacies such as unsynchronized bodily rhythms and deficient organ functions. Normally these are optimized by appropriate development, assuming adequate nutrition, during infancy and childhood. The human brain is particularly slow in its maturation. Our closest relatives, the chimpanzees and gorillas, take roughly one year to attain 70% of their brain growth. However human infants take almost three years for this achievement. Choline, an important chemical for brain growth, for example, exists in breast milk of healthy mothers around the world without much variation in concentration. In addition, all events of life such as behavior and learning, body size and physiology that take place at this time also influence health and longevity throughout life; many events of this period are irreversible. No other food fulfills all those needs so appropriately and economically as breast milk does. In spite of it, approximately 1/10 of infant population of developing countries and equally large number in developed countries are deprived of breast feeding mainly because of mother's poor diet or economic pressures which necessitate weaning. In the U.S., for example, only 25% of infants, are breast fed at the age of one week.

Other general benefits of milk as food

In addition to its importance in brain development, establishment of microbial flora, defense against pathogens and provision of essential nutrients, milk has additional benefits.

- It allows superior absorption of calcium compared to other sources. This benefit applies not only to adults in terms of prevention of clinically significant osteoporosis, but also to children in whom a high calcium intake may prevent or reduce absorption and assimilation of lead.
- Its ratio of calcium to phosphate is protective of the kidney in adults. As a result adults consuming large amounts of milk may have a decreased incidence of renal failure.
- Epidemiologically, consumption of two glasses of milk per day has been associated with decreased incidence of stomach cancer among the Japanese. Perhaps this is because fermented products of milk reduce the levels of toxic wastes generated and promote their elimination.
- Breast milk has a mild laxative effect which not only promotes rapid GI transit but may explain why breast fed infants are rarely constipated, a common problem for formula fed infants.
-

Cow's milk is the only food that matches human milk in many respects including its potentially universal availability. Cow's milk contains three times higher concentrations of protein and minerals, similar amount of fat, and 50% less lactose than human milk. Traditionally, cow's milk rather than that of other animals, has been used as a weaning food for infants. Even in localities where milk supply is scarce the weaning children were traditionally given priority. Milk is not an absolutely necessary food for adults. However, it is notable that in cases of severe malnutrition no other food can bring the kind of recovery that can be achieved by feeding milk. No other single food can help human beings to overcome deficiency of the 50 to 55 different nutrients that humans need as effectively as does milk. Not only does milk provide small amounts of a wide range of nutrients, but also it provides large amounts of some particularly valuable substances. Thus, a quart of milk contributes approximately 90% of calcium; 30-40% of most vitamins, as well as a significant percentage of an individual's daily needs of most other minerals, carbohydrates, fatty acids and proteins.

Milk: a universal standard for human nutrition

Milk is the only food that can close the food gap that exists between "The Haves and The Have nots" because it can benefit both groups while being affordable even for the latter. It represents the most economical and efficient conversion of the field crops and pastures into human food, when corrected for nutritional quality. Milk can be produced for almost the same price as cereals and it is more wholesome than any other animal or plant products. According to the data presented by John Steinhart and Carol E. Steinehart of University of Wisconsin, milk can be produced at a cost of less than 0.5 calorie/calorie output. In contrast distant fishing and feedlot beef production requires nearly 40 times more enery subsidies. Other animal food products are not only more expensive to produce but also have major nutritional drawbacks related to their high protein and fat content and absence of dietary carbohydrate and fiber. Therefore, milk as a supplement to high roughage plant food, is beneficial for both those who need to lose or to gain weight. For the former, non-fat milk assures adequate supplies of essential nutrients during caloric restriction (dieting). For the latter, whole milk can address a range of dietary deficiencies which may be manifest when caloric restriction is relieved. Unfortunately, neither the industrialized countries nor developing countries are taking about the advantages of this unique evolutionarily designed food. Industrialized countries produce enough milk to supply every citizen roughly 25% of their total requirement of protein in the form of milk. Yet milk has been displaced by the popularity of soft drinks. In the developing world lack of awareness of the economy and value of milk has diminished the importance placed on its production and hence it is often in short supply.

Culturally, the superior value of cow's milk can be traced back as far as the time of the Vedas (1400 B. C.). The origin of the "sacred cow" concept came about because the ancient Hindus regarded the cow as an "alternate mother." They seem to have intuitively recognized that milk was essential to protect the health of pregnant women, lactating mothers, weaning children and the elderly (see Chapter 18). Milk also had a special place in American and other western cultures until the recent rise in popularity of soft drinks. According to McCollum "milk is one food for which there is no effective substitute". Three decades ago an average American consumed 33 gallons of milk per year. However, by 1985 per capita milk consumption had dropped to 27 gallons while that of soft drinks jumped from 19.5 gallons to 45.6 gallons. According to recent reports, consumption of milk by the average American is at an all time low and of soft drinks at an all time high.

Milk is an excellent complement to plant staple diets in that plant products provided bulk while milk provides the range of nutrients that insures that particular deficiencies will not develop, even if the variety of plant products consumed is not as broad as is desirable. Both milk and plant products could be made available to all human populations in any parts of the world at the least effort and cost. In contrast the meat-based diets of the modern industrialized countries supply neither variety nor bulk —and are expensive: approximately 10 lbs of food grains are used to produce one pound of meat. As pointeded out to Mahatma Gandhi (p.25, 1949) by the nutrition scientist, Dr. Robert McCarrison : ". . . in the minds of those of us who have devoted a life-time to the study of nutrition . . . milk is one of the greatest blessings given to mankind."

Selected Sources and Suggested Readings

G. Harvey Anderson, Stephanie A. Atkinson and M. Heather Bryan, 1981. Energy and macronutrient content of human milk during early lactation from mothers giving birth prematurely and at term. *American J. Clinical Nutrition,* 34, 258-265

Roslyn B. Alfin-Slater and Derrick B. Jelliffe, 1977. Nutritional requirements with special reference to infancy. *Pediatrics Clinics North America,* 24, 3-16

Jonathan C. Allen, et al 1991. Studies in human lactation: milk composition and daily secretion rates of macronutrients in the first year of lactation. *American J. Clinical Nutrition,* 54, 69-80

Anonymous, 1992. The use of whole cow's milk in infancy. *Pediatrics,* 89, 1105-1109

Anonymous, 1991. Highlights from USDA's Children Research Center. *Nutrition Today,* January/February, 4-5

Anonymous, 1973. Overfeeding in the first year life. *Nutrition Reviews,* 31, 116-118

Anonymous,1970. Intestianl lactase-an inducible enzyme? *Nutrition Reviews,* 28, 138-140

Anonymous, 1968. Present knowledge of ascorbic acid (vitamin C). *Nutrition Reviews,* 26, 33-36

Anonymous, 1943. Colostrum and vitamin A. *Nutrition Reviews,* 1, 206-207

R.L. Atkinson, E.H. Kratzer, and G.F. Stewart, 1957. Lactose in animal and human feeding: A review. *J. Dairy Science,* 40, 1114-1132

Amadu D. Ayebo and Khem M. Shahani, 1980. Role of cultured dairy products in the diet. *Cultured Dairy Products* J. 15, 21-29

F.J. Ballard, 1978. Restricted nutrition and protein turnover. *J. Human Nutrition,* 32, 245-252

Giulio J.Barbero, et al., 1952. Investigations on the bacterial flora, pH, and sugar content in the intestinal tract of infants. *J. Pediatrics,* 40, 152-163

George H. Beaton and Anne Chery, 1988. Protein requirements of infants: a reexamination of concepts and approaches. *American J. Clinical Nutrition,* 48, 1403- 1412

Henri Beerens, C Romond and C. Neut, 1980. Influence of breast-feeding on the bifid flora of the newborn intestine. *American J. Clinical Nutrition,* 33, 2434-2439

B.A. Bernstein, T. Richardson, and C.H. amundson, 1976. Inhibition of cholesterol biosynthesis by bovine milk, cultured buttermilk, and orotic acid. *J. Dairy Science,* 59, 539-543

Marlene W. Borschel, 1986. Fatty acid composition of mature human milk of Egyptian and American women. *American J. Clinical Nutrition,* 44, 330-335

Nancy Butte, et al, 1987. Macro- and trace-mineral intakes of exclusively breast-fed infants. *American J. Clinical Nutrition,* 45, 42-48

A.J. Cant, 1984. Diet and the prevention of childhood allergic disease. *Human Nutrition: Applied Nutrition,* 38A, 455-468

Graham Carpenter, 1980. Epidermal growth factor is a major growth-promoting agent in human milk. *Science,* 210, 198-199

Clare E. Casey, 1989. The nutritive and metabolic advantages of homologous milk. *Proc. Nutrition Society,* 48, 271-281

Kathryn G. Dewey, et al., 1992. Growth of breast-fed and formula-fed infants from 0 to 18 months: The Darling Study. *Pediatrics,* 89, 1035-1041

Sheelagh Donovan, 1983. Milk composition and its implications in the adult diet. *Proc. Nutrition Society,* 42, 375-384

G. Dorner and H. Grychtolik, 1978. Long-lasting ill-effects of neonatal qualitative and/or quantitative dysnutrition in the human. *Endokrinology,* 71, S81-88

Klaus Dörner, et al., 1989. Longitudinal manganese and copper balances in young infants and preterm infants fed on breast-milk and adapted cow's milk formulas. *British J. Nutrition,* 61, 559-572

R.M. English, 1985. Breast-milk production and energy exchange in human lactation. *British J. Nutrition,* 53, 459-466

Ruth M. Feeley, et al., 1983. Copper, iron, and zinc contents of human milk at early stages of lactation. *American J. Clinical Nutrition,* 37, 443-448

Dorothy A. Finley, et al., 1985. Inorganic constituents of breast milk from vegetarian and nonvegetarian women: Relationships with each other and with organic constituents. *J. Nutrition,* 115, 772-781

P.F. Fox, 1978. Milk and dairy products as food materials. *Proc. Nutrition Society,* 37, 247-257

Gun-Britt Fransson. and Bo Lonnerdal, 1984. Iron, copper, zinc calcium, and magnesium in human milk fat. *American J. Clinical Nutrition,* 39, 185-189

M. K. Gandhi. *Diet and Diet Reform.* Navajivan Publishing House, Ahmedabad, 1949

Gerald E. Gaull, et al., 1977. Milk protein quantity and quality in low-birth weight infants. *J. Pediatrics,* 90, 348-355

Robert A. Gibson, and Garry M. Kneebone, 1981. Fatty acid composition of human colostrum and mature breast milk. *American J. Clinical Nutrition,* 34, 252-257

Angel Gil, et al., 1986. Effect of dietary nucleotides on the plasma fatty acids in at-term neonates. *Human Nutrition: Applied Nutrition,* 40 C, 185-195

Roger L. Glass, et al., 1983. Protection against cholera in breast-fed children by antibodies in breast milk. *New England J. Medicine,* 308, 1389-1392

Armond S. Goldman, 1991. Immunology of milk and the neonate conference. *Nutrition Today,* September/October, 30-31

Mavis Gunther, 1975. The neonates immunity gap, breast feeding, and cot death. *Lancet,* 1, 441-442

Michael J. Gurr, 1989. Does nature know best? *British J. Nutrition,* 62, 241-243

Paul György, 1971. Biochemical aspects of human milk. American *J. Clinical Nutrition,* 24, 970-975

P. György, 1957. Development of intestinal flora in the breast-fed infant. *Modern Problems in Padiatrics,* 2, 1-12

Paul György, 1955. Human milk versus cow's milk. Given at *International Nutrition Congress,* Amsterdam, September,1954. Overdruk uit, *Voeding,* Jaargang 16, 1955. 347-362

Barbara Hall, 1975. Changing composition of human milk and early development of an appetite control. *Lancet,* 1, 779-781

Leif Hambraeus, 1982. The significance of mother's milk and breast feeding for development and later life. *Biblithca Nutrtio Dieta,* 31, 1-16

Leif Hambraeus, 1977. Proprietary milk versus human breast milk in infant feeding. *Pediatric Clinics Of North America,* 24, 17-36

G. Harzer, M. Haug and J.G. Bindles, 1986. Biochemistry of maternal milk in early lactation. *Human Nutrition: Applied Nutrition,* 40A, (Suppl. 1), 11-18

Gershon Hepner, et al., 1979. Hypocholesterolemic effect of ypgurt and milk. *American J. Clinical Nutrition,* 32, 19-24

Corinna Hibberd, et al., 1981. A comparison of protein concentrations and energy in breast milk from preterm and term mothers. *J. Human Nutrition.* 35, 189-195

Takeshi Hirayama, 1975. Epidemiology of cancer of the stomach with special refrence. Recent decrease in Japan. *Cancer Research,* 35, 3460-3463

Anthony D. Hitchins and Frank E. McDonough, 1989. Prophylactic and therapeutic aspects of fermented milk. *American J. Clinical Nutrition*, 49, 675-684

Dorothy A. Jackson, et al., 1988. Circadian variation in fat concentration of breast-milk in rural northern Thai population. *British J. Nutrition,* 59, 349-363

Sandra W. Jacobson and Joseph L. Jacobson, 1992. Breastfeeding and intelligence. *Lancet,* 339, 926

Lennart Jansson, Bjorn Akersson, and Lars Holmberg, 1981. Vitamin E and fatty acid composition of human milk. *American J. Clinical Nutrition,* 34, 8-13

D. B. Jelliffe and E. F. P. Jelliffe, Guest editors, 1971. The Uniqueness of human milk. *American J. Clinical Nutrition,* 24, 968-1013

Robert E. Jensen, et al., 1988. Huamn milk as a carrier of messages to the nursing infant. *Nutrition Today,* November/ December, 20-25

Markku J. T. Kallio, et al, 1992. Exclusive breast-feeding and weaning: Effect on serum cholesterol and lipoprotein concentrations in infants during the first year of life. *Pediatrics,* 89, 663-666

Barry S. Kendler, 1989. Taurine: An overview of its role in preventive medicine. *Preventive Medicine,* 18, 70-100

Clemens Kunz and Bo Lonnerdal, 1990. Human-milk proteins: analysis of casein and casein subunits by anion-exchange chromatography, gel electrophoresis, and specific staining methods. *American J. Clinical Nutrition,* 51, 37-46

Joanne Leslie, William C. MacLean,Jr., and George G. Graham, 1979. Effect of an episode of severe malnutrition and age on lactose absorption by recovered infants and children. *American J. Clinical Nutrition,* 32, 971-974

J.L. Linzell, 1967. Diet and milk secretion. *Proc. Nutrition Society,* 27, 44-52

L. Lloyd-Hughes and C. E. J. Daniels, 1988. Substitution of skimmed milk for high-fat milk in the diet of men and women in South Wales. *Europena J. Clinical Nutrition,* 42, 715-723

Bo Lonnerdal, Carl L. Keen, and Lucille S. Hurley, 1981. Iron, copper, zinc, and Manganese in milk. *Ann Review of Nutrition,* 1, 149-174

Bo Lonnerdal, et al., 1976. Breast milk composition in Ethiopian and Swedish mothers. II. Lactose, nitrogen, and protein contents. *American J. Clinical Nutrition,* 29, 1127-1133

I. Macdonald, 1978. Clinical effects of consuming milk and its products. *Proc. Nutrition Society,* 37, 241-245

George V. Mann, 1977. A factor in yogurt which lowers cholesteremia in man. *Atherosclerosis,* 26, 335-340

William Manson, 1978. Aspects of the value and the limitations of milk protein as a food material. *Proc. Nutrition Society,* 37, 217-223

Leonard J. Mata, Franklin Jimenez & Maria L. Mejicanos, 1971. Evolution of intestianl flora of children in health and disease. *Asociacion Mexicana de Microbiologia,* 363-374

Leonard J. Mata and Juan J. Urrutia, 1971. Intestinal colonization of breast-fed children in a rural area of low socioeconomic level. *Annals of New York Academy of Sciences,* 176, 93-109

Leonard J. Mata and Richard G. Wyatt, Host resistance to infection. *American J. Clinical Nutrition,* 24, 976-986

Curtis J. Metlin, Elinor R. Schoenfeld, and Nachimuthu Natarajan, 1990. Patterns of milk consumption and risk of cancer. *Nutrition and Cancer,*, 13, 89-99

Elie Metchnikoff, *Scientifically Soured Milk.* La Société Le Ferment, Paris, 1907

Reynaldo Miranda, et al., 1983. Effect of meternal nutrition status on immunological substances in human colostrum and milk. *American J. Clinical Nutrition,* 37, 632-640

Frank H. Morriss, Jr, et al., 1986. Relationship of human milk pH during course of lactation to concentrations of citrate and fatty acids. *Pediatrics* 78, 458-464

J.H. Moore, 1978. Cow's milk and human nutrition. *Proc. Nutrition Society,* 37, 231-239

F.A.J. Muskiet, et al. 1987. Comparison of the fatty acid of human milk from mothers in Tanzania, Curacao and Surinam. *Human Nutrition: Clinical Nutrition,* 41C, 149-159

Indira Narayanan, 1985. Nutrition for preterm and growth retarded infants: Developing country concerns. *Human Nutrition: Applied Nutrition,* 39A, 242-254

Charlotte C. Neumann and Derrick B. Jellffe, 1977. Symposium on Nutrition in Pediatrics. Foreword. *Pediatric Clinic North America,* 24, 1-2

Margaret C. Neville, et al., 1991. Studies in human lactation: milk volume and nutrient composition during weaning and lactogenesis. *American J. Clinical Nutrition,* 54, 81-92

Molly Niv, Walter Levy and Nathan M. Greenstein, 1963. Yogurt in the treatment of infantile diarrhea. *Clincal Pediatrics,* 2, 407-411

Adewale Omolulu, 1982. Breast-feeding practice and breast milk in rural Nigeria. *Human Nutrition: Applied Nutriton,* 36A, 445-451

Margaret C. Phillips and George Briggs, 1975. Symposium: Milk and dairy products for the American diet. *American J. Dairy Science,* 58, 1751-1763

Thomas A. Picone, 1987. Taurine update: Metabolism and function. *Nutrition Today,* July/August, 16-20

Mary F. Picciano, 1987 Nutrient needs of infants. *Nutrition Today,* January/February, 9-13

J.W.G. Porter, 1978. Milk as a source of lactose, vitamins and minerals. *Proc. Nutrition Society,* 37, 225-331

E.M.E. Poskitt, 1983. Infant feeding: A review. *Human Nutrition: Applied Nutrition,* 37A, 271-286

Surinder K. Rana and T.A. B. Sanders, 1986. Taurine concentration in the diet, plasma, urine and breast milk of vegans compared with omnivores. *British J. Nutrition,* 56, 17-27

David K. Rassin, et al., 1977. Milk protein quantity and quality in low-birth-weight infants. *J. Pediatrics,* 90, 356-360B

G.V. Reddy, K.M. Shahani, and M.R. Banerjee, 1973. Inhibitory effect of yogurt on Ehrlich Ascites tumor-cell proliferation. *J. National Cancer Institute,* 50, 815-817

A.K. Roberts, 1986. Prospects for further approximation of infant formulas to human milk. *Human Nutrition: Applied Nutrition,* 40A (Suppl. 1), 27-37

Susan Roberts and W. A. Coward, 1984. Lactation increases the efficiency of energy utilization in rats. *J. Nutrition,* 114, 2193-2200

Louis L. Rusoff, 1970. Milk: Its nutritional value at a low cost for people of all ages. *J. Dairy Science,* 53, 1296-1302

A. Sanchez-Pozo et al., 1987. Protein composition of human milk in relation to mothers' weight and socioeconomic status. *Human Nutrition: Clinical Nutrition,* 41C, 115-125

Sarah E. Samuels, Sheldon Margen and Edger J. Schoen, 1985. Incidence and duration of breast-feeding in a health maintenance organization population. *American J. Clinical Nutrition,* 44, 504-510

J. Sanguansermsri, P. Gyorgy and F. Zilliken, 1974. Polyamines in human milk and cow's milk. *American J. Clinical Nutrition,* 27, 859-865

Dwayne C. Savage and Julia S. Mc Allister, 1970. Microbial interactions at body surfaces and resistance to infectious diseases. *Proc. International Symposium* By the Western College of Veterinary Medicine. University of Saskatchewan, July 3-4

Dennis, A. Savaiano, et al., 1984. Lactose malabsorption from yogurt, pasteurized yogurt, sweet acidophilus milk, and cultured milk in lactase-deficient individuals. *American J. clinical Nutrition,* 40, 1219-1223

Eugene Schiff, 1989. Benefits of yogurt seen in GI infections, Candidiasis, Highlights issue for the 20th Infection Conferances on *Antimicrobial Agents and Chemotherapy.* Houston, Texas, September: 17-20

Khem M. Shahani and Ramesh C. Chandan, 1979. Nutritional and healthful aspects of cultured and culture-containing dairy foods. *Dairy Science,* 62, 1685-1694

H.C. Sherman and H. L. Campbell, 1924. Growth and reproduction upon simplified food supply. *J. Bilogical Chemistry,* 69, 5-15

P. C. Thomas, 1983. Milk protein. *Proc. Nutrition Society,* 42, 407-418

Rudolph M. Tomarelli, Ruth Hartz and F.W. Bernhart, 1960. The effect of lactose feeding on the body fat of the rat. *J. Nutrition,* 71, 221-228

L. A. Vaughan, C. W. Weber, and S.R. Kemberling, 1979. Longitudinal changes in the mineral content of human milk. American *J. Clinical Nutrition,* 32, 2301-2306

S.F. Villalpando, et al 1992. Lactation performance of rural Mesoamerindians. *European J. Clinical Nutrition,* 46, 337-348

Nicholas Wade, 1974. Bottle-feeding: Adverse effects of a Western Technology. *Science,* 184, 45-48

Emma S. Weigley, 1988. Infant feeding practices- A century of transitions. *Nutrition Today,* March/April 20-24

R.G. Whitehead, M. Lawrence and A.M. Prentice, 1986. Maternal nutrition and breast feeding. *Human Nutrition: Applied Nutrition* 40A (Suppl 1), 1-10

R.G. Whitehead, 1983. Nutritional aspects of human lactation. *Lancet,* 1, 167-169

Elsie M. Widdowson, 1984. Milk and the newborn animal. *Proc. Nutrition Society* 43, 87-100

Dale H. Wytock and Jack A. DiPalma, 1988. All yogurts are not created equal. *American J. clinical Nutrition,* 47, 454-457

Steven H. Zeisel, Douglas Char and Nancy Sheard, 1986. Choline, Phosphotidylcholine and sphingomyelin in human and bovine milk and infant formulas. *J. Nutrition,* 116, 50-58

17

Food for Growth and Productive Life

Abstract: Dietary needs differ during different periods of life. Our dietary need for protein and fat decreases with age while that of fiber and bulk increases, reflecting the generally more sedentary lifestyle, decreased cell and tissue growth, and increased generation of by-products in older age groups. The best way to adapt to these changes in lifestyle and physiology is by a gradual transition in diet in the direction of decreasing nutrient density while maintaining the dietary themes of variety and bulk throughout life. The periods of intra-uterine growth, adolescence, middle age and old age are discussed with respect to their unique nutritional requirements. The importance of minimizing nutritional stress to maximize the duration of productive life in adulthood is emphasized.

One of the great mysteries of life is the development of form and function of living beings. Development involves different processes in particular component tissues. One such process is increase in cell number (hyperplasia). Another such process is increase in cell size (hypertrophy). Differentiation is the process by which cells with many potential forms commit themselves to one particular form. This commitment is manifest when cells take on specialized functions and displaying distinctive nutritional needs. All life forms including humans go through these processes to achieve growth and maturity and respond to a changing external environment. Development is particularly complex in long-lived organisms because their inherited genetic informational units (genes) must contain operational information to maintain form and function for a long lifespan. All animals, for example, posses organs such as kidneys, heart and lungs which are structurally similar but their operational complexity increases with the longevity of the species. The life-span itself is species specific. While genomes (nature) control the maximum longevity, the environment (nurture) influences productivity of life, or the duration of time in adulthood when an individual is healthy and productive. Within a human lifespan the overall need for protein and fat in the diet decreases while the need for fiber and bulk increases. Beyond this generalization, several periods can be distinguished during which nutrition modification may be crucial to optimizing growth and maturation, slowing degeneration, and ultimately maximizing productivity of life. These periods are i) the time of intrauterine growth, ii) puberty, iii) middle age and iv) old age.

Intrauterine growth

Intrauterine growth begins in the mother's womb after the union of two minute cells, the sperm and the egg, forming a zygote. The zygote divides and grows until it reaches a critical mass of cells and differentiation begins. The growth and organization caused by differentiation transforms the zygote into an embryo. During the embryonic period, the rate of hyperplasia and hypertrophy differs from tissue to tissue. Hyperplasia is a much more strictly regulated process than hypertrophy. Differentiation is the key to growth, maturation and aging of tissues. When regulation fails, any cells of the body have the potential to remain as undifferentiated cell masses (tumors). The intrauterine growth rate is exceedingly fast, causing embryos to need large amounts of varied nutrients. In the course of 9 months, a fertilized egg increases its weight six billion times. Human weight increases only 20 times from birth to adulthood.

The intrauterine period is one of tremendous vulnerability to the effects of deficiencies of necessary nutrients and exposure to toxic substances, influencing the individual's life more than what takes place after birth. The embryo, later becoming the fetus, depends upon the homeostatic mechanisms of the mother until about 28 of the 40 intrauterine weeks are completed. The amount and combination of sex hormones present in the mother's amniotic fluid and blood circulation during the fetal stage, for example, may be related to sex characteristics and aggressive behavior expressed by an adult. Other environmental factors such as the deficiency or excess of crucial nutrients, exposure to toxic substances, infection and radiation of the mother also can affect the fetus and cause congenital deformities. Many congenital deformities such as defects of the eyes, bones and muscles have been traced to such influences during the early intrauterine period. The amount of iodine the body needs to ingest in daily food, for example, is so small that it cannot be seen by the naked eye; however, its deficiency or excesses in the mother's diet can cause mental retardation, hyperactivity, mineral imbalance and other health problems in an infant. Likewise ingestion of alcohol, even in moderate quantities, by a pregnant woman, may adversely affect fetal development and subsequent behavior of the infant.

Some body tissues and organs regenerate during the life of the individual, others cannot be replaced after birth, greatly increasing the importance of their optimal development in the intrauterine period.

The majority of neurons in an adult brain, for example, finish their development before the age of two. Even a healthy person may retain only one-third of them by the time he or she is 100 years old. Damaged neurons do not regenerate. Unlike the brain, the liver stops growing when it reaches its genetically determined adult size; if a portion is damaged it regenerates until it reaches its original size. Organs such as the lungs and kidneys operate by developing a limited number of functional units that last for one's life. The functional units of a damaged kidney or a lung do not regenerate, however, the remaining units can takeover the function of damaged parts. Unlike those organs, epithelial cells of the skin, red blood cells and the cells of the intestinal mucosa are replaced daily.

Puberty

Growth can slow down, stabilize and accelerate, as a result of either nature (age, genetic influences) or nurture (nutrition and environmental influences). Infants born prematurely usually catch up with normal growth if they are nursed adequately. Growth slows down between the ages of 4-10 and increases again as puberty starts. After adolescence, very little growth in height takes place but growth in weight continues off and on throughout life. Some metabolic processes also slow down and stabilize before adulthood. Breathing, for example, occurs 30-40 times per minute during infancy and decreases to 20 times by age 6 and 18 times in adults. Similar changes take place in the function of other organs such as the heart and kidneys.

Around age 13 the pubertal growth spurt starts, involving increased appetite, weight gain, and accelerated energy metabolism. It is the result of the unified action of many neuroendocrine hormones such as gonadal steroids, prolactin and growth hormones. The homeostatic mechanism of the body regulates almost all changes including metabolic acceleration and stabilization. The velocity of the pubertal growth spurt is much slower than earlier growth. A newborn, for example, is roughly 2 feet long and weighs 8 pounds. It takes almost 18 years to reach an adult height of 6 feet and weight of 150 pounds.

Dietary and hormonal interactions are highly influential factors in regulating growth, especially during the adolescent period. Anorexia nervosa, a syndrome characterized by extreme weight loss, common during puberty, involves diet/hormonal interactions. Anorectic patients show a marked reduction in the level of gonadotropic hormones in their blood, which normalizes when they undergo nutritional therapy. Malnourished children who show delayed puberty compared to the well-nourished also show reduced plasma hormonal levels. An excess of adrenal corticosteroid hormones is thought to interfere with normal menstrual and menopausal cycles and maintaining resistance to infection and is believed to promote hypertension, atherosclerosis and gastric ulcers. According to one study, 39% of overweight teenagers exhibited early menarche and decreased fertility. Early menarche is also a recognized risk factor for breast cancer.

Middle Age and Old Age and Productivity of Life

Appetite and weight gain slow down at around age 20 and stabilize during middle-age. Menopause in women is the result of the actions of diet and hormones. It is hard to define maturity in a human being. Completion of physical growth takes nearly 20 years, after which the passage of additional time is often necessary for individuals to accumulate the life experiences necessary for them to mature emotionally and intellectually. For most humans, productivity of life is related to maturity. Because of the slow development and long life span of human beings, they cannot achieve full productivity unless middle age is prolonged. Animal studies and many epidemiological studies show that both an inadequate diet that curtails early development, and overnutrition that promotes premature aging, shorten middle-age.

In 1975 Alexander Leaf, professor of clinical medicine at Harvard Medical School, observed that there are communities around the world where many people claim to be centenarians. Subsequently to the initial study, he could not confirm their exact ages, but, undoubtedly, they were very old. He clearly observed that their lifestyle was very vigourous compared to people of their ages in advanced industrialized countries. They also are not afflicted with, or experience much later in life, a wide range of age-related diseases including cataracts, diabetes, obesity, atherosclerosis, arthritis, chronic renal failure, osteoporosis, dementia and cancers.

From Dr. Leaf's descriptions, it is clear that a common finding among the lifestyles of these vigorous individuals of advanced age is consumption of a subsaturating diet, notably low in protein and fat and rich in bulk and variety. It would appear that they have succeeded in achieving a prolonged middle-age and retained fertility and virility for a longer period than is generally true for the population of the U.S. Thus while, in many ways, the genome determines the maximum life span, these observations suggest that homeostasis of the body determines total productivity. Whether an individual ages gradually at an older age or earlier in a more abrupt fashion, depends upon stress-counteracting versus stress-promoting factors in the modern lifestyle. Nutrition is a particularly prominent factor because the diet is easy to modify from one that is stress-promoting to one that is stress-counteracting, without abandoning other aspects of the modern lifestyle.

The Effects of Nutrition on Aging and Productivity of Life

Epidemiological studies show that undernutrition, overnutrition and other adverse environmental factors that increase stress are the main causes of age-related diseases and premature aging. Scientific studies show premature aging correlates with many stressful activities of life that increase auto-intoxication or free radicals produced in the body (See Chapter 10). The only time that humans are even partially spared from stress is during the fetal stage. After birth almost all normal activities of the brain, the body and the microbes impose stress. Reducing stress increases productivity of life. Stress may be elicited by many environmental factors such as adverse nutrition, intake of alcohol and drugs, infection or psychological factors. Stress is measurable even at the molecular level of gene expression in the form of stress protein production. The homeostatic mechanisms of the body favor activities that minimizes stress. The first fermentative microbial system introduced into the infant is one of the most significant stress-counteracting phenomena (See Chapter 16). Many changes that occur during the weaning period enhance carbohydrate metabolism rather than protein metabolism thereby sparing physiological stress.

The balance between protein synthesis and turnover is an age-related function. As summarized by F.J. Ballard, protein synthesis of the body is the most universal metabolic biomarker of aging. When whole body protein synthesis is measured, a gradual but large decrease is evident by old age. A premature infant utilizes roughly 3.2g of protein per kilogram of body weight which decreases to 1.3g between 10 to 20 months of age and declines to as little as 0.42 g/kg body weight by age 80 years. While normal protein turnover declines with age, the body's protein related activities, such as repair, maintenance and immune protection continue.

Scientific investigations have shown that an increase in dietary protein and fat increases the accumulation of free radicals in the body, which are a source of oxidative stress and which speed aging. An increased supply of complex carbohydrates in the diet supplies a variety of micro-nutrients and antioxidants that quench and reduce the levels of such free radicals. A multinational epidemiological study conducted by the World Health Organization (WHO) has associated better overall antioxidants status of the aged with a lower rate of mortality. Other reports correlate consuming foods rich in antioxidants with reduced mortality from age related diseases. According to a longitudinal study done on aging, older people who had higher plasma vitamin C levels also had higher high-density lipoproteins (HDL, HDL2). The consumption of antioxidant rich bulky foods can extend middle-age and support productive longevity for humans.while it freely allows glucose.

Most of the centenarians who lead productive lives probably derive about 75% of their total food calories from complex carbohydrates, and consume only about 35 grams of dietary protein daily, primarily from milk. The work of Morris Ross demonstrated that experimental animals reared on diets restricted in protein and calories, achieve moderate growth, produce healthy offspring, lead more productive lives and more often complete their life-span than do animals allowed to eat as much as they want. While life expectancy in the U.S. increased roughly 25 years at the turn of the century, since 1950 it has increased only 4 years. The earlier increase is attributed to environmental improvements, especially sanitation and the increased availability of protective foods. The more limited increase since 1950 may be attributed to the increased consumption of a low residue, high meat diet, and the consequent increase in degenerative diseases. Even more important, these changes have affected the quality of life: much of the advances in lifespan in modern industrial society has been achieved through introduction of new technologies (e.g. intensive care units, cardiac bypass grafts, mechanical ventilators, organ transplantation). As a result, much of this recent "advance" is of low quality and achieved at an enormous cost which will be difficult to sustain as the age demographics of the U.S. continue to shift.

Selected Sources and Suggested Readings

M. Amador, J. Bacallao and M. Hermelo, 1992. Adiposity and growth: relationship of stature at fourteen years with relative body weight at different ages and several measures of adiposity and body bulk. *European J. Clinical Nutrition,* 46, 213-219

Carlos M.F. Antunes, et al., 1979. Endometrial cancer and estrogen use. *New England J. Medicine,* 300, 9-13

Anonymous, 1989. Aging and dietary fat and cholesterol transport. *Nutrition Reviews,* 47, 334-336

Anonymous, 1979. The development of adipose tissue in infancy. *Nutrition Reviews,* 37, 194-195

Anonymous, 1972. Adipose cell size and number in experimental human obesity. *Nutrition Reviews,* 30, 60-62

Anonymous, 1971. Fat cell size and lipid metabolism. *Nutrition Reviews,* 29, 188-190

Anonymous, 1946. Nutrition in the aged. *Nutrition Reviews,* 4, 172-173

Anonymous, 1944. Diet, retarded growth, and longevity. *Nutrition Reviews,* 2, 3-4

J.M. Bassett, 1986. Nutrition and early development. *Proc. Nutrition Society,* 45, 1-10

J.M. Bassett, 1989. Hormones and metabolic adaptation in the newborn. *Proc. Nutrition Society,* 48, 263-269

Carolyn D. Berdaneir, 1987. The many faces of stress. *Nutrition Today,* March/April 12-17

Jane E. Brody, 1988. Bone loss is not inevitable with age. *New York Times,* October

Elsie R. Carrington, 1974. Relationship of stilbestrol exposure in utero to vaginal lesions in adolescence*J. Pediatrics* 85, 295-296

Kenneth K. Carroll, 1975. Experimental evidence of dietary factors and hormone-dependent cancers. *Cancer Research,* 35, 3374-3383

Maung M. Cho, Pyone M. Han and Myo Thein, 1987. Comparison of human growth hormone levels in children with satisfactory and unsatisfactory growth. *Human Nutrition: Clinical Nutrition,* 41C, 209-213

Ronni Chernoff, 1987. Aging and Nutrition. *Nutrition Today,* March/April, 4-11

Sandhya Chipalkatti, Ajit K. De and Anant S. Aiyar, 1983. Effect of diet restriction on some biochemical parameters related to aging in mice. *J. Nutrition,* 113, 944-950

David B. Coursin, 1971. Central nervous system hypersensitivity to tryptophan. *American J. Clinical Nutrition,* 24, 821-825

Hans-Diedrich Cremer, 1982. Influence of malnutrition on mental development and behavior. *Bibliotheca Nutritio Et Dieta,* 31, 32 39

J.R. Curtis, 1990. Interventions in chronic renal failure. *British Medical J.* 301, 622-624

Howard J. Curtis, 1966. A composite theory of aging. *Gerontologist,* 6, 143-149

Ricahrd G. Cutler, 1991. Antioxidants and aging. *American J. Clinical Nutrition,* 53, 373S-379S

Hilary J. Dimond and Ann Ashworth, 1987. Infant feeding practices in Kenya, Mexico and Malaysia. *Human Nutrition: Applied Nutrition,* 41A, 51-64

G. Dörner, 1982. Hormones, Nutrition and brain development. *Bibliotheca Nutritio Et Dieta,* 31, 19-31

Albert Eisenstein, 1973. Effect of adrenal cortical hormones on carbohydrate, protein, and fat metabolism.*American J. Clinical Nutrition,* 26, 113-120

Peter T. Ellison, 1982. Skeletal growth, fatness, and menarcheal age: A comparison of two hypotheses. *Human Biology,* 54, 269-281

Rose E. Frisch, 1984. Body fat, puberty and fertility. *Biological Reviews,* 59, 161-188

Douglas Gairdner, 1974. The effect of diet on the development of the adipose organ. *Proc. Nutrition Society,* 33, 119-121

Barry Goldin, et al.,1978. Influence of diet and age on fecal bacterial enzymes. *American J. Clinical Nutrition,* 31, S136-S140

R.J. Goss, 1974. Aging versus growth. *Perspectives in Biology and Medicine,* 17, 485-494

William M. Grant, Carol W. McMullen and Kurt S. Laves, 1983. High fetal estrogen concentrations: Correlation with increased adult sexual activity and decreased aggression in male mice. *Science,* 220. 1306-1309

Joan E. Graystone, and D.B. Cheek, 1978. The role of body composition in the assessment of growth and nutrition. *J. Human Nutrition,* 32, 258-263

M.I. Gurr, 1988. Lipid metabolism in man. *Proc. Nutrition Society,* 47, 277-285

N.Y. Haboubi, R.D. Montgomery, 1992. Small-bowel bacterial overgrowth in elderly people: Clinical significance and response to treatment. *Age and aging,* 21, 13-19

D. Harman, 1986. Free radical theory of aging: role of free radical reactions in the origination and evolution of life, aging and disease processes. *Modern Trends in Aging Research,* 147, 77-83

Peter B. Hill, et al., 1986. Gonadotrophin release and meat consumption in vegetarian women. *American J. Clinical Nutrition,* 43, 37-41

Robin Holliday, 1988. Toward a biological understanding of the aging process. *Perspectives in Biology and Medicine.* 32, 109-122

William B. Kannel and Thomas R. Dawber, 1972. Atherosclerosis as a pediatric problem. *J. Pediatrics,* 80, 544-554

Thomas B. L. Kirkwood, 1992. Comparative life spans of species: why do species have the life spans they do? *American J. Clinical Nutrition,* 55, 1191S-1195S

Ronald E. Kalil, 1989. Synapses formation in the developing brain. *Scientific American,* 76-85

Gina Kolata, 1990. Studies find a link between aggressiveness and cholesterol levels. *New York Times,* September 11, 1990

Gina Kolata, 1986. Obese children: a growing problem. *Science,* 232, 20-21

L.F. Koyl, 1976. The health of middle aged and older workers. *Public Health Review,* 5, 299-311

A.A.O. Laditan, 1982. Hormonal profiles in children with progressively worsening nutritional status. *Human Nutrition: Clinical Nutrition,* 360, 81-86

Alexander Leaf, 1982. Long-lived populations: Extreme old age. *J. American Geriatrics Society,* 30, 485-487

Seymour Levine, 1971. Sexual differentiation: the development of maleness and femaleness. *Western J. Medicine,* 114, 12-17

H. J. Lewerenz, 1982. Xenobiotics in the environment of the fetus and the food of the infant and consequences for later life. *Bibliotheca Nutritio Et Dieta,* 31, 83-94

D.W. Lincoln, 1981. Brain, pituitary and nutrition. *Proc. Nutrition Society,* 40, 307-308

Peter S. Lipski, Peter J. Kelly Olver F.W. James, 1992. Bacterial contamination of the small bowel in elderly people: is it necessarily pathological? *Age and Aging.* 21, 5-12

Malcolm Maclure, et al., 1991. A prospective cohort study of nutrient intake and age at menarche. *American J. Clinical Nutrition,* 54, 649-656

S. Manocha, G. Choudhuri and B.N. Tandon, 1986. A study of dietary intake in pre- and post-menstrual period. *Human Nutrition: Applied Nutrition,* 40A, 213-216

Jean L. Marx, 1988. Sexual responses are-almost-all in the brain. *Science,* 241, 903-904

Jean L. Marx, 1974. Aging Research (I): Cellular theories of senescence. *Science,* 186, 1105-1107

Jean L. Marx, 1974. Aging Research (II): Pacemakers for aging? *Science,* 186, 1196-1197

Edward J. Masoro, 1985. Nutrition and aging- A current assessment. *J. Nutrition,* 115, 842-848

C.M. McCay, Mary F. Crowell and L.A. Maynard, 1935. The effect of retarded growth upon the length of life span and upon the ultimate body size. *J. Nutrition,* 10, 63-79

Clive M. McCay, et al., 1941. Nutritional requirements during the later half life. *J. Nutrition,* 21, 45-60

C.R. Moulton, 1923. Age and chemical development in mammals. *J. Biological Chemistry,* 57, 79-96

Annette Natow and Jo-Ann Heslin, 1980. Nature of the aging process. *J. Nutrition for the Elderly,* 1, 89-99

H. F. Newton-John and D.B. Morgan, 1968. Osteoporosis: disease or senescence? *Lancet,* 1, 232-233

Sergio R. Ojeda, 1991. The mystery of mammalian puberty: How much more do we know? *Perspectives in Biology and Medicine,* 34, 365-383

Jana Parizkova, 1973. Body composition and lipid metabolism. *Proc. Nutrition Society,* 32, 181-186

Charles W. Parker, 1991. Environmental stress and immunity: Possible implications for IgE- mediated allergy. Perspective in *Biology and Medicine,* 34, 197-212

June M. Reinisch, 1981. Prenatal exposure to synthetic progestins increases potential for aggression in humans. *Science,* 211, 1171-1173

T. Brailsford Robertson and L. A. Ray, 1920. Experimental studies on growth. XV. On the growth of relatively long lived compared with that of relatively short lived animals. *J. Biological Chemistry,* 42, 71-107

E.T. Rolls, 1981. Neural peptides in nutrition and development. *Proc. Nutrition Society,* 40, 361-362

Chester B. Rosoff and Harvey Goldman, 1968. Effect of the intestinal bacterial flora on acute gastric stress ulceration. *Gastroenterology,* 55, 212-222

M.H. Ross, E. Lustbader and G. Bras, 1976. Dietary practices and growth responses as predictors of longevity. *Nature,* 262, 548-553

M.H. Ross and G. Bras, 1974. Dietary preference and diseases of age. *Nature,* 250, 263-265

Morton Rothstein, 1986. Biochemical studies of aging. *Chemical and Engineering News,* August 11, 26-35

John W. Rowe and Robert L. Kahn, 1990. Human aging: Usual and successful. *J. Clinical Nutrition,* 9, 26-33

D.A. Schoeller, 1988. Energy requirement of obese children and young adults. *Proc. Nutrition Society,* 47, 241- 246

Claire Schofield, Judith Stewart and Erica Wheeler, 1989. The diets of pregnant and post-pregnant women in different social groups in London and Edinburgh: calcium, iron, retinol, ascorbic acid and folic acid. *British J. Nutrition,* 62, 363-377

J.G. Schofield, 1981. The effects of neuroactive peptides on growth hormone release. *Proc. Nutrition society,* 40, 305 – 306

Nevin Scrimshaw, 1969. The effect of stress on nutrition in adlescent and young adults. In *Adolescent Nutrition and Growth,*. Edited by Felix P.Heald, p.101-117

Hans Selye, 1973. The evolution of the stress concept. *American Scientist,* 61, 692-699

H.C. Sherman and H.L. Campbell, 1934. Rate of growth and length of life. *Science,* 80, 547

H.C. Sherman and H.L. Campbell, 1928. The influence of food upon longevity. *Proc. National Academy of Sciences,* 14, 853-855

D. H. Shmerling, 1976. Development of digestive and absorptive function in the human fetus. *Nutrition and Metabolism,* 20, 76-79

Karen Simmer, et al., 1987. Maternal nutrition and intrauterine growth retardation. *Human Nutrition: Clinical Nutrition,* 41C, 193-197

U. Spahn, et al., 1982. Overnutrition and obesity in childhood as a potential risk for chronic degenerative diseases in later life. *Bibliotheca Nutritio et Dieta,* 31, 61-74

T.D. Spector, C. Cooper, A. F. Lewis, 1990. Trends in admissions for hip fracture in England and Wales, 1968-85.0 *British Medical J.*, 300, 1173-1174

Jerzy Staszewski, 1977. Breast cancer and body build. *Preventive Medicine*, 6, 410-415

Robert A Steiner, 1987. Nutritional and metabolic factors in the regulation of reproductive hormone secretion in the primate. *Proc. Nutrition Society*, 46, 159-175

Jannifer Stromberg, Joel D. Howell and W. A. Achenbaum, 1991. Some thoughts about aging from a nineteenth-century Connecticut Yankee. *Perspective in Biology and Medicine*, 35, 140-144

M.R. Turner, 1978. Effect of age and diet on hormone function. *Proc. Nutrition Society*, 37, 295-299

Goya Wannmethee and A.G. Shaper, 1990. Weight change in middle-aged British men: implications for health. *European J. Clinical Nutrition*, 44, 133-142

Elsie M. Widdowson, 1992. Physiological processes of aging: are there special nutritional requirements for elderly people? Do Mc Cay's findings apply to humans? *American J. Clinical Nutrition*, 55, 1246S-1249S

Elsie M. Widdowson, 1987. Fetal and neonatal nutrition. *Nutrition Today*, September/ October, 16-21

J. Willocks, 1977. Nutrition and the foetus. *Proc. Nutrition Society*, 36, 1-7

R.B. Williams, 1977. Trace elements and congenital abnormalities. *Proc. Nutrition Society*, 36, 25-31

O.H. Wolff and June K. Lloyd, 1973. Childhood obesity. *Proc. Nutrition Society*, 2, 195-198

Michelle M. Zive, et al., 1992. Infant-feeding practices and adiposity in 4-y-old anglo- and Mexican-Americans. American J. Clinical Nutrition, 55, 1104-1108

> . . . Thus, whether we are thinking in terms of individual and family *nutrition policy* or that of a nation or a family of nations, any policy which sufficiently recognizes the newer knowledge of nutrition will give a growing place to fruits, vegetables and milk in the food supply.
>
> The shifting into milk production of a part of the grain hitherto fed the meat animals, is a very important feature of the present trend of the food-production goals of the United States Department of agriculture and of the above-quoted statement issued by the National Research Council. . . . A shift to a slightly higher proportion of milk will in nearly all cases mean a better balanced diet and a larger nutritive value from the same expenditure of money. This is permanently true because the grain-fed meat is inherently more expensive of resources to produce. . . .
>
> – Henry C. Sherman, *Selected Works,* 1948

18

Exercise and Weight Control

Abstract: Among animals, exercise occurs as part of the daily struggle for survival and not as an unconnected activity. Prior to the modern era, humans also obtained exercise, typically, in the course of their daily activities. However, exercise, as so commonly practiced today, is an artificial compensation for the sedentary life and increased nutrient density common in modern affluent life. In moderation it serves as a useful adjunct to maintaining homeostasis, but in excess, exercise can upset homeostasis and damage tissues and organs. Rather than exercising to excess, the appropriate way to compensate for a sedentary lifestyle is to decrease nutrient density by use of bulk. This achieves the goals of physical fitness and weight control at an affordable physiologic cost. This approach utilizes homeostatic mechanisms including appetite and satiety to maintain optimal body weight and fitness.

Homeostasis, Weight Regulation and the Body's Rhythms

Exercise, in a most general sense, is activity performed by the mind or the body that consumes energy. This includes activities such as thinking, walking, running,lifting, stretching etc. In a healthy person the body provides a stable supply of glucose to meet the routine energy needs of the brain and other tissues. Under these normal circumstances, the body's preferred energy source is carbohydrate-rich foods. However, when demand exceeds supply, the body taps other resources to provide overall body energy needs, such as protein and fat. These are less economical and more hazardous sources of energy because of their by-products that are a stress to various organs of the body (see Chapter 11). In times of extreme muscular activity, muscle glycogen provides the local needs of muscle. However this fuel reservoir does not contribute significantly to the needs of tissues other than muscle, unlike liver glycogen which is expended to maintain blood glucose (see Chapter 3). Whether exercise is beneficial, resulting in improved fitness, or is a source of stress depends upon many factors. Especially important among these factors is the fuel source that provides the energy during exercise.

Throughout life, the central nervous system (CNS) is responsible for maintaining the energy homeostasis of the body. It regulates homeostasis through hunger and satiety which in turn coordinate food intake in relation to physical activity and the activity of the autonomic nervous system. By coordinating food and activity, non-human animals maintain a stable body weight throughout life. Animals, for example, either fast or eat less during inactive periods such as hibernation. Similarly, carnivores which eat rich (calorie-dense) food do not eat often, and herbivores and omnivores which eat often do not eat rich food. Horses that run fast, elephants that carry heavy loads and chimpanzees that are very active all maintain a carbohydrate-centered energy economy from infancy (see Chapter 16). Non-human animals generally suffer neither from obesity nor other energy related health problems at young ages. In all mammalian herbivores and omnivores, a carbohydrate-centered energy economy is established during nursing, because milk is carbohydrate-rich (lactose). All through the breast-feeding period, the source of carbohydrate and its concentration remains stable. Fluctuating energy needs are met by adjusting the volume of breast milk.

The CNS controls and coordinates the energy mobilizing systems and organs of the body. Rats depleted of serotonin, a neurotransmitter that regulates rhythmic metabolic functions such as appetite and sleep, become obese. Similarly, some studies suggest that obese individuals synthesize a reduced amount of seratonin. Various hormonal signals arising from the G.I. tract stimulate the CNS satiety response which turns off appetite. Energy mobilizing hormones interconnect virtually all organs and metabolic processes and help the CNS maintain stable energy homeostasis. A healthy person, for example, can endure an hour's vigorous exercise or fast for a day without extreme hunger, panic or exhaustion because liver glycogen is consumed to maintain blood glucose through the coordinated actions of the brain, liver, pancreas and the nervous and endocrine controls that operate between them.

From the most primitive animals to humans, energy transactions are carried out through rhythmic signals monitored by biological clocks. Life starts by coordinated rhythmic activities. Rhythmic activity establishes a stable working relationship between the mind and the body. Rhythmic energy transactions also aid the body to cope with the fluctuating external environment. The metabolism of animals and people changes with changing environmental conditions such as light and temperature. Hot weather, for example, decreases the appetite for energy-dense foods. Many metabolic activities such as sleep and urine output change with the changing seasons. According to some scientists, the rhythmicity of the body may play a role in preventing the growth of cancerous cells. Disruption in rhythmicity is known to hasten aging related illnesses.

Almost all traditional cultures used the rhythmicity of the body and the seasons to manage their health and promote longevity. In the Yoga tradition of India, a cultural practice of four thousand years, for example, it is believed that the first sign of sickness is inactivity (alasya) and the first sign of recovery is synchronized activity. Almost all activities in Yoga such as various Asanas (postures) and Pranayamas (breathing exercises), for example, are rhythmic, gentle and coordinated with diet. When the body is inactive such as during sickness and old age, the tradition encouraged reducing the richness of food. The goal is to use foods that help to integrate all functions of the mind and the body and not stress any one part or system. Hippocrates also emphasized coordinating body functions and food moderation to avoid impaired growth, rapid aging and early death.

Consequences of Disruption of Natural Weight Regulation Mechanisms

The cultural practices emphasizing the rhythms of the body and its metabolism became obscured by advancing industrial technology. Hard physical labor is less common in our society, the use of automobiles and other activities are decreasing human energy consumption. These trappings of modern society are not only more common but are necessary for the livelihood of many people today, especially in the industrialized countries. Scientists and policy makers in the industrial nations have made the mistaken recommendation that energy consumption be regulated by control of food calories, irrespective of their energy source. They recommend to a sedentary work force including business executives, factory and office workers, a Recommended Dietary Allowance (RDA) that was initially developed for individuals engaged in hard physical labor (see Chapter 4).

By the 1950's weight gain and other excess energy-related health problems became a trademark of the industrialized nations, especially the U.S. A body fat content of more than 25% in males, and 30% in females is considered overweight. There are 34 million overweight Americans and 11 million of them are more than 100 pounds overweight. Gaining weight has been recognized as a risk factor for many diseases including stroke, diabetes, hypertension, arthritis and cancers of the breast, bowel and central nervous system. These increased risks are greater in young adults. The risk of adult onset diabetes, for example, is 3 times higher among overweight people. Thus sedentary life and rich foods disrupt or override natural weight regulation mechanisms and cause obesity and other health problems.

Vigorous Exercise is the Wrong Compensation for Energy Imbalance

Exercise, which used to occur as a synchronized daily function necessary for procuring food and as communal activity has become a separate regimen, often for the sole purpose of weight control. Before the early 1970's only a few health-oriented people walked and jogged. By the late 1970's more than half of all American adults were exercising through various sports such as tennis, bicycling, swimming, walking and running to keep themselves fit and slim. By the 1990's long distance running became a cultural phenomena with 31 million people participants in the U.S. The American quest for slimness and fitness has led to more than 30,000 methods of weight control and multi-billion dollar diet and sport industries. In spite of this, obesity has increased in prevalence over the past 25 years in the U.S.

According to a recent poll, one in two American adults exercise regularly, and one in 10 suffer from exercise-related injuries every year, elevating sports medicine to a large-scale industry. According to the New York Times, the number of Sport Medicine Clinics in the U.S. has increased from 300 to 1000 since 1980. Sports medicine and other clinics all over the country treat specific injuries such as sprains and fractures and many other non-specific but debilitating exercise-related ailments related to stressed tissues and organs that are exhausted by improper energy mobilization and incomplete elimination of the by-products of the body's metabolism. The ill-effects of vigorous exercise may subside faster in one individual than in another. In some it may aggravate already existing problems such as heartburn, nausea, abdominal pain, cramps and bowel malfunction. In military and athletic programs emphasizing physical fitness, the incidence of kidney and liver damage has been found to be quite high.

Neither exercise, nor the sports medicine industry have succeeded in helping many people achieve long-term stable body weight. Roughly 50% to 80% of the people who join various fitness and dieting programs drop out. Less than 10% follow any one plan. About 95% of individuals who lose weight regain it within the first year. "On and off dieting" and "on and off exercise" which appear to maintain optimal body weight do so at the expense of disrupting energy homeostasis. Many problems such as headache, fatigue and feelings of hunger, nausea and malaise common to exercising people may be signs of disturbed energy homeostasis and physiology that may lead to other complications. Sports anemia, common to many jogging, running, bicycling, tennis playing and swimming athletes has been attributed to many factors that cause iron deficiency. According to some, it is the result of releasing hemolyzing factors by the spleen, a response intended to increased blood circulation. In such cases, increasing iron in the diet may complicate and worsen the situation (See Chapter 10).

Any method of weight control that deprives people of complex carbohydrates and bulk brings temporary results with long-term risks. Many animal and human studies have linked "yo-yo" weight changes with an instability of energy homeostasis. According to Durnin, University of Glasgow, Institute of Physiology, many health enthusiasts have a mistaken idea of exercise and its effect on the body. The ability of an individual to stay thin, run fast, be able to lift heavy weights, or do any other form of exercise may not be an index of general health. Total well-being cannot be achieved when the body is physically fit but stressed. The physiologic stresses of heavy exercise and dieting for weight reduction affect all systems of the body. The affects on the central and sympathetic nervous systems, and the endocrine system (including metabolic and reproductive functions) are especially profound and will be discussed individually in the following paragraphs.

Effects of Vigorous Exercise on the Nervous System

Decreasing blood glucose, as occurs in heavy exercise, changes the activity of many chemicals in the brain. According to Otto Appenzeller, a neurobiologist at the University of New Mexico, the electrical impulses and production of catecholamines and endorphins in the brain increase during running and continue with increased activity after the running is over. The plasma beta-endorphin level of people who ran for 20 minutes on a treadmill at a speed adjustable to maintain heart rate at 80% of maximum increased greatly after exercise. This effect was greater in men than in women.

Vigorous exercise causes increased sympathetic nervous system (SNS) activity, which increases the basal metabolic rate (BMR), which in turn increases oxygen consuming metabolic activities and the generation of their by-products. Increased (SNS) activity is associated with arrhythmias, angina and hypertension, which are more common in both overweight and over-exercised people. According to the Indian nutrition scientists, Shetty and Kurpad, increased sympathetic nervous system activity may be the penalty for the chronic expenditure of excess calories. Physical exhaustion also raises plasma epinephrine (adrenalin), a major neurotransmitter of the SNS.

Endocrine and Metabolic Effects of Vigorous Exercise

Vigorous exercise greatly increases oxygen consumption. This causes a host of biochemical changes including alterations in level of blood glucose and blood pressure. The production of carbon dioxide increases many Kreb's cycle intermediates and by-products including pyruvate and lactate which increase the acidity of the blood. The concentration of anti-oxidants, such as ascorbic acid, in the blood of people who exercise vigorously has been found to reach the level that is commonly found in acute stages of infection and after surgery. According to J. D. Robertson of the Rowett Research Institute of Aberdeen, U.K., the prolonged exercise that stimulates oxygen consumption and stressful free-radicle mediated peroxidation may cause membrane and tissue damages and alter protein functions. This effect may be more severe in those who are deficient in antioxidants (see Chapter 15).

Exercise changes the secretion of hormones which alter many rhythmic functions such as appetite, sleep, reproduction and circulation. Even though only 5 hormones are involved directly in energy transactions, these hormones interact with other hormones, resulting in more widespread effects. When the blood glucose reaches hypoglycemic levels, even for a short period, the sympathetic nervous system activity increases. Hypoglycemia may also influence the effects of thyroid and growth hormones on fat metabolism. In some athletes, circulating beta-endorphin and plasma growth hormone have been reported to increase as much as 440%. Secretion of thyroid hormone is high in people who vigorously exercise. Blood insulin levels are high when one eats foods rich in carbohydrates and go down with a carbohydrate poor diet, starvation, in diabetics and those who exercise to exhaustion.

Vigorous exercise uncouples many rhythmic functions involved in regulating the heartbeat, kidney, liver and bladder functions. The changed activity of the hormone aldosterone, that regulates kidney function through the elimination of sodium and potassium, affects both the body's fluid-holding capacity and its electrolyte balance. Decreased body fluid effects urine output, increases body acidity and slows the elimination of by-products such as lactic and uric acids. Even a so-called beneficial effect of vigorous exercise, reducing plasma cholesterol, has been attributed to a temporary "stop gap" adaptive reaction.

Exercise affects the hormones that regulate the reproductive system of women. Jogging reduces the amount of circulating estrogens which may cause young women to stop ovulating and menstruating. Over 25% of athletic women cease menstruation. Young women who run 15-60 miles per week have been shown to have reduced bone mass in the spine, early osteoporosis and increased bone fractures, probably related to a decrease in estrogens secondary to changes in hypothalamic and pituitary hormone secretion during exercise. Even moderate exercise which does not result in menstrual irregularities has been found to significantly reduce progesterone levels in the second half of the menstrual cycle.

How to Maintain Optimal Body Weight

Body weight can be maintained or reduced by walking, running, fasting, starving or by increasing the bulk (roughage) of the diet. Mild activities such as a daily walk or a weekly fast cause the body to adjust the BMR and energy expenditure, and may help to lose weight with little disruption in homeostasis. Increasing bulk in the diet can achieve weight loss without hunger because it modifies satiety. For example, according to the British scientist K.W. Heaton, when people were given whole apples, pureed apples and apple juice each containing 60 g of sugars, the time required for ingestion averaged 17 min for whole apples, 6 min for purees and 1 1/2 min for juice. The resulting satiety was significantly greater in apples than with puree and juice. The increase in plasma glucose was the same but subsequently decreased significantly more slowly after eating whole apple than puree or juice.

In a study where people were fed either a defined high, moderate or low carbohydrate diet, the people who ate the low carbohydrate diet experienced more fatigue while exercising. A likely explanation is that these individuals failed to fully regenerate their liver glycogen. As early as 1900 Chittenden demonstrated that a person on a low protein and high complex carbohydrate diet could accommodate steady moderate exercise without adverse effects on health, endurance, mental and physical vigor or longevity.

All animals including humans evolved mechanisms to reduce oxidative stress. By utilizing a low lipid, low protein diet rich in bulk and variety through plant products (and hence rich in antioxidants), we can prolong longevity. Exhausting exercise and consumption of calorie-dense foods lacking in bulk and antioxidants work against our evolutionary adaptations.

The consensus of many scientists is that vigorous exercise is not an adaptive mechanism to maintain optimal weight. Scientists such as Roger Williams felt that the common problem of obesity in the U.S. is related to disordered appetite and satiety mechanisms. Controlling weight without controlling appetite is only transiently effective. Thus, a high complex carbohydrate diet with moderate exercise is the safe and effective way to achieve and maintain optimal body weight.

Selected Sources and Suggested Readings

Demetrius Albanes and Philip R. Taylor, 1990. International differences in body height and weight and their relationship to cancer incidence. *Nutrition and Cancer,* 14, 69-77

Gunvor Ahlborg and Philip Felig, 1982. Lactate and glucose exchange across the forearm, legs, and splanchnic bed during and after prolonged leg exercise. *J. Clinical Investigation,* 69, 45-54

Gunvor Ahlborg, er al., 1974. Substrate turnover during prolonged exercise in man. *Physiological Reviews,* 53, 1080-1090

J.F. Andrews, 1991. Exercise for slimming. *Proc. Nutrition Society,* 50, 459-471

Anonymous, 1991. Orderly dieting and disorderly eating: a case report. *Nutrition Reviews,* 49, 16-20

Anonymous, 1990. Saccharin consumption increases food consumption in rats. *Nutrition Reviews,* 48, 163-165

Anonymous, 1985. Diet, exercise, and health. *Dairy Council Digest,* 56, 13-17

Anonymous, 1984. Weight control. *Dairy Council Digest,* 55, 9-13

Anonymous, 1981. Jogging changes brain responses. *Research Resources Reporter,* 5, 11-12

Anonymous, 1980. Nutrition and human performance. *Dairy Council Digest,* 51,13-17

Anonymous, 1980. Nutritional demands imposed by stress. *Dairy Council digest,* 51, 31-35

Anonymous, 1980. Energy balance throughout the life cycle. *Dairy Council Digest,* 51,19-23

Anonymous, 1972. An exercise-induced protein catabolism in man. *Nutrition Reviews,* 30, 108-110

Anonymous, 1970, Anemia during physical training (sports anemia). *Nutrition Reviews,* 28, 251-253

Anonymous, 1970. Exercise and cholesterol catabolism. *Nutrition Reviews,* 28, 211-212

David P. Barr and Harold E. Himwich, 1923. Studies in the physiology of muscular exercise. III. Development and duration of changes in acid-base equilibrium. *J. Biological Chemistry,* 55, 539-549

Carolyn D. Berdanier and M. K. McIntosh, 1991. Weight loss-weight regain. A vicious cycle. *Nutrition Today,* September/ October, 6-12

Howard L. Bleich and Emily S. Boro, 1978. Fasting, feeding and regulation of the sympathetic nervous system. *New England J. Medicine,* 298, 1295-1301

Beverly A. Bullen, et al.,1985. Induction of menstrual disorders by strenuous exercise in untrained women. *New England J. Medicine,* 312, 1349-1353

E.R. Buskirk, 1981. Some nutritional considerations in the conditioning of athletes. *Annual Review of Nutrition,* 1, 319-350

Daniel B. Carr, et al.,1981 Physical conditioning facilitates. The exercise-induced secretion of beta-endorphin and beta-lipoprotein in women. *New England J. Medicine,* 305, 560-562

Britton Chance, Helmut Sies, and Albert Boveris, 1979. Hydroperoxide metabolism in mammalian organs. *Physiological Reviews,* 59, 527-605

C.J. Coscia, et al., 1977. Stimulation of the sympathetic nervous system during sucrose feeding. *Nature,* 269, 615-619

Kelvin J.A. Davies, Lester Packer, and George A. Brooks, 1981. Biochemical adaptation of mitochondria, muscle, and whole-animal respiration to endurance training. *Archives of Biochemistry and Biophysics,* 209, 539-554

Djoeke van Dale and Win HM Saris, 1989. Repetitive weight loss and weight regain: effects on weight reduction, resting metabolic rate, and lipolytic activity before and after exercise and/or diet treatment. *American J. Clinical Nutrition,* 49, 409-416

Michael H. Ebert, Robert M. Post, and Frederick K. Goodwin, 1972. Effect of physical activity on urinary M.H.P.G. excretion in depressed patients. *Lancet,* 2, 766

M. Elia, 1991. The inter-organ flux of substrates in fed and fasted man, as indicated by arterio-venous balance studies. *Nutrition Research Reviews,* 4, 3-31

Peter T. Ellison and Catherine Lager, 1985. Exercise induced menstrual disorders. *New England J. Medicine,* 313, 825-826

Philip Felig, et al., 1982. Hypoglycemia during prolonged exercise in normal men. *New England J. Medicine,* 306, 895-900

A. Ferro-Luzzi, 1990. Seasonality studies in three developing countries: Introduction and background. *European J. Clinical Nutrition,* 44, (Suppl. 1), 3-6

Mary A. T. Flynn and Michael J. Gibney, 1991. Obesity and health: why slim? *Proc. Nutrition Society,* 50, 413-432

Nobuhiro Fukuda, et al., 1979. effects of exercise on plasma and liver lipids of rats. *Nutrition and Metabolism,* 23, 256-265

Henrik Galbo, 1985. The hormonal response to exercise. *Proc. Nutrition Society,* 44, 257-265

J.S. Garrow, 1991. the safety of dieting. *Proc. Nutrition Society,* 50, 493-499

M. Gleeson, J.D. Robertson and R.J. Maughan, 1987. Influence of exercise on ascorbic acid status in man. *Clinical Science,* 73, 501-505

M. Gleeson, J.F. Brown and J.J.Waring, 1980. The effects of exercise and training on the utilization of dietary glucose. *Proc. Nutrition Society,* 39, 35A

Alan G. Goodridge, et al., 1991. Symposium on 'Nutrient-gene interactions'. *Proc. Nutrition Society,* 50, 115-122

Kenneth W. Heaton. Food intake regulation and fiber. In *Medical Aspect of Dietary Fiber.* Edited by Gene A. Spiller and Ruth M. Kay. Plenum Book, 1980

J. Henriksson, 1990. The possible role of skeletal muscle in the adaptation to periods of energy deficiency. *European J. Clinical Nutrition,* 44, (Suppl 1) 55-64

Fumihiko Horio, et al., 1991. Thermogenesis, low-protein diets, and decreased development of AFB_1-induced preneoplastic foci in rat liver. *Nutrition and Cancer,* 16, 31-41

Britta Hylander and Stephen Rossner, 1983. Effect of dietary fiber intake before meals on weight loss and hunger in a weight-reducing club. *Acta Medica Scandinavica,* 213, 217-220

Henry A. Jordan, 1973. In defense of body weight. *J American Dietetic Association,* 62, 17-21

L.J. Koong and C.L. Ferrell, 1990. Effects of short term nutritional manipulation on organ size and fasting heat production. *European J. clinical Nutrition,* 44, (Suppl. 1), 73-77

David Kritchevsky, 1992.Antioxidant vitamins in the prevention of cardiovascular disease. *Nutrition Today,* January/February, 30-33

P.M. Kris-Etherton, 1990. Nutrition and athletic performance. *Nutrition Today,* September/October, 35-37

Marcin Krotkiewski, 1984. effect of guar gum on body-weight, hunger ratings and metabolism in obese subjects. *British J. Nutrition,* 52, 97-105

Ann Leader, 1991. The association of slimming with eating disorders. *Proc. Nutrition Society,* 50, 473-477

Arthur S. Leon, 1984. Forum: Exercise and health. *Preventive Medicine,* 13, 1-2

William R. Leonard and Brooke Thomas, 1989. Biosocial responses to seasonal food stress in Highland Peru. *Human Biology,* 61, 65-85

K. Markiewicz, et al., 1977. Effect of physical exercise on gastric basal secretion in healthy men. *Acta Hepato Gastroenterologica,* 24, 377-380

Roy J. Martin and Barbara J. Mullen, 1987. Control of food intake: mechanisms and consequences. *Nutrition Today,* September/October, 4-10

Gail McBride, 1990. US diet industry under fire. *British Medical J.* 300, 1481-1482

Olaf Mickelsen, et al., 1979. Effects of a high fiber bread diet on weight loss in college-age males. *American J. Nutrition,* 32, 1703-1709

Kathleen Mulligan and Gail E. Butterfield, 1990. Discrepancies between energy intake and expenditure in physically active women. *British J. Nutrition,* 64, 23-36

Stylianos Nicolaidis and Patrick Even, 1985. Physiological determinant of hunger, satiation, and satiety. *American J. Clinical Nutrition,* 42, 1083-1092

N.G. Norgan, 1990. Body mass index and body energy stores in developing countries. *European J. Clinical Nutrition,* 44, (suppl 1), 79-84

Colm O'Herlihy, 1982. Jogging and supression of ovulation. *New England J. Medicine,* 306, 50

L.H. Opie, 1975. Sudden death and sport. *Lancet,* 1, 263-266

S.V. Perry, 1985. Exercise, a stimulus for metabolism and a challenge to nutrition. *Proc. Nutrition Society,* 44, 235-243

Andrew M. Prentice, et al., 1991. Physiological responses to slimming. *Proc. Nutrition Society,* 50, 441-458

F. Xavier Pi-Sunyer, 1985. Effect of exercise on food intake in human subjects. *American J. Clinical Nutrition,* 42, 983-990

Anthony Ramirez, 1991. Keeping the Gobblers, chasing the nibblers. *New York Times,* May 19, 9

J.D. Robertson, et al., 1991. Increased blood antioxidant systems of runners in response to training load. *Clinical Science,* 80, 611-618

James F. Sallis, Melbourne F. Hovell, and C. Richard Hofstetter, 1992. Predictors of adoption and maintenance of vigorous physical activity in men and women. *Preventive Medicine,* 21, 237-251

P.S. Shetty and A.V. Kurpad, 1990. Role of the sympathetic nervous system in adaptation to seasonal energy deficiency. *European J. Clinical Nutrition,* 44(suppl 1), 47-53

R. Jeffrey Smith, 1981. Aspartame approved despite risks. *Science,* 213, 985-987

Maureen P. Smith, et al., 1982. Exercise intensity, dietary intake, and high-density lipoprotein cholesterol in young female competitive swimmers. *American J. Clinical Nutrition,* 36, 251-255

D.H. Snow, 1985. The horse and dog, elite athletes - why and how? *Proc. Nutrition Society,* 44, 271-272

Stephen N. Sullivan, 1981. The gastrointestinal symptoms of running. *New England J. Medicine,* 304, 915

Goya Wannamethee and A. G. Shaper, 1990. Weight change in middle-aged British men: implications for health. *European J. Clinical Nutrition,* 44, 133-142

Roland L. Weinsier, et al., 1982. Dietary management of obesity: evaluation of the time-energy displacement diet in terms of its efficacy and nutritional adequacy for long-term weight control. *British J. Nutrition,* 47, 367-379

Jan A. Weststrate, et al., 1990. Lack of a systematic sustained effect of prolonged exercise bouts on resting metabolic rate in fasting subjects. *European J. Clinical Nutrition,* 44, 91-97

Clyde Williams, Nutritional aspects of exercise-induced fatigue.*Proc. Nutrition Society,* 44, 245-255

Stephen C. Woods, et al., 1985. Insulin: its relationship to the central nervous system and to the control of food intake and body weight. *American J. Clinical Nutrition,* 42, 1063-1071

Alayne Yates, Kavin Leehey and Catherine M. Shisslak, 1983.Running - an analogue of anorexia? *New England J. Medicine,* 308, 251-255

Young and Lewis Landsberg, 1977. Suppression of sympathetic nervous system during fasting. *Science,* 196, 1473-1475

John Yudkin, 1963. Nutrition and palatability with special reference to obesity, myocardial infarction, and other diseases of civilization. *Lancet,* 2, 1335-1338

PART E

Philosophy, Culture and Nutrition

19

Culinary Art: Herbs and Spices

Abstract: Culinary herbs and spices flavor foods and provide valuable nutrients including vitamins, trace minerals and anti-oxidants. They influence flavor in much smaller quantities than sugar and salt, which are also used for that purpose, but have adverse nutritional and health effects. The taste for herbs and spices, and the taste for salt and sugar are acquired early and can be difficult to change. Historically, there have been times when the popularity of spices was so great that their commerce impacted world history. Subsequently, salt, sugar and meat gained popularity and are being consumed in greatly increased quantities, to the detriment of health. By emphasizing the use of herbs and spices rather than sugar, salt and meat from an early age, life-long beneficial dietary habits are established with improvement in health, vitality and longevity through diet.

Traditional Uses of Herbs and Spices

Culinary herbs are generally soft-stemmed plants which may grow a few inches to several feet tall. Most of the herbs do not live more than two seasons. Most spices are barks, roots, leaves, flowers, fruits or seeds which grow mainly in tropical countries in Africa, Asia, and South America. They may be annuals, biennials or perennials. There are many examples where the distinction between herbs and spices blurred. Tender plants of dill (Anethum graveolens, L.), for example, is used as a herb, while the mature seeds are a spice. Herbs and spices have been used since antiquity for their medicinal value and to preserve and flavor foods. They have been so highly sought after that their acquisition and trade has profoundly affected world history. All herbs and spices contribute flavor, micro-nutrients and anti-oxidants to foods. Individual herbs and spices have other notable properties. Cloves, cinnamon and garlic, for example, have significant antibiotic properties which can help to extend the shelf-life of prepared foods. The taste for herbs, spices, meat, sugar and salt is acquired early. Once established, a person's taste for herbs and spices or for meat, sugar and salt can be difficult to change later in life.

The use of plants for flavoring food may be as old as cooking food itself! Archeological findings indicate that even prehistoric people used many leaves, roots and fruits for flavoring their foods. It is difficult to identify the civilization that utilized herbs and spices first. People of the Indus River Valley Civilization knew spices such as black pepper, cinnamon and turmeric before 1,000 B.C. Evidence exists that Chinese, Egyptian and other cultures also used various herbs and spices very early in their civilizations.

People of the Vedic times (1500 B.C.), used herbs and spices in cooking and in medicine (Ayurvedic system). In the Ayurvedic system it was believed that wholesome food should incorporate six tastes (rasa). Rain water that originates in heaven is pure and tasteless (apo). It acquires other tastes such as sweet (madhu), sour (amla), salt (lavana) and bitter (tika) as it flows through rocks and soil. Plants and animals acquire these tastes from water. Humans have to consume a wide variety of food ingredients to include all six flavors because most foods have one predominant flavor. Since antiquity, Indian cuisines have used herbs and spices to create variety, texture, aroma, taste, and color and to improve the keeping quality of food. This reduces the monotony of daily foods (See Chapter 14).

History of Spice Trade

It is the culinary and medicinal values of the herbs and spices of the tropics and subtropics that made the rest of the world interested in acquiring them. Alexander the Great brought a number of spices into Europe from his war expedition to Egypt, Persia and India. The idea that fishes, meats and breads become more palatable and more easily stored without spoilage made spices a most valuable possession of the wealthy Greeks who imported them as symbol of wealth. The Romans used them in cooking meats, flavoring wines and even as dyes. The spices that masked unappetizing meats with rich aroma and flavor became a symbol of honor and passion in many parts of Europe. By the 8th and 9th centuries, Benedictine monks began cultivating herbs such as lavage, marjoram, balm and savory in their cloistral gardens and using them in a variety of ways.

During the 13th century, a book written by Venician merchant, Marco Polo, about the use of spices was regarded as a most valuable possession. Those spices became the major trade for many Europeans. The love of spices was so great that people were willing to trade valuables such as gold, farm animals and land for them. Many explorers were tempted to risk their fortunes to find a means to build a spice trade. To hasten the trade, people ventured to find sea routes from Europe to India and other parts of Asia, Africa, South America and Central America, where spices grew in abundance. In 1498, Vasco de Gamma, a Portuguese merchant, sailed around Africa and reached the west coast of India. Other European explorers tried to find shorter routes. One of them was Christopher Columbus who inadvertently "discovered" North America. European powers involved in spice trade, fought many wars and colonized, enslaved and decimated other cultures such the as Aztec and Mayan. Such expeditions changed the political geography of the world. Around 1616 the British who consolidated their power to monopolize the world spice trade colonized many parts of the world, including India. Activities involving acquisition of spices changed human destiny throughout the world.

Properties of Individual Herbs and Spices

Since antiquity almost all old cultures have used hundreds of spices for therapeutic effects such as calming the emotions, as purgatives, diuretics and antibiotics. Many such properties of spices and herbs are due to the cumulative effects of a vast array of organic compounds present in them. In subsaturating quantities they interact with other food ingredients in various ways to bring about the health benefits attributed to them. Preparations of pungent and irritating spices such as black pepper, ginger, cumin and their combinations are used to relieve congestion of mucous membranes.

Turmeric (Curcuma longa L.) is a rhizome of a monocotyledonous plant belonging to the family Zingiberaceae that has many of the common desirable qualities of spices. It is a native of South Asia, one of the spices of antiquity, and the major food coloring agent of all Indian cuisines. It is an important ingredient of curry powders, and sun-dried and fermented foods. All over India, both the leaves and the roots are used in the cuisine and in therapeutic medicine. The Udipi cuisine uses the dry, bright yellow powder more frequently than the raw rhizome. As a spice, turmeric changes the color of foods to various shades of yellow and red. Its unique pungency modifies the taste of associated ingredients. The changes that turmeric brings to the color and taste of food depends upon whether the food contains acidic fruits such as tamarind and lemon, or non-acidic ingredients such as certain vegetables, lentils and nuts. The coloring of turmeric is due to curcumin which is a pH indicator that is yellow below pH 7.5, orange to pH 8 and red above 8.5.

Recent scientific investigations attribute the therapeutic properties of tumeric to the presence of half a dozen organic compounds such as curcumin and its derivatives. Laboratory experiments have shown that compounds found in turmeric have anti-tumor effects in animals. Inclusion of turmeric in the diet has, in some analyses, decreased the incidence of stomach and mammary tumors. The effect of curcumin on animals varies upon its concentration, whether it is a water or alcohol extract, and on the surrounding pH. The water extract of curcumin shows anti-tumor properties,while concentrated alcohol extract has exhibited cytotoxicity in rats. Curcumin, a strong antioxidant agent has been found to inhibit peroxide induced DNA damage in rats. Two to five percent of turmeric in their diet significantly inhibited induced tumors. Adding up to 12% tumeric to the diet increased glutathione S-transferase activity in the liver by as much as 32%. The liver is known to store and use glutathione as a powerful antioxidant agent. The phenolic derivatives of turmeric suppress environmental mutagens and carcinogens including benzopyrene.

The effect of chili pepper has been attributed to organic compounds such as capsaicin and its derivatives. Many qualities of black pepper have been attributed to piperidine and its derivatives. In addition, many other properties such as preservative, antibiotic and lowering of plasma cholesterol have been correlated with the presence of vitamin C, bioflavinoids and other antioxidant supplying compounds that are found in peppers.

Garlic and onion, which have been used as panacea for health in many ancient cuisines such as Egyptian, Chinese, Greek and Roman, also contain a spectrum of bioactive organic compounds. One of the disulphide derivatives, allicin, found both in garlic and onion contributes to their flavor, aroma and many therapeutic values. Garlic contain many organic compounds such as glycosides, nitrates, sulphides, allin and allicin. It also has many special minerals and vitamins. Garlic may be an effective treatment for many disorders of the circulatory and gastrointestinal systems. It is reported to lower circulating levels of triglycerides and low density lipoproteins, increase high density lipoproteins, inhibit aggregation of platelets and promote anti-inflammatory actions.

The flavor and therapeutic values of ginger root has been attributed to its volatile oil that contains compounds such as gingerol, zingeberene and shogal. It has been claimed to suppress flatulence and has traditionally been used for colic. Ginger root exists in as many as 50 different varieties. The ancient Chinese used many varieties of gingers and more than 1,000 other herbs and spices in their culinary and medicinal arts.

Fenugreek (Trignella Foenum-graecum, L.) is a dull yellowish brown leguminous seed of an annual plant. Its greens and tender stems serve as both herb and vegetable. As a dietary ingredient fenugreek increases the liquid holding capacity of the stool, enhancing elimination. The seeds serve as spice when used in small quantities. They contain an alkaloid, trigonelline, and a steroidal sapogenin, diosgenin. These are biologically active compounds, but what role they play in fenugreek's actions is not known. In large quantities they provide bulk, mucilage and other nutrients. The characteristic bitter flavor fenugreek adds to foods varies with the way it is cooked. Fenugreek is a part of many curry powders and fermented foods of the Udipi cuisine. When used in large amounts it is soaked and combined with yogurt or tamarind to reduce its bitterness. According to epidemiological studies, when people with type I insulin dependent diabetes consume fenugreek seeds, their fasting blood sugar is significantly lowered. Fenugreek in the diet is believed to improve glucose tolerance and lower plasma cholesterol and triglycerides. Possible mechanisms by which these latter effects occur may include alterations in bile absorption. It also increases fecal bulk. Many other properties attributed to fenugreek, such as increasing appetite, and stimulating intestinal secretions and peristalsis, are influenced by its polysaccharide content. Other herbs and spices such as pepper, coriander, ginger, sage, tarragon, thyme, onion and garlic, are also claimed to improve glucose tolerance. They appear to do this without altering plasma insulin levels.

Spices and herbs contain many complex carbohydrates such as pectins and mucilage. They also contain special sugars such as xylose, rhamnose, galactose and arabinose and derivatives. Many of these sugars are specific to each spice or herb. Likewise, as many as 26 organic compounds have been isolated from the milky juice of poppy fruits. Many powerful drugs such as morphine and codeine have been derived from the poppy fruit.

The anti-tumor activity attributed to plants of the mustard family such as mustard, cabbage and broccoli are also due to specific organic compounds such as isothiocyanate and its derivatives. Essential oils are common to many herbs and spices such as thyme, mint, balm, marjoram, fennel, parsley, clove, cinnamon and cumin. Many of them also have special fatty acids such as polyenic acid, along with oleic, lenoleic and lenolenic acids. All such materials also may vary with the species and variety of herbs and spices. Science has not yet identified all of the active organic compounds, including essential oils, that are present in herbs and spices.

Herbs and spices also contribute trace minerals such as iodine, copper, selenium and chromium to the diet. Some of the flavor and therapeutic values attributed to spices are believed to derive from the minerals they contain in tiny quantities. Part of the anti-tumor activity of garlic, for example, has been attributed to the trace minerals selenium and germanium it contains. Likewise, steroidal sapogenins contained in some herbs and spices may be readily converted into biologically active hormones after ingestion. The provitamins and bioflavinoids that many herbs and spices contain are known to contribute more to nutrition than equivalent consumption of purified synthetic forms of vitamins. Vitamin P, for example, which is not available in synthetic form, is contained in many spices including chili pepper and paprika. Vitamin U (a bromine-containing compound) from cabbage and other green leaves has been reported to serve as a natural anti-ulcer compound. The provitamin carotinoids supplied by many herbs and vegetables have greater effects than vitamin A. The antioxidant effects of herbs and spices are due to the cumulative actions of trace minerals, provitamins, bioflavinoids and dietary fiber rather than to any one concentrated compound.

Many herbs and spices are rich in antioxidants. Sage and rosemary, for example, are known to contain as much as 10% of their dry weight as antioxidants. Herbs and spices do not contribute excessive food calories to the diet. Even those herbs and spices consumed in large amounts, such as mustard, onion and garlic, lack concentrated calories because their bulk is mainly due to dietary fiber and water. This bulk, which contributes to the characteristic texture of foods containing those herbs and spices, enhances stool elimination by increasing the liquid holding capacity of the feces.

Problems with Substituting Sugar and Salt for Herbs and Spices

To a large extent sugar and salt have served, like spices, in preservation and flavoring of foods. Like the spices, sugar and salt were also symbols of luxury, health and happiness. However, a much larger quantity by weight of sugar and salt is necessary to contribute to the piquancy and zest of foods. In addition, enormously greater quantities of sugar and salt are needed to preserve foods than are needed of herbs and spices. As sugar production increased it became more readily available than herbs and spices. In England alone,the use of sugar jumped from roughly 10,000 tons in 1700 to 150,000 by 1750. The increased production of sugar led to the increased production of sugar-containing foods such as soft drinks, ice cream, puddings, cakes and confectioneries which became substitutes for fruits and cereal products. As a result, sugar consumption, which was roughly 25 lbs per person per year around 1750, increased to as much as 120 lbs by 1850. Its worldwide production increased nearly 100% between 1937 and 1957. Many countries in South America, Asia and Africa substituted sugar producing crops for other food crops, including herbs and spices. Gradually, the popular taste shifted from spiced foods to sugar-rich foods. Food calories supplied by sugar deprived people of polysaccharides, various other natural organic compounds, antioxidants, trace minerals and dietary fiber previously supplied by herbs and spices.

Many experiments and epidemiological studies show that adapting to foods rich in sugar, salt and other refined products changes appetite, hunger, satiety, and the overall energy metabolism of the body. While hunger brings the urge to eat, appetite stimulates the selection of foods. They are both involved in metabolism and satiety (See Chapter 11). Appetite is acquired and adaptive. All animals, including human infants, adapt to certain type of foods. Such adaptation aids in avoiding monotony and regulates satiety. However, this adaptation is a more complex process in humans than in any other animal.

The food habits established during infancy and childhood are hard to break as an adult, and hence are an important influence on adult health and longevity. Whether one adapts as a child to a diet rich in cereals, fruit and vegetables flavored with herbs and spices or to a diet rich in meat, eggs, sugar and refined products, determines the sorts of foods and flavorings one craves as an adult.

Selected Sources and Suggested Readings

Anonymous, 1984. Research notes. *Science News,* jUNE 2, 349

Anonymous, 1976. The herbs and the heart. *Nutrition Reviews,* 34, 43-44

Magnus A. Azuine and Sumati V. Bhide, 1992. Chemopreventive effect of turmeric against stomach and skin tumors induced by chemical carcinogens in Swiss mice. *Nutrition and Cancer,* 17, 77-83

J.L. Beare-Rogers, et al., 1979. Nutritional properties of poppyseed oil relative to some other oils. *Nutrition and Metabolism,* 23, 335-346

Myung S. Chi, Eunsook T. Koh and Troy J. Stewart, 1982. Effects of garlic on lipid metabolism in rats fed cholesterol or lard. *J. Nutrition,* 112, 241-248

Madeleine P. Cosman, 1983. A feast for aesculapius: Historical diets for Asthma and sexual pleasure. *Annual Reviews of Nutrition,* 3, 1-33

Judith G. Dausch and Daniel W. Nixon, 1990. Garlic: A review of its relationship to malignant disease. *Preventive Medicine*, 19, 346-361

Michael A. Dubick, 1986. Historical perspectives on the use of herbal preparations to promote health. *J. Nutrition,* 116, 1348-1354

Lynnette R. Ferguson, et al., 1992. Adsorption of a hydrophobic mutagen to dietary fiber from Taro (Colocasia esculenta), an important food plant of the South Pacific. *Nutrition and Cancer,* 17, 85- 95

Clifford M. Foust. *Not Just Desserts.* Princeton U. Press, 1992

Louis E. Grivetti, 1991. Nutrition past - Nutrition today. Prescientific origins of nutrition and dietetics. *Nutrition Today,* January/February, 13-24

Louis Grevetti, 1991. Part two: Legacy of the Mediterranean. *Nutrition Today,* July/August, 19-29

C.J.K. Henry and B. Emery, 1986. Effect of spiced food on metabolic rate. *Human Nutrition: Clinical Nutrition,* 40C 165-168

C.J.K. Henry and M. Piggott, 1987. Effect of ginger on metabolic rate. *Human Nutrition: Clinical Nutrition,* 41C, 89-92

N.J. Jardine, D.G. Edwards and C. Mcmenemy, 1990. Implications of nutritional recommendations on sugar for product development. *Proc. Nutrition Society,* 49, 23-30

Dean P. Jones, et al., 1992. Glutathione in foods listed in the National Cancer Institute's health habits and history food frequency questionnaire. *Nutrition and Cancer,* 17, 57-75

Thomas H. Jukes, 1992. Historical perspective. Antioxidants, nutrition, and evolution. *Preventive Medicine,* 21, 270-276

Rosario D. Lamparelli, et al., 1987. Curry powder as a vehicle for iron fortification: effects on iron absorption. *American J. Clinical Nutrition,* 46, 335-340

Walter H. Lewis and Memory P.F. Elvin-Lewis. *Medical Botany. Plants affecting man's health.* John Wiley and Sons, New York, 1977

Zecharia Madar, et al., 1988. Glucose lowering effect of fenugreek in non-insulin dependent diabetics. *European J. Clinical Nutrition,* 42, 51-54

Ching-Liang Meng and Kwai-Wang Shyu, 1990. Inhibition of experimental carcinogens by painting with garlic extract. *Nutrition and Cancer,* 14, 207-217

Hasan Mukhtar, et al., 1992. Tea components: Antimutagenic and anticarcinogenic effects. *Preventive Medicine,* 21, 351-360

M. Nagabhushan and Sumati V. Bhide, 1986. Nonmutagenicity of curcumin and its antimutagenic action versus chili and capsaicin. *Nutrition and Cancer,* 8, 201-210

Narayan G. Patel. *Ayurveda: the traditional medicine of India.* In *Folk Medicine. The Art and the Science.* Edited by Richard P. Steiner, American Chemical Society, Washington, DC, 1986

K.P.S. Raj and N.N. Patel, 1977. Onion-the vegetable drug. *Indian Drugs,* 14, 156-160

K.P.S. Raj and R,M. Parmar, 1978. Garlic- condiment and medicine. *Indian Drugs,* 15, 1-5

Rudolph A. Riemersma, et al., 1990. Plasma antioxidants and coronary heart disease: Vitamins C and E, and selenium. *European J.* Clinical Nutrition, 44, 143-150

Barbara J. Rolls, E.A. Rowe and E.T. Rolls, 1982. How flavor and appearance affect human feeding. *Proc. Nutr. Society,* 41, 109-117

P.Rose, et al., 1986. Dietary antioxidants and chronic pancreatites. *Human Nutrition: Clinical Nutrition,* 40C 151-164

M.J. Salomi, Satish C. Nair, and K.R. Panikkar, 1991. Inhibitory effects of *Nigella sativa* and saffron (*Crocus sativus*) on chemical carcinogenesis in mice. *Nutrition and Cancer,* 16, 67-72

R.D. Sharma, T.C. Raghuram and N. Sudhakar Rao, 1990. Effect of fenugreek seeds on glucose and serum lipids in Type I diabetes. *European J. Clinical Nutrition,* 44, 301-306

Ann R. Stasch, and Mae M. Johnson, 1970. Antioxidant properties of chile pepper. *J. American Dietetic Association,* 56, 409-412

Noritoshi Tanida, et al., 1991. Suppressive effect of Wasabi (Pungent Japanese spice) on gastric carcinogenesis induced by MNNG in rats. *Nutrition and Cancer,* 16, 53-58

M.C. Unnikrishnan, K.K. Soudamini and Ramadasan Kuttan, 1990. Chemoprotection of garlic extract toward cyclophosphamide toxicity in mice. *Nutrition and Cancer,* 13, 201-207

M.C. Unnikrishnana and Ramadasan Kuttan, 1988. Cytotoxicity of extracts of spices to cultured cells. *Nutrition and Cancer,* 11, 251-257

H. Wagner, Hiroshi Hikino and Norman R. Farnsworth. Editors. Economic and Medicinal Plant Research. Volume 1. Academic Press, New York, 1985

Zoe S. Warwick, 1990. Development of taste preferences: Implications for nutrition and health. *Nutrition Today,* March/April, 15-18

Lee W. Wattenberg, 1990. Inhibition of carcinigenesis by minor anutrient consitituents of the diet. *Proc. Nutrition Society,* 49, 173-183

Russell G. Wright, 1988. An update on garlic research. *American Biology Teacher,* 50, 150-151

Jennifer A. Wolf, 1977. The effcet of okra mucilage (*Hibucus exculentus* L) on the plasma cholesterol level in rats. *Proc. Nutrition Society,* 36, 59A

Susumu Yoshida, et al, 1987. Antifungal activity of Ajoenee derived from garlic. *Applied and Environmental Microbiology,* 53, 615-617

In spite of the great advances which have been made in knowledge, some fundamental gaps still remain; matter, life and mind still remain utterly disparate phenomena. Yet the concepts of all three arise in experience, and in the human all three meet and apparently intermingle, so that the last word about them has not yet been said. Reformed concepts of all three are wanted. This will come from fuller scientific knowledge, and especially from a re-survey of the material from new points of view. The fresh outlook must accompany the collection of further detailed knowledge, and nowhere is the new outlook more urgently required than in the survey of these great divisions of knowledge.

— Jan Christiaan Smuts, *Holism and Evolution*, 1926

20

Lacto-vegetarianism: Culture and Science

Abstract: Vegetarianism is both an approach to nutrition with scientific standing and a lifestyle with a long cultural history. In this chapter the roots of vegetarianism are traced in the culture of India and elsewhere. The supplementation of a vegetarian diet with milk assures adequate intake of the full range of necessary nutrients but avoids the risks of nutrient excess inherent in the consumption of most other animal products such as meat. Moreover consumption of milks does not involve killing or harming other living beings and is an extremely efficient nutrient source, unlike meat. Thus lacto-vegetarianism provides a means of improving the health of overnourished affluent peoples with high incidence of degenerative diseases, while improving the health of the undernourished third world where infectious and deficiency diseases are epidemic.

In the preceding chapters we have discussed the importance of a high fiber, high complex carbohydrate, low protein diet. In and of itself this nutritional perspective does not have to eliminate meat, poultry or fish from the diet of those who are accustomed to them. As Mahatma Gandhi believed that the meat eaters must be accorded due respect and love. It should be left to individual's philosophy of life. Lacto-vegetarianism builds this obvious scientific nutritional edifice on a firm foundation of a holistic philosophy of life with historical and cultural underpinnings to eliminate meat from the diet. Some people may wish to follow the general theme of this book and yet maintain a modest intake of meat. However we feel that many people will find the complete lacto-vegetarian perspective makes a great deal of sense in today's world.

Vegetarianism as a cultural philosophy can be traced back to the Vedas, the ancient scriptures of the Hindus which dates back to 2,500 B.C. and earlier.

The Vedas are considered by many historians to be among the earliest documents of human knowledge and aspirations. Scholars trace the origin of the Hindus to the early Aryan immigrant agriculturists who settled on the Indus River valley. The way of life developed by these people evolved into Hinduism. Thus, Hinduism is not an organized religion or doctrine as laid out by a single individual; rather it evolved as a set of beliefs, practices and philosophy involving life, its source, and how it should be led. Even today, while most Hindus share a common philosophy of life they often differ widely in their actual religious practices. To appreciate vegetarianism it is helpful to know something about the philosophy of Hinduism.

Hinduism recognizes polytheistic, monotheistic and even atheistic philosophies. People who conceive of God abstractly as energy (shakti), eternal truth and beauty (nature) and those who idolize God in various forms, including phallic symbols, are all accommodated in the Hindu religion. For example, Ramakrishna a 19th century Vedanti or teacher of Vedantic philosophy, idolized Shakti as both a creative force, and as a female deity, Kali. In worshipping Kali, a Hindu recognizes an all powerful force that can assume the form of a woman as an embodiment of individual and social justice. Ramakrishna's pupil, Vivekananda, another great Vedanti, was an atheist. Mahatma Gandhi equated truth with God. Rabindranath Tagore viewed God as nature. They were all Hindus.

The Rig, Yajur, Sama and Atharva Vedas are four Sanskrit compilations. They consist of mantras (hymns), religious rituals and philosophical discussions. They speculate on the meaning of life and its relation to other creations. They also ponder other subjects such as eternal truth, justice and peace. These concerns are further elaborated upon in the Upanishads which are a series of discourses between teachers and students regarding truth and ignorance. Nearly 200 Upanishads form the basis of Vedantha philosophy. Those who study and interpret the Vedas are the Vedanthis (philosophers). Some of the greatest leaders in the history of India, such as Buddha, Mahaveera, Madhva, Shankara, Basava, Guru Nanak, Kabir, Vivekananda and Mahatma Gandhi, have been influenced by Vedanata philosophy.

According to Hindus, God is the supreme power or energy (shakthi). God may materialize in any form and at any place where injustice predominates, and fairness and truth need to be restored. So far, God has appeared in nine incarnations (avatharas) to restore eternal truth and social justice. Incarnations are not confined to human forms. They start with an aquatic form of fish (Mathsya), move to Kurma, an amphibian, evolving through terrestrial forms including animal, half animal (Narasimha) and diminutive human (Vamana), and finally ideal humans such as Rama and Krishna. The avatars culminate in the arrival of Kalki. The Hindus also believe in reincarnation as higher (or lower) forms culminating in moksha or nirvana (salvation), the ultimate point at which no more janma (rebirths) occur. The simple means to achieving liberation of the self is by conducting one's own daily duties (karma) honestly and fairly. Such an approach leads one towards moksha. Karma is the most powerful tool that promotes or demotes the level of our present and future lives. All creatures are bound by this cycle of rebirths. Some may achieve moksha in one rebirth and others may need many. The number of rebirths needed depends upon the individual.

The Karma philosophy serves as the basis of Jainism and Buddhism which are off-shoots of Hinduism. Karma philosophy interrelates human virtues such as eternal truth (satya), universal justice (dharma), and nonviolence (ahimsa). These virtues can be practiced in one's daily life (Karma). The more an individual conducts his or her daily chores in a path of karma (Karma Marga) the better the future for that person, which shortens the road to moksha. All creatures can follow their karma to attain salvation. They go through many rebirths from nonliving to living stages before they achieve the level of animals,and then humans, a higher stage. A human can continue to advance further as a scholar, a sage and a superior human (devatha), a stage that is closer to moksha. On the other hand, one can also be demoted from the human stage to a lower level, such as that of a worm or a stone. The faster way to advance is to free oneself from greed or ego (aham) and sacrifice one's life for the good of society in the broadest sense.

According to the Hindus, anyone who inflicts pain or suffering or destroys other creations for greed and indulgence contributes to his or her demotion. One can promote oneself by protecting other creatures. himsa is the word for any action that causes pain and violence. It's opposite is ahimsa or nonviolence. Himsa, to some extent, is part of life because everything born is going to be killed and everything killed is going to be reborn. Life is intertwined with birth and death. To be alive one has to destroy other creations. However, the more one is willing to relinquish indulgence and greed, the less one has to destroy. The lifestyle of Ahimsa leads to eternal peace (shanthi). A sage who relinquishes worldly needs achieves moksha faster than a king who relinquishes less. How enlightened a sage can become depends upon how much he or she can minimize the use of anything other than the basic needs of life.

The two great epics of Hinduism, the Ramayana and the Mahabharata, elaborate on the struggles between the forces of good and evil. They date earlier than 500 B.C. In the Ramayana, the compassionate and intellectual Rama fights for the virtues of life and against a most intellectual tyrant, Ravana, and his other demon followers (rakshasas). In the Mahabharata, Krishna clarifies the difficulty of dealing with one's own emotions and such passions as love, sex, greed, jealousy, ego and power. This epic embodies mythology, philosophy, theology, history, politics and law under the unifying authority of Vedas. The essence of the Mahabharata lies in the dialogue (termed the Bhagavad-Gita) between Krishna and his devotee Arjuna on the eve of battle. This religious classic outlines the tenets of Hinduism. Krishna discusses with Arjuna various ways of strengthening justice (dharma) without weakening truth (Satya) on the battlefield between good and evil. The Gita elaborates how the war of emotions can be fought and won by several means. The Gita speculates on issues of human life and social values.

Hinduism involved the entire community through the cast system which distinguished those who were occupied with intellectual persuasions (Brahmins and Vyshayas) from those who pursued bodily strength including warriors and laborers (Kshatriyas and Shudras). Intellectuals, especially Brahmins, occupied a very high place in the society, next to sages. They were also expected to sacrifice the most for the welfare of others. Like sages, Brahmins and Vyshayas, were expected to follow strict lacto-vegetarianism; however, sages sacrificed further by living on one meal a day or less. Sages also had no homes and no belongings. Their meager lifestyle earned them great respect from the society. Practicing nonviolence through a lacto-vegetarian lifestyle was required in the social hierarchy. Even wild animals and poisonous snakes were not to be harmed needlessly.

Brahmins were expected to be conscious of their actions towards others. Even daily chores such as milking a cow, for example, was done only after feeding her and letting her feed her calf. Harvesting plant products was done with great care to minimize destruction. The cutting down of old trees that provided food and shelter for birds and animals was condemned. The Brahmins were expected to lead a life of sacrifice. The sacrifices expected of Brahmins on a daily basis were performed by non-Brahmins on special occasions, such as festivities or after the age of 60. Traditional Hinduism never condoned indulgence. It held spiritual and intellectual achievements above all other accomplishments in life. Philosophers such as Shankara and Ramakrishna relinquished worldly involvements at a very early age in life. Vegetarianism developed as a part of this philosophy rather than as a religious doctrine. Indeed, only a relatively small percentage of the Hindu population maintained strict vegetarianism.

While vegetarianism among the Hindus started as a profound philosophy of life, it later became an empty and even cynical ritual. For example, proscriptions against killing a cow, became more important than taking responsibility for the care and well-being of cows. The society that found god in all creations began exploiting all creations including humans for pleasure and profit. Greed and indulgence corrupted all levels of Hindu society. What was supposed to be a caste distinction based on a persons' character and aptitude became a rigid hereditary system. Society became stratified.

The deterioration of the Hindu society lead to the evolution of Jainism and Buddhism as offshoots striving to uphold the principles of ahimsa. In 623 B.C. Buddha was born as prince Gautama. He was raised by a ritualistic and indulgent Hindu ruling family. Spiritually troubled, Gautama spent his youth in search of the eternal truth that would make nirvana achievable to all. When he realized that following karma principles through the ahimsa path would lead to nirvana, he preached it to all and earned the title of Buddha. In sanskrit, the name "Buddha" refers to one who has "buddhi" (knowledge and wisdom). He emphasized achieving nirvana through karma, dharma and ahimsa, not idol worship or rituals.

Verdhamana Mahaveera, who established Jainism, was also born in a royal family, a century before Buddha. He too realized that one can escape from the turmoils of life and rebirths and achieve moksha by following karma through ahimsa principles. Both Buddhism and Jainism believe that protecting all God's creations is a human responsibility. Both promoted vegetarianism as a means of practicing ahimsa and decried the practice of rituals and idol worship.

The popularity of Jainism and Buddhism diminished in India for various reasons. However, Buddhism made a comeback in the third century B.C. during the Gupta Dynasty. An incident that took place in the life of King Ashoka made him revive Buddhism and propagate the ahimsa principles in India and elsewhere in Asia, strengthening the connection of vegetarianism to nonviolence. King Ashoka (269-232 B.C.) had engaged in a war with a neighboring kingdom. While victorious, the death and destruction of the battlefield led him to vow to prevent future wars. In his quest for eternal peace, he embraced Buddhism and sought to derive peace and happiness through ahimsa principles. He sent messengers all over India and other parts of Asia to spread Buddhism, vegetarianism and the philosophy of nonviolence. No other ruler in history of India was as protective of the environment and of animals as this enlightened monarch. His reign is considered a "golden age" in Indian history. The "Dharma Chakra," a wheel representing universal justice, created by King Ashoka, remains the emblem of India.

After the 10th Century A.D., waves of Arabs, Turks, Moguls and finally Europeans conquered India. Even before these invasions however, the religions of Islam and Christianity had taken root in India. Nevertheless Hinduism remained the dominant religion. Because of significant differences in their value systems, the principles of ahimsa, and its associated vegetarian lifestyle were further de-emphasized during the periods of Islamic and Christian rule.

Mahatma Gandhi's movement for the independence of India revived the ahimsa philosophy once again. Gandhi was born in a traditional vegetarian Hindu family. In addition, the community he grew up in was strongly influenced by the Jain commitment to nonviolence. However, along with many reform minded young people, the young Gandhi was led to believe that meat-eating was essential to a modern outlook and that vegetarianism was an historical anachronism. This peer pressure lead him to experiment with eating meat secretly with friends. After half a dozen trials he was overwhelmed with intense guilt and revulsion. At age 18 he went to England for higher studies. During his stay in England he had many opportunities to read about, ponder, and discuss vegetarianism. For many reasons he decided to remain vegetarian and to establish it as a firm moral foundation of his philosophy of life. He came to believe that "making food into flesh was better than making flesh into food."

Gandhi felt that adherence to vegetarianism would decrease extravagant consumption, a reform he thought was essential to improving the Indian economy and environment. Gandhi's unalterable devotion to ahimsa philosophy strengthened his commitment to vegetarianism which in turn helped rejuvenate the deteriorating philosophical and moral conviction of

Indian youth. It gave a new meaning to his political movement and uplifted a confused younger generation. The authors of this book grew up in that environment during the 1940's and were profoundly influenced by Gandhi's convictions. Gandhi felt that leading a vegetarian lifestyle would boost many important virtues such as maintaining self-sufficiency, conserving natural resources and protecting the environment of the country. He also thought that consuming less would preserve health and improve spiritual well-being.

Another reason that made Gandhi favor vegetarianism was that it served as a defense against malnutrition and improper food distribution to many in the country. He motivated young people to grow basic crops of vegetables and fruits and adapt their taste and diet to those crops rather than to the habits of the affluent class. These ideas gave a new meaning to the Vedic ahimsa philosophy and vegetarianism. He used every opportunity to set an example of preserving health by minimizing intake, and of protecting the world environment by adhering to vegetarianism. Yet, in spite of his enthusiasm for vegetarianism, Gandhi never made its propagation a religious crusade. Rather he espoused vegetarianism as a thoughtful intellectual philosophy that Hindus should recommend to non-Hindus for the benefit of all. As a result Gandhi's disciples included many non-Hindus as well as non-Indian foreigners.

Pure vegetarianism versus lacto-vegetarianism

Mahatma Gandhi was a purist. He wrote in his book, *Key to Health* (1948) that he was in favor of an exclusively vegetarian diet. Yet he declared that experience had taught him that in order to keep perfectly fit, a vegetarian diet must be supplemented with milk and milk products. By his own personal experience, he wrote that he was forced to admit the importance of adding milk to the strict vegetarian diet. He nevertheless expressed the hope that, some day, plant products would be identified which would supply sufficient nutrients as to replace milk.

In a letter to Gandhi, the well-known nutrition scientist of British India, Robert McCarisson wrote:

"There can be no doubt in the minds of those of us who have devoted a life-time to the study of nutrition that milk is one of the greatest blessings given to mankind." Commenting on this advice, Gandhi wrote back: "I personally favor a pure vegetarian diet, and have for years been experimenting to find a suitable vegetarian combination . . . . It is one of the many inconsistencies of my life that, whilst I am in my own person avoiding milk, I am conducting a dairy which is producing cow's milk . . . .

The view of the authors of this book is that milk (or defatted milk or yogurt) is an essential dietary supplement for all people.

Vegetarianism outside of India

Many ancient Egyptians and Greeks who believed in the transmigration of souls from human to animals practiced vegetarianism. Pythagoras and other Greek intellectuals were vegetarians. According to Daniel Dombrowski, the idea that it is morally wrong to eat animals prevailed among the ancient Greek and Egyptian philosophers for nearly a thousand years. Dombrowski explored the basis of vegetarianism in the ancient Greeks and found it to be similar to that of many of today's humanists. He correlates the demise of the ancient vegetarian tradition with the rise of Judeo-Christianity.

Occasional vegetarian movements started by individuals or groups kept this philosophy and lifestyle alive in Europe and America over the last two centuries. An early vegetarian society was established in Manchester, England in 1809. Vegetarianism then spread to Germany, France and Ireland. It has always attracted writers, philosophers and intellectuals like Leonardo da Vinci, Voltaire, Shelley, Annie Besant, George Bernard Shaw. In 1978, the Nobel Prize winning American agronomist, Norman Borlaug, was reported to have stated that thousands of people around the world were alive because Americans were eating less meat. It is quite well-known by now that about six people can live on the grain that it takes for one person to eat meat. The Bible Christian Society, Trappist monks and Seventh-Day Adventists are groups in America which espoused vegetarianism. Many American intellectuals such as Benjamin Franklin, Ralph Waldo Emerson and Henry David Thoreau supported the vegetarian philosophy. Leaders of health movements such as Sylvester Graham and his ardent followers William Alcott and J.H. Kellog kept the tradition alive during the 19th century. Those who popularized protective foods in the 20th century (e.g. McCollum and Chittenden, see Chapters 3, 4, 5) also were influenced by the vegetarian movement. The affluence of the 1950's in the U.S. supported the rise of a "meat culture" and downgraded vegetarianism to the position of fringe groups. During the post-war period vegetarianism was completely misrepresented in the West, especially in the U.S. Vegetarians like ourselves felt humiliated, in part by our inability to defend our culture in that environment. Most of us lacked the knowledge needed to repudiate the cultural distortions such as the misrepresentation of the Hindu concept of the sacred cow. Likewise scientific misinformation, such as the belief that vegetarians lacked dietary protein and suffered from iron and vitamin B12 deficiencies ran rampant in the absence of rebuttal. As a result, the majority of the U.S. population were led to believe that vegetarianism was an tasteless, unhealthy form of extremism. Many who would be vegetarians were thus intimidated into reluctant meat consumption or to referring to vegetable dishes by popular names of meat dishes, such as vegetable cutlets and veggie burgers.

People's attitudes in the U.S. towards a vegetarian diet began changing again in the 1970s and 1980s, for both philosophical and scientific reasons. The credit for raising philosophical awareness goes to people active in groups concerned with world hunger, civil rights, peace and social justice, animal rights and the state of the environment. They popularized various sorts of vegetarianism such as lacto- and ovo-vegetarianism, fruitarianism and veganism. Frances Moore Lappé explored it as a means to alleviate world hunger. Peter Singer and animal welfare groups supported it to avoid cruelty to animals. From the scientific community, it received attention only from those who wanted to promote dietary fiber but not as part of a larger view of the optimal human diet. Such a diet had been proposed by outstanding physiological chemist Chittenden and others early in this century. The purpose of this book has been to fill a part of this gap in the scientific basis for lacto-vegetarianism.

In 1987, the First International Congress on Vegetarian Nutrition was held in Washington D.C. to draw attention to the scientific evidence of the potential health benefits of a vegetarian diet. The speakers included Johana Dwyer of Tufts University and many others. David Nieman of Loma Linda University spoke about the athletic endurance that a vegetarian diet provides. David Snowdon, Epidemiologist at the University of Minnesota, reported on a 21 year study done on 25,000 Seventh-Day Adventists (SDA). The SDAs studied had lower cholesterol than non-SDAs. Males who began a vegetarian diet early in life had a relatively lower risk of heart disease than those who became vegetarians later. In males, meat eating was strongly associated with diabetes. Ritva Butram of the U.S. National Cancer Institute stressed that there is enough data to recommend reducing fat intake to 30% of total calories, and increasing daily fiber intake to about 30 g by consuming more fruits and vegetables.

M. L. Burr of the Medical Research Council, in Cardiff, U.K. reported on a twelve-year study of nearly 11,000 vegetarians and non-vegetarians that demonstrated that vegetarians are leaner and have lower blood cholesterol levels than non-vegetarians. Sheila Bingham of the Medical Research Council of Cambridge, England, brought up the association between dietary meat and colon cancer. Lawrence Berlin of the University of Western Australia presented the role of the vegetarian diet in lowering blood pressure in a study of 300 Mormons and SDAs. Many investigators also presented data on older vegetarian women who possess higher bone mineral density than women eating a meat based diet who lose more urinary calcium. Andrea Boyar of the American Health Foundation pointed out that vegetarians have a headstart in the attainment of optimal health.

Reports after report that have come from the U.S. Senate, National Academy of Sciences, National Institute of Health of Canada, and World Health Organization clearly attest to the superiority of a predominantly vegetarian diet in maintaining health. No other diet can balances bulk, protein, calcium and variety of micronutrients as well as does a lacto-vegetarian diet.

Thus it appears that vegetarianism may be on the verge of a new revival as appreciation of its scientific merits is more widely recognized. In the preceding chapters of this book we have seen a survey of the scientific bases for lacto-vegetarianism. The lacto-vegetarian diet is the most suitable diet to protect the human body's own internal ecosystem (see Chapter 12). Humans have evolved in an environment that provided the microflora with plenty of bulky carbohydrates, and even today no other diet can maintain the supportive environment and provide healthy food for them. All our surviving relatives such as chimpanzees and Great Apes depend predominately upon a plant staple diet. There are people in all cultures who have maintained their health on plant staples. The lacto-vegetarian diet is scientifically sound, philosophically satisfying and prudent both medically and economically for a diverse and growing world population.

Selected Sources and Suggested Readings

Mohammed Abdulla, et al., 1981. Nutrient intake and health status of vegans, chemical analyses of diets using the duplicate portion sampling technique. *American J. Clinical Nutrition,* 34, 2464-2477

Catherine F. Adams. *Nutritive value of American Foods.* Agriculture Handbook No 456, United States Department of Agriculture, Washington, D.C. 1975

William Aiken and Hugh La Follette edited. *World Hunger and Moral Obligation.* Prentice Hall, New jersey, 1977

B. Akesson, et al., 1981. Content of trans-octadecenoic acid in vegetarian and normal diets in Sweden, analyzed by the duplicate portion technique. *American J. Clinical Nutrition,* 34, 2517-2520

Bonnie M. Anderson, et al., 1981. The iron and zinc status of long-term vegetarian women. *American J. Clinical Nutrition,* 34, 1042- 1048

Anonymous, 1990. *Diet, Nutrition and the Prevention of Chronic Diseases.* A report of the WHO Study Group on diet, Nutrition and Prevention of Noncommunicable Diseases. Technical Report Series 797. World Health Organization, Geneva, Switzerland

Anonymous, 1990. Risks and benefits of Vegetarian diets. *Nutrition Today,* March/ April, 27-29

Anonymous. *Diet and Health.* National Academy Press, Washington, D.C. 1989

Anonymous, 1988. Inhibition of free radical chain oxidation by alpha-tocopherol and other plasma antioxidants. *Nutrition Reviews,* 46, 206-207

Anonymous, 1984. Eating away at cancer risk. *Science News,* 125, 124

Anonymous, 1980. Position paper on the vegetarian approach to eating. *J. American Dietetic Association,* 77, 61-69

Anonymous, 1980. Environmental out look grim for year 2,000. *Chemical and Engineering News,* 58, 21-22

Anonymous, 1979. Nutrition and vegetarianism. *Dairy Council Digest,* 50, 1-6

Anonymous, 1979. Growth of vegetarian children. *Nutrition Reviews,* 37, 108-109

Anonymous, 1972. *A Blueprint for Survival.* Editors of the Ecologist, New American Library, New York, 1974

William Aiken and Hugh La Follette edited. *World Hunger and Moral Obligation.* Prentice Hall, Englewood Cliffs, NJ, 1977

B. Akesson, et al., 1981. Content of trans-octadecenoic acid in vegetarian and normal diets in Sweden, analyzed by the duplicate portion technique. *American J. Clinical Nutrition,* 34, 2517-2520

Bonnie M. Anderson, et al., 1981. The iron and zinc status of long-term vegetarian women. *American J. Clinical Nutrition,* 34, 1042- 1048

Bruce Armstrong, et al., 1979. Urinary sodium and blood pressure in vegetarians. *American J. Clinical Nutrition,* 32, 2472-2476

Atif B. Awad, Peter J. Horvath, and Martha S. Andersen, 1991. Influence of butyrate on lipid metabolism, survival, and differentiation of colon cancer cells. *Nutrition and Cancer,* 16, 125-133

Francis G.Benedict and Paul Roth, 1915. The metabolism of vegetarian as compared with the metabolism of non-vegetarians of like weight and height. *J. Biological Chemistry,* 20, 231-241

Agehananda Bharati. *The Ochre Robe.* Doubleday, New York, 1970

Paul C. Billings, et al., 1990. Protease inhibitor content of human dietary samples. *Nutrition and Cancer,* 14, 85-93

Gladys Block, 1991. Dietary guidelines and the results of food consumption surveys. *American J, Clinical Nutrition,* 53,356S- 357S

Letitia Brewster and Michael F. Jacobson, 1984. *The Changing American Diet.* Center for Science in the Public Interest, Washington DC

Jane E. Brody. *Jane Brody"s Nutrition Book.* W. W. Norton & Co., New York. 1981

Jane E. Brody, 1983. New research on the vegetarian diet. *New York Times,* October 12

Jane E.Brody, 1982. How diet can affect mood and behavior. *New York Times,* November 17

Nicola L. Bull and Sigrid A. Barber, 1984. Food and nutrient intakes of vegetarians in Britain. *Human Nutrition: Applied Nutrition,* 38A, 288-293

M.L. Burr, et al., 1981. Plasma cholesterol and blood pressure in vegetarians. *J. Human Nutrition,* 35, 437- 441

Marian Burros, 1992. Eating well. *New York Times,* July 8, 1992

Kenneth K. Carroll and Heli I. Parenteau, 1991. A proposed mechanism for effects of diet on mammary cancer. *Nutrition and Cancer,* 16, 79-83

Barbara J. Culliton, 1992. Eat your broccoli (and brussels sprouts). *Nature,* 356, 377

Jared M. Diamond, 1992. Diabetes running wild. *Nature,* 357, 362-363

Margaret D. Doyle, et al., 1965. Observations on nitrogen and energy balance of young men consuming vegetarian diets. *American J. Clinical Nutrition,* 17, 367-376

Daniel A. Dombrowski. *The Philosophy of Vegetarianism.* University Massachusetts Press, Amherst. 1984

Alizon Draper and Erica F. Wheeler, 1990. *Proc. Nutrition Society,* 49, 60A

Alizon Draper, Nina Malhotra and Erica F. Wheeler, 1990. Who are 'vegetarians' and what do they think about food? *Proc. Nutrition Society,* 49, 61A

René Dubos, 1979. The intellectual basis of nutrition science and practice. *Nutrition Today,* July/August, 31-34

Johanna T. Dwyer, et al., 1982. Nutritional status of vegetarian children. *American J. Clinical Nutrition,* 35, 204-216

Frey R. Ellis and V.M. Montegriffo, 1970. Veganism, clinical findings and investigations. *American J. Clinical Nutrition,* 23, 249-255

Frey Ellis, et al., 1972. Incidence of osteoporosis in vegetarians and omnivores. *J. American Clinical Nutrition,* 25, 555-558

E. Ernst, et al., 1986. Blood rheology in vegetarians. *British J. Nutrition,* 56, 555-560

M.K. Gandhi. *An Autobiography or the Story of My Experiments with Truth.* Navajivan Publishing House, Ahmedabad, India, 1927

M. K. Gandhi. *Diet and Diet Reform,* Navajivan Publishing House, Ahmedabad, India, 1949

B.R. Goldin, et al., 1982. Estrogen excretion patterns and plasma levels in vegetarian and omnivorous women. *New England J. Medicine,* 307, 1542-1547

Leslie Goodman-Malamuth, 1986. Cruciferous veggies. *Nutrition Action, March 1986, 12*

C.Gopalan, B.V. Rama Sastri and S.C.Balasubramanian. *Nutritive Value of Indian Foods.* National Institute of Nutrition, Indian Council of Medical Research, Hyderabad, India, 1984

Francisco Grande, Joseph T. Anderson and Ancel Keys, 1965. Effect of carbohydrates of leguminous seeds, wheat and potatoes on serum cholesterol concentration in man. *J. Nutrition,* 313-317

A.M. Greco, et al., 1985. Effects of an overload of animal protein on the rat: Brain DNA alterations and tissue morphological modifications during fetal and post-natal stage. *International J. Vitamin and Nutrition Research,* 55, 107-112

Leif Halberg, Mats Brune, and Rossander, 1989. Iron absorption in man: ascorbic acid and dose-dependent inhibition by phytate. *Americn J. Clinical Nutrition,* 49, 140-144

Suzanne Havala, et al., 1987. Position of the American Dietetic Association: Vegetarian diets-technical paper

Peter B. Hill, et al., 1986. Gonadotrophin release and meat consumption in vegetarian women. *American J. Clinical Nutrition,* 43, 37-41

Fumihiko Horio, et al., 1991. Thermogenesis, Low-protein diets, and decreased development of AFB_1- induced preneoplastic foci in rat liver. *Nutrition and Cancer,* 16, 31-41

N.L. Jacobson, 1974. The controversy over the relationship of animal fats to heart disease. *BioScience,* 24, 141-147

Gunnar K. Johansson, Ludmila Ottova, and Jan-Ake Gustafsson, 1990. Shift from a mixed diet to a lactovegetarian diet: Influence on some cancer-associated intestinal bacterial enzyme activities. *Nutrition and Cancer,* 14, 239-246

Robert Kowalski, et al., 1987. Congress investigates vegetarian nutrition. *Nutrition Today,* July/ August, 30-33

Martin J. Lee, 1991. Relationship between stool pH and butyrate levels. *Nutrition and Cancer,* 16

Bonnie Liebman, 1983. Are vegetarians healhtier than the rest of us? *Nutrition Action,* June, page 8

P. H. M. Lohman, K. Sankaranarayanan and J. Ashby, 1992. Choosing the limits of life. *Nature,* 357, 185-186

I.A. Macdonald, Robert Webb and David E. Mahony, 1978. Fecal hydroxysteroid dehydrogenase activities in vegetarian Seventh-Day Adventists, control subjects, and bowel cancer patients. *American J. Clinical Nutrition,* 31, S233-S238

Sanat K. Majumder, 1972. Vegetarianism: Fad, Faith, or fact? *American Scientist,* 60, 175-179

Margarete Malter, Gerlinde Schriver, and Ursula Eilber, 1989. Natuarl killer cells, vitamins, and other blood components of vegetarian and omnivorous men. *Nutrition and Cancer,* 12, 271-278

Elizabeth A. Melcher, Michael D. Levitt, and Janne Slavin, 1991. Methane production and bowel function paramenters in healthy subjects on low- and high fiber diets. *Nutrition and Cancer,* 16, 85-92

Jawaharlal Nehru. *The Discovery of India.* Edited with a foreword and comments by Robert I. Crane. Anchor Books, Doubleday, New York, 1960

Prabhudas Palan, et al., 1991. Plasma levels of antioxidant B-carotene and alpha-tocopherol in uterine cervix dysplasias and cancer. *Nutrition and Cancer,* 15, 13-20

David Pimentel, et al., 1973. Food production and the energy crisis. *Science,* 182, 443-449

A. Pronczuk, Y. Kipervarg and K.C. Hayes, 1992. Vegetarians have higher plasma alpha-tocopherol relative to cholesterol than do nonvegetarians. *J American College of Nutrition,* 11, 50-55

Rebecca Purves and T. A. B. Sanders, 1980. An assessment of the nutritional status of preschool vegan children. *Proc. Nutrition Society,* 39, 79A

Sarvepalli Radhakrishnan and Charles A. Moore, Edited. *A Source Book in Inian Philosophy.* Princeton University press, Princeton, New Jersey, 1957

U. D. Register, and L.M.Sonnenberg, 1973. The vegetarian diet. *J.American Dietetic Association,* 62, 253-261

Daphne A. Roe, 1986. History of promotion of vegetable cereal diets. *J. Nutrition,* 116, 1355-1363

Ian L. Rouse, et al., 1983. Blood- pressure-lowering effect of a vegetarian diet: controlled trial in normotensive subjects. *Lancet,* 1, 5-9

Joan Sabate et al., 1991. Attained height of lacto-ovo vegetarian children and adolescents. *European J. Clinical Nutrition,* 45, 51-58

Eduardo n. Siguel, 1983. Cancerostatic effect of vegetarin diets. *Nutrition and Cancer,* 4, 285-291

H. C. Sherman, 1920. Protein requirement of maintenance in man and the nutritive efficiency of bread. J. Biological Chemistry, 41, 97-109

Eduardo N. Siguel, 1983. Cancerostatic effect of vegetarian diets. *Nutrition and Cancer,* 4, 285-291

R. B. Singh, et al.,1990. Dietary modulation of blood pressure in hypertension. European *J. Clinical Nutrition,* 44, 319-327

Terry D. Shultz and James E. Leklem, 1983. Nutrient intake and hormonal status of premenopausal vegetarin Seventh-Day Adventists and premenopausal nonvegetarians. *Nutrition and Cancer,* 4, 247-259

P. V. Sukhatme, 1970. Size and nature of the protein gap. *Nutrition Reviews,* 28, 223-226

P. V. Sukhatme, 1969. Incidence of protein deficiency in relation to different diets in India. *British J. Nutrition,* 24, 477-487

Louis Tobian, 1988. Potassium and hypertension. *Nutrition Reviews,* 46, 273-283

Delores D. Truesdell, Eleanor N Whitney and Phyllis B. Acosta, 1984. Nutrients in vegetarian foods. *J. American Dietetic Association* 84, 28-35

Pierre Würsch, Simone Del Vedovo, and Brigite Koellreutter, 1986. Cell structure and starch nature as key determinants of the digestion rate of starch in legume. *American J. Clinical Nutrition,* 43, 25-29

Appendix 1

Key Concepts as they are introduced in each chapter

PART A WISDOM OF THE BODY

CHAPTER 1 Understanding the Human Body and its Three Entities

- From a nutritional perspective, a human being can be viewed as three interacting and interdependent entities: the brain, the other organs of the body, and the intestinal microflora. The optimal human diet provides nutrients in a manner that meets the diverse needs of each entity, but provides no excess to upset the balance within and between entities.

CHAPTER 2 Homeostasis, Holism and Holistic Nutrition

- Homeostasis: the concept that dynamic mechanisms operate to maintain constancy of the internal environment.
- Holism: the perspective that the Whole is more than the sum of its parts and that complex systems cannot be understood solely by the study of their individual components.
- Nutrition modification in support of homeostasis is an important holistic approach to maintenance of health, promotion of longevity and fighting disease.

CHAPTER 3 Physiological Economy: Complex Carbohydrates are Special

- Complex carbohydrates are the optimal food source for all three entities:

For the brain because complex carbohydrates are broken down directly (but slowly) into simple sugars such as glucose, the brain's preferred fuel; For the other organs of the body, because glucose is readily stored as, and released from, liver glycogen in response to minute by minute needs and does not require extensive intermediary metabolism with generation of potentially toxic byproducts; For the normal intestinal microflora because undigested complex carbohydrates arriving in the colon supports their characteristic fermentative metabolism.

- Carbohydrates are best absorbed in a slow-release fashion. This pattern of absorption, which is ideal for the proper functioning of homeostatic mechanisms, is characteristic of complex carbohydrates.
- Liver glycogen is central to fuel homeostasis and is a manifestation of the special role of complex carbohydrates in human nutrition.
- The work of Russell Chittenden was a practical application/validation of this insight into physiological economy: How you get calories is more important than how many you get.

CHAPTER 4 What is Wrong with Our Nutrition?

- The affluent American diet is NOT based on sound principles of human nutrition.
- Plant products are high in complex carbohydrates and fiber and contain small amounts of all other necessary nutrients, making them superior dietary staples.
- Animal products are high in protein and fat but essentially devoid of complex carbohydrates and fiber making them a poor choice of dietary staple.
- Highly processed foods are generally rich in protein, fat, salt and sugar while unprocessed plant products are generally rich in fiber and complex carbohydrates.
- Sound holistic nutritional concepts have been ignored for the last 50 years as a consequence of the efforts of commercial interests and reductionist thinking. As a result, the incidence of diseases of affluence (e.g. obesity, cancer, atherosclerosis, diabetes mellitus, arthritis) are on the rise. The current sorry state of Western nutrition is likely to continue or get worse until this situation is changed.

PART B THE DIETARY CONSTITUENTS: SUBSATURATION IS OPTIMAL

CHAPTER 5 Protein: Essential in Moderation; Harmful in Excess

- As currently over-consumed in the typical American diet, protein often does more harm than good.
- An excess of protein in the diet can be viewed as any amount greater than necessary to provide adequate amino acids for protein synthetic purposes.
- The consumption of calories in the form of protein to be expended for energy is an excess.
- A consequence of protein excess is breakdown products of amino acid metabolism which are toxic to the kidney and ultimately may contribute to kidney failure.
- A consequence of protein excess is to elevate the levels of amino acids to saturating levels. Such levels supply the needs of pathogens and established or potential cancer cells which would be unable to compete with normal cells for these nutrients when present at subsaturating levels.
- A consequence of protein excess is that it alters the character of the intestinal microflora from fermentative to putrefactive species with negative health consequences.
- A consequence of protein excess is its metabolism by microbes generating by-products including toxic amines which can affect the brain and have been implicated in some cases of schizophrenia and depression.
- Just because a small amount of something is good for you does NOT mean that an excess is even better.

CHAPTER 6 Fats Are Also Essential

- Small amounts of certain fats (e.g. essential fatty acids) play a crucial role in normal development and in maintaining health.
- Dietary excess or deficiency of certain fats result in disease. In excess, fats can contribute to obesity, cardiovascular disease and certain cancers (e.g. breast and colon cancer). Deficiency of essential fatty acids contributes to learning disorders.
- Just because an excess of something is bad for you does NOT mean that a small amount is not beneficial.

CHAPTER 7 The Value of Vitamins and Antioxidants

- Plants are the primary source of vitamins and antioxidants.
- An excess of certain vitamins (e.g. fat soluble vitamins) may be as harmful as their deficiency.
- Diversity is more important than quantity in determining the value of a diet with respect to vitamin and antioxidant content, because there are a wide range of vitamins and antioxidants needed in very small amounts.

CHAPTER 8 The Role of Minerals

- Not only deficiency but also excess supplementation of trace and ultra-trace minerals in more than trace or ultra-trace amounts causes disease. The risks associated with management of mineral nutrition through supplementation are significant.
- Unprocessed plant products contain these substances in the trace or ultra-trace amounts in which they are needed. A problem with modern processed foods is that some of these substances have been removed while others have been replaced in excess.
- Thus, the best approach to preventing mineral deficiency or excess is through a mixed diet of unprocessed plant products supplemented with milk.

CHAPTER 9 Complex Carbohydrates Provide Variety and Bulk

- Individuality of complex carbohydrates: The precise structure of the fiber and the precise mix of nutrients differs for complex carbohydrates from one plant source to another. Thus, eating different plant foods provides true variety. This is not the case for different meats.
- Complex carbohydrates provide bulk in the form of indigestible fiber.

CHAPTER 10 Dietary Fiber, Sedentary Life and Affluent Diseases

- Fiber facilitates elimination of toxic and potentially toxic products both direct binding and indirectly by speeding transit time through the GI tract.
- Fiber contributes to homeostatic regulation by altering rates of nutrient absorption. One mechanism is simply by dilution. As a result, transport mechanisms are no longer saturated and rates of absorption are altered (increased for some nutrients, decreased for others) in ways that are

optimal for homeostasis. Another mechanism is by binding certain nutrients (e.g. simple sugars), which slows their absorption.

- Fiber supports the normal fermentative intestinal microflora not only by providing a source of nutrients but also because the products of microbial metabolism of fiber result in an acidic environment inhospitable to pathogens.
- Fiber stimulates peristalsis thereby serving to "exercise the gut" preventing degenerative diseases such as diverticulosis which are epidemic in the American population consuming a low fiber diet. @bl = Relationship of fiber deficient diet to sedentary life: both are associated with obesity.
- Relationship of fiber deficient diet and sedentary life to modern disease.

PART C OUR INTERNAL ENVIRONMENT

CHAPTER 11 Digestion, Absorption and Beyond

- The composition of food affects the amount of acid secretion (increased by protein), transit time out of the stomach (slowed by protein and fat) and transit time out of the small intestine (slowed by fiber).
- Rate of absorption of specific nutrients depends on the overall composition of ingested food. For example, excess phosphate interferes with absorption of other minerals; for example iron absorption is dependent on pH in the stomach; for example, fiber delays absorption of simple sugars
- Satiety is a subjective feeling of sufficient food consumption which can be achieved by several different mechanisms including high fat, high glucose or high bulk diets. Satiety achieved by a high fat/protein diet brings with it negative aspects of excess protein consumption. Satiety achieved by a diet of simple sugars is transient and counter homeostatic as rapid absorption raises and then lowers blood glucose. Bulk contributes to satiety by distension of the stomach which, via signals to the brain, removes the desire to eat. Thus a diet of complex carbohydrates provides the advantages of glucose-mediated satiety without the disadvantages, due to the effect of dietary fiber.
- Rates of nutrient absorption can also affect satiety. For example seratonin competes with tryptophan for absorption from the small intestine. In a high complex carbohydrate diet seratonin is preferentially absorbed serving to signal satiety to the brain. ???
- Once again a connection between nutrition of the three entities: complex

carbohydrate-mediated satiety affects both the brain and body homeostasis; the same complex carbohydrates support the intestinal microflora as described previously.

CHAPTER 12 Elimination Decreases Internal Pollution

- Organisms, and the cells and tissues of which they are composed, have evolved mechanisms for both acquiring nutrients and for eliminating wastes. The renal, GI (including liver), circulatory and respiratory systems are all involved in elimination.
- The human body is a limited ecosystem with respect to capacity for waste elimination. Moreover, that capacity for elimination of wastes normally decreases due to cell loss and dysfunction with age. Therefore it is prudent to maintain homeostasis by minimizing waste generation rather than by making the excretory organs work harder to eliminate a larger amount of waste.
- Excess nutrients, toxic by-products and Xenobiotics (e.g. ingested drugs and environmental pollutants) all can cause disease and degeneration through mechanisms including direct toxicity, inappropriate deposition of substances (e.g. cholesterol deposits in arteries causing atherosclerosis), and carcinogenic effects.
- Rapid transit of fecal waste through the colon is important because prolonged exposure to toxic fecal material results in local irritation and other effects on the epithelial cells of the colonic lumen that can cause cancer, and increased absorption of compounds that can be harmful.

CHAPTER 13 Our Microbes in Nutrition and Health

- The normal microbial population of the GI tract, largely limited to the colon, comprises species that are permanent residents as well as transients which enter from the outside world.
- This third entity within human beings is unlike the other two (the brain and the other organs of the body) in that it is not inherited, but rather, develops after birth under the influence of the diet.
- When well established colonic microflora is a powerful player in maintaining homeostasis. When developed inappropriately, the result is susceptibility to a wide range of disease.
- The beneficial role of normal microbial flora includes the establishment of a GI tract environment inhospitable to most pathogens and the production of beneficial substances including certain vitamins and short-chain fatty acids.

- The diet is a powerful influence on the composition and stability of the colonic microbial flora. Fermentative bacteria are the natural inhabitants of the colon on a diet of plant products and complex carbohydrates while a range of proteolytic species are favored in high-protein, meat-staple diets.
- Fermentative bacterial populations are associated with improved longevity and quality of life, and a range of disorders can be ameliorated or, in some instances possibly, even prevented, by maintenance of a fermentative colonic bacterial population.

PART D A DIET TAILORED BY EVOLUTION

CHAPTER 14 Human Evolution, Traditional Culture and Diet

- Omnivores (including primates) have evolved to be nourished by complex carbohydrates.
- Ancient populations had firm ideas as to what constituted wholesome food based on the experience of earlier generations and necessity determined by their environment, technology and economy. These diets were, in general, characterized by the presence of a variety of complex carbohydrate food types, especially prior to the full scale development of commercial agriculture. These diets were also characterized by low nutrient density due to the presence of bulk (indigestible fiber), simply because the technology for extensive food processing (by which modern preparation removes indigestible fiber), was not in existence. The traditional philosophical and medical systems incorporated these diets. The Indian systems of Yoga and Ayurvedic Medicine are discussed as examples.
- Since our ancestors and other primates evolved consuming such diets, it is not surprising that our physiological economy is optimized when nourished by complex carbohydrates. Likewise, it is only natural that the subsequently such diets would be incorporated into culture as it developed.
- The scientific and industrial revolutions of the last century have changed the way people live and the diets they eat. Unfortunately they have done so in a manner largely disconnected from the evolutionary history that determines what constitutes the optimal diet for humans as reflected in cultural dietary traditions characterized by bulk and variety of complex carbohydrates.

CHAPTER 15 Protective Foods Prevent Disease

- The value of a diet is determined not only by its caloric and specific nutrient content, but also, by the ability of some foods to offset deleterious features of others, as first enunciated as the concept of "protective foods" by McCollum 70 years ago.
- High dietary fat and protein, low dietary fiber and saturation of nutrients as occurs in a meat-staple diet, contribute to the widespread problems of obesity and constipation and are causally associated with degenerative diseases and cancer.
- Protective foods allow us the benefits of certain nutrients while mitigating their deleterious aspects: glucose is better than amino acids as an energy source, however simple glucose would be, by itself, absorbed too rapidly to maintain a stable supply; dietary fiber is beneficial for many reasons – but more so when taken as a natural product than as a medication, due to the accessory nutrients, vitamins, antioxidants etc. that unprocessed fiber provides.
- Protective foods are those such as complex carbohydrates which display all of these beneficial features (e.g. of glucose for energy metabolism of mineral, vitamin and antioxidant variety, or nutrient dilution and binding) while either mitigating the negative aspects of each of these components in isolation or providing additional benefits (e.g. the possibilities of substitution through variety, see Chapter 7).
- Such "protective foods" were plentiful in traditional diets, but have been neglected in recent decades by a nutrition science obsessed with reductionist views of food value and food industries geared to refined products.
- Studies suggest that an increase in consumption of protective foods would result in improved heath of the population: decreased constipation and obesity, decreased nutritional deficiencies and diminished incidence of degenerative diseases would be a likely outcome of dietary modification.

CHAPTER 16 Milk: Food Tailored by Evolution

- Milk is a quintessential "protective" food unique to mammals. Through evolution, the composition of milk has been optimized for the distinctive needs of individual species.
- The special role of milk in nutrition are that i) it contains an enormous diversity of nutrients, ii) these nutrients are present in a very dilute solution at subsaturating concentrations, and iii) milk is rich in lactose, a sugar with distinctive and crucial nutritional properties.

- The diversity of nutrients in milk prevents deficiencies that might otherwise interfere with development.
- The subsaturating concentration of nutrients in milk permit optimal establishment of homeostatic mechanisms and forms a barrier to pathogens by forcing them into unfavorable competition for nutrients. Examples include iron, lipid, carbohydrate, and protein metabolism of the developing infant.
- The importance of lactose includes its being the only simple sugar whose absorption is sufficiently slow as to mimic complex carbohydrates. Because of this slow absorption, lactose has a special role in promoting calcium absorption and initiating the selection of an optimal fermentative intestinal microbial flora.
- Milk provides a cornerstone around which a universal standard for human nutrition can be built. While human milk is the optimal diet for human babies, cow's milk as a dietary supplement provides a reasonable nutritional standard readily attainable for adults.

CHAPTER 17 Food for Growth and Productive Life

- The periods of intrauterine growth and adolescence are times of great sensitivity to the effects of deficiencies of necessary nutrients and exposure to toxic substances, influencing the individual's life more than what takes place later.
- Our dietary need for protein and fat decreases with age while that of fiber and bulk increases, reflecting the generally more sedentary lifestyle, decreased cell and tissue growth, and increased generation of metabolic by-products during aging.
- The best way to adapt to these changes in lifestyle and physiology is by a gradual transition in diet in the direction of decreasing nutrient density while maintaining the dietary themes of variety and bulk throughout life. This minimizes the high nutritional stress that high nutrient density and high protein foods place on the body, which cause accelerated degeneration of organs and decreases the productive life-span in adulthood.

CHAPTER 18 Exercise and Weight Control

- Among animals, exercise occurs as a daily routine, part of the struggle for survival, and not as an activity unconnected to survival needs. Prior to the modern era humans also obtained exercise, typically, in the course of their daily activities.
- Exercise, as so commonly practiced today, is a highly artificial compensation for the sedentary life and increased nutrient density that are

common in modern affluent life. In moderation however, it serves as a useful adjunct to maintaining homeostasis.

- In excess, exercise is a stress which can damage tissues and vital organs.
- Rather than exercising to excess, the appropriate way to compensate for a sedentary lifestyle is to engage in moderate physical activity and decrease nutrient density by use of bulk (fiber-rich complex carbohydrates). This achieves the goal of weight control without an unacceptable long-term physiologic cost. Such an approach utilizes the homeostatic mechanisms of appetite control through satiety to maintain optimal body weight and physical fitness.

PART E PHILOSOPHY, CULTURE AND NUTRITION

19 Culinary Art: Herbs and Spices

- The taste of food can be influenced either by small quantities of herbs and spices or by larger quantities of sugar, salt, fat and meat.
- In addition to flavor, herbs and spices make other valuable contributions to food, namely as micro-nutrients and anti-oxidants. The flavor they impart to foods allow more extensive consumption of high bulk plant ingredients. In contrast, the much larger amounts of sugar, salt and meat that are necessary to affect palatability of foods have other decidedly negative health consequences.
- The taste for herbs, spices, meat, sugar and salt is acquired early and once established, can be difficult to change.
- By emphasizing use of herbs and spices rather than sugar, salt and meat from an early age, life-long beneficial dietary habits are established. This is a crucial foundation for improvement in health and longevity through diet.

CHAPTER 20 Lacto-vegetarianism: Culture and Science

- Vegetarianism is not only an approach to nutrition with scientific standing, it is also a lifestyle with a long cultural history.
- The supplementation of a vegetarian diet with milk assures adequate intake of the full range of necessary nutrients to maintain health, but avoids the risks of nutrient excess inherent in the consumption of most other animal products such as meat.
- Lacto-vegetarianism provides a means of improving the health of over-

nourished affluent societies with high incidence of degenerative diseases by eliminating nutrient-dense animal products such as meat.

- Lacto-vagetarianism is the surest means of improving the health of the undernourished third world where infectious and deficiency diseases are epidemic. It does this by providing the minimum concentration of the full range of nutrients necessary to maintain health in the most affordable manner.
- Lacto-vegetarianism is the surest way to expand world food resources and reduce world hunger while protecting the environment.

Governments should consider their investment and subsidy policies in both agriculture and the food industry to ensure that they are consistent with the nutritional concepts contained in this report. Policies should be geared to promoting the growing of plant foods, including vegetables and fruits, and to limiting the production of fat-containing products.

– Recommendations to national governments. Diet, nutrition, and the prevention of chronic diseases. World Health Organization, Technical Report Series 797, p. 160, 1990.

Appendix 2

SAMPLE RECIPES OF THE UDIPI CUISINE

1 Introduction to the Udipi Cuisine

1.00 Historical overview
1.10 Buying groceries
1.20 Pretreatment of ingredients
1.30 Utensils and table setting
1.40 Cooking procedures
1.41 Deep-frying
1.42 Cooking rice
1.43 Cooking lentils
1.44 Roasting
1.45 Making *ghee*
1.46 Preparing *oggarnay*
1.50 Herbs, spices and curries
1.51 Masala
1.60 Synthetic additives
1.70 Traditional eating
1.80 Leftover foods
1.90 Miscellaneous

2 Yogurt Dishes

2.00 The place of yogurt in Udipi cuisine
2.10 Making low-fat cultured yogurt
2.20 *Pulikajipu* (Yogurt curry)
2.21 *Southay Raitha* (Cucumber salad)
2.22 *Badanay Pachadi* (Eggplant salad)

3 Vegetable Dishes

4 Cereal Dishes

4A Combination Rice Dishes

4B Dishes of Grits

4C Breads

4D Fermented Dishes

5 Legume Dishes

RECIPES OF THE UDIPI CUISINE

1 Introduction to the Udipi Cuisine

1.00 *Historical overview*. Nearly 1,200 years ago, a major revival of Hinduism began in India. In broad terms, movements were started to reestablish the doctrines that were rooted in the *Vedas*, the ancient Hindu scriptures. As a result, three major systems of metaphysics were established between 800 and 1,300 A.D.: The *Adwaita* (Absolute Monism) philosophy of Shankaracharya, the *Vishishtadwaita* (Qualified Monism) of Ramanujacharya and the *Dwaita* (Dualism) of Madhwacharya. The three *Achryas* (teachers) who came from different parts of India, propagated their interpretations from the state of Karnataka. Madhwacharya established his school of *Dwaita* philosophy in Udipi (Udupi), a small coastal town in Mangalore district of Karnataka. The town is famous for the Sri Krishna temple of the 13th century and it is the administrative center of the *Madhwas (Dwaitas),* the followers of Madhwacharya. The *Madhwas* believe that the human soul is saved by the grace of God and God bestows grace on true devotees.

Devotional worship is central to the lives of the *Madhwas*. Worship invariably involves offering delicious foods without causing pain to or destruction of any creatures. For example, milking a cow is allowed on the basis of mutual sharing of food (milk) but slaughtering a cow is a sin. The followers of the three *Acharyas* are strict lacto-vegetarians. Following the *Vedic* rituals, the *Madhwas* worship the sun, the earth, the wind, the fire and the rivers, in addition to idolizing *Sri Krishna* (an incarnation of *Vishnu*). These include, offering a variety of creative and wholesome foods to Krishna. Even today, serving sumptuous dinners is a part of worship at the temple in Udupi.

The Udupi area is warm (70-90°F) and gets nearly 80 inches of rainfall a year. As many as three major crops a year may be harvested, one after another, from the same field. The area did not experience devastating foreign invasions as did many parts of India. Furthermore, the rulers were benevolent and they harbored many minorities. Under the conditions of bountiful nature, tolerance of philosophy and religion were nurtured. The followers of Shankara, Ramanuja and Madhwa were living harmoniously with other religions (Islam and Christianity) and sects. Under such an environment they developed an elaborate cuisine as an integral part of their lifestyles which included celebration of numerous "feasts" and observance of "fasts".

The intermixing of the cultures and cuisines of the broad geographical regions of India has taken place continuously over the centuries. Consequently, the Udipi Cuisine outlined in this book is broadly applicable to the food of India in general and those of Karnataka, Tamil Nadu, Andhra, Kerala and of the bordering regions of Maharashtra in particular. Although the basic terminology used in this cuisine is from Kannada, the official language of Karnataka, words from other languages such as Tulu, Konkani and Hindi are also used. They are defined in the glossary.

This book is not a cookbook as such; recipes are intended as a guide to the broad features of Udipi cuisine. We tested this cuisine while raising our family in the U.S. during the past 40 years. We have entertained our friends using many of these recipes. In addition, we put those years of experience for use in operating Annapurna Restaurant in Massachusetts for 16 years. As a result, many North Americans expressed genuine interest in learning more about this cuisine and its nutritional relevance. There are no books on Udipi cuisine. This book, therefore, is the outcome of both a cultural background and a contemporary scientific outlook. There are nutritionally sound lessons to be learnt from this and other ancient cuisines. We are research biologists and teachers who have remained the practitioners of this diet.

In order to avoid repetition, some general culinary procedures are described and variations are indicated wherever they are used in specific recipes, which we have adapted to suit the conditions of North America. Therefore, many North American ingredients and cooking procedures are used. For example, the use of sour cream, cottage cheese, defatted milk powder, frozen vegetables or the use of a microwave in the Udipi style cooking may appear strange, as part of an ancient cuisine, but their effects are marginal.

1.10 *Buying groceries*. Most North American cities have Indian grocery stores. The ingredients may also be bought throughout North America in supermarkets or in natural food stores. The specialty items may be found in Middle Eastern, Spanish or Chinese grocery stores. Individuals with an Indian background and Indian newspapers are good sources of information on locations of Indian groceries. Buy the rarely used spices and specialty items in small quantities and store them in refrigerated. If available, whole spices should be bought, stored in jars and ground as needed. If a specialty item listed in a recipe is not available, do not hesitate to experiment by either substituting the item or omitting it. Most of the groceries bought from Indian grocery stores are natural, untreated and unprocessed. They should be carefully inspected for any extraneous materials such as sand grains, chaff and insects, and cleaned. The lentils, grains and nuts may be dried overnight in an oven at about 45°C and stored in covered glass jars with tight lids preferably in the refrigerator. As with any organic (natural) food ingredients, prolonged storage in cartons and plastic bags is not desirable; insects can easily gain access and disseminate through them.

1.20 *Pretreatment*. Fresh fruits and vegetables from the market or from the garden must be thoroughly washed to remove pesticides and preservatives are used these days. In spite of government regulations and inspections, commercial food ingredients may carry undesirable chemicals. Even the produce from a kitchen garden may accumulate chemicals from the atmosphere from the atmosphere. Soaking and washing in cold water not only removes the particulates and soil, it also makes the vegetables crisp. To prevent the leaching of nutrients, vegetables should be soaked and washed before chopping them. However, certain vegetables such as eggplant are, soaked in water after cutting, to reduce chemicals that cause browning. The addition of fresh lemon or tamarind juice to the soak also prevents browning. Sprouting seeds, grains and lentils enhances their appearance, taste and nutritional values. Essential processing of some of the ingredients are given below.

Asafoetida or *asafetida* is a very strong smelling resin from roots and rhizomes of a plant, *Ferula foetida*, (carrot family). It is called *Hing* in Hindi. Rarely it is sold as pure resin; mostly as powder compounded with inert ingredients (gum arabic, wheat or rice flour). The quantities indicated in the recipes refer to compounded material. If it is pure, as little as 10 mg may be enough to spice 4 servings.

Coconut is available as fresh fruit, as dried, shredded, shredded and sweetened and, as concentrated extract (milk). The fresh coconuts sold in the groceries have 3 eye spots at one end, one of which is soft. The soft spot may be easily opened by digging with a screwdriver or a penknife and a clear watery juice may be drained into a glass. If the juice is cloudy, ropy or rancid, both the nut and the juice are spoiled. If the juice is clear and sweet to taste, the nut is edible. The fresh nut may be cracked by a hammer and the meat lifted from the shell. The dried coconut is sold as *Copra*. Either of them may be shredded and used as needed. We prefer using unsweetened shredded coconut. It stores well in the refrigerator.

Mango pulp is sold in cans in Indian stores. During the summer fresh mangoes are available; they may be used instead. The pulp of fresh mangoes may be stored temporarily in the refrigerator. It does not freeze well.

Oils and fats. Except butter, only vegetable oils are used in this cuisine. Corn, cotton, peanut, sesame, or soybean seed oils are equally suitable for frying, or as ingredients. Oil for frying may be reused after treating with fresh lemon juice and decanting and storing in a jar in the refrigerator. This treatment reduces oxidized products in the oil and improves its flavor.

Raw sugar (*Gud*) is available in lumps in Indian stores. *Gud* is the unpurified concentrate of sugarcane juice and it is rich in minerals. It is inexpensive. Two parts of *Gud* may be heated with one part of water and made into a syrup and stored in the refrigerator. Wherever *gud* is indicated in the recipes, honey or molasses may be substituted.

Tamarind is available as dry fruit with or without shells and seeds, as a concentrate (pulp), and as juice. The dry fruit is shelled, seeds removed, pulp cooked in water and juice extracted several times by squeezing. The juice may be used as such or pooled and concentrated by boiling. It may be stored in the refrigerator. We suggest buying concentrated juice when available. Approximately 1/2 cup of juice equals two tablespoon pulp for use in the recipes. Experiment using rhubarb stalks or lemon juice when tamarind is not available.

1.30 *Utensils and table setting*. Most common kitchen utensils, equipment and gadgets such as saucepans, skillets, griddles, mixing and serving bowls, casserole dishes, measuring cups, spoons (wooden and metal), knives, peelers, pressure cooker, double boiler and colander, are suitable for use in this cuisine. A stone grinder if available is used extensively in this cuisine. A good blender somewhat replaces it. Any deep metal bowl or a skillet may substitute for the Indian deep-frying pan. An egg poacher may substitute for the steam cooker.

For making curries of any vegetables it is better to use a large (6 quarts) saucepan or a pressure cooker vessel and then transfer the finished preparation to serving dishes. The fresh vegetables occupy a lot of space before cooking and, they shrink after cooking. A pound of fresh greens or a head of shredded cabbage fills a large pan but when cooked makes only about four servings of curry. Therefore, 4 quarts or larger utensils are preferred for vegetable cooking.

Traditionally, Udipi dinners are served on approximately 12"x20" fresh banana leaves. Nowadays, special stainless steel plates, the *Thali*, accompanied by small cups for individual items, are used all over India. The arrangement provides an opportunity to taste individual dishes as such or in combinations. A *Thali* is fun to use and may be bought in any Indian grocery store. We have also served Udipi dinners with the western table settings.

1.40 *Cooking Procedures*. Many kinds of cooking procedures are used in this cuisine; they include pressure cooking, steaming, grilling, griddling, frying, roasting, popping, and the use of acidic and mixed fermentations.

Vegetables are cooked in a covered saucepan, at low heat, and without the addition of water. They may be also cooked in a pressure cooker or in a microwave oven. If water is added, do not drain and discard it because most of the nutrients will be lost. Instead, any excess liquids of cooked vegetables may be made into a soup such as *ganji*, *saru* or *Huli*(Section 5).

1.41 *Deep-frying* is done in a variety of frying pans, preferably in a deep metal bowl. Make sure that the vessel used for deep-frying is filled with oil to no more than 1/2 its capacity. If for any reason oil begins to froth turn off the heat immediately. Under no circumstance should hot oil be left on the stove unattended. Hot oil ignites very easily. Do not let children play near where you are deep-frying.

Generally deep-frying is done on medium heat, at about 400° F. Frying too many pieces at a time lowers the oil temperature and fried items become excessively oily. Adding items into the fryer requires care; of all the cooking procedures, deep-frying requires the most precautions.

Depending upon the size of the vessel used, as much as 4 cups of oil may be required to deep-fry items for 10-12 servings. However, nearly 1/2 the oil may remain after deep-frying. The leftover oil has a spicy flavor and it may be saved in the refrigerator for making *oggarnay* (see section 1.46) or to saute vegetables. Remember, consumption of repeatedly fried oil is unhealthy.

1.42 *Cooking rice*. Parboiled (converted) rice is our preference because it is an Udipi tradition, it does not become mushy on cooking and it refrigerates well. Above all, it has many good features that make it superior even to brown rice (Table, Appendix 1.1). However, if any other kind of rice is used, follow the cooking instructions. Many recipes describe cooking rice by boiling in excess water and draining it. In such a procedure much of the nutrients are leached out. Therefore, we suggest using the cooked extract in making a soup such as *ganji*(see Section 8.10), rather than discarding it. Alternatively, we prefer, cooking rice by evaporation: parboiled rice is cooked in two volumes of water for about 15 minutes in a pressure cooker or in a double boiler until the water evaporates. Parboiled rice so cooked will be fluffy. It may be refrigerated and rewarmed in a microwave or double boiler with a sprinkling of water. It will remain fluffy. Refrigerated rice is good for making combination rice dishes because individual grains remain separate. Chilled rice may be mixed with *Palya* or *Huli*, topped with nuts or herbs, and cooked in an oven like a casserole (35°F for 20 minutes).

1.43 *Cooking legumes*. A large number of different kinds of whole or split legumes *(dal)* are used in this and other Indian cuisines. However, split peas, chickpeas and mung beans available in any grocery stores may be substituted for *dal*. Split peas or chickpeas, often used in *oggarnay* (see Section 1.46), may be either dry or soaked. Either way, they should be added to *oggarnay* when the mustard seeds start popping. If dry lentils are used, add vegetables after *dal* turns brown, cover and cook until they are slightly soft. If soaked lentils are used, browning makes them slightly hard. In either case do not fry them dark brown as they become too hard instead of soft and nutty.

For soups, *Saru* or *Rasam*, (see Section 5.11), lentils should be cooked until very soft. For a curry, *(Huli)* cooking should be stopped just as the legumes turn soft so that individual seeds remain. In either case, bring water to boil, add lentil with 1/4 teaspoon of oil and 1/4 tsp turmeric powder, turn down heat and keep the lid ajar to reduce boiling over. Other details of cooking are specified in the recipes.

1.44 *Roasting*. Sesame seeds and nuts may be freshly roasted in a skillet over low heat, and stirring with a wooden spatula. They may also be roasted by spreading them thinly on a cookie sheet, and cooking in the oven set at 350°F for 15-30 minutes and stirring once or twice. After cooling, they may be put in a heavy bag and crushed with a rolling pin. Prerosted, salted and packaged seeds are rarely used.

1.45 *Making ghee*. *Ghee* is clarified butter. It has a pleasant aroma and longer shelf life at room temperature. Traditionally, in Indian cooking, *ghee* is used more frequently than butter. *Ghee* is prepared by melting unsalted or low-salt butter in a saucepan, 1/3 full, over medium heat. When it starts to crackle, turn to low heat and continue heating until the crackling sound dies down. Turn off the heat. There will be a light brown sediment which carries the salt that the butter may contain. The sediment is separated by decanting the supernatant oily liquid, the *ghee*. *Ghee* is used on rice, breads and wherever butter or oil is called for. *Ghee* may be flavored by adding herbs of your choice just before turning off the heat. In all the recipes given here, vegetable oil may be substituted for *ghee*.

1.46 *Preparation of oggarnay.* This is an essential requirement in South Indian cooking, especially, in the Udipi cuisine. It is a special garnishing process. It gives a finishing touch to all spicy curries. The specific ingredients of each *oggarnay* are given in the recipes. The general procedure is as follows: Heat a table spoon of *ghee* or vegetable oil in a saucepan over medium heat. Add *black* mustard seeds, keep stirring until they begin popping. Lower the heat. Spices such as turmeric and asafoetida are added after turning off the heat near the end of popping, whereas spices such as cumin are added earlier. Either way, garnishing is done by quickly pouring the sizzling mixture of *oggarnay* on top of a finished soup or curry. *Oggarnay* is also used to saute vegetables. For this purpose, add ingredients such as *dal*, nuts and spices as the mustard seeds start popping and add the cut vegetables at the end of popping. Then stir and cook as outlined under each recipes. Pieces of dry chili peppers may be added along with spices, but we do not recommend it to the novice because the pungent aroma may be very irritating. Yellow mustard seeds are not suitable for *oggarnay*. The sediment, however, is used to flavor *Palya* and curries or mix with plain rice. oggarnay.

1.50 *Herbs, Spices and Curries*. Botanically, flowering plants which do not become woody and remain relatively small are known as herbs. In popular terms any plant that is used to flavor or color the foods or used medicinally are herbs. Invariably, herbs are aromatic, pungent and flavor enhancing tender parts of plants.

The most commonly used herbs in the Udipi cuisine are greens of coriander, dill, mint, onion, and curry leaves. Anise, asafoetida, black pepper, cardamom, cayenne (chili) pepper, cinnamon, clove, coriander, fennel, fenugreek, garlic, ginger, mace, mustard, nutmeg, onion, poppy seeds, sesame seeds, saffron, tamarind and turmeric are commonly used spices. Sometimes, as in the case of coriander and dill, the tender parts serve as herbs and the mature seeds are spices. Some tender herbs such as the leaves and stems of dill and fenugreek are used as vegetables.

Spices such as fenugreek are mild, in contrast, asafoetida has a strong aroma. Black pepper is mild compared to cayenne pepper. All spices, especially hot spices such as cayenne and jalapeno peppers, may serve as mild stimulants that increase the secretion of digestive juices and cause a sensation of thirst. Use them in moderate quantities. Excessive consumption of spices, especially the hot ones, may irritate and injure mucous membranes. Those who are not used to eating spicy food should be particularly cautious in using chili peppers.

Curries are formulations made up of several spices and herbs. Each region of India and even individual families have their own variations of curries. Many varieties of curry powders and pastes are made by mixing and blending various spices, herbs, lentils and nuts. Variation of curries are also made by adding some ingredients raw and some roasted.

Making curry is a highly developed art. In this cuisine, a curry which is thick in consistency is called *Huli*, The thin curries that contain less lentils and no vegetables are called *Saru* or *Rasam*. A curry made of one or more vegetables without liquid is known as *Palya*. Curries are served warm. *Raitha* and *Pachadi*, which contain yogurt in addition to spices and vegetables are served cold. In general, curries contribute many valuable nutrients in minute amounts and enhance the flavor and appearance of foods. A sample of a curry base, a *Masala*, is described below. Small quantities of masala are added as indicated in the recipes, or as desired, to impart curry flavor to soups, sauces, salad dressings, dips, sandwich spreads, cooked vegetables and condiments.

1.51 *Masala* (A curry powder)

1 tsp cumin seed
1/2 tsp black mustard seeds
1/4 tsp fenugreek seeds
1/3 cup coriander seed
1/2 cup yellow split peas
1/2 tsp vegetable oil
8-10 whole dried red pepper pods.

Fry the cumin, mustard and fenugreek seeds together in a skillet over medium heat, until the mustard stops popping and transfer them to a bowl. Using the same skillet brown the split peas and coriander separately. Add them to the mustard mix. Finally, add oil into the skillet and fry red pepper until light brown. Turn on the exhaust fan to clear the pungent aroma. Mix and grind them together into a fine powder in a blender. Store the powder in a covered glass jar, preferably in the refrigerator. Use it as a curry base as suggested in the recipes.

1.60 *Synthetic additives*. Synthetic flavors, colors and preservatives are not used in traditional Udipi cuisine. Instead, spices, herbs and their mixtures (curries) are used to enhance flavor, color, shelf-life and nutritional value of foods. Turmeric (yellow), saffron and safflower (red, orange), tamarind (brown) etc. serve also as coloring agents. Spices such as garlic, onion, ginger, cloves, cinnamon and red pepper are flavoring agents which also have powerful antibiotic, antioxidant and preservative properties.

Traditionally, food preservation was accomplished by what may be called *egrated pest management practices,*ther than by chemical overkill. These included effective combination of dehydration, fermentation, clarification, acidity, osmotic pressure, unsaturated vegetable oils, pickling, *oggarnay*, steaming, use of herbs and spices, and hygienic practices. Nowadays, ready availability of pressure cooking, refrigeration and freezing provide additional protection.

1.70 *Traditional eating.* Indian dinners involve eating with free use of fingers. Therefore, traditionally, hands are washed thoroughly before and after eating. Morsels of rice are mixed with lentil, vegetable and yogurt dishes and tasted. Mixes are varied to suit ones's taste. The dishes are also used as dips or dabs to make small bite-size sandwiches with pieces of breads, parata, puri, or wadapay. Both traditional and modern styles of serving are acceptable.

1.80 *Leftover Foods*. The cooked vegetable dishes in general and those that contain yogurt in particular, do not spoil readily. Also dishes that contain sour fruits such as tomato, tamarind and lemon juice resist spoilage. The cereal dishes ferment rather than spoil in contrast to lentil and coconut dishes which develop rancidity and ropiness when stored for several days even in the refrigerator. In all these cases of vegetarian cooking, even rancidity only makes the dishes unpalatable but do not cause food poisoning. The excessive fermenting flavor of foods may be reduced by adding a little milk (in the case of yogurt dishes) or a little honey (in the case of dishes that contain sour fruits) and a little flour (in the case of fermenting dough).

1.90 *Miscellaneous*. Hot (green) peppers, along with a variety of other ingredients, are used in moderate amounts to generate infinite variations in tastes and allure. Ground cayenne pepper may substitute but it imparts different flavors. If you are not familiar with the use of hot peppers, start with 1/4 of the amount given in the recipes. While chopping peppers or squeezing tamarind wear disposable plastic gloves, unless you are sure that your skin is not sensitive to them. If you feel a burning sensation due to the peppers dab the area with yogurt. By and large, irritations caused by spices are alleviated by yogurt.

Cooking ahead. The majority of dishes in this cuisine taste better if they are served at least an hour after cooking. The spices take time to seep into the vegetables. During this intervening period, the dishes should be kept hot. As a general rule store food for longer than 4 hours in the refrigerator to prevent spoilage.

Servings. The number of servings that a recipe makes depends upon the number of different dishes being served and other factors such as how much the diners like spicy foods. Spicy foods stimulate drinking water which also reduces consumption of food. Therefore, the servings indicated for each recipe are only approximate estimates.

YOGURT DISHES

2.00 **Place of Yogurt in the Udipi Cuisine.**

We are starting our section on recipes with yogurt dishes in order to accentuate the place of yogurt in this cuisine. Yogurt is a food of antiquity which has gained nutritional importance in North America only in the recent decades. Yogurt has been such an important ingredient in the Udipi Cuisine that no traditional dinners are served without yogurt or yogurt dishes. Yogurt is used in a variety of beverages such as *Lassi* and *Neeralay*, in salads such as *Pachadi* and *Raitha*, in entrees such as *Butti anna*, in curries such as *Pulikajipu* and in desserts such as *Rasayana*. In other words, no other single food ingredient contributes to the completion of a meal as much as yogurt does. Yogurt dishes. therefore, are described under different categories. A few tested recipes are included.

2.1 Preparation of low-fat natural yogurt

3 cups of instant nonfat milk powder
3 cups of cold water
1/2 cup of cultured yogurt (starter)

All utensils and tools used in yogurt making must be clean and rinsed in boiling water. In a mixing bowl, take a cup of water, add the milk powder and mix with a wire beater. Add remaining water, mix, place in a double boiler or in a water bath and heat to scalding over low heat. Let it cool to touch (approximately 45° C). In the meantime, place the starter yogurt in a separate bowl, smooth with a wire beater and combine it with milk. Then pour the mix into a quart jar. Leave the jar in a warm place (an old type of oven with a pilot flame provides the right temperature). At about 40°C, the lactic acid bacteria of the starter will multiply rapidly and bring about the desired fermentation and sets the yogurt. If the temperature and starter are just right, the yogurt should be set within 3 hours. If it takes longer than 3 hours, the yogurt will not be firm and sweet. Before starting to use the newly prepared yogurt, save about 1/2 a cup of it in a clean jar (treated with boiling water) for use as a starter. Notice that the amount of milk powder used in this recipe is more than twice the amount suggested by the manufacturer for reconstituted milk.

2.2 *Pulikajipu* (A yogurt curry)

2 large cucumbers
4 medium sweet peppers
4 Tbsp *ghee* (see Section 1.45)
1 tsp black mustard seeds
1 Tbsp cumin seeds
2 Tbsp salt
1 Tbsp raw sugar or honey
1 tsp turmeric powder
1/2 tsp cayenne pepper powder
4 cups water
2 cups yogurt
1/2 cup sour cream
3 Tbsp chickpea flour
1 Tbsp rice flour
1/2 cup shredded coconut

Mature (yellow) cucumbers are ideal. If the cucumbers are fresh and unwaxed do not peel. Cut them and the peppers into one inch cubes including seeds and rind. In a saucepan, prepare *oggarnay* (see Section 1.46) using *ghee*, black mustard and half the amount of cumin seeds. When the mustard seeds stop popping, add the cut vegetables, salt, sugar, turmeric and pepper and saute. Close the lid and cook on medium heat for 5 minutes or until the cucumber pieces begin to soften. While the vegetables are cooking, grind the coconut, the remaining cumin seeds, rice and chickpea flour into a slurry, in a blender, adding the yogurt and sour cream, a little at a time. Blend and pour into the cooking vegetables. Rinse the blender with water and pour into the mix. Keep the heat on and the lid off until the curry starts to boil. Turn off the heat and replace the lid. It may be eaten hot or cold; and with rice or bread. It is a very good curry to make during cucumber season and may be frozen in small batches. Increase or decrease the cayenne pepper to suit your taste. Makes 8-10 servings.

2.21 *Southay Raitha* (Cucumber salad)

1 large cucumber
1 cup yogurt
1/2 cup sour cream
1 tsp honey
1 tsp salt
1/2 tsp cayenne pepper powder
1 tsp cumin seeds
2 Tbsp *ghee* (see section 1.45)
1 tsp black mustard
1 Tbsp fresh chopped coriander greens

Chop cucumber into fine pieces. In a mixing bowl, using a wire beater or a wooden spatula mix the yogurt, sour cream, honey, salt and pepper. Fold in the chopped cucumber. In a small saucepan, roast 1/2 tsp cumin until the seeds turn dark brown. Powder the seeds when cool and add to the yogurt mixture. Prepare *oggarnay* (see Section 1.46) using remaining cumin and mustard seeds. Pour the sizzling *oggarnay* over *Raitha* mixture. Chill before serving. Eat as such, or with rice or breads. Makes 4-6 servings.

2.22 *Badanay* Pachadi (Eggplant salad)

1 large eggplant
2 large potatoes
1 1/2 cups yogurt
1/2 cup sour cream
1/2 cup light cream
1 tsp raw sugar or honey
1/2 tsp cayenne pepper powder
2 tsp salt
5 Tbsp *ghee* (see Section 1.45)
1 tsp black mustard seeds
1/8 tsp asafoetida powder
1 Tbsp fresh coriander greens, chopped

Smear 1/2 tsp *ghee* over eggplant and potatoes, wrap them suitably and bake or cook (approximately 20 min in microwave oven) until a fork or a toothpick can be inserted easily. They may be cooked ahead of time and refrigerated. Mash the cooked eggplant and potatoes without removing their skins and set them aside. Mix yogurt, cream, honey, pepper and salt in a mixing bowl using a wire beater. Fold in mashed vegetables. Heat *ghee* a small saucepan and prepare *oggarnay* (see Section 1.46) using black mustard and asafoetida. Garnish the eggplant-yogurt mix with sizzling hot *oggarnay*. Transfer the contents of the mixing bowl to a serving dish, sprinkle coriander greens, chill and serve. Eat as a salad or with rice or with bread. It tastes better several hours after making. Makes 6-8 servings.

2.23 *Tharkari Pachadi* (A vegetable salad)

1 large cucumber
1 sweet pepper
1 carrot
2 tomatoes
2 baked potatoes
1 tsp finely chopped fresh ginger
1/4 tsp cayenne pepper powder
1 cup natural plain yogurt
1/2 cup sour cream
1/2 cup coffee cream
2 tsp salt
1 Tbsp honey
4 Tbsp *ghee* (see section 1.45)
1 tsp black mustard seeds
1 tsp cumin seeds

Use all the vegetables except carrots without peeling or removing seeds.

Peel and cut the carrot. Chop the cucumber, pepper and tomatoes. Mash the potatoes into about i/4 inch lumps. In a bowl, mix the cream, sour cream, yogurt, ginger, salt and honey. Fold in the vegetables. Make *oggarnay* (see Section 1.46) using *ghee*, mustard and cumin. Garnish the *Pachadi* with sizzling *oggarnay*. Chill before serving. Eat as a salad or with rice as a mix and as a spread on breads. Makes 6-8 servings.

2.24 *Lassi* (A cold drink)

1 1/2 cups yogurt
1/3 cup sour cream
1/3 cup light cream
1 Tbsp raw sugar or honey
1/8 tsp cardamom powder
1/8 tsp nutmeg powder

Mix all ingredients in a blender and serve with ice cubes. Makes 3-4 servings.

VEGETABLE DISHES

3.00 **The kinds of vegetables used.** Commonly available vegetables such as beans, broccoli, Brussels sprouts, cabbage, cauliflower, carrot, cucumber, eggplant, onion, okra, peas, pepper, potato and tomato are all used in this cuisine. We have served delicious dishes made of the greens and tender stems of amaranth, beet, grape, kale, pigweed, purslane, squash, and spinach. In addition, flower buds, fruits and seeds of squash and radish, orange and water melon rinds, the skins of squash and the tender stems of kohlrabi and cauliflower also make popular dishes. We have also adapted vegetables such as Jerusalem artichoke tubers, rhubarb stalks and comfry leaves and stems which are common in North America but not in India.

We have created tasty dishes from many kinds of fruits such as crab apple, gooseberry, pineapple, peach, cranberry, immature grapes, and nuts. Edible plants, when cooked with combinations of cereals, lentils, fruits, nuts and spices, make attractive and appetizing dishes balanced nutritionally without being loaded with empty calories. They are rich in fiber, potassium and calcium, and low in fat, sodium and phosphate. They contain little cholesterol. They are good sources of needed essential fatty acids. They are choice foods for people with sedentary lifestyle. Vegetables in general, contain moderate amounts of protein, minerals and vitamins. They provide a variety of complex carbohydrates and antioxidants. Being the primary biomass, vegetables are high in yield per unit land area and, therefore, economical for growing anywhere in the world.

Raw vegetables contribute fewer calories than cooked vegetables because they occupy more space per unit weight and our system digests the intact plant tissue only partially. However, one has to be cautious in consuming large amount of raw vegetables for two main reasons: 1. It may cause stomach pain, diarrhea and intestinal discomfort unless the person's G.I. system is accustomed to eating them 2. In many third world countries vegetables are grown under unsanitary conditions and they may be

contaminated with human parasites and pathogens. Casual washing may not remove the contaminants; cooking destroys them.

3.10 *Tharakari Saru* (A vegetable soup)

2 sweet peppers
1 large carrot
1 small head of cabbage
1 large onion
4 Tbsp *ghee* (see Section 1.45)
1 tsp cumin seeds
1 tsp black mustard seeds
2 Tbsp tamarind pulp (see Section 1.20)
1/2 a cup split peas
5 cloves of garlic, chopped
1 tsp coriander powder
1/2 tsp asafoetida
1/2 tsp turmeric powder
1/2 tsp ginger powder
2 tsp salt
1 tsp raw sugar or honey
8 cups of water

Cut the pepper and carrot into 1" x 1/2" pieces. Chop the onion and cabbage. In a large saucepan bring 4 cups of water to boil, add 1/4 tsp *ghee*, turmeric and split peas. Cook until split peas are mushy. Transfer to a bowl. Using the same pan, prepare *oggarnay* (see Section 1.46) with *ghee*, mustard and asafoetida. Saute the garlic until it is light brown, add cut vegetables and mix. Add salt, tamarind, honey and a cup of water. Cover and cook until the vegetables are soft. Add the cooked peas and the remaining water and bring to a boil uncovered. Wait for about 30 minutes before serving. It may be eaten as such or mixed with rice and eaten. It refrigerates well. Makes 8-10 servings.

3.11 *Soray Palya* (Summer squash curry)

1 large mature summer squash
2 sweet peppers
1/2 cup rhubarb pieces
1/4 cup shredded coconut(see Sec. 1.20)
3 Tbsp *ghee* (see Section 1.45)
1 tsp black mustard seeds
1 tsp cumin seeds
1 Tbsp grated fresh ginger
1 tsp chopped fresh hot pepper
1 Tbsp fresh chopped coriander greens
1 cup red lentil
1 tsp turmeric powder
2 tsp salt
1 tsp raw sugar or honey

Cut the squash into one inch pieces (including the skin and seeds). Cut the pepper into large pieces. Prepare *oggarnay* (see Section 1.46) with the *ghee*, mustard and cumin. Saute the ginger, peppers and coriander and add the squash, rhubarb, turmeric, salt, honey, lentils and coconut to *oggarnay*. Mix, cover and cook for about 10 minutes, until the lentils are soft but not mushy. Turn off the heat and leave the lid on. This can be eaten as salad, or with bread or rice. Makes 8-10 servings.

3.12 *Tharakari Palya* (Vegetable curry)

1 medium size cauliflower
1 lb carrots
3 large sweet peppers
1 small head of cauliflower
1 cup chickpeas
3 Tbsp tamarind paste(see Section 1.20) 1/4 cup shredded
coconut(see Sec. 1.20)
4 Tbsp *ghee* (see Section 1.45)
1 tsp black mustard seeds
2 tsp cumin seeds
1/4 cup yellow split peas
10 cloves of garlic
2 tsp salt
1 tsp coriander powder
1 tsp turmeric powder
1 1/2 tsp cayenne pepper powder
1 tsp raw sugar or honey

Soak the chickpeas overnight in cold water and drain. Peel and slice the carrot into 1/2 inch pieces. Cut the cauliflower (including leaves and soft stems) and cabbage into approximately 1"x 1/2" pieces. Peel and chop the garlic. Heat *ghee* in a large saucepan and prepare *oggarnay* (see Section 1.46) using mustard, cumin and split peas. Add chickpeas along with chopped garlic and saute. Then add the cut vegetables, salt, coriander, turmeric, cayenne and honey to *oggarnay*. Mix, cover, and cook for about 10 minutes or until the chickpeas are soft. Cover, turn off the heat. This may be eaten as such, or with rice, bread or yogurt. It refrigerates well. Serve warm. Makes 8-10 servings.

3.13 *Kosu Palya* (cabbage curry)

1 medium size cabbage
1 medium size potato
4 Tbsp ghee (see Section 1.45)
1 tsp black mustard seeds
1 tsp cumin seeds
1/3 cup yellow split peas
1 tsp grated fresh ginger
1 tsp chopped fresh hot pepper
1 1/4 tsp salt
1/2 tsp turmeric powder
1 tsp honey
juice of 1/2 lemon
12 oz frozen or fresh green peas
1/3 cup shredded unsweetened coconut

Chop the cabbage without discarding any parts. Cut the potato into 1/2 inch pieces without removing the skin. Heat *ghee* in a large saucepan and prepare *oggarnay* (see Section 1.46) using *ghee*, mustard, cumin and split peas. Add the potato, ginger and pepper into the *oggarnay* and saute. Add the cabbage, turmeric, salt, honey, lemon juice and mix. Cover the pan and cook for about eight minutes. Add the green peas and coconut, mix, cover and cook over low heat for approximately 5 minutes. Turn off the heat. Serve warm. May be eaten as a salad or with rice, spaghetti, bread or yogurt. It refrigerates well. Makes 6-8 servings.

3.14 *Elay Menasinakai* (Curry of greens)

2 lbs assorted greens
1 large onion
4 Tbsp sesame seeds
4 Tbsp *ghee* (see Section 1.45)
1 tsp black mustard seeds
1/3 cup split peas
1 tsp chopped fresh ginger
1 tsp salt
1 Tbsp raw sugar or honey
1 tsp Masala (see Section 1.51)
1 tsp turmeric powder
1/2 tsp asafoetida powder
1 tsp chopped fresh cayenne pepper
1/2 cup water

A variety of greens such as amaranth, comfry, kale, purslane, mustard, water cress, spinach and Swiss chard may be used as available. Chop the assorted greens and onion. Roast and crush the sesame seeds (see Section 1.44). Prepare *oggarnay* (see Section 1.46) using *ghee*, mustard and split peas. Saute the onion and ginger. Add the chopped greens and stir while adding salt, turmeric, honey, Masala, sesame, asafoetida and cayenne. Cover and cook for about 5 minutes. Add water and continue cooking for about 10 minutes. Turn off the heat and wait for about 30 minutes before serving. May be eaten with rice. Refrigerates well. Makes 4-6 servings.

3.16 *Pudina Pakoda* (Mint savory)

2 medium onions
1 cup fresh mint greens
1/2 cup freshly roasted peanuts
1 cup chickpea flour
1/2 cup rice flour
2 tsp salt
1/2 tsp cayenne pepper powder
1/2 tsp turmeric powder
2 Tbsp *ghee* (see Section 1.45)
1 cup water
oil for deep-frying

Chop the onions and mint. Crush the peanuts. Mix them with chickpea flour, rice flour, salt, pepper and *ghee* in a bowl using a fork. Add small amounts of water at a time and mix the contents of the bowl with a wire beater or by hand into soft ball consistency. Drop approximately one inch diameter lumps of batter at a time gently from the sides of the frying pan into the hot oil.

Deep-fry them to a golden brown color at medium high heat and drain excess oil on paper towels. Serve warm as a snack or as an appetizer with soup. Makes 20-24 pieces.

4. CEREAL DISHES

Since antiquity cereals have been the main staple of human food in almost all parts of the world. Rice, wheat, corn, and millets are the major cereals. In the U.S. there is a growing tendency to use them as cattle feed. Unless the tremendous importance of whole grains as human food is recognized, the well-being of future generations will suffer. In the Udipi cuisine, rice, wheat and millets are the most commonly used grains. Rice, however, is the main staple.

4A Rice. Rice, when harvested is known as **paddy**. It becomes **brown rice** when outermost rough coat is removed by milling. The thin brown coat that remains is rich in nutrients; when it is removed by further polishing, it becomes **white rice**. White rice is poor in important nutrients and fiber which are lost along with the germ and the bran.

In the Udipi area, the paddy is briefly treated with boiling water, dried and then hulled. This process drives the nutrients of the outer coats deep into the kernels of the grains and enriches the grains in addition to giving them a yellow tinge. This specially treated rice is known as **parboiled rice (converted rice)**. Using parboiled rice is an Udipi tradition. It stores and cooks better than white or brown rice. Rice is served plain or in various combinations with vegetables, lentils, herbs, spices, fruits, nuts and yogurt as **Combination rice** or **Pilaf**.

If cooking is compared to an art, then rice is like a blank canvas which inspires the painter to express his or her talent. Rice, more than any other cereal, lends itself to creation of innumerable dishes by blending with vegetables, lentils, fruits, herbs, spices, and with other cereals. The additives also bring changes in texture, aroma and color of rice preparations. Rice is non-allergenic and easily digested by the young and the old alike. The recipes given below demonstrate the possibilities.

4A COMBINATION RICE DISHES

4.00 *Kesari Anna* (Saffron rice)

1 cup parboiled rice
2 cups water
4 medium size carrots
4 Tbsp *ghee* (see Section 1.45)
1/2 tsp black mustard seeds
1/2 cup raw cashew nuts
1/3 cup raisins
1 cup green peas (fresh or frozen)
1/2 tsp salt
A pinch of saffron (6-8 filaments)
1/4 tsp safflower petals (optional)

Cook the rice and chill it in the refrigerator. Wash, peel and grate carrots. Heat *ghee* in a saucepan and prepare *oggarnay* (see Section 1.46) using mustard seeds and add cashews, when they turn slightly brown add raisins. When the raisins swell up, add carrots and salt and saute. Cover and cook until the carrots are soft (about 5 minutes). Add the peas and continue cooking for about 3 minutes on low heat. In the meantime, break up the chilled rice into individual grains and soak the crushed saffron and safflower in a tablespoon of warm water. Add the rice, saffron and safflower to the carrot-oggarnay mixture. Cover and cook on low heat until you smell its aroma (approximately 5 min.). Serve warm with *Pachadi* as a side dish. Makes 6-8 servings.

4.01 *Butti Anna* (Traveler's rice)

1 cup parboiled rice
2 cups water
3 large sweet peppers
1 small Spanish onion
1/3 cup cream (half and half)
1/4 cup cottage cheese
2 cups plain yogurt
1 tsp grated fresh ginger
1 tsp salt
4 Tbsp *ghee* (see Section 1.45)
1 tsp black mustard seeds
1/4 cup yellow split peas
1/4 tsp cumin seeds
1/4 tsp turmeric
1/8 tsp asafoetida

Cook the rice (see Section 1.42), and chill it. Chop the onion and pepper into 1/4" pieces. Mix yogurt, cream, cottage cheese, ginger and salt in a mixing bowl. Fold in chopped onion and pepper. Break up the chilled rice into individual grains by hand and combine it with the yogurt mix in the bowl using a wooden spoon. Prepare *oggarnay* (see Section 1.46) using *ghee*, mustard, split peas, cumin, turmeric and asafoetida. Garnish the rice-yogurt mix with a sizzling *oggarnay* and mix. Serve with any palya, appetizers and hot soup. Makes 6-8 servings.

It is called Traveler's rice because it lasts for several days without refrigeration even in warm weather. The lactobacillus population of yogurt coats the starchy rice grains and acts as a preservative. It is known to prevent traveller's nausea and diarrhea. It supplies much needed energy and roughage during travel. When supplemented with fruits it helps to relieve constipation and reduces stress.

If necessary, the fat content of this dish may be reduced by replacing the cream with buttermilk or yogurt made of defatted milk powder (see Section 2.10). Presence of cultured yogurt on rice surface encourages lactic fermentation under ambient temperatures (20-30°C). It results in lactic fermentation and preservation of the preparation.

4.02 *Belluli Anna* (Garlic rice)

1 cup parboiled rice
2 cups of water
4 large potatoes
10 cloves of fresh garlic
1 tsp grated fresh ginger roots
6 Tbsp *ghee* (see Section 1.45)
1 tsp black mustard seeds
1/2 tsp cayenne pepper powder
1 tsp salt
1/3 cup grated coconut
1/3 cup broken cashew nuts

Cook the rice and chill it. Bake the potatoes and crush them into 1/2" pieces. Peel and chop the garlic. In a large saucepan prepare *oggarnay* (see Section 1.46) with *ghee* and mustard. Add nuts and brown them. Then add potatoes and stir. When they are brown, add garlic and ginger and saute. Add salt, pepper and coconut and mix. Break the rice into individual grains and add it to the vegetable spice, mixture. Cover and cook over low heat for about 5 minutes. Turn off the heat and leave for about 30 minutes before serving. Serve warm with *Pachadi* or soup. Makes 6-8 servings.

4.03 *Chitra Anna* (Picturesque rice)

1 cup parboiled rice
2 cups of water
4 large sweet peppers
1/2 fresh lemon
1 tsp grated lemon rind
5 Tbsp *ghee* (see Section 1.45)
1 tsp black mustard seeds
1 tsp cumin seeds
1/3 cup yellow split peas
1/3 cup cashew nut, toasted
1 tsp chopped fresh chili pepper
1 Tbsp fresh ginger, grated
1 Tbsp green coriander leaves, chopped
1 tsp raw sugar or honey
1 tsp salt
1/2 tsp turmeric powder
1/4 cup grated coconut

Cook the rice and chill it. Soak the split peas for about 1/2 an hour and drain. Cut the pepper into 1/4" pieces. Prepare *oggarnay* (see Section 1.46) in a sauce pan using *ghee*, mustard and cumin. Add the split peas, stir and as they begin to brown add cashews and brown them together. Saute ginger, hot and sweet peppers and coriander. Break up the rice into individual grains and add to *oggarnay*. Add salt, pepper, lemon juice, rind, coconut and mix. Cover and cook for about 10 minutes on low heat. Turn off the heat. Serve warm with soup and *Pachadi*. It refrigerates well. Makes 6-8 servings.

4.04 *Puliyogaray* (Tamarind rice)

1 cup parboiled rice
2 1/2 cup water
1/2 cup sesame seeds
1 cup shelled peanuts
5 Tbsp tamarind (see Section 1.20)
1/3 cup vegetable oil
1 Tbsp black mustard seeds
1/3 cup yellow split peas
1 Tbsp salt
4 Tbsp raw sugar or honey
1 tsp cayenne pepper powder
1 tbsp *masala* (see Section 1.51)
1 tsp turmeric powder

Cook the rice with 2 cups of water and chill. Roast the peanuts and sesame seeds (see Section 1.44). Roast and crush the sesame (see Section 1.44). Dissolve tamarind paste in 1/2 cup of hot water. In a large saucepan prepare *oggarnay* (see Section 1.46) using oil, mustard seeds and split peas. Add tamarind juice, salt, sugar, pepper and Masala to *oggarnay* and boil for about 5 minutes. This tamarind sauce may be made and saved in the refrigerator. Crumble the rice into individual grains and mix the tamarind sauce, sesame and peanuts with it. Cover and let it simmer for about 10 minutes. It may be stored in the refrigerator and reheated before serving. Serve warm with *Pachadi*, yogurt and soup. Makes 6-8 servings.

4B GRITS

Upma and *Bath* made out of cereal grits. These are used as breakfast foods, as snacks and as low calorie special dietetic foods. They refrigerate well.

4.10 *Upma* (Spicy grits)

1/4 cup cream of wheat or bulgur
1/4 cup corn meal
5 Tbsp *ghee* (see Section 1.45)
1 large onion
1 tsp fresh hot pepper
1 Tbsp coriander greens
1 tsp fresh ginger
1 tsp black mustard seeds
1/3 cup yellow split peas
1/2 fresh lemon
1 tsp salt
1/3 cup shredded coconut
2 1/2 cups water

Soak the split peas in water for about 30 minutes and drain. Heat one tablespoon *ghee* in a saucepan, add the grain mixture and fry until dull brown; set aside. Chop onion, pepper, ginger and coriander. In a large saucepan prepare *oggarnay* (see Section 1.46) using remaining *ghee*, mustard and soaked peas. Add hot pepper, onion, ginger and coriander greens. Add water, salt and coconut and, when the mixture starts boiling, lower the heat. Add grits slowly and mix with a fork. Cover the pan and continue cooking on low heat for about 10 minutes. Turn off the heat. Serve warm with yogurt or Pachadi as a wholesome light meal. Refrigerates well. Makes 6-8 servings.

4.11 *Wangibath* (Eggplant grit)

1 medium eggplant
8 Tbsp *ghee* (see Section 1.45)
1 1/2 cup regular cream of wheat
1/3 cup sesame seeds
1/2 cup cashew nut pieces
1 tsp black mustard seeds
1/4 cup yellow split peas
1 tsp turmeric powder
1/4 tsp clove powder
1 tsp cinnamon powder
2 Tbsp *Masala* (see Section 1.51)
1/2 tsp cayenne pepper powder
3 Tbsp tamarind (see Section 1.20)
2 tsp salt
1 tsp raw sugar or honey
3 cups of water

Cut the eggplant into 1/2" x 2" pieces including skin and seeds and soak them in cold water. Roast the sesame seeds and powder. Heat two tablespoon of *ghee* in the saucepan and fry cream of wheat until it is dull brown and set aside. Use a teaspoon of *ghee* to brown cashew nut separately. Prepare *oggarnay* (see Section 1.46) using mustard and split peas. Add drained eggplant and saute. Add turmeric, clove, cinnamon, Masala, pepper, salt, sugar and tamarind. Mix, cover the pan and continue cooking over low heat for about 10 minutes. This mixture could be saved in the refrigerator. Add water and continue cooking until it starts to boil. Lower the heat, add cream of wheat, cashew nut and left over *ghee* while stirring with a fork and continue cooking until the mass starts to solidify. Cover and allow it to simmer for about 5 minutes, then turn off the heat. Serve warm with yogurt, salad or *Pachadi*. It refrigerates well. Makes 8-10 servings.

4.8 *Ksheera* (Sweet grit)

1 cup regular cream of wheat
2/3 cup *ghee* (see Section 1.45)
1/2 cup raisins
1/2 cup cashew nuts, chopped
1 cup sugar
2 cups water
1 tsp cardamom powder
6-8 filaments of saffron
1/4 tsp safflower (optional)

In a skillet heat 1 tablespoon of *ghee* over low heat, then fry the cream of wheat until it is dull brown, then set aside. Using the same pan, heat an another teaspoon full of *ghee* and fry cashews until light brown, add raisins and continue frying until the raisins become plump. Soak saffron and safflower in a tablespoon of water. In a saucepan heat water, add remaining *ghee* and sugar bring to boiling. Lower the heat and add cream of wheat, cardamom and saffron while mixing with a fork. Cover the pan and simmer for about 10 minutes. Turn off the heat but leave the pan covered for about 30 minutes before serving. Serve as a breakfast food, dessert or snack. Refrigerates well. Makes 6-8 servings.

4C BREADS

Traditional breads of India are unleavened. They are made of whole-grain flours and grits of cereals such as wheat, rice and millets. In the Udupi cuisine, bread is subsidiary to rice as a staple. There are many types of breads including *Rotti*, *Parata*, *Chapathi*, *Puri* and *Wadapay*. *Parata* and *Wadapay* are cooked on a griddle. **Puri** is deep-fried. *Rotti* may be partly cooked on a griddle and then briefly roasted on a grill or directly on hot cinders. Some kinds of breads are stuffed with spicy vegetables and lentils, some are spiced but most are bland. Breads are eaten with other dishes such as *palya, chutney* or *pachadies*. These breads taste best when freshly made. They may be wrapped, and refrigerated and warmed for 1 minute in a microwave oven before serving. Below we have given just a few of the many bread recipes.

4.20 *Alu Parata* (Potato bread)

2 cups whole-wheat flour
1/2 cup all purpose flour
2 Tbsp vegetable oil
1 tsp salt
4 un-peeled, boiled potatoes
1 tsp coriander powder
1 tsp ginger powder
1 tsp cayenne pepper powder
1/4 tsp asafoetida
4 Tbsp *ghee* (see Section 1.45)
2 cups water

Stuffing: Mash the potatoes along with a 3/4 tsp salt, coriander, ginger and cayenne. Add asafoetida dissolved in a teaspoon of water. Mix and make walnut-size lumps and set them aside.

Dough: In a bowl, mix flour, oil and the rest of the salt, add water, a little at a time, to make a ball of dough. Knead dough and break it about 1" diameter lumps. Knead them individually into balls.

Roll each ball into an approximately 5" diameter disk on a piece of wax paper. Place the potato-spice stuffing on a dough disk, and press with fingers to spread the stuffing evenly. Place a second dough disk over the potatoes, align the edges of the two disks, press and seal the edges of the disks. Flatten the stuffed disks gently with a rolling pin.

In the meantime, heat 1/2 a teaspoon of *ghee* on a griddle, turn over the stuffed disk on the griddle and peel the wax paper off slowly. When one side begins to turn light brown, flip to the other side, add 1/2 teaspoon of ghee and brown both sides. Serve warm with *Pachadi*, *Chutney* and soup. Makes 6-8 *parata*.

4.21 *Wadapay* (Spread bread)

1 1/2 cups of whole-wheat flour
1/2 cup cream of wheat
2 Tbsp vegetable oil
1 tsp salt
1/2 tsp cayenne pepper powder
1 tsp ginger powder
1 onion, chopped
1/3 cup yogurt
1 Tbsp fresh coriander greens, chopped
1 1/2 cups of boiling water
4 Tbsp *ghee* (see Section 1.45)

In a bowl mix flour, cream of wheat, salt and oil with a fork. Continue mixing while adding pepper, ginger, onion, yogurt, coriander and water to make a soft dough. Pinch the dough into lemon-size lumps, and flatten the individual balls gently into about 6" diameter disks on pieces of wax paper with fingers. Heat griddle on medium heat and spread 1/2 a teaspoon of *ghee*. Gently turn over the disks, one at a time, on the hot skillet and peal the paper off as the bread cooks. Turn the bread over to the other side when one side turns brown. Add 1/4 teaspoon more *ghee* and brown both sides. Serve warm with *Chutney, Palya* or *Pachadi*. They refrigerate well. Makes 8-10 *Wadapays*.

4.22 *Puri* (Deep-fried bread)

1 1/2 cup whole-wheat flour
1/2 cup all purpose flour
3 tsp vegetable oil
1/4 tsp salt
1 cup water
Vegetable oil for deep-frying

Mix flour, salt and oil in a bowl with a fork. Adding water a little at a time, continue mixing and finally make a large ball of dough. Pinch off 1" diameter lumps. Knead them individually by hand into balls. Roll the balls to about 4" diameter disks either on wax paper or on a floured board. In the meanwhile, heat oil over medium heat in a deep bowl. Deep-fry one disk at a time by slowly sliding it into hot oil and immersing it gently by pressing with a ladle. At the right oil temperature, it rapidly puffs full of steam. The disks should be taken out without letting them become brittle. It is convenient for the beginners that one person rolls and an another concentrates on frying. With experience one should be able to make all the puries puff. Improper dough, imprecise rolling and insufficient heating of oil contribute to failure of puffing. Drain them on paper towels and serve warm with plain honey, or with *Palya, Chutney, Pachadi* or *Huli*. Makes 15-20 puries.

4.23 *Nippitu* (A fritter)

2 cups whole-wheat flour
1/2 cup split peas
3 Tbsp *ghee* (See Section 1.45)
1 tsp salt
1\4 tsp baking powder
1/2 tsp ginger powder
1/2 tsp cayenne pepper powder
1/8 tsp asafoetida (optional)
1 cup of water
vegetable oil for deep frying

Soak the split peas for an hour and drain. Mix the flour, split peas, salt, *ghee*, ginger, pepper, asafoetida and baking powder with a fork, in a bowl. Continue mixing while adding water a little at a time. Knead the dough well and divide it into 1" diameter balls. Roll them into 2" diameter disks on wax paper or a floured board. Alternatively, roll the entire dough into one large disk, about 1/8 inch thick, and cut out 2" diameter disks using a sharp rimmed cup or a cookie cutter. Heat oil in a deep bowel, 1/3 full, over medium heat. Deep-fry two or more of the disks at a time in oil until both sides are light brown. These will not puff but will remain crisp and crunchy. They are great for parties. They are also good as a side dish for soups and as snacks. They last for days without refrigeration. They may be frozen and reheated. Makes about 25 pieces.

4D FERMENTED DISHES

Fermenting batter before cooking is a very old technique of Udipi cuisine. Rice along with other cereals and lentils are soaked and ground into a paste and allowed to ferment. Fermented batter is mixed with ingredients such as yogurt, coconut, herbs, spices and vegetables before cooking by steaming or deep-frying. Under warm conditions (70-90°F) mixed fermentation ensues. The process enriches the food with cells of various beneficial microbes and their products such as vitamins, organic acids and esters, and also prevents spoilage. These benefits are especially appreciated in warm countries where food and water contamination is widespread and refrigeration is scarce. In India, fermented dishes of Udipi cuisine such as *Idli* a kind of rice cake, *Masala Dosay*, a stuffed pancake and *Uttapa*, a pancake sprinkled with vegetables are popular. Here are a few sample recipes.

4.30 *Masala Dosay* (Stuffed pancake)

Preparation of pancake batter

2 cups rice
1/3 cup udid dal (black gram)
1/2 tsp fenugreek seeds
2 tsp salt
1/8 tsp baking powder
4 cups water

Masala Preparation (Spicy stuffing)

4 boiled potatoes
3 medium onion, chopped
1/4 cup yellow split peas
4 Tbsp vegetable oil
1 tsp black mustard seeds
1 tsp fresh ginger root, grated
1 Tbsp coriander green, chopped
1 fresh cayenne pepper, chopped
1 tsp cayenne pepper powder
1/2 tsp cinnamon powder
1/2 tsp turmeric powder
1/2 tsp *Masala* (see Section 1.51)
1/4 tsp clove powder
1/2 fresh lemon
1 tsp raw sugar or honey
2 tsp salt
6 Tbsp *ghee* (See Section 1.45)

Soak rice, black gram and fenugreek separately overnight in water. Drain and grind rice into a smooth paste in a blender, at medium speed using 1 cup of water. Transfer it into a mixing bowl. In the same blender, grind the black gram and fenugreek also into a smooth paste adding the rest of the water a little at a time. Continue blending for about 5 minutes to whip some air into the batter. Transfer it into the bowl containing the rice paste. Add salt, mix and allow the batter to ferment for 12 to 24 hours in a warm place. The Udipi cuisine relies heavily on highly efficient wet grinder to prepare the batter. Simple but reliable motorized versions of wet grinders are now available.

Prepare *oggarnay* (see Section 1.46) for *Masala* with vegetable oil, mustard and split peas in a pan. Add the onion, ginger and fresh pepper and saute while adding coriander, cinnamon, turmeric and clove. Add salt, juice from the lemon and raw sugar. Mix, cover and cook for about 5 minutes. Crush potatoes into 1/2" pieces, add to the cooking mixture and continue cooking over low heat for 5 more minutes. Turn off the heat. Let it cool.

Add small amounts of water or rice flour to the batter, if necessary, to bring it to the right consistency. Add baking powder and mix.

Heat griddle over medium heat, spread 1/2 teaspoon full *ghee* on it and make a thin Dosay (pancake); spreading approximately 1/4 cup of batter into a disc 6" or larger in diameter. When one side turns brown, spread 1\2 tsp *ghee* and turn over the other side. Spread about 2 Tbsp of *Masala* on one hemisphere of the Dosay, fold the opposite half over the *Masala*, press with a spatula and remove the stuffed pancake into a serving tray. Serve warm with *Chutney, Pachadi* and *Huli*. Both batter and *Masala* refrigerate well. All batter need not be used up. Part of it can be used as a starter for the next preparation. Makes 12 -14 *Dosays*.

4.31 *Uttapa* (Vegetable pancake)

2 cups of batter made for Idli or Dosay 1 medium onion
1 medium tomato
1 medium green pepper
4 Tbsp *ghee* (see Section 1.45)

Chop onion, pepper and tomato into small pieces and keep them separately. Heat a griddle on medium heat, spread 1/2 teaspoon of *ghee*, pour about 1/4 cup of the batter (see Section 4.30) and spread it to about 5" diameter disk by using the bottom of the cup itself. While *Dosay* is cooking spread any one or combination of the chopped vegetables over the fresh batter. Cover with a lid and cook until the contact side is brown. Turn to the other side, spread more *ghee* and cook without the lid, until brown. It may be cooked to be soft or crisp. Serve warm with *Chutney* and *Huli* as dips. Makes 6-8 *Uttapas*.

4.32 *Southay Dosay* (Cucumber flapjack)

1 cup rice
1 medium size cucumber
1/2 cup shredded coconut
1/3 cup yogurt
4 Tbsp corn starch
1 tsp salt
1 tsp black pepper corns, crushed
1/2 cup water
4 Tbsp *ghee* (see Section 1.45)

Soak rice in water overnight and drain. Cut cucumber into small pieces. Add rice, water, coconut, pepper, salt and yogurt into a blender and grind them into a smooth while batter adding cucumber pieces a few at a time. Transfer batter to a bowl and set aside to ferment in a warm corner. Before making *dosay* add corn starch made into a slurry 1\2 cup water and mixing with a wire beater. Place skillet over medium heat, spread 1/2 teaspoon of *ghee* on it and make thick *dosays* as in Section 4.30 & 4.31 except that nearly 15% more batter is used for each pancake. Cover the pan and cook until one side is brown, then uncover, turn over the other side, brown both sides and serve warm. Serve with *Palya, Huli* or *Rasayana* as dips. Makes 8-10 pancakes.

4.33 *Idli* (A fermented rice cake)

2 cups parboiled rice
1 cup *udid* dal (black gram)
1/2 tsp fenugreek seeds
2 cups water
1 tsp salt
1/2 tsp baking powder
4 Tbsp *ghee* (see Section 1.45)

Soak fenugreek and *udid* overnight. Fry rice in a skillet, over medium heat, for about 5 minutes. Cool, and grind it dry using the slow speed of a blender, adding a little at a time to make grits. Set it aside. Then, grind black gram and fenugreek, adding water a little at a time. Continue grinding for about 5 minutes to whip in some air. Mix grits and batter. Let the batter ferment overnight in a warm place (70-90°F). Mix salt and baking powder with the fermented batter just before cooking *Idli*. Bring water to boil in a poacher, smear 1/4 teaspoon *ghee* into each cup and pour batter into cups 1/2 full. Cover and continue boiling the water over medium heat. After about 10 minutes of steaming, check whether the batter in the cups has set firm by stabbing with a toothpick. If the toothpick comes out clean, turn off the heat and let it cool slightly. Turn each cup over a plate and dislodge the *Idli* with a butter knife. Adding *ghee* or oil can be avoided altogether by overlaying the cups with pieces of wet cheese cloth or tender grape leaves. After steam cooking the *idli* will come of the cups easily.

Serve warm with *Chutney, Huli*, *Rasayana*, honey or other spicy or sweet sauces. *Idli* by itself tastes bland. Both batter and *Idli* refrigerate well. Makes 18-20 *Idlis*.

LEGUME DISHES

5.00 **Dietary Value of Legumes.** Legumes include edible pods and seeds of the Pea family, *Leguminosae*. Legumes are also called pulses or grams and they are referred to as lentils if the seeds are flat. Bengal gram *(chickpea)*, black gram (*udid*), green gram (*mung*) and red gram (*tur*) are some of the common legumes used in this cuisine. Split legumes are called *Dal* in *Hindi* or *Belay*, in Kannada language.

The family *Leguminosae* comprises of about 13,000 species which are important sources of food and fodder. They grow throughout the world. Use of legumes as a major protein source became unpopular in the U.S. when the agro-industries popularized them as "cattle feed" or as "poor man's 'meat'. In fact, meat does not supply as many different nutrients as legumes do. In addition to proteins, legumes supply complex carbohydrates and 4 to 5% dietary fiber. Another advantage of legumes is that the human digestive system can use only 80% of legumes compared to nearly 98% of meat, egg or cheese which directly reduces the available calories. Furthermore, most legumes are very low in fat. Mature peas and many beans have as little fat as 1.3%, several common kinds of beans (pinto, calico, red Mexican) 1.2%, lentils 1.1 %, and horse gram has 0.5%. Some exceptions are peanuts (40% oil) and Soybeans (20% oil), but these oils are rich in polyunsaturated fatty acids. Most legumes also have cholesterol lowering properties; the mechanism is not very clear. Therefore, for our sedentary population, beset with the problem of over-nourishment in fat and undernourishment in fiber, legumes are to be viewed as a better source of protein than meat, eggs or cheese.

In addition, legumes are also relatively inexpensive (in real costs, for the cost of one pound of meat one may be able to produce 5 to 8 pounds of legumes). Since antiquity, legumes have been a major source of dietary protein to the rich and the poor alike. The nutritional value of legumes needs more recognition by the sedentary populations of industrialized countries everywhere.

5.10 *Thoway* (*Dal*; A mild legume curry)

1 cup split mung beans
3 cups water
1/2 tsp turmeric powder
2 Tbsp *ghee* (See Section 1.45)
1 tsp black mustard seeds
1/2 tsp cumin seeds
1/8 tsp asafoetida
1 tsp fresh ginger root, grated
1 tsp fresh coriander greens, chopped
1 tsp fresh hot pepper, chopped
1/2 fresh lemon
1/2 tsp raw sugar or honey
1 tsp salt

Bring water to boil in a saucepan, add mung, turmeric 1/2 teaspoon of *ghee* and cook for about 30 minutes on low heat until mung is soft. Set it aside in a bowl. Prepare *oggarnay* (see Section 1.46) in the same pan using the rest of the *ghee*, mustard, cumin and asafoetida. Saute ginger, pepper and coriander in it. Add cooked mung, salt, lemon juice and honey. Bring the preparation to a boil. Serve warm and mix with rice or use as a dip for breads, *Dosay* or *Idli*. Makes 6-8 servings.

5.11*Saru* or *Rasam* (Spicy lentil soup)

1/2 cup tur dal (or yellow split peas)
4 cups water
1/2 tsp turmeric powder
2 Tbsp *ghee* (see Section 1.45)
1 tsp salt
1 tsp *Masala* (see Section 1.51)
1 tsp black mustard seeds
4 or 5 curry leaves (optional)
2 Tbsp tamarind (See Section 1.20)
1 tsp raw sugar or honey
1/2 tsp cayenne pepper powder
1/4 tsp asafoetida powder

Cook *dal* or split peas in a saucepan with 2 cups of water, turmeric and 1/2 a teaspoon of *ghee*. Mash the cooked peas. Add salt, tamarind, honey and cayenne and mix. Add the rest of the water, bring to boil over medium heat and then turn off the heat. In a separate small saucepan, prepare *oggarnay* (see Section 1.46) using the rest of the ghee, mustard, asafoetida and curry leaves. Garnish *Saru* with sizzling *oggarnay*. The addition of a Tbsp each of *Masala* and tamarind paste will make it into *Rasam*. Good for sipping or for eating with rice. Makes 6-8 servings.

5.12 *Khara Pongal* (Mung-rice & sauce)

1 cup rice
1 cup split mung beans
1/2 cup roasted cashew nuts, crushed
1 Tbsp black pepper corns, crushed
1 tsp black mustard seeds
1 tsp turmeric powder
1 tsp salt
1 tsp raw sugar or honey
6 Tbsp *ghee* (see Section 1.45)
5 cups water

Soak rice and mung beans in water for about 10 minutes, drain and set aside. Prepare *oggarnay* (see Section 1.46) with *ghee*, mustard and black pepper in a large pan. Add pepper after mustard pops completely and fry until a strong aroma appears. Add cashew pieces and brown them slightly. Add rice-mung mix and fry them until dull brown. Add water, mix and cook for about 15 minutes, over medium heat, until it starts boiling. Continue cooking until there is no liquid on the rice. Gently mix the contents to prevent burning at the bottom. Close the lid, and simmer for about 10 minutes and leave it warm for about 30 minutes before serving. Serve with *Hunasay Gojju* (tamarind) sauce). Makes 6-8 servings.

Hunasay Gojju (Tamarind sauce)

1/3 cup tamarind (see Section 1.20)
1 cup water
2 tsp salt
1 tsp chickpea flour
2 Tbsp raw sugar or honey
1/2 tsp cayenne pepper powder
2 Tbsp *ghee* (see Section 1.45)
1 tsp black mustard seeds
1/2 tsp asafoetida
1/2 tsp turmeric powder

Mix tamarind paste, water, salt, raw sugar, chickpea flour and cayenne pepper in a 1-2 quart saucepan. Bring it to a boil over medium heat, continue boiling for about 10 minutes and save it in a jar. In an another saucepan prepare *oggarnay* (see Section 1.46) with ghee, mustard, asafoetida and turmeric. Garnish the sauce with sizzling *oggarnay*, and cover the jar. It refrigerates very well. Makes 8-10 servings.

5.13 *Huralikai Huli* (Green beans curry)

1 cup *tur dal* or yellow split peas
3 tbsp *ghee* (see Section 1.45)
7 cups water
1 tsp turmeric powder
2 pounds tender green beans
2 large onions
2 large potatoes
1 tsp black mustard seeds
2 tsp salt
2 Tbsp *Masala* (see Section 1.51)
1 tsp cinnamon powder
1/4 tsp clove powder
1 Tbsp raw sugar or honey
2 Tbsp tamarind pulp

Bring 2 cups of water to a boil in a sauce pan, add 1/2 teaspoon *ghee*, turmeric, *dal* and cook with the lid ajar until individual lentils begin to soften and set aside. Cut green beans into 1-2" pieces, wash and drain. Cut potato and onion into 1" pieces separately. Prepare *oggarnay* (see Section 1.46) in a large saucepan using the rest of the *ghee* and mustard. Add the onion and saute. Then add the potato and continue stir-frying while adding green beans, salt, *Masala* powder, clove and cinnamon; mix and fry for about 5 minutes. Then add tamarind, cover and cook over medium heat until the potato is soft. Add the cooked split peas and the rest of water into it, mix and bring to boil uncovered. Turn off the heat, leave it covered for about 30 minutes before serving. Huli keeps well in the refrigerator. Serve warm with rice or as a sauce or dip for *dosay* and breads. Makes 8-10 servings.

5.14 *Waday* (Lentil patty)

1 cup dry chickpeas or yellow split peas
3/4 cup water
1/3 cup rice flour
1/3 cup chickpea flour
1/8 tsp asafoetida
1/2 tsp turmeric powder
2 tsp salt
1/2 tsp cayenne pepper powder
1 Tbsp fresh ginger, chopped
1 Tbsp fresh coriander leaves, chopped
1 tsp green chili pepper, chopped
Vegetable oil for deep-frying

Soakpeas in water overnight, drain and crush coarsely in a blender, adding a little water at a time (do not make into a paste). Transfer crushed peas into a mixing bowl. Add rice flour, chickpea flour, asafoetida, turmeric, hot pepper, ginger, salt and coriander and mix well. Make the batter into walnut-sized balls. In the meantime, heat oil over medium heat for deep-frying. Using wet fingers flatten each ball into a patty on a piece of waxed paper. Slowly slide the patties into hot oil one at a time. Using a slotted ladle, turn them slowly, one at a time, as one side turns brown. When both sides are brown, take them out and drain on paper towels. Serve with *Chutney* and *Huli* as dips. They may be prepared ahead of time, frozen and rewarmed. A good appetizer and a good snack for children. Makes 20-24 pieces.

5.15 *Payasa* (A legume porridge)

1 cup split chickpeas
2 Tbsp *ghee* (see Section 1.45)
4 cups water
1/2 cup raw or brown sugar
1 cup cream (half and half)
1/8 tsp cardamom, ground
1/4 tsp nutmeg powder
1/2 cup cashew nuts, chopped
1/2 cup raisins

Bring 2 cups of water to boil, in a 4 quart saucepan, over medium heat, add 1/4 teaspoon *ghee* and chickpeas and cook until soft. Turn down to low heat. Add sugar, the rest of the water, cream, cardamom and nutmeg. In the meantime, heat the rest of the *ghee* and fry the cashews in a skillet. As they start turning brown, add raisins and fry until they swell. Garnish *Payasa* with the nut and raisin mixture. Bring to simmering, turn off the heat, cover, and serve after about half an hour. Serve as dessert, as breakfast food or as snack. Payasa refrigerates well but the consistency will change. Makes 8-10 servings.

6. FRUIT DISHES

6.00 **Dietary Importance of Fruits:** In this cuisine, both fresh fruits and fruit dishes are served as breakfast dishes, as desserts and as snacks. Fruits are also valued as food to start and end fasting.

Immature, raw as well as ripe fruits are used for different preparations. Some spicy curries are made from raw or very ripe fruits. Unripe fruits such as orange, lemon, lime, mango, papaya, crabapple, goose berries and grapes are examples which provide primary ingredients for making several kinds of pickles and relishes. Many condiments (*Happala* and *Sandigay*) are made from unripe or ripe plantain, jackfruit, and other fruits. Varieties of fruits are salted, candied, fermented and dried for snacks, for flavoring and for enriching foods. Only a few fruits such as avocado contain large amounts of protein and/or fat and they are unsuitable. In general fruits are rich in complex carbohydrates, fiber, minerals and vitamins. Fruits and fruit dishes are offered to God during worship, and serving them to the worshipers is a common practice. Fruits are served, without concern for ill effect, to people of any age or physical condition. So much so, according to the *Sanathana Dharma*, the traditional way of life, persons past the age of sixty, should live mainly on fruit diets.

6.10 *Rasayana* (A spicy fruit dessert)

2 cups mango pulp
1 cup natural plain yogurt
1/2 cup sour cream
3 Tbsp honey
1/2 tsp cardamom powder
1/8 tsp nutmeg powder
2 peaches
2 ripe bananas
3 Tbsp sesame seeds

In a bowl mix mango pulp (select 3 ripe mangoes, peel, cut and scrape the pulp off the seed and mash), yogurt, cream, honey, cardamom and nutmeg with a wire beater. Immerse ripe peaches in boiling water for about 2 minutes, wash in cold water to help slip skin off easily. Remove pits and cut peaches into 1/2" pieces. Peel and cut bananas into 1/4" inch thick semi-circles and fold into the mixture. In place of mangoes and peaches chunks of any ripe fruits may be tried. Chill in the refrigerator. Before serving top with freshly roasted and crushed sesame seeds (see Section 1.44). Makes 8-10 servings.

6.11 *Panaka* (A fruit drink)

1 apple
1/4 lemon
2 Tbsp raw sugar or honey
2-3 filaments of saffron
1/8 tsp cardamom powder
1 quart of water

Core apple, discard core and cut apple (including the skin) into quarters. Discard the seeds from lemon and cut into pieces. Quince and other fruits may be substantiated for apple. Lemon may be reduced or omitted if the fruits are sour. In a covered saucepan, cook apple and lemon pieces in a cup of water over medium heat for about 5 minutes (2 minutes in microwave oven). Puree both apple and lemon pieces in a blender along with the honey, saffron and cardamom. Add the rest of the water, mix and transfer from the blender to a pitcher and refrigerate. Serve with ice. Makes 5-6 glasses.

6.12 *Sapatha* (A grits & fruit dessert)

2 medium apples
1 banana
1 cup pineapple
1 cup cream of wheat
2/3 cup *ghee* (see Section 1.45)
1/2 cup raisins
1/2 cup cashew nut pieces
1 cup raw sugar
2 cups water
1/2 tsp cardamom powder
6-8 filaments saffron

Discard core and seeds and chop apples into 1/4" pieces. Chop banana and pineapple into similar size pieces and set aside. Heat one tablespoon of *ghee* in a skillet over medium heat and fry the cream of wheat until it is a dull brown and set it aside. Using the same pan and heat an another teaspoon of *ghee* and fry the cashews until light brown. Add raisins and continue frying until the raisins swell up. Soak saffron in a spoonful of water. Add water, the remaining *ghee* and sugar to the pan and heat to boiling. Add fruits and cook for three minutes over low heat. Continue cooking and mixing with a fork while adding the cream of wheat, nuts, raisins and saffron. When the mass begins to solidify let it simmer for a few more minutes. Quickly, transfer the simmering mass into a pie plate coated with *ghee*. Shape the surface with a spatula while still hot. Decorate with nuts. Makes a birthday cake. It refrigerates well and it may be served rewarmed. Makes 8-10 servings.

7. ENSEMBLES

7.00 **What is an Ensemble ?** Ensembles consists of a variety of dishes created by using one primary vegetable, lentil or fruit, . This is accomplished by mixing or blending a variety of compatible food ingredients. The technique is ideal for making use of abundantly available seasonal produce without making meals monotonous. Ensembles embody the philosophy of conservation and creative frugality. It epitomizes culinary creativity. The technique utilizes every part of plants or plant products. This kind of preparation helps to add varied nutrients to our diet without burdening the body with overnutrition. As an example of this technique we are using one of the common winter squashes, the butternut squash, in the recipes below.

The squashes belong to the Gourd family

Cucurbitaceae, which has nearly 750 species known for their characteristic fruits that are eaten raw or variously cooked. They include varieties of cucumbers, gourds, marrows, melons, pumpkins and squashes. Nearly all parts of most of these plants are edible. The tender stem tips, flower buds and all parts of the fruits may be cooked into a variety of dishes. Butternut squash grows well in New England and needs very little care. A single vine may bear in 110 days of growth 10 or more fruits, each weighing about 5 lb. The ripe fruits keep for several months when stored indoors in dry cool part of a basement.

We have selected butternut squash to demonstrate how a variety of dishes, for an elaborate meal, can be prepared from a single vegetable. The seven dishes outlined below serve 8-10 people when accompanied with rice.

7.10 **Preparation** : Cut a ripe butternut squash into eight pieces with a butcher knife or hacksaw. Peel the skin and separate the seeds from the pulp and the fibrous material around them.

1. Save the seeds for making *Huri beeja;* there is no need to wash them.
2. Save the skin, pulp, fibrous center material and any excess seeds. If available tender stem tips and flower buds may be incorporated in making *Chutney* and *Menasinakai*
3. Slice one piece of the squash into 1/4" thick pieces of about 2 x 1" for making *Bujji*.
4. Grate one piece for making *Sasiway*.
5. Cut three pieces into 1/2" cubes for making *Kootu*.
6. Cut two pieces into 1/2" cubes for preparing *Menasinakai*
7. Slice eighth piece into 1/2 x 1/4"x 1/8" slices to make *Wadapay*. Set them all aside separately.

7.11 *Huri Beeja* (An appetizer)

1 tsp *ghee* (see Section 1.45)
1/4 tsp black pepper powder
1/4 tsp salt
1/2 cup squash seeds

Heat *ghee* (see Section 1.45) in a skillet, add pepper and fry until a strong aroma of pepper emanates. Then sprinkle seeds with salt and fry until they are light brown. Serve as an appetizer.

7.12 *Bujji* (An hors d'oeuvre)

squash (as in step #3 in Section 7.10)
1/2 cup chickpea flour
4 Tbsp rice flour
1/4 tsp salt
1 tsp *ghee* (see Section 1.45)
1/2 tsp cayenne pepper powder
1 Tbsp lemon juice
1 Tbsp fresh coriander leaves, chopped
1/8 tsp asafoetida
1 cup water
oil for deep-frying

Mix together chickpea flour, rice flour, salt, pepper, ghee, asafoetida and coriander with a fork. Add lemon juice and water and continue mixing with a wire beater until it resembles pancake batter. Heat oil to 400°F (see Section 1.41). Coat squash slices individually with batter by dipping, slowly slide them through the edge of the bowl, one at a time, into hot oil and deep-fry them to golden brown color. Drain on paper towels and serve warm with *Chutney* as a dip. Makes 20-24 pieces.

7.13 *Chutney*

3 cups peeling and rind
1/3 cup *udid* or split peas
4 Tbsp *ghee* (see Section 1.45)
2 Tbsp tamarind (see Section 1.20)
1 tsp salt
1 tsp raw sugar or honey
1/2 tsp cayenne pepper powder
1 tsp black mustard seeds
1/2 cup water

Heat 1/2 tsp ghee in a skillet and fry udid or split peas to golden brown and set aside. Cook squash peeling, rind, any remaining seeds with tamarind, salt, sugar, cayenne and water in a saucepan, over medium heat. Cool the mixture and crush it in a blender along with fried *udid* into a paste (do not add excess water). Transfer into a bowl. Prepare *oggarnay* (see Section 1.46) using the rest of the *ghee* and mustard. Garnish *Chutney* with sizzling *oggarnay*. *Chutney* may be used as a dip to *Bujji*, *Wadapay* or to mix with rice. It refrigerates well. Makes 8-10 servings.

7.5 *Sasiway* (A salad)

1 cup grated squash (#4 in Section 7.10)
4 tsp black mustard seeds
1/2 cup yogurt
1/4 cup sour cream
1 tsp salt
1 tsp honey
1/4 cup shredded coconut
1 Tbsp rice flour
1/2 tsp cayenne pepper powder
4 Tbsp *ghee* (see Section 1.45)

Blend 3 tsp mustard seeds, coconut, yogurt, sour cream, salt, honey and pepper into a smooth paste. Lower blender speed. Add grated squash little by little and blend. Transfer the mixture into a bowl. Prepare *oggarnay* (see Section 1.46) using *ghee* and remaining mustard seeds. Garnish *Sasiway* with sizzling *oggarnay*. Chill and serve cold. May be eaten as salad or with rice or as a dip for *Wadapay*. Makes 8-10 servings.

7.15 *Kootu* (A curry)

2 cups squash pieces (#5 in Section 7.10)
3 Tbsp *ghee* (see Section 1.45)
1 tsp black mustard seeds
1 tsp freshly crushed black pepper
1 tsp raw sugar or honey
1 tsp salt
1/2 tsp turmeric powder
1/2 cup shredded coconut
2 Tbsp rice flour
4 cups water

Prepare *oggarnay* (see Section 1.46) in a large using *ghee*, mustard and black pepper and saute squash pieces in it. Add sugar, salt, turmeric and 2 cups of water. In the meantime, put coconut, rice flour and 1/2 cup of water into a blender and grind them into a paste. Add this to the cooking mixture.

Use remaining water to rinse the blender and add it to the mixture. Bring the contents of the pan to boiling and turn off the heat. Prepare *Kootu* 30 minutes before serving. Serve warm as a mix for rice or as a dip for Wadapay.Makes 8-10 servings.

7.16 *Menasinakai* (A sweet/sour curry)

2 cups squash pieces (#6 in Section 7.10) 3 Tbsp ghee
(see Section 1.45)
1 tsp black mustard seeds
1/2 tsp turmeric powder
1/3 cup sesame, roasted and crushed
1/3 cup shredded coconut
1 Tbsp raw sugar or honey
1 tsp cayenne pepper powder
3 Tbsp tamarind paste
1 tsp salt
1 Tbsp rice flour
4 cups of water

Prepare *oggarnay* (see Section 1.46) using *ghee* and mustard. Saute squash pieces and add turmeric, sugar, salt and tamarind and 1/2 cup water. Cover and turn down heat to low. In the meantime, put sesame, coconut, rice flour and pepper into a blender and blend into a paste, using 2 cups of water a little at a time. Transfer blended mix to the saucepan. Use the remaining water to rinse the blender and add it to the curry and mix. Remove the lid and turn down heat to medium. Let it boil once. Replace lid and turn off the heat. Serve warm to mix with rice and with *Wadapay* as a dip. Prepare curry 30 minutes before serving. Serves 8-10.

7.17 *Wadapay* (A bread)

1 cup squash slices (#7 in Section 7.10)
1 1/2 cups rice flour
1 Tbsp vegetable oil
1/4 cup shredded coconut
1/2 tsp black pepper powder
1/2 tsp asafoetida powder
1 tsp salt
1 cup water
3 Tbsp *ghee*(see Section 1.45)

Mix flour, oil, coconut, pepper, asafoetida and salt in a mixing bowl using a fork. Continue mixing while adding water and squash pieces a little at a time. Break the soft dough into lumps of about 2" diameter. Heat griddle over medium heat with a teaspoon of *ghee*. Flatten a lump of dough on a piece of wax paper with wet fingers to about 6" diameter disk. Turn it over the hot griddle and peel off the paper. Cover with a lid and cook until the surface looks dry or the side facing the griddle is slightly brown. Turn and cook with an additional smear of *ghee*. Do not cover. Remove when both sides are brown and stack them on a plate. Serve warm. May be eaten as such or with curries and *Chutney* as dips. Makes 8-8 servings.

8 LOW CALORIE DISHES

8.00 **Meaningful ways to reduce calories**. Low calorie dishes should be designed to help reduce the body weight by reducing appetite through satiety. It includes, readapting the body economy to a metabolism that will provide the body of all essential nutrients and supply only the needed amount of calories. The only natural way to do this is by increasing consumption of adequate fiber- and water-rich vegetables and fruits. Unlike other methods of reducing body weight by semi-starvation which promote constipation and cause stress, reducing calories through increased consumption of fiber and water-rich vegetables stabilizes the metabolism, satiates the appetite, relieves constipation and provides adequate antioxidants and reduces stress.

People who gain weight easily and those who have already gained more weight than necessary need to incorporate even more fiber-rich food in their daily diet. This kind of diet fills the stomach, adjusts satiety, and reduces the craving for high calorie foods such as candies, rich deserts or even alcohol.

Almost all the recipes given here are rich in fiber and milk or yogurt. Among animal products, milk is the most valuable food and it contributes a minimum of calories, cholesterol and salt. Our approach to calorie reduction is to avoid all animal products other than fat-free milk and yogurt. In addition, the quantity of rice, breads, pasta and potatoes may be reduced to a great extent by increasing the proportion of fiber-rich, unprocessed vegetables and fruits in the diet. Drinking dilute beverages such as *Panaka* or *Neeralay* will reduce calories without the undesirable effects of soft drinks. An orange containing nearly 11.5% dietary fiber is a low calorie snack but pure orange juice containing virtually no fiber is not.

Giving priority to cooked leafy vegetables as salad (*Palya*) with whole grain cereals (rice & breads) with lentil soups, fat-free milk and yogurt before or dessert or fried snacks will help cut down appetite, provide adequate calories, bulk and with snacks of apples, oranges and some nuts all the three entities of the body, the mind, body and microflora will be nourished. A variety of leafy vegetables and lentils may be used to make ensembles along the lines of the butternut example. These will provide all the nourishment the human body needs. Additional examples of low calories items are given below.

8.10 *Ganji* (A rice extract soup)

1/4 cup rice
4 cups water
1/2 cup yogurt
1 tsp *ghee* (see Section 1.45)
1/8 tsp asafoetida
1/8 tsp turmeric
1 tsp black mustard seeds
1 medium carrot, grated
1 sweet pepper, chopped
1 tsp salt

Cook rice using 5 cups of water until individual grains are mushy (30 min in the pressure cooker). Mash and strain through a colander. Mix yogurt with the strained rice extract using a wire beater. Prepare *oggarnay* (see Section 1.46) using *ghee*, mustard, asafoetida and turmeric. Saute carrot and pepper in it, add the yogurt with rice extract mixture and salt, bring to boil and turn off the heat. May be served hot or cold. Makes about 6 servings.

Nutrient Composition of Soups

Soup	Cal	Prot	Fat	Ca	Na	K
Ganji	32	1.2	1.4	33	946	108
Bean	350	17.0	12.0	133	2,138	837
Onion	132	10.8	3.10	56	2,144	211
V.V.	180	4.5	4.8	40	1,710	350
Tomato	180	4.0	3.8	28	1,880	470

Per Cup = 225 ml, Cal = Calories, Prot. = protein in grams, F = Fat in grams, Ca = calcium in milligrams, Na = sodium in milligrams, Mg = magnesium in milligrams, K = potassium in milligrams. V.V = vegetarian vegetable,

8.11 *Neeralay* (A cold drink)

1/2 cup low fat yogurt
1/2 tsp salt
1 tsp fresh ginger, chopped
1 tsp coriander greens, chopped
1/8 tsp asafoetida
1/8 tsp fresh chili pepper
1/2 lemon juice
1/4 tsp honey
5 cups of water

In a blender, mix, salt, ginger, coriander, asafoetida, chili pepper, lemon juice and honey with yogurt. Add water, blend the mixture and refrigerate.

Serve with ice. Very thrust quenching. It refrigerates well. Makes 5-6 servings. Five calories/glass.

8.12 *Kosambari* (Cucumber/lentil salad)

1/4 cup split mung beans
1 medium cucumber
1 tsp grated ginger
1 tsp coriander green, chopped
1/2 tsp salt
2 Tbsp fresh lemon juice
1/2 tsp honey
1/2 tsp fresh chili pepper, chopped
1 tsp *ghee* (see Section 1.45)
1/2 tsp black mustard seeds
1/8 tsp asafoetida

Rinse and drain split mung beans. Add finely chopped cucumber, ginger, coriander, salt, lemon juice, honey and pepper. Mix thoroughly, cover and leave for about an hour (Salt extracts water from the cucumber and lentil absorbs it and becomes soft). Prepare *oggarnay* (see Section 1.46) with *ghee* mustard and asafoetida. Garnish *Kosambari* with sizzling *oggarnay*. Chewy and nourishing. Chill and serve. Approximately 15 calories/ tablespoon. Makes 8-10 servings.

8.20 **Specific suggestions to lower calories**: *Ghee* may be reduced in quantity or replaced by sesame, safflower or other vegetable oil. Most of the ingredients used here are very low in lipid content and, therefore, we do not have to be too stingy in the use of *ghee*! Items such as *Huli* (Section 5.13) or *Palya* (Section 3.11) may be made of leafy vegetables such as spinach, dill, cabbage or amaranth deleting potatoes. *Mung-rice* (Section 5.12) and *Wadapay* (Section 4.21) are better than plain rice or deep fried breads such as *Puri*. *Wadapay* may contain leafy vegetables of about 10% of the weight of flour. Vegetables used in this cuisine can be more mature than those used in general American dishes. Older vegetables such as squashes or carrots, have more fiber than the very tender ones. We suggest selecting *dal*, fruits or other vegetables that include skin. As long as the vegetables and fruits are thoroughly cleaned and they are free of pesticides we should try to retain edible portions of skin on them. Popcorn and roasted nuts (without butter or sugar coating) and fresh fruits should replace all kinds of commercial items that are loaded with salt, sugar, cheese and chemical additives.

8.30 Our daily diet.

The following is a brief account of our daily diet, when we are home, for the past 15 years.

Breakfast: 1/2 a grapefruit, 2 tbsp whole grain cereal (a homemade granola) with 1/2 cup whole milk and 1/2 a banana.

Lunch:1 medium size carrot pealed, cut and soaked in cold water, a stick of celery, a medium size apple or pear and a glass of fat-free milk or a cup of yogurt. A glass of vegetable juice for snack.

Supper: One serving each of *soup*, *Palya*, rice and 1/2 a *rotti* and a curry. One serving of dessert made of different fruits such as orange, melon and banana combined into a fruit salad or *Rasayana*. A cup of yogurt with half a teaspoon of honey, raw sugar or molasses. A cup of tea or herb tea with 1/3 lemon.

Late night snack: A glass of hot milk with a teaspoon of honey or raw sugar (*gud* and a fruit if desired.

Occasional snacks: A serving of roasted peanuts, roasted chickpeas, pop-corn, and on very rare occasions ice cream and a slice of pie.

Supplements: One 90 mg tablet of vitamin B complex with vitamin C and one 500 mg of vitamin C daily.

Variations : We vary the kind and varieties of cereals, breads, fruits and vegetables every day. We exchange rice for pasta, local breads etc. They are amenable to replacement or modification to take care of special individual needs of calories, nutrients or supplements or likes and dislikes.

We have never taken laxatives, antacids or sleeping pills. We also do not smoke or drink alcoholic drinks or any kind of soft drinks and limit drinking coffee or tea, with cream, to three cups per day. The result of this kind of diet has been briefly discussed in the foreword of this book.

We walk to work, up a steep hill, at least one way (1.5 miles) and do 20 minutes exercise indoors.

The diet described above will provide a daily supply of apaproximately 2,000 Calories, 60 g protein, 50 g lipids (23% of total calories, mostly oils), 40 g fiber and about than 2 g of salt but more than 4 g of potassium and 2 g of calcium. The Recommended Daily Allowance (1989) for a 70 Kg male past the age of 51, is 56 g protein (44 g for females) and 800 mg Calcium. Lipids (mostly vegetable oils) 30% of the calories.

We feel that there is no need to calculate the adequacy of other minerals and vitamins as long as we consume a variety of fresh protective food ingredients. After each of the meals we feel full. As a result we do not crave for commercial "delicacies" such as doughnuts, cakes, pastries and snack foods. Because of the high roughage content of our food we eat full dinners and do not have any desire to eat dessert. As a result our body weight has remained constant for the past several years.

Appendix: 3

Answers to Some of Your Questions

1. Is it true that we do not need all the parts of our digestive system?

The loss of some part of any system in the body burdens other parts and impinges on the maintenance of homeostasis. In the 1950's tonsils were considered dispensable, but today we know that they are of much greater value than previously thought. Similarly, at one time, very few physiologists and nutritionists thought that our colon or it's microbes play any role in nutrition and health. However, today few will dispute the major contributions that our colon and it's microbes make towards the maintenance of optimal health. We must understand our body before we disturb its ecological equilibrium. Each tree is important to the forest, and yet the loss of a few trees does not necessarily imperil the forest ecology. Similarly, each cell of the body contributes its share toward maintaining the homeostasis of the whole body. However, the body has evolved to survive without many of it's cells and parts. Often the choice is ours to make.

2. Should a woman's diet differ from a man's?

As Dr. Roger Williams pointed out, all of us are born with biochemical individuality in nutrition. While all individuals have the same needs for the basic nutrients, the specific proportions of each nutrient may differ between each individual. Specific differences in diet exist not only between men and women, but also between the young and old or between sedentary and active individuals. For example, energy and calcium are essential for all humans; although a woman's body can manage with less energy, they also require more calcium than men. Another important feature of a woman's diet is that her diet can have a tremendous effect on the next generation. Fertility , behavior and even aspects of sexual characteristics, and aging are all influenced by nutrition. Blood levels of hormones, the chemicals that play such a great role in many of these features, are greatly influenced by nutrition.

3. How do we know whether or not our body homeostasis is balanced?

Animals in nature are much more aware of homeostatic imbalances. People in more traditional cultures appear to have managed reasonably well too. It should therefore not be especially difficult for us to become more aware ourselves. Just as we are taught to recognize many automotive problems by sound and feel or handling, similarly the instability of the body homeostasis can also be recognized by many indicators such a change in sleep patterns , appetite, digestion, elimination, pain, stability of body weight, performance and fatigue. What is lacking in our present society is an awareness of these facts at a young age. We need to teach the 'health education of prevention' to our children. A greater awareness of preventative health management at an early age could prevent many problems before they become serious medical conditions. For example, the prevention of constipation requires only an awareness of the importance and sources of fiber; but the treatment of diverticular disease or colon cancer is much more painful and expensive.

4. Why do I gain weight in spite of dieting?

It is fundamentally incorrect to approach the nutrition of our complex human bodies in terms of calories alone. The body metabolism doesn't consume fuel like a fire indiscriminately burning anything it is given. Much to the contrary, the body homeostasis operates by prioritizing and delicately balancing the multiple internal and external influences with the resources that are available. In other words, dieting should not imbalance the body homeostasis.

Hunger and satiety can be regulated by increasing the bulk of the diet and reducing the density of nutrients while maintaining the variety. Such modifications will aid in resetting the biological clocks that drive hunger and satiety. While there will be more subtle individual variations, generally increasing foods such as fresh fruits and vegetables, and milk or yogurt while minimizing pasta, nuts, cheese and lentils can serve to stabilize body weight. This is done in a manner that utilizes the 'currencies' that allow the physiological economy to continue to function smoothly.

5. How much complex carbohydrate should we eat?

Regardless of one's concern for weight loss, gustatory preference or ethnic background, a balanced diet should revolve around a varied intake of plant materials as a source of complex carbohydrates. This source of nutrition provides the variety of nutrients the body needs to function smoothly. Milk is the only animal food that can also provide a similar variety of nutrients without saturation of any one nutrient in quantity. Breast milk, which supplies more than 100 different nutrients to an infant, provides a greater diversity of nutrients than any other single source. Although the milk of different animals (such as human's versus cow's) provide differing proportions of each nutrient, they still provide a similar diversity. Although a cow's milk is not suitable for a human infant's immature G.I. tract, it is an excellent supplementary food for older children or adults. Therefore, a cornerstone of good nutrition is to maintains a varied plant diet supplemented with milk or yogurt. Additional food consumption in the form of nutrient-rich food versus bulk and fiber-containing food can be based on your individual need for weight reduction or more energy.

6. I do not consume many calories, but still I gain back the weight that I initially lost. Why?

A person's diet must be appropriate to their physiologic economy at all times if a stable weight and health are to be maintained. Unfortunately, many people alternate between draconian diets and meals that are excessively rich in nutrients. Their diet is so stringent and limited that they cannot continue it and stay healthy and satiated for long periods of time. As discussed above, a diet that is based on flavorful preparations of plant materials supplemented with milk or yogurt will provide all the basic nutrients (such as proteins, fats and trace minerals and vitamins) that one requires to stay healthy regardless of weight concerns. By varying the amounts of complex carbohydrates versus fiber-rich food sources one can help your own body to regulate it's weight gain or loss while maintaining a single healthy diet. In this way you can avoid the starvation and splurge cycle that frustrates so many people.

7. Why did my grandmother have the confidence to raise her nine children with minimal access to food and education, while I struggle to raise three children with an abundance of both?

Your grand mother had the support of cultural wisdom and the help of many extended family members (some might refer to this as 'family values'). Getting a prudent diet, education and security in early childhood should be a birthright of all children. This would contribute to both the health and longevity of individuals to say nothing of it's benefits to society. To paraphrase Professor René Dubos, measuring growth by the pound may be acceptable for animal husbandry, but raising a well-adjusted, whole human being is a considerably more complex challenge.

8. If I become a vegetarian, how can I get enough protein?

As is discussed in greater detail in the text of this book, the popular nutrition perspective has overemphasized the importance of protein in our diet. Protein is an essential nutrient. However either a deficiency or an excess of protein will cause disease. if you follow a general diet that maintains a variety of plant products with adequate bulk (as described in the previous questions and the text of the book) you will get all necessary nutrients, including protein, while not imbalancing the homeostatic mechanisms of the body.

9. If you, Drs. Lingappa, are such staunch vegetarians, why did you not raise your children that way?

In the 1950s surviving as a vegetarian was not easy for anyone because people believed that meat was absolutely necessary for good health. Additionally, at the time we neither had the nutritional understanding to guide us nor the confidence to stand up for what we believed in our heart to be correct. Life and death are far more complex than many of our parents taught us. While it is true that millions of microbes that we harbor get killed every day, and we kill many pests and plants for our survival. Nonetheless, we cannot escape from our responsibility to protect this planet. We felt that our children had to be aware of these complexities and responsibilities. It was then for them to choose. We are very pleased with the choices that they have made. Our aim is to emphasize milk and yogurt in place of meat in the diet.

The kind of vegetarian one wants to be is a matter of personal choice. However, educating our children to be concerned about our environment (both internal and external) is the responsibility of all.

10. As a vegetarian how can I balance my diet?

It is essential for everyone, vegetarians and non-vegetarians alike, to have a balanced diet. Non-vegetarians who do not consume plant products in variety and bulk are damaging their health as much as vegetarians who rely upon an isolated food (e.g. such as cottage cheese) rather than a diet notable for variety. Vegetarians as well as non-vegetarians can become less anxious about their nutrition if they can incorporate low-fat milk or yogurt and a variety of plant products into their diet.

11. Is milk or yogurt an absolute necessity in the diet of a vegetarian? Do adults need it?

All animals, including humans, can survive and even maintain good health without any particular food, including milk or yogurt. However, incorporating milk or yogurt into your diet makes achieving a balanced diet much easier than would be the case otherwise. This is because no other single food can provide as many required nutrients – in the low concentrations that is optimal for body homeostasis – as does milk or yogurt. No other food optimally integrates the needs of the brain, body and intestinal microflora as well as milk or yogurt. Milk is, in many ways, an evolutionary food and drinking 2-4 glasses daily can improve health at all ages.

At any age milk is not a harmful food unless one has a valid medical reason - and this does not include a dislike for the taste. Taste for any food is cultivated either by adapting to it from childhood or being motivated by necessity.

12. Can I substitute cottage cheese for milk?

Lots of foods including cheese, cottage cheese, eggs, meat, whole grains and beans may provide a particular nutrient (such as protein, vitamin or a mineral) in larger quantities than milk. However, none can provide all the materials that milk provides and in a manner that brings health and stability to the brain, body and intestinal microflora. Cottage cheese for example, may contain as much or even more calcium than an equivalent amount of milk, but it's bioavailability (the amount that actually is able to be taken into the body) is considerably less than milk. Therefore, many foods may partially compensate for a lack of milk in the diet, but only yogurt can serve as a true substitute for milk.

13. Is carbohydrate good for health?

Many foods qualify as 'carbohydrate including sucrose (white sugar), fructose (fruit sugar), purified starches and synthetic sugars. However, if we consider their effects on health and longevity, natural foods with a minimum of processing are best for maintaining health. The presence of dietary fiber, trace minerals and anti-oxidants in unprocessed natural foods means that consumption of these foods provides more than carbohydrate. Moreover, features such as the presence of fiber influence the physiologic response to different carbohydrates (such as the rate of rise in blood sugar). Thus, while grapes and oranges are both sources of carbohydrates, their nutritional value and physiologic effect are far superior to equivalent amounts of pure glucose, sucrose or fructose.

14. Is it not better to provide some egg and sea-foods in the diet of young children?

Other than for taste, seafood and eggs are not required to maintain health at any age and eating them in excess can be harmful. What a family or an individual prefers to eat is dictated by cultural traditions, personal philosophy, the environment and available resources. However, generally the acquisition of a taste for a certain food is either adapted from childhood or cultivated by personal motivation. Children who learn to eat fresh fruit early on rarely develop an excessive taste for candies and pastries. Conversely, once a taste for junk foods has been developed it is not easy to switch to fresh fruit. Therefore childhood is the best time to cultivate taste.

15. I don't eat meat. How can I provide iron in my diet?

Unless mineral homeostasis exists in the body, providing any amount of iron or other trace mineral may not help the body. For example, in the face of a chronic infection or disease an individual may develop an anemia that will be resistant to resolution with extra iron until the chronic disease is cured. When mineral homeostasis exists in the body, a good mixed diet should provide all trace minerals, including iron. The body's efficient recycling mechanism recovers most trace minerals. What little is lost can be provided by a wholesome complex carbohydrate rich diet. Most fruits, including dried fruits such as raisins, and nuts contain trace minerals. Unless some unusual genetic or physiological problem exists, a wholesome diet emphasizing variety in unprocessed plant products and supplemented with milk or yogurt, should easily meet the body's needs.

16. Is it true that one can develop iron deficiency anemia if you don't eat meat or seafood?

It is common misperception that consuming meat is the only way of avoiding iron deficiency. The small quantity of iron present in milk and plant products satisfies the body's needs better than the large quantity of it present in meat. This is because the former source goes a long way towards maintaining the homeostasis of the body, while the latter, by disturbing the intestinal microflora, and via other mechanisms, can impair homeostasis.

17. Is a meat diet required during nursing to provide adequate nutrition to my baby?

No. As long as you drink plenty of milk and eat many varieties of fruits, vegetables and whole grains, you do not need to eat meat either during pregnancy nor during lactation.

18. When I eat a lot of salad, I develop gas. How can I increase my vegetable consumption without this unpleasant side effect?

Many 'gas' problems arise from a change in the gut microbial population. This in turn may arise from eating too much uncooked salad vegetables and not consuming enough starch in the diet. Cooked or partially cooked vegetables (see Palyas and Pachadis in the recipe section) will let you consume more vegetables in a non-monotonous way while avoiding the development of gas. Consuming more yogurt may also help with gas.

19. How much bran and cereals should one consume to get enough fiber?

Culturally fiber used to be a major entity of the diet. It was obtained from whole grains in bread, pasta and rice, legumes, beans, vegetables and fruits. If your diet contains all these foods you don't need to eat bran specifically. Bran refers only to cereal fiber. Ideally, our diet should include fiber from a variety of sources to take advantage of the variety of micronutrients (such as different vitamins, minerals and antioxidants) present in different fiber-containing foods.

20. Is it true that vitamin B12 deficiency will develop if you do not eat meat.

No. The primary source of vitamin B12 for all animals including human beings is a normal gut microbial flora. Moreover, if the microflora is not normal, consumption of additional vitamin B12 may simply contribute to the establishment of unnatural microbes rather than to meeting the body's needs.

21. Is it true that by increasing the lean meat in our diets we can avoid fat?

This is not really true because even the leanest meat has more fat than a vegetable-based diet. Thus, if you really want to cut your fat consumption, it would be better to increase your consumption of fiber-rich plant products and decrease your consumption of meat. Moreover, unlike the fat in meat, that of plants serves some essential roles while not contributing to the increased risk of atherosclerosis arising from a diet high in animal fats.

22. I am past 50 years old. Can I quit eating meat?

Meat is not necessary at any age. Moreover, as we grow older it becomes progressively more important that we decrease the nutrient density of our diets (e.g. eat more fiber-rich plant products and less rich foods such as meat) if we are to avoid problems such as obesity and degenerative disease.

23. Can I avoid all the fats from my diet?

Among the 50-52 nutrients that our body needs to maintain health are various kinds of fats —including cholesterol. How much of each of these is needed varies with age, environment and activity, in ways that are not easy to separate and distinguish. The easiest way to avoid providing an excess of fat to the body (which increases your risk of cardiovascular and metabolic disease) is to increase the variety and bulk of plant products consumed while decreasing nutrient density by avoiding meat. This way, body homeostasis is able to operate to conserve or eliminate nutrients, depending on physiologic needs. These dietary changes also makes it easier to maintain a steady weight without much dietary fluctuation.

24. Do we have to consume fresh vegetables to be healthy?

No. The majority of necessary nutrients such as vitamins minerals and fiber, are not affected by the degree of freshness of vegetables. Moreover, eating too much of raw vegetables may cause problems of digestion and encourage non-beneficial microbes in the colon. The main nutrient not well preserved in canned vegetables is vitamin C. However, no one can dispute the palatability of fresh vegetables, which therefore encourages a plant product-based diet.

26. What kind of synthetic vitamins should we take?

If not for our sedentary life, the consumption of many varieties of foods such as whole grains, nuts, vegetables and fruit would provide all the needed vitamins. However, in modern times, the advance of middle age brings more need for vitamins, especially water soluble vitamins such as vitamin B complex and vitamin C. Consumption of 250 milligrams of vitamin B complex and 250-500 milligrams of vitamin C may be able to compensate for changing nutritional needs. Since these are water soluble vitamins, they pose no risk of overmedication at reasonable levels of intake.

27. Are spices dangerous to health?

In moderation, very few nutrients are harmful while in excess, even healthy foods such as milk may cause adverse effects. Spices perform multiple functions such as enhancing taste without adding calories, stimulating the gastrointestinal mucosa and providing various antioxidants in minute amounts.

28. Is black coffee good for health?

Like meat, alcohol or spices, small quantities of coffee (e.g. one or two cups a day) are likely to be harmless. The addition of milk or cream to coffee not only provides a means of enhancing one's consumption of this valuable nutrient, but also may mitigate any harmful effects from coffee by colloids in elimination of toxic components. Milk is a colloidal suspension of protein and it can be an agent to complex the undesirable tannins and related substances.

29. Does starchy foods such as potato and rice make one gain weight?

No more than do other nutrients such as meat, eggs, nuts or beans. Any source of carbohydrates, protein or lipids in excess of the energy needs of the body will result in weight gain. However, as important than the absolute amount of food calories is the metabolic effects of the source of those calories (e.g. carbohydrates vs protein vs lipids) as discussed in the text. To prevent weight gain then, one need simply titrate down the amounts of starchy foods and increase the amount of fiber-rich plant products that provide satiety through bulk thereby sparing consumption of calories.

30. What is the best way to cut down one's weight?

Except in rare cases, all individuals should plan on gradually reducing their food calorie consumption beyond the age of 20, in anticipation of a progressively more sedentary lifestyle in their 30s and beyond. The reason for starting so early is that dietary preferences are easiest to change when carried out gradually. Beyond the age 35 when one really needs to decrease caloric intake, it is more difficult than it would be if one has developed taste for a high roughage diet over the years. The dietary change we recommend beyond 30s is to replace whole milk with low fat or defatted milk or yogurt and increasing the amount of bulk containing whole grains, vegetable and fruits in the diet while decreasing all other nutrient dense foods.

31. Why do you recommend yogurt (and yogurt rice) for travellers?

Most of the sickness that commonly occurs during travelling is caused by the invasion of the gastrointestinal tract by microbes with which our body is not familiar. This results in symptoms ranging from upset stomach and nausea to vomiting and diarrhea. Yogurt with any kind of starchy food not only replaces the foreign bacteria with beneficial normal flora, but also lowers the pH of the gut which supports their establishment and is inhospitable to transient and pathogenic microbes.

32. Does increased plant products in the diet cause excessively loose bowel movements?

No. While the lack of plant products can cause hard stools, a diet plentiful in plant products does not cause excessively loose stools or diarrhea. Many people in Western societies are so accustomed to constipation and hard feces, that they mistake what are normal stools to be excessively loose. The normal bowel movement is relatively loose and soft and should move effortlessly. The epidemic of hemorrhoid and diverticular disease in Western societies reflects our low fiber diets and the consequence of decades of excessively hard stools.

33. Why do you recommend supplementation of the diet with vitamins B complex and C?

We are impressed by the arguments for "biochemical individuality" pioneered by Roger Williams and other eminent nutrition scientists. Since these are water soluble vitamins, a moderate excess of intake is harmlessly excreted, while deficiency may cause disturbance of homeostasis in ways that contribute to ill health. Moreover, modern living is associated with increased stress, necessitating increased consumption of antioxidants (such as vitamin C), perhaps even more than is practically achieved by eating fruit and vegetables. We do not recommend fat soluble vitamin supplements because they have a greater risk of toxic effects in excess, since they are more difficult to eliminate from the body.

34. If taking fat soluble vitamin supplements is not recommended, how can I be sure that I do not have a deficiency of these vitamins?

We believe that consumption of a wholesome diet that supports a fermentative microbial flora is sufficient to ensure that adequate amounts of vitamin K produced by endogenous microbes will be available to the body. One carrot and related vegetables consumed daily will provide the needed vitamin A. Vitamin A should be derived from a varied plant product-based diet. Finally consuming 2-3 glasses of milk or the equivalent in yogurt will provide adequate vitamin D.

35. Can I get used to a vegetarian diet even after decades of acclamation to a meat-staple diet?

More than two-thirds of the world's population lives on such a diet. While many of these people are malnourished, their deficiency results from restricted availability of amount and variety of plant products and are not at all due to their vegetarian diet. The recipes provided in this book were tested by us in North America on a broad group of people and diverse American clientele in Annapurna Restaurant for over 17 years. Many of our customers made the transition from meat-based diets to predominantly lacto-vegetarian diets. The key lies in the use of herbs and spices to make vegetable dishes enticing and in gradually developing taste for milk or yogurt. Please try the recipes. Like so many of our customers at Annapurna over the years, I believe you will find that you no longer miss meat and experience satiety.

One thousand five hundred years ago our ancestors recognized no duties outside the circle of kinsfolk. Today we recognize duties to all mankind, although our thought is so bound up with the idea of duties to our kin that we have to disguise that fact by using metaphors such as the brotherhood of man. We are also beginning to recognize duties to the higher animals, although so far we can only say that we have the negative duty of not causing them unnecessary suffering. Have we any duties to plants and inanimate nature beyond preserving them for the delight, instruction, and use of our own species? I do not know the answer to that question, but I expect it is yes. It is a poor man who does not love his country, which is not the same thing as loving his countrymen. That is something in addition. If we love it, then I think we have a duty to it. Only posterity is going to be able to decide this question of whether we have a duty to nature, but on the general principle that every step in man's technical achievement broadens the sphere of his duties, I expect that posterity will decide it in the affirmative.

—J.B.S. Haldane, *What Is Life?*, 1947

Glossary*

Acidogenic bacteria Those that produce acids

Aerobe Organism that require oxygen to live

Ahimsa Nonviolence; not causing pain or suffering (S)

Alu (H) Potato

Amaranth Amaranthus tricolor var. an annual

Anaerobe Organism that can live without oxygen

Anna Any food (S); cooked rice (K)

Antioxidants Compounds that prevent oxidation

Asafoetida A plant resin of strong odor used as spice

Badanay (K) Eggplant

Bajji (K) A spicy cooked vegetable salad

Banana leaves 10-14" x 18-20" piecs on which food is served traditionally in Karnatka and nearby states

Belay (K) Split legumes, peas, beans, lentils

Belluli (K) Garlic

Bioamine Biologically acitve ompounds containing aminogroups

Black mustard A variety preferred for oggarnay

Butti Anna A combination of yogurt, soft vegetables and rice

* 1 (H) Hindi, (K) Kannada, (S) Sanscrit; Weights and measures given here are drawn from U.S.Department of Agriculture, Handbook No.456, 1975.

°C Degrees Celsius; a scale in which water frezes at 0 and boils at 100°. In that scale our body temperature is about 37°C

Calorie A unit of heat required to raise the 1 gram of water from 15 to 16°C abreviated as c; in nutrition and metabolism it is x1000 or kilocalorie (kcal) or C. 1000 calories = 1 kcal or 1 Calorie. Calorie content of carbohydrates and proteins are 4 kcal/gram; of fats and oils are 9 kcal/gram. Alcohol gives 7 kcal/gram.

Candida albicans A yeast that may be a normal inhabitant of the human body but under debilitated states, it may be come pathogenic.

Carcinoma A malignant growth, a kind of cancer.

Chapathi Unleavened bread made of whole wheat flower.

Chutney a spicy relish made of fruits, vegetables and legumes.

Cup (one), measuring. 236.6 g; 16 tablespoons or 48 teaspoons

Curries special combinations of spices in Indian cooking

Dal (H) see Belay; also Thovay

Dietary fiber Plant cell walls and fibers and associated items

Ensemble Refers to an entire meal of several dishes prepared with a primary plant ingredient but blended and supplemented with other ingredients such as lentils, herbs, spices and fruits and nuts

Facultative anaerobe An organism that can function as well under absence of oxygen as in presence of it.

°F Fahrenheit scale. To convert to Celsius scale: °F-32 x 5/9; to convert °C to F: 9/5 x °C + 32.F

Fenugreek Seeds (or tender plants) of Trigonella used as spice

Fermentation, mixed More than one kind of acid, alcohol or related products are produced such as in the Idli or Dosay batter.

Fermentative flora Organisms thriving and producing acids, alcohols and related compounds by breaking down carbohydrates.

Fermented milk Yogurt or similar products that result from the activities of Lactobacilli, Streptococci and like organisms.

Food Equivalents (approximate portion) 3 Bananas = 1 lb; Beans (dried), 2 cups = 1 lb; Butter 2 cups = 1 lb; Whole wheat flour 4.5 cups = 1 lb; 4 Lemons = 1 lb; 1 lemon = 8 Tbsp juice; Peanuts 13/4 cup = 1 lb; Raisins 3 cups = 1 lb; Rice 2 cups = 1 lb; Sugar 2 cups = 1 lb; Raw sugar 2.5 cups = 1 lb; Gallon (one), 3,785.6 milliliters (ml) or 3.79 liters (l) 4 quarts or 8 pints = 1 gallon (gal)

Ganji Soup made from rice (or other) grain extracts.

Ghee The liquid remaining after butter is slowly heated to evaporate water and after the nonfat solids settle as light brown precipitate.

Gud Unpurified, dark brown, raw sugar made by evaporating crude extract of sugarcane. A cottage industry in India.

Gut microflora Normal inhabitants of our lower intestines; highly specialized microbes which have symbiotic relation with our bodies.

Inch (one), 2.54 centimeters, (cm); 25.4 millimeters, (mm)

Kesari Saffron. Also a cereal dessert that contains saffron.

Kg 1,000 grams; 1,000 ml of water; 2.2 pounds (lb)

Kilocalorie (one), 4.184 kilo Joules; 1 calorie = 4.184 Joules

Kitchen Measures 3 teaspoons = 1 tablespoon; 4 tablespoons = 1/4 cup; 16 tablespoons = 1 cup; 2 cups = 1 pint; 4 cups = 1 quart; 2 pints = 1 quart; 4 quarts = 1 gallon; 16 ounces = 1 pound.

Lassi (H) Sweet or salty drink of yogurt

Lentils legumes, beans, gram and pulses are edible seeds of the Pea family or leguminous plants.

Masala Any special mixture of spices that are used in making curries. There are different masala for different dishes.

Oggarnay A specialty of Udipi cuisine. Spicy dishes are garnished at the end of their preparation by a sizzling hot oil and spices. It gives and added zest to the preparation.

Ounce (one), fluid. 29.6 g or 29.6 milliliters (ml)

Oven Temperatures in degrees Fahrenheit (approximate): Low 250 to 350; Medium 350 to 450; High 450 to 550.

Palya Curried single or mixed vegetables

Panaka A cold drink made of blended fruits, spices and raw sugar.

Payasa A porridge of cereals or lentils made with milk, raisins, nuts and raw sugar and served as a dessert.

Pint (one), 473.2 milliliters (ml); 2 pints = 1 quart (qt)

Pongal Abland preparation of rice and mung beans (Phaseolus) that is eaten with a ginger flavored spicy tamarind sauce.

Pound (one), 453.6 g or 456.6 milliliters

Proteins Polymers of 20 different amino acids

Proteolytic flora Microorganisms that are able to break down proteins into small peptides, amino acids and their products.

Putrefaction Anaerobic microbial degradation of proteinaceous matter resulting in foul smelling products as from decomposing meat.

Quart (one), 946.4 milliliters

Soray A gourd. It is a member of Cucurbit family.

Rancidity Acid odor of decomposing fatty materials

Sterile condition Where there are no microorganisms

Symbiosis When two or more organisms live together helping each other. Our gut microflora is an example.

Tablespoon (one), 14.8 milliliters

Tamarind A tropical fruit with sour pulp. Tamarindus indica

Teaspoon (one), 4.9 milliliters

Tharakari (H) Edible vegetables

Thoway (K) A mildly spiced thick lentil sauce; a Dal

Three entities Our body is conceived a harmonious organization of three entities, Mind, Body and Microflora, without the full development of which we will not function well.

Udid Black gram, Phaseolus Mungo, a close relative of mung beans.

Xenobiotics Synthetic chemicals such aspesticides that find their way into our bodies.

Index

The dietary factors most effective in the production of meat, milk, and eggs also bring about a rapid growth of children; but growth rates are not the most significant values of human life. Life span, resistance to disease, intellectual performance, emotional responsiveness and perceptiveness, etc. are characteristics that cannot be measured on a weight scale and are of little relevance to the production of market pigs or chickens, yet should be of paramount importance in judging the value of a diet for man.

– René Dubos, *Man Adapting*, 1980.

About the Authors

Yamuna Lingappa was born in 1929 in Nanjangude, Karnataka State, India. She obtained the Bachelor of Science (B.S.) degree from Mysore University and the Bachelor of Teaching (B.T.) degree from Madras University, both in India, and Master of Science (M.S.) and Doctorate (Ph.D.) degrees in Biological Sciences from Purdue University, in the United States. She has done post-doctorate research in microbiology at the University of Michigan, Michigan State University, and the College of the Holy Cross and at the University of Geneva in Switzerland. She has published over 30 original scientific articles in international scientific journals. She has taught courses in human nutrition and world hunger at Worcester State College, Clark University and the College of the Holy Cross, in Worcester, Massachusetts, during which many of the arguments expressed in this book were developed. For the past 17 years she has been President of Annapurna Incorporated, Worcester, Massachusetts which operates a lacto-vegetarian restaurant dedicated to the practical application of the nutritional principles explained in this book. Married to her co-author, B.T.L., she has raised two sons and a daughter.

Banadakoppa T. Lingappa was born in 1927 in Hulimane, Karnataka State, India. He obtained B.S. and M.S. degrees in agriculture at Banaras Hindu University in India and Ph.D. from Purdue University in the United States. After post-doctorate research in microbiology at the University of Michigan, Michigan State University, he joined the faculty of the College of the Holy Cross in Worcester, Massachusetts where he is Professor of Biology. He has been a visiting scientist at the Massachusetts Institute of Technology and at Harvard University and at the University of Geneva in Switzerland. He has published 45 original scientific articles in international scientific journals. He and his associate (Y.L.) have research interests which include development of a novel anaerobic (methanogenic) bioconversion project, and an another dealing with gene expression in *Candida albicans*. Married to his co-author, Y.L., they have two sons and a daughter.

युक्ताहारविहारस्य युक्तचेष्टस्य कर्मसु ।
युक्तस्वप्नावबोधस्य योगो भवति दुःखहा ॥ १७ ॥

Yoga killeth out all pain for him who is regulated in eating and amusement, regulated in performing actions, regulated in sleeping and waking.

– *The Bhagavad-Gita*, 6:17, translated by Annie Besant

To, Dr. Burday.

From: Jaya & BT
Sreedhara

Behalf of my sis-in-law
Dr. Yamuna Lingappa